ISLAMIC SPAIN, 1250 TO 1500

ISLAMIC SPAIN 1250 TO 1500

L. P. HARVEY

THE UNIVERSITY OF CHICAGO PRESS
Chicago and London

THE UNIVERSITY OF CHICAGO PRESS, CHICAGO 60637
THE UNIVERSITY OF CHICAGO PRESS, LTD., LONDON

Paperback edition 1992
Printed in the United States of America
99 98 97 5 4

Library of Congress Cataloging in Publication Data

Harvey, L. P. (Leonard Patrick)
Islamic Spain, 1250 to 1500 / L. P. Harvey.
p. cm.
Includes bibliographical references (p.

ISBN 0-226-31962-8 (pbk.)
1. Spain—History—711–1516. 2. Muslims—Spain—History. 3. Granada (Kingdom)—History. 4. Mudéjares. 5. Nasrides. I. Title.
DP102.H34 1990
946'.02—dc20
90-30225
CIP

♾ The paper used in this publication meets the minimum requirements of the American National Standard for Information Sciences—Permanence of Paper for Printed Library Materials, ANSI Z39.48—1984.

This study is dedicated to
Shaykh Aḥmad Zakī Yamānī
with gratitude and respect.

CONTENTS

PREFACE

Two distinct categories of Muslims were to be found in the Iberian Peninsula after the middle of the thirteenth century. On the one hand, there were the inhabitants of the small but crowded independent Muslim Kingdom of Granada; on the other, the many Muslims who lived out their lives as subjects of the Christian kingdoms in the lands of the Crown of Castile, in the lands of the Crown of Aragon, and in the small Pyrenean Kingdom of Navarre.

It is normal for these two groups to be treated quite separately. Islamic, Arabic-speaking Granada is rightly held to form part of the Islamic world, and so its history often is seen as a mere eccentric far-western appendage to that of the Middle East. The Muslim subjects of the Christian monarchs, on the other hand, in almost all cases quite small minorities in the regions where they lived, for that reason became in some accounts almost irrelevant footnotes to a story that is not their own. A quarter of a millennium of the history of Islamic Spain at the end of the Middle Ages has thus been subjected to a double process of marginalization, and in consequence has not always been well understood.

Relations between the various regions of the Islamic world and the West (with all *its* divisions) have occupied a disproportionately large amount of space on the agendas of our twentieth-century international bodies. Those relations have usually been characterized by mutual incomprehension, often by exasperation and recrimination. It has always surprised me that so little attention has been paid to the period at the end of the Middle Ages when Islam was in the process of being eliminated from Europe. Many of the attitudes that help to generate modern misunderstandings were formed at this time. The crusading endeavors of Europeans in the Middle East are certainly formative influences on those attitudes, but contact, largely hostile, between Christendom and Islam went on much longer in the Iberian Peninsula. The experience of Islam in Spain needs to be understood.

It is to be hoped that the type of treatment here accorded to Spanish Islam will prove to have more in its favor than the mere convenience of broader coverage. The Muslims of the peninsula were at all times deeply divided, it is true, even in the great days of the Caliphate of Cordova in the tenth century, but they were also from remarkably early on conscious of an underlying religious and cultural unity and proud of the common cultural inheritance of their *jazīrat al-Andalus,* "peninsula of al-Andalus," as they called their home. This consciousness of their own identity and worth, this self-respect, was to continue even after the period covered in these pages. In the sixteenth century, when Granadans and subject Muslims alike were to be condemned to forcible conversion, they still retained their pride in their religion and culture. They eventually took their pride with them into exile in North Africa and elsewhere. Even today in Tunisia (as for example in Zaghouan and in parts of the region of Cap Bon), in Algeria (in Blida and Tlemcen), in Morocco (in Chaouen and in Tetouan and in countless other places besides), there are families who cherish the heritage their forebears brought with them from al-Andalus, who still consider themselves to be, in some sense, "Andalusians."

It seems eminently reasonable to attempt to cover in one volume the history of both the Granadans and the subject Muslims of the rest of Spain. True, for long periods interaction across the frontiers was limited, but the two streams of Muslim life were never entirely separate, and in the end they come together again after the Christian occupation of Granada in 1492. That event spelled disaster for all Muslims in the peninsula without exception. The continued existence of an independent Muslim state had provided the ultimate guarantee that Muslims everywhere would be respected. Within five years of the conquest of Granada, the process of forcible conversion had begun. A quarter of a century later the conversion was virtually complete, in name and outward appearance at least.

Neither 1250 nor 1500 is put forward as a date important in itself: they are merely round figures marking off the quarter of a millennium during which Islam in the peninsula was catastrophically transformed. At about 1250 Christian military supremacy had been established, but there were still large Muslim populations in both Christian and Muslim lands. By 1500 not only had the last independent enclave been overwhelmed, but the process of forcible conversion and of the destruction of the distinctive culture of al-Andalus was under way.

The year 1500 certainly does not mark the conclusion of Muslim presence in the peninsula. Even after that date, Muslims from all regions managed to preserve their faith and something of their distinctive culture in secret, but the clandestine Islam of the sixteenth century is something quite new and distinct, and demands separate treatment. The Moriscos are a subject that must be reserved for another occasion.

Underlying the great diversity of the phenomena studied here, there is one constant. All the communities, as they met a daunting series of challenges over many periods, unwaveringly struggled to preserve their identity and to hand it on to their descendants. One might say that eventually Spanish Islam failed, for that Hispano-Islamic identity did not survive into the modern world (apart from those nostalgic memories of al-Andalus present in North Africa). This study is not conceived as a study of failure, however, rather as a record of a courageous and stubborn defense.

ACKNOWLEDGMENTS

When I began to set down the names of those to whom I am indebted for help and kindness received during the writing of this book, I soon realized that the long list occupied more space than my tolerant publisher could conceivably accord me, for in a sense the work has been in preparation since the mid-1950s. I must therefore ask all those, librarians, archivists, friends and colleagues, who over the years have responded to my inquiries and requests for help to accept this general expression of my gratitude. There are, however, a few names I cannot fail to mention because of their contribution at some crucial point in the development of this study. At the outset the late Professor Sir Hamilton Gibb encouraged me to turn my attention towards the problems of late Spanish Islam, and then the guidance of Professor A. F. L. Beeston enabled me to bring my early research projects to a successful conclusion after Gibb had left Oxford for Harvard. The late Father Pedro Longás, librarian of the Instituto de Valencia de Don Juan, Madrid, patiently taught me to read the Andalusī script of the manuscripts of the Mudejars of his native Aragon. Professor Emilio García Gómez kindly made available to me the manuscripts of the Almonacid hoard kept in the Escuela de Estudios Árabes, Madrid, and then in 1956 opened the pages of *Al-Andalus* to my first, brief publication.

During the quarter-century that followed, the study of the Mudejars, of the Kingdom of Granada, and of the final Morisco period has developed enormously. Whereas in the 1950s research into late Spanish Islam occupied the attention of a few isolated individuals, nowadays there are scholars and even well-organized and active research groups in all regions of the Iberian Peninsula, in North Africa and in other parts of the Arab world, in the Americas, in most European countries, and even as far afield as Japan and Australia. All contribute to the late twentieth-century explosion of information. My indebtedness to the new generation of scholars and researchers will be obvious from my bibliography, and from my references to their published works.

By the early 1980s I could see that the time had come to attempt a new synthesis. So as to be able to devote all my time to research, I resigned my chair of Spanish at King's College, University of London.

Such a decision is not arrived at lightly, and I will always be grateful to Dr. William R. Polk for spending several days with me, discussing my decision and evaluating my research projects. His sustained support over the years has been invaluable.

The course of action on which I embarked was not without its consequences for my wife, and I wish to thank her for the unfailing encouragement she has given me (as also for her collaboration in various aspects of this project).

Among those to whom I am particularly indebted for help received over the last decade, I would like to mention: Father Feliciano Delgado of the University of Cordova; Professor A. Deyermond of Queen Mary and Westfield College; Professor Mikel de Epalza of the University of Alicante; Professor A. Galmés de Fuentes, formerly of Oviedo, now of the University of Madrid; Dra Mercedes García-Arenal of the Consejo Superior de Investigaciones Científicas; Dr. Antonio Gavira, Sr. Martín Gavira, and his wife Ellen Etzel for assistance with photography; Dr. David Hook of King's College, University of London; Professor Abdeljelil Temimi of the University of Tunis and of the Centre d'Etudes et de Recherches Ottomanes, Morisques, de Documentation et d'Information, Zaghouan; Professor A. Vespertino Rodríguez of the University of Oviedo; Mr. Gerard Wiegers of the Faculteit der Godgeleerdheid, University of Leiden.

Finally, and above all, I must place on record my profound indebtedness to the generous patron to whom this volume is dedicated. Thanks to him I had the means to carry my researches to a successful conclusion.

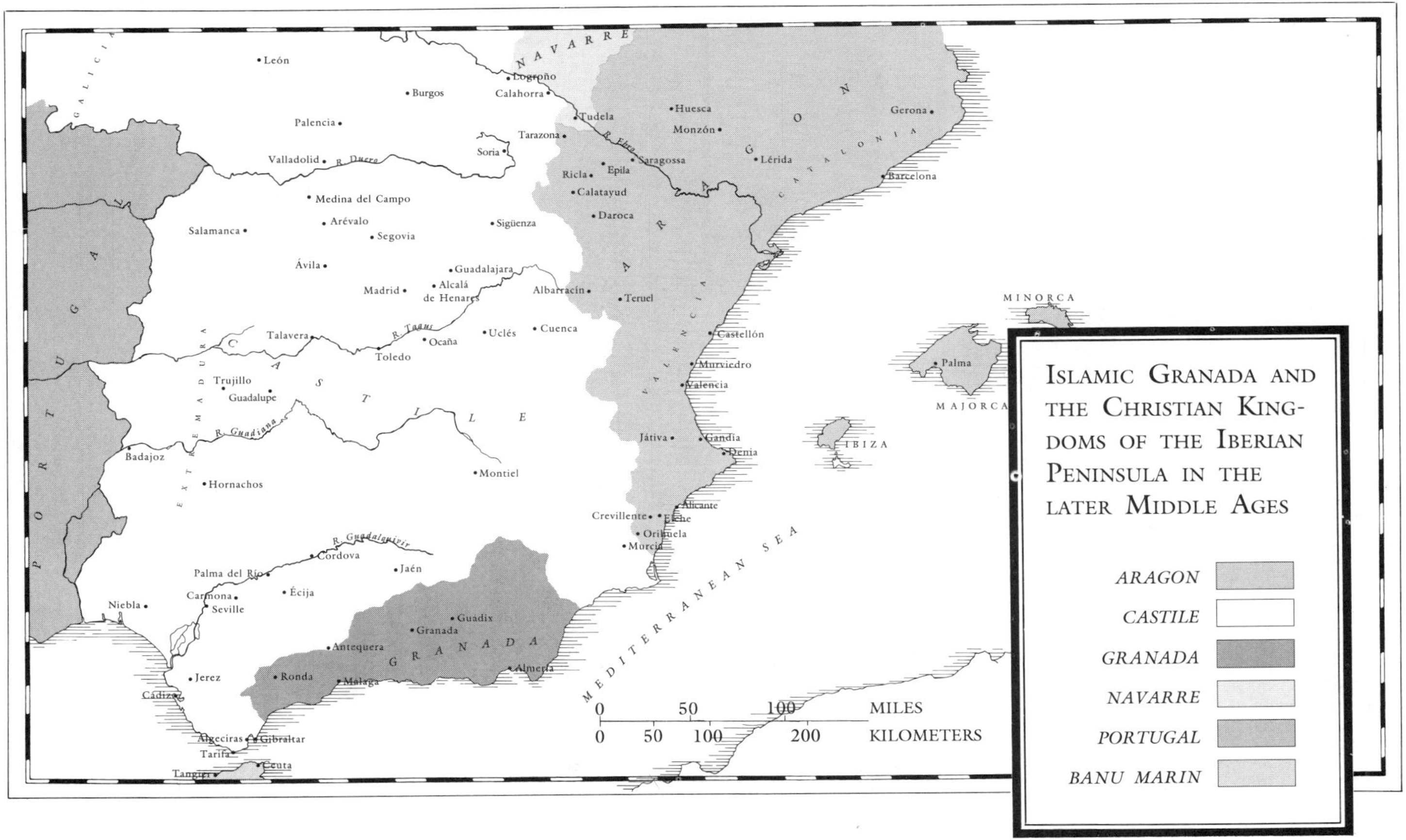
Islamic Granada and the Christian Kingdoms of the Iberian Peninsula in the later Middle Ages
ARAGON
CASTILE
GRANADA
NAVARRE
PORTUGAL
BANU MARIN
MILES
KILOMETERS
0
50
100
200
NAVARRE
ARAGON
CATALONIA
VALENCIA
CASTILE
EXTREMADURA
PORTUGAL
GALICIA
GRANADA
MEDITERRANEAN SEA
MINORCA
MAJORCA
IBIZA
Palma
León
Burgos
Palencia
Valladolid
R. Duero
Soria
Logroño
Calahorra
Tudela
Tarazona
R. Ebro
Saragossa
Huesca
Monzón
Lérida
Gerona
Barcelona
Ricla
Epila
Calatayud
Daroca
Medina del Campo
Arévalo
Segovia
Salamanca
Sigüenza
Ávila
Guadalajara
Madrid
Alcalá de Henares
Albarracín
Teruel
R. Tagus
Talavera
Toledo
Ocaña
Uclés
Cuenca
Castellón
Murviedro
Valencia
Trujillo
Guadalupe
R. Guadiana
Badajoz
Hornachos
Montiel
Játiva
Gandia
Denia
Alicante
Crevillente
Elche
Orihuela
Murcia
R. Guadalquivir
Cordova
Jaén
Palma del Río
Écija
Carmona
Seville
Niebla
Guadix
Granada
Antequera
Ronda
Malaga
Almería
Jerez
Cádiz
Algeciras
Gibraltar
Tarifa
Tangier
Ceuta

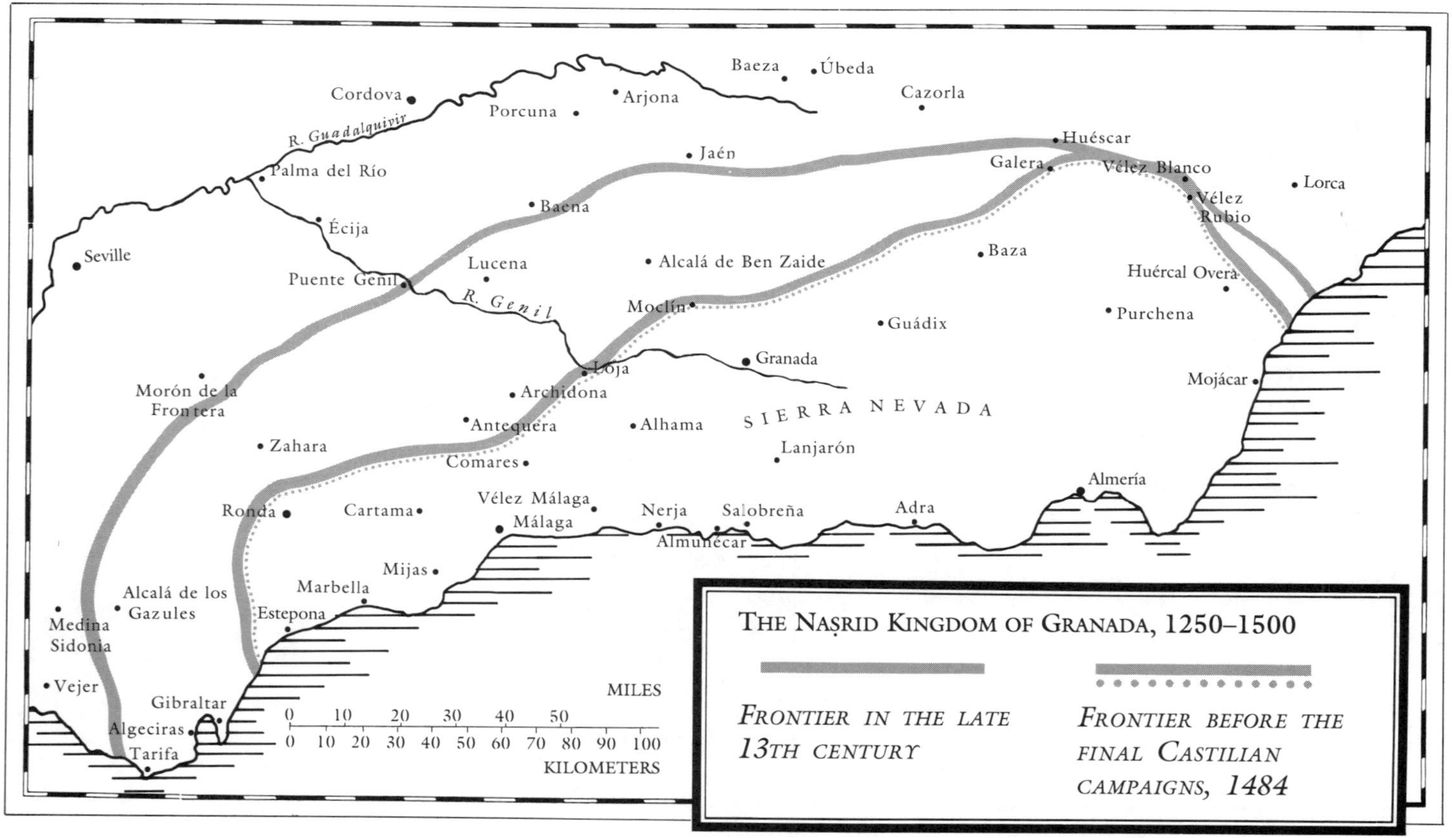
THE NAṢRID KINGDOM OF GRANADA, 1250–1500
FRONTIER IN THE LATE 13TH CENTURY
FRONTIER BEFORE THE FINAL CASTILIAN CAMPAIGNS, 1484
MILES
0 10 20 30 40 50
0 10 20 30 40 50 60 70 80 90 100
KILOMETERS
Cordova
R. Guadalquivir
Porcuna
Arjona
Baeza
Úbeda
Cazorla
Jaén
Palma del Río
Écija
Baena
Seville
Puente Genil
Lucena
R. Genil
Alcalá de Ben Zaide
Moclín
Granada
Loja
Archidona
Antequera
Alhama
SIERRA NEVADA
Lanjarón
Guádix
Baza
Huéscar
Galera
Vélez Blanco
Vélez Rubio
Lorca
Huércal Overa
Purchena
Mojácar
Almería
Adra
Salobreña
Almuñécar
Nerja
Vélez Málaga
Málaga
Comares
Cartama
Mijas
Marbella
Estepona
Ronda
Zahara
Morón de la Frontera
Alcalá de los Gazules
Medina Sidonia
Vejer
Gibraltar
Algeciras
Tarifa

ONE

Geographical Environment and Historical Context

Problems of Terminology

If we wish to discuss the Muslims of Spain at any period in their history, we encounter a series of terminological problems. What are we to call the Muslims themselves, and the land they inhabited? The difficulties arise in part because the geographical and ethnic terms available to us themselves arose in the course of nine long centuries of contact and conflict, and while reflecting that conflict, they do not always help to throw much light on it. *Moor* (*moro*), for example, is a historical term which is authentic in the sense that it occurs in source materials of the period, but it is a term we can rarely use nowadays. It is not merely geographically imprecise, leaving us uncertain whether the person it describes is of North African origin or simply a Muslim, it is ambiguous with regard to the value judgment it implies. Often *Moor* conveys hostility, but there are contexts where Muslims refer to themselves as Moors with evident pride. Even such an apparently straightforward term as *Spain* places pitfalls in our path. Does Spain include or exclude those places not under Christian rule? (And does it imply the inclusion or exclusion of what is now Portugal?). If we seek to escape from the difficulty created by *Spain* by using such an apparently unambiguous expression as "the Iberian Peninsula," we find we have created a new problem, because the inhabitants of the peninsula cannot be called Iberians (that is an expression limited to ancient history, or to the contrived ecumenicism of modern times).

If we adopt the Arabic name for the Iberian Peninsula, *al-Andalus,* we do not avoid all difficulties, because in English (and indeed in other modern European languages) the word is used of Islamic as distinct from Christian Spain, but since in Arabic the *jazīrat al-Andalus* was the whole peninsula, there is always the possibility that the broader sense may be intended.

In the Iberian Peninsula in the Middle Ages two major civilizations came into conflict. The words we use to describe that conflict inevitably reflect it in their very semantic structures, and there is no way available to us to talk about what went on in neutral terms, nor is there any way of achieving flat uniformity except from the most biased of partisan viewpoints. What we must do is be aware of the ways in which our vocabulary may lead us astray.

Spanish possesses a rich vocabulary to designate the minority religious and cultural groups that existed in the peninsula over the centuries, and English has adopted many of these words. It seems at first sight that we have a tidy set of terms to meet each logical possibility. Besides straightforward Christians and Muslims, we need terms for (*a*) Christians living under Muslim rule, (*b*) Christians who are converts from Islam (or descendants of such converts), (*c*) Muslims living under Christian rule, and (*d*) Muslims who converted from Christianity (or their descendants). We do indeed find (*a*) Mozarab (*mozárabe*), (*b*) Morisco, (*c*) *Mudéjar,* and (*d*) *muladí,* but it is important to realize that these are *not* terms universally applicable over the whole chronological range of peninsular history, and each one of them has a problematical aspect. The question of the proper use of *Mozarab(ic)* affects a multiplicity of groups over a very long period of time (say, from 711 to ca. 1200). Some would apply it to all subject Christians without exception; the extreme opposite viewpoint restricts the word to those culturally Arabized Christians from the south who took refuge in León in the eleventh and twelfth centuries. The resolution of the problem of how the word *Mozarabic* ought properly to be employed must be left to specialists; the sole purpose of mentioning the word here is to point out that it gives rise to disagreement and controversy. Of the other three terms mentioned, it should be noted that two, *muladí* and *Morisco,* are subject to chronological limitations. By and large *muladí* is used only of converts from Christianity to Islam in the days of Umayyad rule. (Later the term *elche* is sometimes used, but it seems to imply that the converts in question are outsiders to the community that has adopted them.) *Morisco* in the special sense indicated at (*b*) is not in use until well after 1500 (modern historians may use it from 1500 or so, but it is doubtful whether it actually came into use until about mid-century: before that the Moriscos *avant la lettre* were simply referred to as *nuevos convertidos*).

The word *Morisco* illustrates particularly clearly the dangers inherent in vocabulary. To make the point very briefly (and there would be a great deal more to say), by employing this term *Morisco* (rather than *Spanish Muslim,* say) we are tacitly accepting and approving of the forcible reclassification of this group of Muslims as something other, although all the documentary evidence indicates that most (not all) of them continued until the end to be crypto-Muslims who would have rejected the conversion if they had been at liberty to do so. The very use of the word seems to signify assent to the marginalization of the people so designated. Not to use it, however, is to court misunderstanding, as it is a standard part of the Spanish historical vocabulary.

The term that will concern us most in the course of the present study is *Mudejar:* "a Muslim who, after the surrender of a territory to a Christian ruler, remained there without changing religion, and entered into a relationship of vassalage under a Christian king" (a slightly modified translation of the entry *Mudéjar* in the *Diccionario de la Real Academia Española*). Are we, by referring to such Muslims as *Mudejars,* also endorsing their marginalization? As we shall see, the problem is really more complicated than that posed by *Morisco.*

Against the view that *Mudejar* is a term that relegates those so described to an inferior status, it may be argued that in recent critical usage the word has occurred in neutral and purely descriptive senses, and indeed some ascribe to it a strongly positive value judgment. In art history, Mudejar architecture has been much esteemed; even in literary criticism, López-Baralt has discerned positive aspects in "Mudéjar" writing "from Juan Ruiz to Juan Goytisolo" (the latter a twentieth-century author preaching what he sees as a *mudejarismo* for our times).[1]

A difficulty facing those who would advocate a revaluation of *Mudejar* lies in its etymology. Etymology is no absolute bar to upward mobility, of course, and words which have begun as terms of oppro-

1. López-Baralt 1985:esp. 181–209 ("Hacia una lectura 'mudéjar' de *Makbara*").

brium may sometimes be adopted as proud banners. (In British history, the rise of *Tory* out of the bogs of Ireland provides a particularly striking example of the phenomenon.) Yet etymology can be a useful guide to early usage and is not to be ignored. Let us see what it tells us about *Mudejar*.

The phonetic changes the word has undergone mean that its origins are by no means transparent, and erroneous guesses have abounded. The attempt to associate the word with Arabic *dajjāl,* "he who leads astray," an epithet applied to Satan, can be discounted at the outset as an obvious clumsy product of anti-Islamic polemics. To associate it with Spanish *dejar* "to leave" (presumably because these Muslims were "left behind") implies that *dejar* was borrowed in a rather strange way: we have no evidence that the Arabic of Spain adopted *dejar* as a loan word. The obvious place to look for light on this problem is in Arabic texts themselves speaking of the Mudejars; usually they simply have *Muslims,* but a few, notably al-Wansharīshī's *Kitāb al-Miʿyār,* use the expression *ahl al-dajn,* "people who stay on" (al-Wansharīshī 1908:XII, 198). As will be seen below (chapter 4), al-Wansharīshī is an author who strongly disapproves of the very idea of Mudejar status, and we can be sure that in his usage it carries a charge of opprobrium. *Mudajjan,* the participial form, would have the same sense as *ahl al-dajn,* namely "having stayed on."

There is another aspect of the semantics of this word. Cognate to *mudajjan* are forms such as *mudājin* and *dawājin* which are used of "domesticated" or "tame" animals, particularly poultry. It would seem that a semantic link exists between the animal, which passes under human protection and acquires "domesticated" status, and human populations, which pass under the protection of a dominant power and become safe subjects.[2] To be tame and domesticated is not a characteristic of which any man will boast. What we have here is probably a taunt, perhaps at first directed by free Muslims at subject coreligionists. Since the new "subject Muslim" status was one for which no existing term was available, the name stuck and even passed into Spanish usage.

Can the term *Mudejar* be part of our modern historical vocabulary? "Muslim subject to a Christian ruler" is a clumsy expression; a word is needed, and it would be perverse not to employ the one that is to hand,

2. Watt (1965:151) gives "'permitted to remain', with a suggestion of 'tamed, domesticated'."

but we must be aware that there are contexts in which it will not function as a bland and colorless adjective, that it can be an emotive and possibly, on Muslim lips, an offensive epithet. (The theological implications of the acceptance by Muslims of Christian rule are discussed in chapter 4.)

Problems of Demography

How people are to be counted has always been a problem, and one of the difficulties experienced by medieval historians is that sometimes their sources will be making honest if unsuccessful attempts to reflect reality as it was perceived, while at other times they will be using numbers because of the symbolic or magical properties attributed to them. The preeminence of mathematics in our culture and the reliance we put on statistics place historians under pressure to find ingenious ways of extending back into the past sequences of demographic statistics of the same kind as we expect to have available for the twentieth century. That is rarely, if ever, possible.

We are far from possessing reliable statistics for any of the periods or areas that concern us. Occasionally, and for certain areas, we know a great deal, but alongside the extraordinarily detailed information which some medieval archives do preserve, there are black holes of ignorance which will never be filled. It is always necessary to remind ourselves that thirteenth-century statistics are not the same as twentieth-century statistics (which are not the same as the full and objective truth).

In general, of course, the nearer we approach the present day, the more information we have. We would expect to have more information about the sixteenth century than about the fifteenth, but there is also the special circumstance that during that period the "Morisco question" was on the agenda of Spanish statesmen and administrators. When the Final Expulsion of the Muslims came in the early seventeenth century, the consequent movement of populations was documented as fully and as bureaucratically as the Final Solution of the Jewish question in the twentieth. Thus the careful and comprehensive studies of Muslim populations in Spain in the final period have been made on the basis of full and apparently reliable statistics. Henri Lapeyre, in his *Geography of Morisco Spain (Géographie de l'Espagne Morisque)*, was able to assemble a remarkably complete set of figures for almost all the Muslims who were expelled in 1609–1611, and to extend this coverage to earlier periods of the sixteenth century.

Lapeyre's survey can often be used to project even further backwards into the later Middle Ages information about the distribution and relative sizes of Muslim settlements, but it has to be employed with all due precaution, for the sixteenth century was a period of particularly large movements of population (affecting the Muslims of Granada more than others, but leaving few areas untouched).

We may form some idea of the degree of uncertainty with regard to population statistics at about the outset of our period by comparing two estimates. J. N. Hillgarth estimates as follows: "Reckoning back from an estimated 7,000,000 or 8,000,000 in 1482, it is conjectured that the population of Castile-León in 1225 was about 4,000,000 (another estimate is 3,000,000) and that the conquests added 300,000 more" (Hillgarth 1976:I, 30). J. O'Callaghan (after remarking on the hazardous nature of population estimates) cites Vicens Vives' estimates of the population of "Castile, the largest of the peninsula states, at about the middle of the thirteenth century, as four or five million people, including about 300,000 Muslims and Jews" (O'Callaghan 1975:459). Estimates for the Crown of Castile, we see, vary between 3 million and 5 million. As O'Callaghan points out, "For the crown of Aragon there are a number of statistical records that scholars have used to advantage. On the basis of the census of households of 1359, the population of Catalonia has been estimated at about 450,000 people, including about 18,000 Jews and 9,000 Muslims, located mostly in the south. Vicens Vives believed the population had dropped from about 500,000 in the thirteenth century because of emigration to Valencia, Majorca, Sicily, Sardinia and Greece. The estimate for Valencia is about 300,000, for Aragon about 200,000 and for Majorca about 45,000. This would give a total population of one million in the crown of Aragon" (460). He goes on to put all the figures together into a global estimate for the peninsula as between 6,200,000 and 7,200,000 before the Great Plague. The proportion of Muslims in these total populations is likewise not known with accuracy. Both O'Callaghan (1975:462) and Hillgarth (1976:I, 32) quote the estimate given by Sobrequés that about half the population of the crown of Aragon were Muslims.[3] "This very high figure is less improbable than some others given for Jewish population, but it is reached by the same process of arguing back from figures of later

3. The reference is to S. Sobrequés Vidal in J. Vicens Vives (ed.), *Historia de España y América,* Barcelona, 1961:II, 61.

centuries, in this case from those calculated for the Moriscos expelled in the seventeenth century. Only in the Kingdom of Valencia (and its extension southward to Alicante) did Mudejars constitute a large majority of the population: in Majorca they may have formed 50 per cent. They were very numerous in Aragon proper" (Hillgarth 1976:I, 32).

As for Granada itself, the figure of 200,000 given by Aragonese envoys at the Council of Vienne in 1314 (O'Callaghan 1975:460) is undoubtedly far too low, although we have no reliable figures. Hillgarth declines even to conjecture what it might have been; Ladero gives an estimate of 300,000 for the years before 1492 (Hillgarth 1976:I, 30).

If we add to the population of approximately 5,000,000 in Castilian lands, the 1,000,000 for Aragon, we have perhaps 6,000,000 in total (with a considerable margin of uncertainty, as we have seen). The population of Muslims may have been the 300,000 for the Crown of Castile. (O'Callaghan [1975:459] gave 300,000 for Muslims and Jews together; his estimate seems low bearing in mind the numbers of Muslims remaining behind at least until the Mudejar revolts of 1264.) For the Crown of Aragon one-half of the total population of 1,000,000 is clearly too high, but 300,000 is probably on the low side bearing in mind the dense settlements in Aragon proper and in Valencia. For the Kingdom of Granada we can only guess at least 300,000 or more. The total for Muslims in the whole peninsula must have approached 1,000,000. Perhaps one in six of the total population in the whole peninsula may have been Muslims. (Navarre with its steady small population of about 100,000 in all, and perhaps 1,000 Muslims,[4] does not really affect our estimates as these figures fall well within our margins of error.)

If these very rough estimates are anywhere near the mark, they give rise to considerable problems when we seek to relate them to estimates for earlier periods in the Middle Ages. Thomas Glick's survey of these problems may be cited verbatim: "Assuming that there were seven million Hispano-Romans in the peninsula in 711, and the numbers of this segment of the population remained level through the eleventh century, with population growth balancing out Christian migration to the north, then by 912 there would have been approximately 2.8 million indige-

4. García-Arenal 1984:esp. 15–20, "La Población." The various *morerías* she lists total 1,088 in 1366 (her statistics derive from J. Carrasco, *La población de Navarra en el siglo XIV,* Pamplona, 1973:150–52.).

nous Muslims (*muwalladūn*) plus Berbers and Arabs. At this point Christians still vastly outnumbered Muslims. By 1100, however, the number of indigenous Muslims would have risen to a majority of 5.6 million" (Glick 1979:35).

The theoretical basis for this assertion by Glick is the "conversion curve" established by Bulliet[5] for Christian-Muslim conversions in the Middle East; Glick posits that the same conversion rates would apply in Spain (1979:34–35). If Glick is right, the Muslim population must have dropped from 5,600,000 to 1,000,000 in two centuries. Such rapid change seems highly unlikely, even though there must have been a rapid decline as a result of all the fighting and emigration to North Africa. It seems to me that Glick's figure of 5,600,000 is too high, and that Bulliett's curve is not replicated exactly in the history of the peninsula. This does not mean I do not agree with Glick's general view of an Islamic Spain which was demographically buoyant during the earlier Middle Ages, and which benefited from the self-confidence that flowed from that buoyancy. Glick makes the telling point that

> The basic element in the perception of the frontier by Castilians and Leonese of the ninth and tenth centuries was the awareness of the paucity of their own population in comparison with the great numbers of their Muslim adversaries. Such perceptions emerge regularly in accounts of early battles with the Muslims: for example, the tens of thousands of Muslim troops said in the Chronicle of Alfonso III to have been defeated by Pelayo's tiny band at Covadonga. In the *Poema de Fernán González* the same point is made in the assertion that "thirty wolves" (that is, the Castilians) can kill 50,000 sheep (the Muslims). A much quoted line from the same poem (stanza 217) describes the Castilians of the tenth century as "a few men gathered together in a small land" (*eran en poca tierra pocos omnes juntados*). This line occurs in some recensions of the poem in the opposite sense, *muchos hombres juntados,* which Sánchez-Albornoz used to support the picture of a Castile expanding through the dynamism of an exploding population. The first reading, that stressing low numbers, is supported by the corresponding section in the *Crónica General,* but moreover is more in

5. Bulliett 1979. The graph for al-Andalus is reproduced by Glick (1979:35).

> line with what I believe was a general perception of the insignificance of Christian numbers compared to the Islamic colossus. (Glick 1979:63)

There did indeed take place an enormous change in attitudes between 1100 and 1300, and Christians in this period switch from the underdog mentality of the earlier Middle Ages to confidence in the rightness of their cause. Castilians and Aragonese alike possessed this confidence as they put into effect in the thirteenth century their plans to advance southwards. Even though Glick's projection of the Muslim population along a Bulliett-type curve may well lead to too high a figure in the Almohad period, it is nevertheless the case that by about 1250 Muslims were looking back on two centuries of catastrophic decline, retreat, and shrinking population. Whereas Christians surely can hardly have believed in their good fortune.

From many points of view it is difficult to understand why the Christians did not maximize their mid-century advantage and push ahead to complete the enterprise which was not to be completed until 1492. Demography acted as a brake on expansion. Even though Castile enjoyed the advantage of a larger population base, its manpower resources were by no means infinite. Castile's rulers could accomplish only what they had men enough to do. And alongside these considerations (and linked with them), there were considerations of morale. For Chiristians to think in 1250 of eliminating completely the power which had so recently in the past been utterly predominant would have been very difficult. The Castilians and the Aragonese, but above all the Castilians, needed thus to persuade *themselves* that victory might be possible. There is a psychological dimension to demography.

A New Map of Spain

In the middle of the thirteenth century, the map of the Iberian Peninsula had just been profoundly transformed by Christian military successes right across the peninsula—from the Algarve, in southern Portugal, to Murcia and Valencia in the east. The mere listing of the major cities and the key towns that had just been conquered at this time is sufficient to indicate what an immense readjustment must have taken place. The city of Valencia had fallen to James the Conqueror. The Muslims of Valencia ruled by Ibn Mardānish had hoped to oppose the attack with the assistance of Abū Zakariyā', the Ḥafṣid emir of Tunis, but although Abū

Zakariyā᾽ had sent arms and money by sea, these could not reach the city itself because of an effective blockade. Valencia capitulated on September 29, 1238 (García Gallo 1967:II, 616).

The next important center to the southwest is Murcia, which fell in 1243 to Alfonso, the future Alfonso X, on behalf of his father Ferdinand III. This is the stretch of the frontier between Christians and Muslims which was also disputed between Castile and Aragon. Here the southward drive of the Catalan speakers of the lands of the Crown of Aragon intersected with the southeastward thrust of Castile. The agreements in force at this time assigned Murcia to Castile, and the eventual outcome was that it became Castilian, but that was by no means a foregone conclusion. Moreover on the Muslim side there were a number of claimants to power there. Ibn Mardānish, displaced from Valencia, imposed himself in Murcia, but also in contention were the Banū Hūd, descendants of the dynasty that for so long dominated Saragossa. The leader who was to emerge as Muḥammad I, Ibn al-Aḥmar of Granada, had his interest in this key area too. The outcome was therefore uncertain, but on April 2, 1243, Murcia surrendered to Castilians led by Alfonso.[6]

Events elsewhere on this Murcia sector of the frontier were somewhat confused, for not only did Castile take some towns assigned to Aragon, but Aragon took towns in the Castilian zone, so that a further treaty (that of Almizra, 1244) was necessary to settle the division of the valuable spoils, and Aragon went on to take Alcira, Játiva, and Biar in 1245. The willingness of the Aragonese to moderate their demands for territory in this part of the conquest was no doubt due in part to the fact that their territories elsewhere were still so largely peopled by Muslims, with the Aragonese political hold on the new conquests as yet by no means firm. Valencia, captured in 1238, had to be pacified again in 1248 when, as we shall see, one al-Azraq led a revolt.

Turning now westwards, it was at the city of Jaén that was forged the Castilian frontier policy which prevailed during the rest of the Middle Ages, for it was here that Castile met resistance led by Muḥammad I, Ibn al-Aḥmar, and reached an accommodation with it. The nature of that accommodation was continually redefined and renegotiated in the course of the next quarter-millennium, but it was at Jaén that the new style of politics was created. The details of the Jaén conquest must be left

6. O'Callaghan 1975:348; Huici 1970:III, 262. See also Cagigas 1949:II, 40n53.

for analysis in the chapter on the creation of the Naṣrid state. Ferdinand III had failed before Jaén in 1225 and 1230, but thanks to his deal with Muḥammad he took the city in 1246 (Cagigas 1949:II, 432–33).

From Valencia to Jaén the pattern of events on the frontier had been one of a number of rival forces engaged on each side, and advances taking place in no clear linear sequence. Westward from Jaén the pattern is much clearer, and the chronological sequence runs from the conquest of Cordova in 1236 to the conquest of Seville in 1248. The swiftness of the Castilian thrust down the rich valley of the Guadalquivir towards the Atlantic seems to speak of a determination and a close coordination which turn out to be absent when we examine the record. The capture of Cordova was the result of uncoordinated opportunistic raiding by individuals acting outside Castilian royal control. Indeed Fernando III was many leagues away in Benavente (in the province of Zamora) when the news came, and the monarch had to undertake a dangerous and arduous journey through the flooded countryside across half Spain to arrive in time to take charge of what must be seen as the key event in the whole of the Christian reconquest, the taking of Cordova. Cordova in the thirteenth century was not the great metropolis of all the west which it had been in the tenth century, but the symbolic force of the celebration of a Te Deum of victory in the great mosque will have been lost on nobody. Nevertheless there had been a ludicrous side to Fernando III's precipitate dash from Benavente. At one point on his journey, at Bienquerencia, he had to spend the night in a tent in a field outside the local castle, which was still in Muslim hands. The governor of this castle, unnamed for us in the *First General Chronicle,* came to him bearing hospitable gifts: bread and wine and meat and barley (the standard fodder for working horses in the peninsula). Ferdinand asked for the castle itself, only to receive mocking refusal (*en manera de escarnio*) from the Muslim who "thought the king could not bring off what he desired." The refusal was hardly surprising, as all Ferdinand had with him was thirty "peers at arms," so that we may wonder at the way in which the commander of this castle allowed free passage to the Castilian king (PCG:II, 729–33, esp. 731). The conquest of Cordova, then, was the culmination of no great military plan, and we have seen that the logistics of the monarch's own journey there could not have been more rapidly improvised or more primitive. Cordova, 1236, nevertheless, marks a key point in the whole advance, for this city was never again to be in danger of being lost (as Seville itself was), and throughout our period, right up to the final campaign, it provided the base, the source of supplies, the headquarters for much of the military activity, not only in the swift compaign against Seville (captured 1248), but also in that against Granada (captured 1492).

Something of the Seville campaign must figure in the account of the rise of the Banū'l-Aḥmar in the next chapter. This was an advance so swift that it left enclaves at Niebla and at Cadiz, but by and large by 1248 the new map of the frontier had been drawn. The Christians had made a great bound forward. They had in the east come to occupy the fertile lands of the Valencian coastal regions, and the irrigated paradises of Murcia as well. In the center and the west they had come down across a frontier which had run along the southern fringes of the Meseta Central, and had occupied the valley of the great river, the Guadalquivir, itself. The economy of the Meseta Central was one of stock raising and of transhumance. The economy of the new lands was based on more settled forms of agriculture.

Not only was this a period of redrawing of frontiers, it was also a period of the movement of populations. There were broadly two ways in which the Muslim populations were treated. Those who surrendered by treaty might be allowed to remain and become Mudejars, subject Muslims, as described above. Those who had lived in areas that held out to the bitter end and refused terms of surrender were expelled (the place of refuge they eventually found was almost always somewhere in the Kingdom of Granada). However, there were many exceptions to this pattern. Many of those allowed by the terms of surrender to remain behind would not wish to do so. The teaching of the Muslim religious leaders was overwhelmingly in favor of emigration to Muslim territory. And in those areas from which all Muslims ought by the terms of surrender to have been expelled, some Muslims often managed to live on, either by keeping out of view, or because they had services to offer which made them valuable and acceptable to the new Christian masters. The territories newly acquired by the Christians were now areas where there was a great unsatisfied demand for labor, and those who were willing to make themselves useful were welcome, so long as their religion was discreetly practiced. Powerful nobles, desirous of developing estates, seem at times to have encouraged new Muslim settlements, as at Palma del Río.

The shift of population, the replacement of Muslims by Christians, was thus not nearly as tidy and complete a process as might at first be expected. Nevertheless there was a massive influx of Christian folk from the north, attracted by the opportunities of this new frontier. We have full documentation of the process of settlement in the case of some cities and other areas where the division of spoils (*Repartimiento*) was recorded in documents which were often carefully preserved because these were in effect foundation deeds of the new Christian communities. *Repartimientos,* like all historical documents, pose problems of interpretation. What was set down as being granted in the immediate aftermath of the fighting did not necessarily remain true as the years wore on and new local Christian power structures emerged. Some of the powerful recipients of grants might wish to realize their assets and move on, some of the financially weaker new settlers might fail to adapt to the new economic requirements of Andalusian trade and agriculture and be driven to the wall. For entrepreneurs from outside—and not necessarily from other parts of Spain, because traders from Italy, and particularly from Genoa, were quite active—these rich lands were full of promise and colonialist opportunity.

The opening up of the new conquests to Christian settlement had repercussions in the old possessions of the Castilian crown, both Castiles, León, and elsewhere, and what was at first a welcome relief of the pressure of a dangerous rise in population in the central areas soon began to be perceived as an unwelcome drain on human resources. The opposite phenomenon is to be detected in the Muslim communities. It is difficult to find any direct witness to the upheaval, and to the human suffering that must have taken place in the course of the immense transfer of population from the conquered cities, Jaén, Cordova, Seville, and elsewhere, and from the conquered fertile agricultural areas, where intensive forms of cultivation must have required large gangs of farm workers, into areas that were not already notably underpopulated and often enjoyed soils and climatic conditions by no means as favorable as those the Muslims had been obliged to leave. The influx of population, however, far from creating insuperable difficulties for the new state of Granada, seems to have opened the way to the creation of a medieval economic miracle. (There are many other examples in history of stress and hardship acting as a stimulus to growth and prosperity.)

To argue from historical silence is always extremely dangerous, but mention must be made here of the probable absence of any indigenous Christian element in the new Islamic state of Granada. The mountainous redoubt of the Sierra Nevada, and of the mountains to the north of

Malaga, had undoubtedly in early times, during the Caliphate, been places of refuge for Mozarabic Christians, with shrines and hermitages which can hardly have subsisted without the support of some surviving peasant community of the faithful. Quite when the Andalusian Mozarabs were eliminated in such an area we do not know. The assumption must be that the unwise expedition of Alfonso I of Aragon (the Battler) into Andalusia in 1125 was the principal cause. Not only were Mozarabs shifted northwards in large numbers as refugees, and some shipped off to North Africa where they could constitute no military threat, but Mozarabs in general from that time on were identified as dangerous potential subversives by their Muslim rulers. Whatever the reason may be, from the thirteenth century onwards we do not hear of native Christians anywhere in Muslim Andalusia. Such few Christians as are mentioned are resident foreigners, merchants or slaves or political refugees, or members of the groups of Castilian nobles who sought the backing of the Granadan authorities at various times. This gave a special character to the Islamic society of Granada. The existence side by side of three religious communities, which had been such a marked characteristic of Islamic Spain in the days of the Caliphate, was no feature of Islamic Granada in our period. With the exceptions already mentioned, the protected (*dhimmī*) community was largely limited to the Jews, and they seem to have tended to concentrate in certain places: Lucena, Granada itself, and Malaga, which as a great seaport offered them scope to practice their skills as merchants and entrepreneurs. Alongside this tendency for Granada to evolve towards being a purely Islamic state with only small *dhimmī* elements, and in particular scarcely any Christians, we note a tendency towards a culture that was purely Arabic in its expression. The place names of the area show that there must have been strong Romance influence in the language at one time in the past, but none of the Muslims of Granada used Romance in the way that Muslims in Aragon or Castile did. By a process of cultural filtration and concentration, as the years went by those who wished to live a purely Islamic life, to express themselves in Arabic, and to owe cultural allegiance to Islamic rather than European culture, went to live in the kingdom of Granada. The twentieth century can perhaps understand what went on better than earlier ages could, because it has seen examples of peoples opting for the revival of languages as the best expression of the culture they wish to preserve. The Arabization of Granada at the end of the Middle Ages is not as strange a phenomenon as the readoption of Hebrew by Zionist Jews in Israel in the twentieth century, because Granada had already had the basis of Arabic existing there as a majority tongue. Nevertheless, the strength of the Arabic language there until the very end is indeed remarkable. There is no sign at all that Arabic in Granada was in any danger of being replaced by Castilian at any time before the military defeat of 1492. To be a Granadan implied a positive affirmation of identity: to dress, eat, sleep, wash, speak, sing, pray, and be, in quite distinctive ways. The new frontier drawn on the map at about 1250 became a frontier of the mind also.

The very success of this fortress-redoubt mentality in Granada created problems for the rest of the Muslims of the lands of the Crown of Castile and Aragon. The Mudejars of the Christian north were Romance speakers who had to work out their own way of being Muslims, distinct from that of their Arabic-speaking coreligionists in Granada. The new Islam of the Mudejars of the north is an interesting phenomenon which in many ways anticipates the Islam of the modern world. A new interpretation of the pillars of the faith, and above all a readiness to translate the Koran into the vernacular, may seem unsurprising nowadays in an Islamic world where the old distinctions between *dār al-ḥarb* (abode of war) and *dār al-islām* no longer apply, and where the Koran has been translated into so many languages, but in Spain in the thirteenth century the Mudejars had no accepted models to follow, and had painfully to evolve their new manner of Islamic submission. It might seem that the Valencians, conquered and yet Arabic-speaking, constituted an exception to this division between Arabic-speaking Granadans and Romance-speaking Mudejars. What made this exception possible was the sheer size of the Muslim community, reinforced by the fact that the Valencian seacoast kept it in communication with Muslims overseas. Theirs was a quite special form of Mudejarism, which gave proof of little cultural religious creativity, if we compare its achievements with those of their brethren in Granada or in Castile or Aragon. The survival of the massive archives of the Crown of Valencia (and the scholarly attention lavished on those archives by R. I. Burns and others) have made the Valencian Muslims one of the groups about whom we know the most, and yet we know least, because they appear to have been, at the end of the Middle Ages, a people to whom nothing occurred, and who did nothing but survive. Survival was no mean achievement. We ought not to forget that it was Valencia that kept Arabic alive after it had died in Granada, and Valencian Muslims, of all the Muslims of the peninsula, who came nearest to negotiating effective aid from overseas allies, but to speak in this way of the Valencian Muslims' power of survival is to follow their story into the sixteenth century and beyond the purview of this book. In our period they are largely inert.

Islamic Spain in the mid-thirteenth century then emerges as divided into a number of strongly differentiated groups, each with a distinct past and without institutions, even religious ones, which would have enabled them to envisage united action. In such circumstances what happened to the largest single group, that of Granada, swollen at mid-century with its influx of refugees, inevitably had great effect on the fate of Islam in the peninsula as a whole. The rise of the state of Granada, therefore, is a key development in the history of Spanish Islam, and an examination of that rise must be the beginning both of the study of Granada itself and of the Mudejars of the rest of the peninsula. Muḥammad I's kingdom was a brilliant success against all the odds. It assured the continued existence of Islam in Spain for hundreds of years after the point when it seemed doomed to disappearance, but there was a dark side to that success: the deal struck at Jaén in 1246, the inglorious participation of Granadan forces in the conquest of Seville in 1248, the disastrous failure of the Granadan-inspired Mudejar revolt of 1264, all show Muḥammad as much more able to look after the interests of his own regime than those of Muslims in the peninsula at large. We owe it to Muḥammad I to attempt to understand the nature of the decisions he had to reach in the course of his crucial reign.

Since the study of the Muslims of the Iberian Peninsula during this period entails constant references to the rulers of the various Christian states as well as to the Naṣrid sovereigns, a parallel listing of regnal dates will be found in Table 1.

Table 1 The Rulers of Granada and of the Christian Kingdoms of the Iberian Peninsula

GRANADA	ARAGON	CASTILE	NAVARRE	PORTUGAL
Muḥammad I (1237–1273)	James I (1213–1276)	Ferdinand III (1217–1252)	Theobald I (1234–1253)	Alfonso III (1248–1279)
		Alfonso X (1252–1284)	Theobald II (1253–1270)	
			Henry I (1270–1274)	
Muḥammad II (1273–1302)	Peter III (1276–1285)	Sancho IV (1284–1295)	Jeanne I (1274–1305)	Dinis (1279–1325)
	Alfonso III (1285–1291)		m. Philip (1285–1314)	
Muḥammad III (1302–1309)		Ferdinand IV (1295–1312)		
Naṣr (1309–1314)	James II (1291–1327)		Louis (1314–1316)	
Ismāʿīl I (1314–1325)			Philip V (1316–1322)	
Muḥammad IV (1325–1333)	Alfonso IV (1327–1336)	Alfonso XI (1312–1350)	Charles (1322–1328)	Alfonso IV (1325–1357)
			Jeanne II (1328–1349)	
Yūsuf I (1333–1354)				
			Charles II (1349–1387)	
Muḥammad V (1354–1359)	Peter IV (1336–1387)	Peter I (1350–1369)		Peter (1357–1367)
Ismāʿīl II (1359–1360)				

Table 1 (continued)

GRANADA	ARAGON	CASTILE	NAVARRE	PORTUGAL
Muḥammad VI (1360–1362)				
Muḥammad V (1362–1391)		Henry II (1369–1379)		Ferdinand (1367–1383)
		John I (1379–1390)	Charles III (1387–1425)	John I (1385–1433)
Yūsuf II (1391–1392)	John I (1387–1395)	Henry III (1390–1406)		
Muḥammad VI (1392–1408)				
Yūsuf III (1408–1417)	Martin I (1395–1410)	John II (1406–1454)		
	Ferdinand I (1412–1416)			
Muḥammad VIII (1417–1419)	Alfonso V (1416–1458)			
Muḥammad IX (1419–1427)			Blanche (1425–1441) m. John/John II of Aragon (1425–1479)	
Muḥammad VIII (1427–1429)				
Muḥammad IX (1430–1431)				
Yūsuf IV (1431–1432)				
Muḥammad IX (1432–1445)				Edward = Duarte (1433–1438)

Table 1 (continued)

GRANADA	ARAGON	CASTILE	NAVARRE	PORTUGAL
Muḥammad X (1445)				Alfonso V (1438–1481)
Yūsuf V (1445–1446)				
Muḥammad X (1446–1447)				
Muḥammad IX (1447–1454)				
Muḥammad XI (1451–1452)				
Sa ʿd (1454–1462)		Henry IV (1454–1474)		
Yūsuf V (1462)	John II (1458–1479)			
Sa ʿd (1462–1464)				
Abū᾽l-Ḥaṣan ʿAlī (1462–1482)				
Muḥammad XII (1482)	Ferdinand V (1479–1516)	Isabella (1474–1504)	Leonor (1479)	John II (1481–1495)
Abū᾽l-Ḥasan ʿAlī (1482–1485)			Francis (1479–1483)	
Muḥammad XII (1486–1492)			Catherine (1483–1512) (throne claimed by Ferdinand V of Aragon)	Manuel (1495–1521)

TWO

The Rise of the Banūʾl-Aḥmar

Muḥammad I

The Muslim dynasty which ruled over Granada up to 1492 first came to prominence in 1232 not in Granada itself, but in Arjona. The small town (in our days it has perhaps ten thousand inhabitants) is in the modern province of Jaén, northwest of that city, and south of Andújar. There Muḥammad Ibn Yūsuf Ibn Naṣr Ibn al-Aḥmar set himself up as ruler of a small area that stretched eastwards as far as Baeza, southwards to Guádix, and which included the city of Jaén. We can give a precise date to the raising of the standard of revolt: 26th Ramadan 629, as the faithful came out of the Friday prayer.[1] The month of Ramadan is, of course, not only a month of fasting but one of gathering together in family and kinship groups to feast after dark, and we may assume that the date of the last day of community prayer in Ramadan was a particularly propitious one on which to seek to summon fellow citizens and fellow Muslims to an enterprise calling for confidence and a sense of mutual solidarity. We may imagine the disquiet experienced by Muslims of the towns of the frontier who had seen the Almohad protection disappear, who had heard tales of one warlord after another being picked off up and down the frontier, and who were conscious of the pressures exerted by the Castilians, not to mention the Aragonese and Catalans.

1. Arié (1973:55) refers to al-Nubāhī, *Nuzhat al-baṣāʾir waʾl-abṣar* (Escorial MS 1653 fol. 38).

What Muḥammad b. Yūsuf b. Naṣr had to offer to his anxious fellow Muslims was a reputation as a doughty fighter won already in the rough and tumble on the frontier, and the backing of his clan, variously known as the Banū Naṣr or Banū' l-Aḥmar. With them were associated another family grouping with Arjona connections, the Banū Ashqilūla (or Banū Escayola, as they were known to the Castilians), who claimed ultimate descent through the Tujībīs from the Arab tribe of Kinda. In this generation they were linked by marriage with the Banū' l-Aḥmar, as we shall see. Arjona was lost to Islam as early as 1244, but the human links which were formed in that little town continued to function within the large society of the whole Kingdom of Granada. The great North African historian Ibn Khaldūn in his justly renowned Introduction to his *History of the Berbers* discusses the ways in which the Berber polities, such as the Almoravids and the Almohads, acquired their cohesive social bonds (the word he uses in Arabic is *ʿaṣabiyya,* perhaps "tribal solidarity") as the result of the exigencies of life in the harsh conditions of the desert. He traces the stages whereby this *ʿaṣabiyya* fades and is lost in the gentler lands that were so easily conquered by tribesmen imbued with such esprit de corps: each empire is in turn swallowed up by the latest waves of tribesmen out of the deep desert (Mahdi 1964:196 and n.1). As an analysis of the workings of history as experienced by the Berbers the account is brilliant, and the theory even has its wider human application outside the world of nomads and desert empires ("clogs to clogs in three generations" is a northern English saying which charts a similar process among textile entrepreneurs). But the remarkable thing about the history of Naṣrid Granada is that Granada defied Ibn Khaldūn's law, for the *ʿaṣabiyya* on which Granada was constructed was prolonged over many generations.[2]

Still, it cannot be said that Muslim Granada disproves Ibn Khaldūn's law of diminishing *ʿaṣabiyya,* for it might be argued that the vital factor in Granada was the continuous *omnipresence of the frontier.* Nowhere could anyone forget the frontier, for all the luxury and refinement of Granadan life (solvents, according to Ibn Khaldūn, of the martial virtues), so that the cohesion of this society, even if constantly called in question by treason and bad faith, never wasted away altogether.

2. Ibn Khaldūn had personal knowledge of both Granada (which he first visited in 1362) and of Christian Spain (he was sent on a diplomatic mission to Seville in 1364 and met King Peter there).

The self-same year of the revolt, Muḥammad Ibn al-Aḥmar extended his influence as far as Cordova, thanks to the help of the family of the Banū'l-Mawl, who saw in Muḥammad a useful tool to frustrate their arch-enemy, Ibn Hūd. However, for the inhabitants of the city of Cordova, with its memories of caliphal glories, there can have been little attraction in being included in the *ṭā'ifa* of a chieftain from such an unimportant place as Arjona. Cordova rejected him and fell back into the hands of Ibn Hūd. During these early years of his political career, Muḥammad set himself policy objectives of piecemeal expansion similar to those of earlier *ṭā'ifa* rulers, and sought to extend his rule to Seville. There, as in Cordova, it was not impossible to find allies: in Seville the Bajji (or Peche) clan threw in their lot with him, but the triumph was again short-lived, and indeed lasted only about a month. Like Cordova, Seville once again accepted the rule of Ibn Hūd, and so in 1234 Muḥammad had to acknowledge the suzerainty of Ibn Hūd in exchange for recognition of his rights over his original home area of Arjona, to which was added the more important Jaén to the southeast and Porcuna to the south.

Muḥammad's role in the events immediately following show him in a very dubious light as betraying not only his new lord, Ibn Hūd, but also the fellow Muslims of Cordova, by entering into dealings with Ferdinand III and actively assisting him in the conquest of the old caliphal capital. In this period of kaleidoscopic reversals of alliances, there were no Muslim leaders in Spain, not even the Almohads, who had not at various times done deals with the Christians. Muslims fought for Christians, and Christians fought for Muslims. Nevertheless, there is something disturbing about the skill and rapidity with which Muḥammad trimmed and maneuvered in order to survive.

With our hindsight we can see that a vitally important stage in Muḥammad's maneuvering was the moment when, almost certainly in 1237, he succeeded in taking over Granada. As we know, only this mountain-girt city could provide the refuge that was to permit Spanish Islam to survive for as long as it did. At the time, the extension of Muḥammad's power to Granada was probably but one move in a complex game, and was not even clearly remembered, for there are disagreements among the authorities with regard to its date (Arié 1973:57n.5). Almería fell in May 1238, and Malaga sent envoys to invite Muḥammad to take over there, probably in 1239 (though here again sources disagree).

Thus it was that at the moment when the crusading thrust of the Castilians gave them Cordova (1236), and that of the Aragonese gave them Valencia (1238), there emerged as most powerful on the Muslim side the one-time lord of Arjona, now ruler of all the great cities of the south, Muḥammad Ibn al-Aḥmar. We have seen Muḥammad in 1236 subservient to the policy of the Castilians in the final stages of the Christian capture of Cordova. He was soon to find himself in direct conflict with the Castilians, who, after securing that city, were driving east towards Jaén. It is hardly surprising that the accounts we have from Muslim and Christian sources do not agree as to the responsibility for commencing hostilities: the Christian *First General Chronicle* (PCG:II, 743–45) speaks of Muslim raiding, whereas Ibn Khaldūn places the blame on the Christians.[3] The balance sheet of the exchange was that successful Muslim raids in the region of Andújar and Martos in 1242 were followed by Christian counterblows which led to the siege and capture of Arjona in 1244. Thus at a relatively early stage in his career Muḥammad lost the original seat of his power. We may suppose that this defeat was a grievous personal blow to him, but we may also speculate that the loss, coming when it did, forced him to a sound appraisal of the balance of power in southern Spain at this time, and perhaps guided him in hammering out a viable policy for survival.

For Ferdinand III, Arjona was no more than another small frontier town, and the prize in this area was, of course, Jaén—no easy city to take, for it was dominated by an immensely powerful, apparently impregnable, castle. Rather than making a frontal assault, the Castilians set about cutting Jaén off from the rest of Muslim territory, particularly from Granada, and then in 1245 closed the ring and began a tight siege. The fact that the Castilians did not undertake a frontal assault did not mean that fighting was not costly. An attempt had been made by Muḥammad to drive fifteen hundred head of sheep into Jaén to relieve the famine, but it is hardly surprising that such an operation was detected by Castilian espionage, and frustrated (PCG:II, 744–45). There was, however, no protracted bloody siege, which would certainly have been a difficult undertaking, for this is a land of harsh contrasts and extremes of temperature. In spite of the strength of the defensive positions, Muḥam-

3. Ibn Khaldūn 1969:IV, 74 (*Berbères*): "The Muslims had to endure the capture of their castles, the invasion of their territory, the loss of their provinces, the occupation of their cities."

mad must have calculated that Jaén was too exposed to attacks from the north to be defensible with the forces available, and he concluded a peace settlement whereby he yielded Jaén itself, committed himself to payment of a considerable amount in tribute, and accepted Ferdinand as his overlord (PCG:II, 746).

It must have been extremely difficult to carry through this policy and not lose the public support which was essential. At all stages in the Reconquest the Muslim divines (*ʿulamāʾ*), powerful shapers of public opinion, were more inclined to preach in favor of last-ditch resistance than statesman-like compromise. From the early point in the Reconquest when Alfonso VI's pressure on al-Muʿtamid of Seville drove the *ṭāʾifa* of Seville to conjure up the dangerous demon of North African Berber support, to the final stages of the Reconquest—when the negotiations for the surrender of the city of Granada had to be carried on in conditions of the greatest secrecy for fear that some of the religious leaders would frustrate the peace settlement by stirring up the faithful to make a desperate stand to the death—we find tension between the politicians of Muslim Spain and the theologians of Islam. The politicians' aim must have been to achieve the best that was materially possible in the light of the realities of the situation, while the theologians had no acceptable theoretical framework into which permanent retreat and the yielding up of lands to the polytheistic enemy could be fitted. If we may speculate on the military and political consequences of this theological phenomenon, we may suppose that at times Muslim resistance was stiffened by the intransigence of the clergy, but we may also wonder whether Islam would have stood a better chance of survival rather than elimination if the secular leaders had been freer to maneuver and negotiate without fear of alienating the more hard-headed among their own supporters. All the Naṣrids had to tread a tightrope, and the two perils their state faced were, on the one hand, defeat by Christians arising from an unrealistic assessment of what was militarily possible and, on the other hand, losing the support of Muslim opinion (we must bear in mind that the Islamic nature of their state was, after all, its prime reason for existence).

Ibn Khaldūn would seem to have concurred with Muḥammad in his appreciation of the strategic situation in 1245.

> In the western region of Andalusia the military forces of Ibn al-Aḥmar were insufficient to defend the lands adjoining the vast

> plains of the frontier. Recognizing that defense of the country would have called for more troops than were available to him, and that such defense would so wear down his capacity to resist as to provoke further attacks from the enemy, he yielded it to the Christian in exchange for peace. Wishing to be safe from threats of aggression, he led the Muslims into the harsh and mountainous terrain along the coast, selected Granada as his abode, and built the Alhambra there as his palace. (1969:IV, 74 [*Berbères*])

Ibn ʿIdhārī says that the peace made in 1245 was for a period of twenty years (Huici 1956:162). Whether or not this was formally written into the settlement we cannot confirm, but in fact such a period of relative peace did ensue, and it was badly needed by the Naṣrids. During it they created for Muslims a mountain redoubt that was to prove an enduring political entity. The material resources of this new state were scanty, but there Islam could survive on Spanish soil, there Islamic literature, art, and architecture could continue to flourish. The surrender of Jaén in 1246 is thus an event of the greatest importance, and Ladero Quesada is absolutely correct to describe it as the "birth certificate of the Granadan emirate" (Ladero 1969b:75). It may seem surprising to us now that the Castilians were prepared to give the Muslims such respite, just as it is difficult to understand why the Muslims in the early eighth century did not complete their conquest of the peninsula by eliminating resistance in the north, such as Pelagius and his little band. In the middle of the thirteenth century Castilian policy succumbed to the temptation to bypass the tough redoubt constituted by the Sierra Nevada, and the whole mountain complex backing onto the sea, to which Ibn Khaldūn referred. The Castilians thought instead of carrying the war over into North Africa. No doubt if Castilian policy had been successful there, the Granadan centers of resistance would have withered away soon enough. However, it was surely an incorrect assessment of the situation to hope that Castile, overstretched by the need to digest all the vast territories acquired in the course of the second great phase of the Reconquest, would ever be able to produce resources sufficient to conquer North Africa. From 1252 the Granadans had to deal not with Ferdinand III but Alfonso X. Alfonso deserves the epithet "Wise" (*Sabio*) for his contributions to Castilian letters and intellectual life in general, but he was remarkably unwise in his political enterprises. The disastrous debacle of Alfonso's North African campaign is to be compared with the expensive frustration he experienced when he set out to win the title of Holy Roman Emperor, or with his inability to carry through the reform of the Castilian legal system which he so mush desired (the famous *Partidas* were in his day nothing but theoretical studies), or with his ill-judged attempts to determine who would succeed him (Ballesteros-Beretta 1963:254–81, 674–734, 781).

From the Naṣrid point of view it was, to say the least, extremely fortunate that the critical years of weakness at the beginning of the existence of the Granadan state coincided with a period when the attention of Castile, which had been focused with such success by Ferdinand III on the enterprise of the Reconquest, was now dispersed by Alfonso X on so many ill-judged will-o'-the-wisp enterprises. Alfonso may have undertaken some of his unwise policies—the African crusade, the bid for empire, the attempted legal reforms—out of pious respect for the clearly expressed wishes of his father Ferdinand, or in deference to family interest, but this in no way diminishes his own responsibility for what he did.

Vassalage and Religion

While historians have not failed to ascribe importance to the role of religion in the rise of the Naṣrid state, they have rarely emphasized it. By and large the aspect of the new regime that has received most attention has been Muḥammad I's decision in 1246 to become Ferdinand III's vassal. For Ladero, for example, Muḥammad "managed to set his power on a firm basis by transforming himself into vassal and tributory of the King of Castile" (Ladero 1969:75). Arié holds the view that this last Muslim kingdom "could only be set up under vassalage to the Christians," and this is clearly a considered opinion of hers, because it is repeated in her more recent Spanish-language publication on the subject: "the Kingdom of Granada could only exist as vassal to the Christians" (Arié 1973:60, 1984:37).

The theme of its vassal status occurs repeatedly in the history of the Islamic state of Granada from its inception to its destruction in 1492, but it would be misleading to suggest that throughout this period Granada sought or accepted such subordination to Castile. As we shall see, the initial period of vassalage was unambiguously interrupted by Muḥammad I's sponsorship of the rebellion of many of Castile's Muslim subjects in 1264. The initial period of vassal status thus lasted twenty-two years at the maximum. Vassalage was subsequently frequently renewed, but was equally frequently rejected by the Granadans in the course of a long history of wars. To describe the kings of Granada as the vassals of the kings of Castile is to give to the term *vassal* a sense quite different from what it has elsewhere in the Iberian Peninsula, let alone elsewhere in Western Europe.

It is not surprising that the picture of Granada as a subject state, as a vassal, albeit an unreliable one, is projected repetitiously by medieval Castilian chronicle sources. The *First General Chronicle* in speaking of the Jaén agreement of 1246, assures us that Muḥammad "wanted nothing other than to become [Alfonso's] vassal in respect of all his lands," and when Ferdinand passed away in 1252, "the King of Granada, his vassal, caused great lamentation to be made throughout his realm" (PCG:II, 746, 774). The most striking manifestation of Muḥammad I's loyalty to his lord came during the campaign to take Seville in 1248. Far from striving to help his fellow Muslims besieged for six months in that city, Muḥammad provided Ferdinand III with a force of five hundred men for that campaign.

That Muḥammad I made an act of feudal submission to the Christian monarch at Jaén in 1246 is confirmed by all the Christian sources, and his political conduct over the next two decades is consonant with his continuing acceptance of such status. But equally clear from Muslim sources is that Muḥammad also made repeated acts of submission to Muslim suzerains, first to the ʿAbbāsid caliph of Bagdad, to Ibn Hūd, to the Almohad al-Rashīd (these before the surrender of Jaén), and to Ibn Zakariyāʾ, Ḥafṣid ruler of Tunis, in 1242 and 1264 (Cagigas 1949:II, 504). He was also in the later years of his reign within the political orbit of the Marinids. Nowhere in any Arabic source is there any mention of Muḥammad being Alfonso's vassal or liege man.

It seems likely that we have to do with a problem at once political and linguistic: a lack of communication between two incompatible worlds. In the mid-thirteenth century in countries where Latin or one of the Romance vernaculars was in use, it was difficult to speak of a relationship of political subordination without making use of the vocabulary of feudalism. The conceptual framework created by the language of course had its influence on the practicalities of relationships. Nothing of this applied within the Islamic world and in areas where Arabic was the language of culture. Arabic has a vocabulary to express suzerainty and subordination, but has no term exactly to convey the concept of vassal, although the word *mubāyaʿa* may be very close to it in some ways. It is hardly surprising that the picture of the rise of Granada that stems from the Arabic sources should be different from what we get from the Christian chronicles. To speak of "treason" on one side (and Ballesteros-Beretta still chooses to use the particularly emotive Spanish term *alevosía* [1963:362]), or of apostasy on the other, does not help us grasp what was happening, or appreciate the peculiarly delicate form of equilibrium on the frontier between two civilizations, which the Naṣrids were striving to maintain.

This point about the classification of the Granadan regime may seem obvious. The Castilian assertion of Granada's vassal status has been so successful, however, that the theory underlies most thinking on this aspect of peninsular history. Luis Suárez Fernández, summarizing the period in 1967, stated the Castilian view thus: "In 1246 Muḥammad I secured the recognition of Ferdinand III of Castile in return for a vassalage which, though often ignored, remained in force until the Kingdom's disappearance."[4] In the face of such statements it is necessary to assert Muḥammad's staunch allegiance to Islam, and to give our reasons for regarding religion as particularly important in the formation of the new state.

The first mention of Muḥammad I Ibn al-Aḥmar in the Castilian *First General Chronicle* is as follows: "And after that [the death of Ibn Hūd in Almería] an Arab called Mahomad Auenalahmar gained control over the land. But a short while before he had been a farmer [*quintero*] with no other occupation than following the oxen and the plough, but thereafter he was lord of Arjona and of Jaén and of Granada and of . . . Écija" (PCG:II, 722). One of the points being established by this passage in the chronicle is the humble social background of Muḥammad, presumably because that makes us the more prepared to accept that such a ruler is not to be regarded as a fully independent king. The choice of the word *Arab* (*alarbe*) is even noteworthy: it is a word often suggesting the penniless tent-dweller.

In Arabic our principal source of information is beyond question Ibn al-Khaṭīb. We must pay attention to his numerous writings because as secretary to the *dīwān al-inshā'* or chancery of the Naṣrid state, he had access to Granadan state papers, including those of the archives. As holder at one period of the "double vezirate" (he was *dhū' l-wizāratayn*) he was in a most privileged position. On the other hand it would be

4. *Encyclopaedia Britannica* 1967:X, 670, s.v. Granada, Kingdom of.

unwise to accept all he says without question, for he was by training a man skilled in giving to the truth various guises, and it was for many years his task to project the Naṣrid dynasty in a particular light. We are dealing with a great historian—one might almost call him a compulsive historian—but we are also dealing with a public relations expert.

In Ibn al-Khaṭīb's greatest work, the *Iḥāṭa* ("All-Embracing") we find a genealogy not in essential conflict with the Castilian source (which, one suspects, may have been drawing on very similar material):

> *His origins:* there are abundant references in many writers to the fact that the Naṣrid house descends from Sa'd b. ʿUbāda, lord of the tribe of Khazraj and Companion of the Prophet (o.w.b.p.) . . . Al-Rāzī said that there entered Spain two men of the family of Sa'd b. ʿUbāda, one of whom settled in the area of Tarragona, the other in a village near Saqrastuna [? the emendation Saragossa is offered by the Egyptian editor of the text, but the garbling of such a familiar name as Saragossa is, perhaps, unlikely], known as the village of the Khazraj. He made his home in Arjona in the *campiña* of Cordova, a region with good soil and high yields. This was his home town, and his forebears lived there in prosperity, dedicating themselves to agriculture. It was then that the crisis developed in political life, and his thoughts turned to obtaining the emirate. (Ibn al-Khaṭīb 1974:II, 92)

Ibn al-Khaṭīb next gives a long account of how Muḥammad obtained a particularly fine steed, an account one feels must be loaded with symbolism, and then: "Within a year he proclaimed his mission (*daʿwa*) in Arjona, and gained control over Jaén. There is conflicting information over those to whom the mission was directed. Some say it was the laboring folk [*ʿummāl*] who were readiest to undertake the task, but others disagree."

By the time of Ibn al-Khaṭīb (b. 1313), we can see that there were conflicting stories in circulation with regard to the new dynasty. Elsewhere in the *Iḥāṭa* the religious and specifically Sufi nature of the early Naṣrid propaganda is more explicit. "Abū Muḥammad al-Basṭī relates: 'I with my own eyes saw him when he entered the city [of Granada]. He was wearing on his head a *shāshiya* [plain wool cap] and had wrapped himself in ribbed material, the shoulders of which were torn.' " We are elsewhere in the same work told that he "wore sandals (*naʿl*) on his feet and coarse cloth (*khāshin*)" (Ibn al-Khaṭīb 1974:II, 94, 97). This was the traditional garb of the Sufi. There is a further allusion to the essentially religious nature of Muḥammad's role at the outset in an enigmatic conversation reported in another of Ibn al-Khaṭīb's works, the *Aʿmāl al-Aʿlām,* where after the accession to power he came to the following arrangement with his associate Ibn Ashqilūla: "When he established himself in Granada he turned over to his relative by marriage [i.e., Ibn Ashqilūla] the giving of all orders, and said to him, 'I am an illiterate [*ummī*] man, and cannot write, what is power for you is power for me, and what is kingdom for you is kingdom for me.' So he assigned him quarters in the Alcazaba, and set him in command of the army" (Ibn al-Khaṭīb 1934:331).

Are we really to take it that Muḥammad I was illiterate? The statement is quite unambiguous. Islam is, of course, the religion proclaimed by the Prophet who was illiterate (*ummī*). The statement concerning Muḥammad I's avoidance of the exercise of power himself fits into the pattern of values of the Islamic ascetic. We will never know what Muḥammad I's exact religious beliefs were (any more than we will know whether he really was illiterate), but we do know that the rhetoric of asceticism and the vocabulary of piety and humility predominate. Ibn al-Khaṭīb (again) put it at the beginning of the section of the *Iḥāṭa* headed "his condition" (*ḥāl,* itself a word replete with associations in Islamic mysticism): "This man was a portent and a sign among Allah's signs because of his lack of guile (*sadhāja*), his integrity (*salāma*), and his spirit of fellowship (*jumhūriyya*) when on service, fighting to defend the frontier, when he displayed his audacity" (1974:II, 93).

That statement acquires added force if we bear in mind that the expression employed to signify "one of God's signs" was *ayatan min ayātillahi.* The concept of the signal virtues of the Naṣrid is certainly not the same as that of the *ayatollah* as it was subsequently to be developed in Shi'ite Iranian Islam, but the religious dimension of this leader's early career can be passed over in silence only at the expense of falsifying the nature of the Islamic state he founded.

Why, then, is this aspect of Muḥammad I's rise to power, so explicitly present in the sources, at times ignored? It is not sufficient to say that it accords ill with the picture of a vassal to a Christian monarch which Spanish historiography has propagated, for Muslim historiography also avoids mention of it. We must take into account also the orthodox Mālikī theological stance, which became such an important part of the propaganda of the Naṣrid dynasty in its later period. Nobody, therefore, had any motive to keep green the memory of this aspect of the Naṣrid past. In order to understand the Sufi beginnings of the Granadan regime, and the switch away from that particular religious emphasis which ensued as the thirteenth century went by, it is necessary for us to focus on the clan that was so closely associated with Muḥammad at the outset, the Banū Ashqilūla.

The Banū Ashqilūla and the Naṣrids

The period of Ashqilūla political activity is relatively short, spanning from the 1230s to the end of the century. This family first comes into prominence in 1232 when their then leader, Abū᾿l-Ḥasan ʿAlī Ibn Ashqilūla al-Tujībī assisted Muḥammad Ibn Naṣr Ibn al-Aḥmar to make his *pronunciamento* in Arjona, and they provided invaluable assistance to the Naṣrid cause up to the takeover of Granada, and beyond. For the first twenty years of the regime, the Ashqilūla clan were close and loyal associates and collaborators of Muḥammad in all his enterprises—both the many early ones which proved abortive, such as the brief assumption of power in Seville, and the successful positive response in 1237 to an invitation from the notables of Granada to come and assume control of that city.

The basis of the relationship between them and the Banū᾿l-Aḥmar was a series of marriages: Abū᾿l-Ḥasan ʿAlī is described as the *ṣihr* of Muḥammad I (Ibn al-Khaṭīb 1934:331). This word is usually rendered as "son-in-law," probably correctly in this case, but it should not be forgotten that this word can also be used to describe other relationships by marriage, particularly that of brothers-in-law. The two families were, in the colloquial English usage, "in-laws," but the strongest link between them is probably alluded to by Ibn al-Khaṭīb in the "Memoir" on the rift between Ibn Naṣr and the Banū᾿l-Ashqilūla which is contained in his *Aʿmāl al-Aʿlām* where, after mentioning the links created by the marriages between members of the two families, he speaks of Muḥammad I's son-in-law as being *mumāthil lahu* (1934:330). This expression might in other contexts be rendered as "bearing a likeness to him," "analagous," "comparable to him," but anyone familiar with the patterns of relationships in Andalusia as described by other anthropologists may find the term *compadrazgo* springing to mind. Through the bonds of *compadrazgo* the two individuals concerned become "faithful friends for life": *compadres*. The bonding may well be reinforced by marriages, but these are secondary to the lifelong pact of mutual help and trust between the two males (Pitt-Rivers 1954:107–8). The words already quoted, "what is power for you is power for me, and what is kingdom for you is kingdom for me," seem to articulate just such a pact. In dividing out the spoils of government not only among the members of his own family, but also among the Banū Ashqilūla, Muḥammad would have been conforming to a well-known pattern of behavior in an Andalusian society of small cultivators.

Another parallel springs to mind for such a cohesive and tightly knit group of associates acceding to power: the Almohads. The Almohad preaching was initiated by Ibn Tumart (1078–1130), but power in that case passed on Ibn Tumart's death (ca. 1130) to his faithful friend and ally ʿAbd al-Muʾmin. Ibn Tumart provided the original charismatic leadership, ʿAbd al-Muʾmin the continuity of administration which prevented the movement from foundering. There was one significant difference between the Almohad experience and that of the Naṣrids. With the Almohads it was the practical man of affairs who ensured that the new regime lived on, leaving behind as a pious memory the preaching of a prophetic figure. With the Naṣrids the charismatic leader, Muḥammad, after initially appearing to spurn power, leaving the army and most other practical matters in the hands of his *compadre* Abū'l-Ḥasan ʿAlī, later asserted himself and took over, leaving the erstwhile practical politician outmaneuvered. The Banū Ashqilūla were consigned to exile. In the case of the Almohads, the pious rhetoric of the fundamentalist preaching of Ibn Tumart was retained and used as eventually the only ideological cement that held together the empire ruled by the descendants of ʿAbd al-Muʾmin. In the case of the Naṣrids the preacher (*dāʿī*) of the period of the struggle for power himself initiated the transition away from a religion of enthusiasm, and he kept the kingdom for himself and his own family—a transition that was paid for by his acceptance of the doctrinal guidance of the orthodox religious establishment of Andalusia, a group that was profoundly attached to the teachings of the law school of Mālik ibn Anas.

The marriage links between the two clans were multiple. Abū'l-Ḥasan ʿAlī's daughter Fāṭima was married to Yūsuf b. Naṣr. His son Abū Isḥāq Ibrāhīm, whose seat was the virtually impregnable castle of Comares, was married to a Naṣrid princess, Muʾmina: he later came to control Guádix. In all parts of the kingdom the Banū Ashqilūla gave devoted service. In the farthest west in 1233, when Muḥammad had made his unsuccessful bid to wrest Seville from Ibn Hūd, Abūʾl Ḥasan ʿAlī had been the governor on the spot, ready even to carry out the unpleasant task of doing away with the local Muslim leader, al-Bājjī. In the farthest east in 1265 Murcia was to be ruled by an Ashqilūla governor, Abū Muḥammad, nephew of Muḥammad I. If geographically they ranged wide, their center of focus from an early date was Malaga, and from 1255 Abū Muḥammad was the governor there.

The two families were so closely intertwined in their grip on power that it is difficult to understand how they fell out, why they became such bitter enemies. According to Arié the dissension arose because in 1257 Muḥammad I went back on his promises to share the kingdom eventually with the Banū Ashqilūla: he declared his own sons Muḥammad and Yūsuf to be his heirs. Also, in 1266 Muḥammad announced that one of his daughters was to marry not an Ashqilūla but one of her Naṣrid cousins, Faraj (Arié 1973:66). Against such a reading of events, María Jesus Rubiera alleges that the Banū Ashqilūla "made no show of being displeased" at the news of 1257 (Rubiera 1983:89). She suggests that the real cause of the rift was Muḥammad I's decision to call in North African assistance to deal with the crisis stemming from the collapse of the Mudejar revolt of 1264: the Banū Ashqilūla feared they would be replaced as the military mainstay of the regime. And the marriage, in her view, must have been that of Muḥammad II's daughter, not Muḥammad I's. It is probable that both historians are in essence right. The Naṣrid decision to begin to restrict power to the Naṣrid family group cannot have failed to alarm the Banū Ashqilūla, and the decision to call in North African aid will have been a danger signal. From about this point the differences between the two clans begin to be perceived in such religious terms that the Arabic word *fitna* is used (a word usually reserved for the most serious of violent doctrinal disagreements).

That Granada was a territory beleaguered by outside threats is a familiar enough idea, that it was often in danger of foundering because of internal dissensions is perhaps not sufficiently taken into account. It was not only in riots and battles that the *fitna* was manifested; we also find trials for heresy culminating in public executions.

Evidence on the nature of the battle of beliefs which underlay the strife is sparse. Ibn al-Khaṭīb writing in the *Aʿmāl al-Aʿlām* uses the word *khilāf* 'dispute', 'divergence of opinion' (1934:330). After describing these disagreements, he makes the point that the Banū Ashqilūla nevertheless desisted from making their own appointments of judges and from striking their own coinage, so long as Muḥammad I was alive. But after his death (1273) "the *fitna* grew worse, discords abounded, and they began to wage open war and sought the assistance of the Christians, until the Sultan [the Naṣrid] with his superior resources brought an end to all that" (Ibn al-Khaṭīb 1934:331).

Ibn al-Khaṭīb's mention of the question of the appointment of judges is an allusion to religious discord, but for information on what was going on inside Ashqilūla territory (i.e., mainly in Malaga) we have to turn to the more indirect source of al-Qashtālī's *Kitāb tuḥfat al-mugtarib bi-bilād al-Magrib,* a work that sets out to document the claims of a religious leader, al-Yuhānisī, to spiritual authority. Precisely because its center of focus is outside the Banū Ashqilūla problem, it brings us occasional invaluable insights in incidental remarks.

We read of a Malaga rent by sectarian discord, a place where wild and heretical preachers flourished. And these preachers, we are told, received Ashqilūla support:

> We arrived in Malaga in the year 666 (1267–1268) and found the city consumed by a conflagration, for one al-Fazārī, Ibrāhīm, had erected there a beacon to deceit by his false claims to be prophet and messenger. It had been one of the matters of contention between the Ashqilūla and the sultan whether this man was the one who was awaited to humble the pride of the devil and to reinforce the pillars of the faith. What he used to say was: "I am naught but a prophet from heaven" . . . and when the people had fallen for this deception, he proceeded to preach his prophethood, and his role as messenger. If any of the scholars opposed him, he incited the *ra'īses* [i.e., the Banū Ashqilūla] against them, and he spread slander abroad. Matters eventually reached the pitch of him having one of the leading scholars publicly humiliated without any justification: he was scourged with lashes and then paraded through the markets. Some people believed al-Fazārī to be a holy man (*walī*) and others said he was a prophet (*nabī*). (al-Qashtālī 1974:81)

Al-Qashtālī is here more concerned with a conflict between *his* holy man, al-Yuhānisī, and the Ashqilūla protégé al-Fazārī. He is delighted that al-Fazārī comes to a bad end, crucified in Granada, after being cursed by al-Yuhānisī. The text therefore provides valuable independent confirmation that al-Fazārī was executed in Granada. Ibn al-Khaṭīb had given details of this incident:

> There arose between him [al-Yuhānisī] and the Tujībī governors of the Banū Ashqilūla who were in command in Malaga bad relations made ever worse by slanders disseminated by a charlatan who practiced the arts of magic and who on the basis of charismatic power (***karāma***) laid claim to prophetic status. He was known as al-Fazārī and his name was Ibrāhīm. [Perhaps, Fazārī was an epithet, cf. ***fazzura*** 'riddle', 'puzzle', etc.] He was weird in his behavior, outrageous in his manner of acting, an extravagant enchanter claiming he knew what would happen in the future. He overstepped the bounds with his development of asceticism and enchantment. His following consisted of worthless people of the basest sort who led no settled life. (1973:I, 191)

Ibn al-Khaṭīb tells us how al-Fazārī incited the mob against the worthy orthodox scholar Ibn al-Zubayr, whose house was broken into, whose valuable library was scattered, and who was finally driven to seek refuge "under the wing of the Sultan of Granada, the emir, son of the emir Ibn Naṣr [i.e., Muḥammad II], who accorded him asylum and acknowledged his claims." Then later "power returned to the emir in Malaga, and so he sent a summons for al-Fazārī, and called witnesses against him, and took great pains to have his teachings refuted. Finally he had him executed in Granada" (1973:I, 192).

There is a pathetic final paragraph to this account, which does not modify in any way the heartless gloating tone of Ibn al-Khaṭīb's account: "Our ***shaykh*** Abū'l-Ḥasan Ibn al-Jayyāb said, 'When orders came for him [al-Fazārī] to be got ready for execution, while he was still in the prison where he was kept awaiting his fate, he began to recite the ***Sūra Yā-sīn*** aloud. One of the common folk who had crowded into the jail called out to him, "You stick to your own Koran! What are you stealing ours for today!" Or words to that effect. This has become a well-known example of wit.' "[5]

This tells us that in the opinion of his enemies al-Fazārī had written a Koran of his own. We also learn that when confronted with imminent

5. Ibn al-Khaṭīb 1973:I, 192. The text as edited reads نعرة, which I emend to دعرة, and translate as "common folk," although "lewd fellows" might be preferable.

death he sought consolation in the *Sūra Yā-sīn* as any orthodox Muslim might.

Such an anecdote throws a flood of light on the religious life in Malaga and in Granada. Whether al-Fazārī's mountebank version of prophetic religion was actively encouraged by the Malagan authorities, or whether the breakdown of public law and order opened the way for popular preachers whom the rulers could not control, we shall never know, but the Banū Ashqilūla came to be perceived as enemies by the orthodox whose stronghold was Granada. The orthodox felt themselves under threat. They struck back.

Out of this turmoil two groups emerged victorious. Muḥammad II *al-faqīh* (the "canon lawyer" now we can see the significance of the epithet) and his family gained a grip on power which was to continue for two centuries. But also victorious were the lawyers themselves, the *fuqahā'*, and the scholars. The regime had begun under the leadership of Muḥammad *al-shaykh*. The epithet cannot mean "the old man," for it seems to have been used from an early date. More likely is the sense of "leader of a religious confraternity or mystic brotherhood." The leader of a fraternity of frontiersmen, Muḥammad came to power with the assistance of his *compadre* Ibn Ashqilūla, but once established on his throne he switched the basis of his authority from the self-authenticating legitimacy of a leader of a group of religious enthusiasts to the institutionally more secure (because externally legitimized) authority afforded by the institutions of Sunni Islam.

To convey the determination with which Muḥammad I enforced Mālikī orthodoxy, no illustration is more striking than the case of the offending gestures of the poet Abū Jaʿfar Aḥmad b. Ṣābir al-Qaysī. During some parts of the ritual prayers (*ṣalāt*), this man had the custom of raising his hands to the level of his head at moments when the normal Mālikī practice was to keep the hands much lower. (It should be explained that such an apparently insignificant gesture was regarded by some as indicative of Ẓāhirī sympathies. Ẓāhirism, a form of Islamic fundamentalism that asserted the supremacy of "obvious"—*ẓāhir*—interpretations of the Word of God and held in suspicion logic-chopping in Koran exegesis, had in the past had some minority hold in the Iberian Peninsula. Ibn Hazm, nonetheless, was a Ẓāhiri.) Now Aḥmad b. Ṣābir's practices at prayer might well have escaped attention had he not been secretary (*Kātib*) to Muḥammad I's own son Abū Saʿīd Faraj. Muḥammad issued a simple but terrible threat: either the *Kātib* conformed to standard Mālikī practice in this matter or Muḥammad would have the offending hands hacked off. Aḥmad b. Ṣābir's response was as remarkable as the king's threat. He refused to conform and fled to Egypt, where he put it about that "the *sunna* of the Prophet is dead in Al-Andalus."[6]

These anecdotes tell us that Islam in Granada at this period was no relaxed religion about to merge into a form of syncretism or to be abandoned. The rulers of Granada themselves took religious issues very seriously and knew that their subjects were equally zealous. We must read Muḥammad I's "vassalage" in the light of what we know about his religious beliefs.

Because the cause of Spanish Islam has sometimes been espoused by the liberal opponents of Catholic extremism, there is a tendency for it to be assumed that Catholicism's enemies were liberal and tolerant. We have seen that nothing could have been further from the truth.

Muḥammad I and the Castilian Nobles

Focus has so far been directed on the Banū Ashqilūla and their role in the rise of the Granadan state, and on the primary importance of religious issues in the history of the regime. The explanation this provides for what happened seems coherent and satisfactory. On the Castilian side and in Castilian sources there is no awareness of all this. The Castilians certainly knew of dissensions within the Granadan state, but they appear not to have realized the motivation for these dissensions. What we hear are a set of parallel alternative explanations, in a sense valid as far as they go. The Castilian accounts center on relations between the Castilians themselves, the king of Granada (seen as vassal of the Castilian monarch), and the Banū Ashqilūla (referred to as the *arrayaces,* etc.): the Castilians seek to weaken the position of the enemy king by allying themselves to his internal enemy. This tripartite pattern then changes towards the end of the reign of Muḥammad I, when about 1272 there emerges on the Castilian side a rebel group of nobles under Nuño González de Lara, thus making a symmetrical pattern with on each side a band of rebels in opposition to the monarch, so that an interesting crossover of loyalties takes place.

6. For the offending posture, see the "posture of prayer" depicted by E. W. Lane in *The Manners and Customs of the Modern Egyptians,* London/New York (Everyman edition), n.d.:78.

As so often in Granadan history, the analysis of what went on in this particular affair resembles an account of the moves in a game of chess (perhaps it was not for nothing that chess was at this period looked upon as intellectual training for the ruling class rather than a distracting pastime). We may begin to follow the moves of the game in 1266 when, as we have seen from the Arabic accounts, Malaga was in an uproar of religious conflict and civil disorder. The rulers of the city (Banū Ashqilūla) were afraid that Muḥammad I would take their city from them. They may have been concerned about the possibility that Muḥammad would call in North African help (thus bringing in a new factor which would have further upset the equilibrium). Muḥammad I moved to open conflict with his rebel subjects and laid siege to the city, but he soon realized that he lacked the necessary military strength. (We must remember that from the beginning of the Naṣrid regime the Banū Ashqilūla had been powerful within the armed forces, and so had had ample opportunity to consolidate their power base.)

The Banū Ashqilūla response to Muḥammad's attack was to seek alliance with Castile. Alfonso X, perceiving how this provided him with an effective means of keeping Muḥammad in check, accorded to them the assistance of one thousand Christian knights under the great leader Nuño González de Lara. It was as a result of this move that Muḥammad withdrew from his siege of Malaga and himself entered into negotiations with Alfonso. The resultant agreement concluded at Alcalá de Benzaide gave to Alfonso territory (Muḥammad yielded his claims in the regions of Jerez and Murcia, i.e., those outlying regions he could not hope to control from Granada anyway), and money (2,500,000 maravedis annually). What did Alfonso yield in exchange? Besides such an insignificant concession as pardon for al-Wāthiq of Murcia, what Castile had to offer was abandonment of its compact with the Banū Ashqilūla, who were to return to being Muḥammad's loyal subjects within a year.

Alfonso X had no intention of carrying out his side of the bargain, and if the game could have been stopped at that point he would have come away the clear victor. However, Nuño González de Lara, sent to Granada to put down Muḥammad I's rebellious subjects for him, was himself in the process of becoming a rebel, in company with a number of other magnates (the *Ricos Hombres*) who used Granada as a safe base in which to organize opposition to Alfonso. Muḥammad was understandably disgruntled at Alfonso's reluctance to move against the Banū

Ashqilūla; the Castilian chronicle (of Alfonso X, c. XVI) tells the story as follows:

> While the king of Granada was in his tent, there came to parley with him Nuño González, who said that King Alfonso had done certain wrong things to him and to his father and to his brother, Juan Núñez, and that if they were to find help from the king of Granada, he, Nuño González, would speak to the others and persuade them to join him. Immediately the king of Granada heard this he was delighted, and he spoke, saying that the *arrayaces* [i.e., the Banū Ashqilūla] were occupying his land by force, and doing him much harm, and that King Alfonso had done him harm in not keeping the terms of the agreement made at Alcalá de Benzaide. If Nuño González would speak with his relatives, and with other powerful nobles of the kingdom, to persuade them to join him, then he, Muḥammad, would assist them to force King Alfonso to put to rights all the complaints they had against him. In token of this the king of Granada gave to Nuño González some of his jewels, and shared with him his money, and departed for Granada. (BAE:LXVI, 11)

By this move Muḥammad had won. At one stroke he crippled Alfonso's ability to operate effectively by depriving him of his best troops, and himself acquired these same troops for use against his own recalcitrant Ashqilūla subjects. However, so fine was the balance always in Granadan politics, that the slightest move could lead to far-reaching changes. One obvious possibility was a reconciliation between Muḥammad and the Banū Ashqilūla, and indeed negotiations were attempted under the sponsorship of a reliable intermediary, al-Tahurtī from Morocco, but the attempt got nowhere.

And at this juncture, on January 22, 1273, while on a minor military expedition quite near to Granada itself, Muḥammad fell from his horse and was killed (Ibn al-Khaṭīb A.H. 1347:36).

Muḥammad had by this time so securely set out the lines of Granadan policy that his death did not bring any catastrophic collapse in the regime. His son Muḥammad II was able to take over from him and to implement the actions Muḥammad had in hand. That he was able to bequeath a functioning state to his successor was a major achievement. He had managed to construct a house on quicksands that had appeared to offer no secure foundations. Against the background of the greatest defeat suffered by the Muslims of the peninsula (the loss of the valley of the Guadalquivir), a man with no secure base at all (his native town of Arjona occupied in 1244), after a career initial phases of which were characterized by unheroic compromises with the enemy all along the line from Seville to Jaén, and the later phases of which were marred by internal discords arising from the alienation of his principal supporters, yet managed to snatch from disaster the one thing he perceived to be feasible: a relatively secure refuge for Islam in the peninsula. The price to pay for the preservation and development of that refuge would be continual vigilance, readiness to enter into all sorts of compromises, readiness to switch alliances as the shifts of power politics required, anything and everything that was necessary to prevent Granada from being absorbed. One thing alone mattered: survival.

Underlying all the shifts of politics and international relations was a religious stability, itself based, as we have seen, on a doctrinal switch. The religion of a frontier *shaykh* who at the outset displayed all the austere symbols of the fundamentalist believer—threadbare coarse robes, sandals, simplicity of life—was exchanged for Sunni orthodoxy blessed with the approval of the *fuqahāʾ* (lawyers) and the *ʿulamāʾ* (scholars), securely in the mainstream of Islamic culture.

THREE

Enclaves and Anomalies

For a quarter of a millennium at the end of the Middle Ages Muslims of the Iberian Peninsula had a simple choice: either to accept subject Muslim (Mudejar) status within one of the Christian states (Aragon, Castile, Navarre) or live within the Islamic kingdom of Granada. However, at the beginning of the period which concerns us there were, during a brief transitional period, a number of exceptions to the simple bipartite division, a number of areas besides Granada with pretensions to independent status. None of the these would-be Islamic states was to last for very long, and most of the political entities mentioned here were very small indeed. It might be more in accord with a sense of historical proportion to treat some of them as the estates of feudal lords, of which the only peculiarity was that the lord and most of his men were Muslims. Perhaps they should at least be listed, because these unsuccessful Islamic states of the thirteenth century provide us with a measuring stick against which to judge the degree of success of the Naṣrid kingdom.

If these Islamic enclaves, Niebla or Murcia or Crevillente, failed to survive where Granada lived on, that was not due to any initially superior legitimacy possessed by Granada; the differences were geographical, demographic, and strategic rather than constitutional. None of the would-be states that failed possessed all the elements—a mountainous situation facilitating defense, distance from centers of Christian population, and a long sea coast, through which could pass military aid from North Africa—which in combination were probably the underlying reasons for Granada's success. Nevertheless at the outset, in the middle of the thirteenth century, it could not have been predicted with any certainty that all these Muslim enclaves would be obliterated and only

Granada would survive. These petty states were not so much potential allies in the fighting on the frontier against the Christian foe as rivals. The readiness of their rulers to plot and intrigue against one another has led some to speak of this as the third *ṭāʾifa* period. Whether it is legitimate to extend the use of the term *ṭāʾifa* analogically from the confused maelstrom of the eleventh century (when the term *mulūk al-ṭawāʾif* 'party kings' first came into use) to other confused periods of transition is dubious. In the eleventh century it is clear that there was a *ṭāʾifa* of the Berbers, a *ṭāʾifa* of Slavs, and so forth—sectional loyalties that provided nuclei for the petty states that sprang up in the chaos created by the collapse of the Caliphate, so that it is meaningful to speak then of a *ṭāʾifa* period. It is by no means certain that the petty states that emerged in the thirteenth century did so in response to the same mechanisms of power. If the term *ṭāʾifa* is to be used at all, it must simply serve to recall that in the history of Islam in Spain there was a constant pattern of alternation between stability under central rule and near-anarchic proliferation of petty states wherever the central authority was absent or unable to function effectively. It may be of some advantage to have a term that correctly implies that before the situation eventually polarized unambiguously into free Muslims on one side, subject Muslims on the other, there was in the thirteenth century a fairly long phase during which Granada was but one of a number of Islamic petty states and enclaves, all obliged to confront the problem of how to survive in the face of powerful Christian enemies.

If we follow the east-to-west order adopted in chapter 2, we must begin with the Islamic enclaves and states of the lands of the Crown of Aragon, all of them, of course, in the Kingdom of Valencia. The Islamic enclaves that existed within Aragonese territory (that ruled by al-Azraq, and that ruled by the Banū ʿĪsā) will be dealt with in chapter 8 (and the other, more dubious case of the Muslims of the Balearics at the end of chapter 7). However, its singularity obliges us to look at the case of Crevillente here.

Crevillente

The tiny lordship of Crevillente was not in fact incorporated into Valencia until 1304. From 1243 to 1296 it was a Mudejar state under Castilian overlordship. This area near Elche lies on the borders of the spheres of Castilian and Aragonese power, and its survival must be attributed to this circumstance, and perhaps also to the recognition by Christians of the usefulness to them of a small political unit which could constitute no political or military threat to any of their essential interests, but which through its continuing open relations with Granada could serve as a channel for diplomatic contact and perhaps for espionage. In this village-state there ruled a dynasty (if we may employ such a word in speaking of so insignificant an entity) which lasted until 1318, longer than any of the other Muslim ruling families of this age, apart from the Naṣrids.

Guichard (1973) in his study of the lords (*raʾīs*) of Crevillente at this period traces the existence of separate rule in this area back to the period of anarchy before the Christian conquest, and infers that this family was exercising effective rule there from the fact that when James I of Aragon, acting on behalf of the Castilians, intervened to repress the Mudejar revolt in 1265, he received the lord after having taken over from him two castles (Soldevila 1983:153 [Jaume I No. 422]). This appears to be the earliest evidence of the existence of this local dynasty, that of the Banū Hudayr. We are not even certain of the personal name of the ruler at this early period, but he must have been of service to Alfonso X in the course of the rising of the Mudejars, because in 1266 Alfonso awarded him an extra hamlet (*alquería*) to add to his domains, and there are traces in the documentation of the continued existence of this political unit (which in 1282 at least was for administrative purposes being treated as subordinate to Orihuela). That Crevillente did not function merely as a fief of the lowest rank, but as an entity that had some independence even at the level of interstate relations, is suggested by a document of 1284: the letters of credence of the Aragonese ambassador to Granada are copied to Royç Abuabdilla Abenhudeyr, lord of Crevillente. The good relations which obviously existed between the ruler of Crevillente and the Aragonese throne must have facilitated the transfer of this entity to Aragonese suzerainty in 1296. The *raʾīs* gave homage ("es féu son hom e son vassall") after Aragonese arms had taken Alicante (Soldevila 1983:835 [Muntaner]).

Guichard characterizes the attitude of Crevillente towards the Aragonese in their fighting with Alicante (i.e., Naṣrid Granada) as "at the least one of friendly neutrality" (1973:292), and when after these campaigns the time came for an allocation of territories between Castile (Alfonso de la Cerda) and Aragon, the *raʾīs* were able to opt for Aragon rather than Castile. From these negotiations there accrued to Crevillente yet another minor territorial addition, Beniopa in the direction of

Gandía. It would seem that the *raʾīs* up to 1296 was called Aḥmad and that he was succeeded by a Muḥammad (up to 1306), followed by another Muḥammad (up to 1316), and finally by Ibrāhīm up to 1318.

The ruler of Crevillente at times was used by the Aragonese authorities as the collector of taxes for other areas in the region of Murcia. In case one should draw from all this the picture of a ruler servilely subordinate to Christian rulers and cut off from other Muslims, it is important to bear in mind that the Aragonese at this time actually had in their service a Marīnid detachment under al-ʿAbbās Ibn Raḥo based in the Val de Ricote, and the *raʾīs* and his men were for operational purposes grouped with these North African warriors in fighting against Castile in 1303. Not only this, but Muḥammad (I) appears to have acted as recruiting agent for Aragon in Granada itself, bringing in more "Zanāta."

In the face of all this evidence of the astute success of the rulers of Crevillente in remaining afloat in the troubled waters of peninsular politics, the question arises of why they did eventually go under. Guichard shows that on the death of Muḥammad II in 1316, a conflict arose within the ruling family between his widow Finda (presumably "Hind") acting on behalf of his son and successor Ibrāhīm, and another member of the family, ʿAlī. Bartolomeo de Vilalba, the emissary of the Aragonese crown, played a key role in these maneuvers, the outcome of which was that some compensation was given to some surviving members of the family, but the crown assumed effective control (Guichard 1973:303–13). Presumably the Aragonese were only interested in permitting this anomalous entity to subsist for so long as it constituted a political advantage. Divisions within the Banū Hudayr family would have meant that outside troublemakers could easily have suborned them, thus converting Crevillente into a potential liability, and so it was astutely liquidated. The remainder of the story of the Muslims of Crevillente will be found in the chapter on Valencia (chapter 8).

Murcia

From Crevillente, Murcia lies fifty kilometers to the southwest. It was for the Christians an incomparably more important prize. Not surprisingly the period of transition here is complex in the extreme. At the death of Ibn Hūd in 1238, Murcia had declared for his son al-Wāthiq billāh, but his rule was short, and in August 1238 we find a *faqīh* ruling under the absurdly pretentious honorific title of Ḍiyāʾ al-Sunna ("resplendence of the custom of the Prophet"), a style which did not save him from assassination in 1239. For a time the authority of Zayyān b. Mardānish extended over Murcia, and he seems to have set al-Wāthiq free. Al-Wāthiq, as we shall see, was to demonstrate a rare talent for survival. One of the Ibn Hūd clan, known as Abenhudiel to the Castilians, was ruling in 1240 under the title of Bahā᾽ al-dawla, and this prince in 1243 entered into a relationship of vassalage with Castile after negotiations, first in Toledo and then in Alcaraz, with Alfonso. The *First General Chronicle* narrates this stage in relationships as follows:

> The Moors surrendered the castle of Murcia to the Prince Alfonso, and acknowledged his authority over the whole domain, agreeing that he should receive all its income with the exception of certain concerns left to the benefit of Abenhudiel and to other lords of Crevillente and Alicante and Elche and Orihuela and Alhama and Alacado and Ricote and Cieza and all the other places in Murcia where the lords were independent [*señoreados sobre si*]. In this way the Moors acknowledge the authority of Prince Alfonso in the name of his father King Ferdinand over the whole of the kingdom of Murcia with the exception of Lorca and Cartagena and Mula, places which did not surrender nor enter into these negotiations with the others. Little did they gain thereby, for in the end they had to surrender unwillingly. (PCG:II, 742)

The importance of this surrender will readily be appreciated; not only did it set up a Mudejar state in Murcia itself, but also a host of other similar areas in the region, the number of which it is impossible to determine. We might well be suspicious of the loose wording of the Castilian chronicle as being a way of obscuring a de facto reverse or failure without loss of face, were it not for the case of Crevillente, already described, where the surviving documentation as studied by Guichard, even though it is sparse, still does make it clear what kind of puppet regime must have operated in a number of zones in the southeast.

The regime of Bahā᾽ al-dawla (Abenhudiel) after the settlement with Castile continued to manifest most of the external signs of an independent state. It had its own army and its own administrative structure. The ruler struck his own coinage. He would appear to have behaved much as Muḥammad I of Granada did: he offered his vassalage while opportunistically watching for a chance to break free. True, we do not find Bahā᾽ al-dawla committing himself quite so deeply to the service of the Castilian monarch as did Muḥammad I of Granada, who participated in the Castilian attack on Seville, but Bahā᾿ al-dawla certainly signed documents from Alfonso's chancery alongside other principal vassals on a number of occasions—1253, 1254, and 1259—and the arrangement was not personal to him, for in 1259 his name is replaced by Abu Jaffer, king of Murcia, on a great *privilegio rodado.*[1] Abū Jaʿfar, Bahā᾿ al-dawla's son, ruled for less than two years and was then replaced by al-Wāthiq (Cagigas 1949:II, 372). The reappearance of this name after a gap of a quarter century is surprising, and one must wonder whether the al-Wāthiq active in the 1260s is the same as the one who so briefly held power in 1238–1239. It seems probable that it is the same man, certainly he was equally unsuccessful. By this time the Naṣrids' power extended far enough for al-Wāthiq to feel constrained to acknowledge Muḥammad I as his suzerain. Muḥammad entrusted to one of the Banū Ashqilūla, ʿAbdallah b. ʿAlī, the task of bringing aid to Murcia. (Another way of describing what happened might be to say that ʿAbdallah took over and remained in command until the inhabitants of the city recalled al-Wāthiq for a third period of rule; the situation was confused.) The Kingdom of Murcia and its affairs now became embroiled both in the fate of the revolt of the Mudejars and in Naṣrid policy aims. The Aragonese forces, acting for Castile, marched in, and it was to James that al-Wāthiq surrendered his city in 1266.

James tells us of his dealings with the Muslims of the city:

> At the time of vespers, the *wazīr* [*algutzir*] appeared in our presence, and told us that they had done all that they were asked, but the Christians were entering the city, and were taking for themselves things which they ought not to. We said we would send three men to stop anybody going beyond the castle, and that the

1. Cagigas 1949:II, 372 and n.55. The *privilegio rodado* of 1260 (Ballesteros-Beretta 1963:1082 No. 472) is in favor of the Cathedral of Seville. Clearly it was not felt odd for a non-Christian to append his name to such a document. (See also *Mem. Hist. Esp.,* 1:166.) Bahā᾿al-dawla signs the document of 1253 as "Don Mahomad aben Mahomad abenhuc, Rey de Murcia, vassallo del Rey" (see Fernández y González 1866:335 [also 338, 342, and 345]). Interestingly, one of these documents, dated December 8, 1254, is the foundation deed of a *studium generale* in Seville for Latin and Arabic.

> next morning we would enter the city, and that in company with their elders we would divide the city up.
>
> When morning came, after mass we climbed up to the castle, and he [the *wazīr?*] was with us and five of the chief Saracens of the city of Murcia. . . . We said that the mosque near to the castle should belong to the Christians . . . and be included in our sector of the city, but they said that would not be right, for the treaties said they were to have their mosques, and keep them just as in Saracen times. We said that was correct, but they did not understand: we wanted them to keep their mosques, but what were the Christians to do, they had no church to which to go? And the church should be at the castle gate. For us to be able to hear the muezzin right by our head when we were asleep is, if you think about it, not fitting. You have two mosques in the city, pray in them, and leave us this one. They said they agreed.[2]

The attitude of James seems very reasonable, but the text shows us how weak and unenforceable were any "rights" guaranteed in surrender documents. It would have been most unwise for the Muslims to attempt to hold out for what was "theirs."

This intervention by James was not, of course, limited to Murcia alone, and most of the centers of population that had negotiated for themselves some kind of independent Mudejar status from 1243 onwards were now swallowed up by outright conquest: Villena, Elda, Elche, Alicante, Orihuela. After the Christian takeover in Murcia, al-Wāthiq appears to have been given a castle in which to reside. In Arabic the name appears as the consonant outline *Y-S-R,* of uncertain vocalization, but no doubt translated by the Romance name of "Fortuna." Perhaps from the Muslim viewpoint the most important long-term consequence of the disastrous Revolt of the Mudejars (see below) was this conversion of the Kingdom of Murcia, for two decades an area where Muslims still lived under Muslim rule, into Christian territory held on

2. Soldevila (1985: 159 [Jaume I No.445]) has variant readings in the passage where I have translated "muezzin." One text reads *sabaçala* (i.e., *sāḥib al-ṣala* or *imām*), another *ala lo sabba o alla,* apparently hopelessly corrupt. The uncertain reading in no way affects the relevance of the anecdote: James was in a position to expropriate the mosque, whatever the surrender terms had said.

the same basis as Cordova or Seville. In Cordova and such cities, of course, after the conquest "those Arabs left in the city could go out alive, and that was all," as the *First General Chronicle* puts it (PCG:II, 733). We have to turn to the far west to find another example of an Islamic enclave left in being in the second half of the thirteenth century. To understand what happened in that region, it is necessary to bear in mind the circumstances of the final stages of the Reconquest, which, of course, involved the Portuguese as well as the Castilians.

Enclaves in the West

The final stages of the Portuguese advance down the Atlantic coast brought them in 1238 to Mértola, in 1239 to Tavira, and finally in 1249 Alfonso III took Faro. As in the east, the final stages of the Christian advance were bedeviled by tension between the Castilians, fanning outwards in their southward drive, and the maritime power coming down the coast. In the east the region in dispute was Murcia, and that eventually went to Castile. In the west the disputed zone was the Algarve, where Castile abandoned its claim. One factor in this decision must have been that a short distance from Huelva there subsisted a powerful Muslim center. Niebla under its ruler, Ibn Maḥfūẓ, did accept vassal status under Alfonso X, and Alfonso made no attempt at first to conquer the zone; he must have realized that it would be dangerous to extend Castilian lines far to the west in an area open to incursions from the sea.

Mūsā b. Muḥammad b. Naṣr Ibn Maḥfūẓ had originally come from Seville, and in the confused years following the collapse of the Almohads had created for himself a domain which included not only the greater part of the Algarve, but the coast as far as Huelva and inland as far as Gibraleón as well. He also adopted the pretentious honorific title of al-Muʿtaṣim. After Ferdinand's capture of Seville, Ibn Maḥfūẓ gave allegiance to him in 1237 and fell back on Niebla, defensively a very strong position. His more westerly lands went to the Portuguese, and other areas, such as Gibraleón (Jabal al-ʿAyūn) and even Saltes, were ceded to the Castilians. The wisdom of Ferdinand in not attempting to oust Ibn Maḥfūẓ in the 1230s became clear when Alfonso X did finally undertake siege in 1262. It took nine months for the forces Castile could deploy to get the better of the defenders of Niebla (Ballesteros-Beretta 1963:313–20).

A curious anecdote about this final battle is to be found in the

Chronicle of Alfonso X. There would seem to be no reason to doubt its veracity.

> And because the whole of the Algarve was in the hands of the Moors, at whose head was a Moor called Aben Mafot, King Alfonso summoned all the men of his kingdom, and the nobles and the town councils, and assembled an army, and set out to besiege Niebla. As soon as he had reached it, he gave orders for encampments to be constructed, and they brought up many siege engines, for the place then had very strong fortifications, and was protected on all sides by a wall with strong towers, all of stone construction. Aben Mafot had the town well supplied with ample food, and it was defended by good troops, so that King Alfonso had to maintain the siege for a long time, and attack the enemy hard with siege engines and engage him in fierce hand to hand skirmishes.
>
> It so happened that while the king was engaged in this siege, a great plague of flies afflicted the troops of his besieging army, so that none of them could eat anything without the flies spoiling it. This caused them to suffer from a wasting sickness from which many died. The king and all his men therefore decided to abandon that siege after sustaining it for seven months.
>
> Now at that time there were in the camp two friars, one called Friar Andrew and the other Friar Peter, and they presented themselves to the king, and told him that it was a mistake for him to have it in mind to leave when he had almost captured the town, for the Moors would bring in fresh supplies and would repair the defensive works knocked down by the siege engines, so that when he came to make a second attempt to capture it, he would not be able to reduce it to the point which he had already reached. The king replied that he did not know what to do, for the suffering in his camp was very great, and men were dying. The friars replied that they had advice to give, and immediately a public proclamation was made throughout the army that whoever brought in one *almud* [a measuring capacity] of flies to the friars would be paid two silver *torneses* for each measure. The poorer folk struggled hard against the flies in order to earn the coins, and they brought in such quantities that they filled up two disused grain silos that were there. In consequence the suffering diminished and they began to get the better of the sickness that had been causing so

> many deaths, so that the Christians were able to attend to what was necessary in order to capture the town.
>
> Aben Mafot had reached the point of having no food left for himself or for his men and when he saw that Alfonso and his men were still going to keep the siege up after nine and a half months, he sent asking for the king's mercy, and begged to be allowed to leave safely with his men and their possessions. He asked to be assigned estates to assure his maintenance for life, in exchange for the surrender of the town of Niebla and the area of the Algarve. This King Alfonso accepted, and in this way Niebla was handed over. King Alfonso assigned King Aben Mafot a place to live all his life [and the chronicle goes on to mention all the dues and rents so assigned]. (BAE:LXVI, 6)

One of the properties given to Ibn Maḥfūẓ was a residence on the outskirts of Seville, which for long continued to be called the *Huerta del Rey* (Ballesteros-Beretta 1963:319). Whether he did live out his life there is not known, but is unlikely, for we hear of him crossing to the court of al-Murtaḍā in Marrakish (where the Almohad regime was about to be swallowed up by the Banū Marīn) (*Dhakīra* 1920:106).

The Fate of the Enclaves

To recapitulate, in the Iberian Peninsula the Islamic state ruled over by Banū'l Aḥmar emerged alongside at least two other major centers of Islamic power, Murcia in the east, Niebla in the west, not to mention other smaller enclaves. The Muslim rulers of these areas do not seem to have been less resolved than the Naṣrids to maintain their independence. They were also as ready as the Naṣrids were to negotiate with the Christians, and to find compromises which would enable them to live on in their homeland.

All these petty states were incorporated in the 1260s into Castile (the exceptions being a few localities in the region of Orihuela and Elche which fell to Aragon). These were, in a way, the victims of the ill-conceived Mudejar uprising in Castilian territories. The decade of the 1260s, by the same token, marks the point in Naṣrid history when Granada came to realize its destiny as an effective even if limited refuge for Islam in the peninsula. That new policy was clearly not acceptable to all Muslims, and the Ashqilūla wars were probably one aspect of the crisis during which the new state policy was forged.

One of the puzzles of this period is that it is difficult to understand the policy of Granada towards the lands to the west of the valley of the Guadalquivir. We hear of Muḥammad I's participation in the Castilian conquest of Jerez in 1261, and he did nothing to deflect Alfonso from the siege of Niebla in 1262. We may speculate that Muḥammad may have taken the risk of allowing the Castilians to eliminate potential Muslim rivals for him, thus putting him in the position of being the sole leader of all Muslims in the peninsula. With Ibn Maḥfūẓ of Niebla (and others) out of the way, Muḥammad could set about his campaign of 1264 to shake the Castilian hold over the recently captured lands. And even if the Mudejar revolt were to fail—as we shall see it did—the balance would be far from purely negative. Granada emerged as the unquestioned Islamic successor state in the peninsula, heir to the whole Andalusi heritage. And with each area that was captured by Castile, Granada received a further wave of "immigrants," refugees from Christian rule. In a sense, although Muḥammad I was playing a game of uncertain outcome, every possible result but one was in his favor. And since the only really dangerous outcome, the Castilian conquest of Granada itself, was excluded because, for all their rhetoric, the Christians were not militarily prepared for it, Granada could hope to flourish when all about her was in collapse and decline. The game being played was, nevertheless, a very dangerous one, and the conduct of Granadan policy at this period must have demanded a cool nerve.

The Revolt of the Mudejars

From the beginning of the reign of Alfonso X we may divide the Mudejars under Castilian rule into two broad groups. On the one hand there are those Muslims from Old and New Castile and contiguous lands (those listed under A and B in chapter 5) who had for many generations been loyal subjects of the crown, with the Mudejar status of these Muslims written into the charters of their native towns and cities. The second group (largely C, D, and E in chapter 5) were the Muslims of the areas conquered in the thirteenth-century expansion.

There were many differences between these two groups. The first was made up of stable communities, well integrated into the life of the larger communities in which they lived (although in some cases they might live separated from the Christians in "Moorish quarters" or *morerías*). These older Castilian Mudejars counted among their number many skilled craftsmen, carpenters and joiners in particular, and potters, builders, and architects. We cannot be certain what language they used within their own homes, although the presumption is that it was Castilian. However, since in the mid-fifteenth century the writings of Castilian Muslims frequently contain laments at the decline of Arabic, we must assume that Arabic had at some time in the past had some status, at least as a language of community organization and written record.

The situation was quite different where the Mudejars of the Guadalquivir valley were concerned. In contrast with the stability of the Castilian *morerías,* these largely Andalusian groupings were in the thirteenth century subject to violent upheavals. Even in those towns and other areas where the terms of surrender to the Christians had permitted a Muslim community to stay on, it was often relocated, usually in an outer suburb or outlying hamlet. There can have been little feeling of continuity in such towns between the old days of Muslim independence and the new days of subject status. The advice these people had received from their own spiritual advisors had been to leave, to emigrate to a safe Islamic territory. Although some made the journey into North African exile, that was an adventure beyond the purse of many. For most of them, love of their homeland and slender economic means limited their choice of refuge, so that the only place to which they could emigrate was Granada. There was an enormous flow of Muslims into that city from all the recently conquered lands. Those who did not emigrate, or who were still assembling means to do so, lived in a state of unrest, unable to accept their new Castilian masters, but with no idea of what might effectively be done to change their situation.

The revolt of the Mudejars which occurred in 1264 affected the recently acquired lands very seriously, but affected the stable Mudejar communities of Old and New Castile hardly at all. The name by which this episode is known in history, the "Revolt of the Mudejars," thus merits two corrections. In the first place to leave *Mudejars* unqualified fails to indicate that very many Muslim quarters (in Ávila, in Burgos, in Arévalo, in Madrid, etc.) were in no way implicated. In the second place it leaves out of account the role played by the Naṣrids, for the rising was concerted with the ruler of the largest group of Muslims in the peninsula, Muḥammad I of Granada. The revolt of 1264 was in fact an attempt to achieve in Andalusia and Murcia the unity that Muslim resistance had lacked all through the long campaigns of Ferdinand III, from Cordova, lost in 1236, to Seville, lost in 1248. It was the last in the series of battles in which Muslim resistance attempted a stand against the Christian capture of the Guadalquivir basin. In the chapter of Ballesteros-Beretta's life of Alfonso X that deals with this episode, the rising is entitled "La alevosía del Nazarí," which we might render as "The dastardly treason of the Naṣrid." Treason it was, in that many of the participants in the fighting against the Castilians had sworn fealty to Alfonso, but looked at from the Muslim side of the frontier there is no doubt that this was thought of as a desperate last stand.

It was a rising that came dangerously near success. Its effects rocked Alfonso X's complacent self-confidence; from this point onwards none of his major enterprises succeeded, none of his policy objectives was secured. It brought substantial groups of the Castilian aristocracy into open rebellion, and, as we have seen, many of them betook themselves to Granada to pursue their campaign against Alfonso and his allies from that base. Our knowledge of the revolt naturally rests largely on Castilian sources, and Castilian historiography has its good reasons for playing down what the Mudejars, the Andalusian Muslims as a whole, were able to achieve in 1264. It was an event of prime importance.

> The Moors of Jerez realising that the king would be able to do nothing to stop them for some time, surrounded the castle of that town with Garci Gómez Carrillo in it, and his men; the Moors attacked them ruthlessly by night and day, giving them no rest. To help them came Moors from Algeciras and Tarifa, and in spite of all the Christians' efforts, the Moors forced their way into the castle.
>
> The Moors made their way to the tower being defended by Garci Carrillo, and attacked it, burning the gate down and killing the men with him. He defended the gateway as long as he could, to stop them getting in. They did not wish to kill him because of his great goodness, and so they brought up steel hooks to take him, and they hooked him through the flesh with them, but he allowed his flesh to be pulled away rather than be captured. But finally those Moors caught him alive with the hooks, and took the castle and everything else besides. (BAE:LXVI, 9)

It was not only Jerez that fell, so did Lebrija, Arcos, and Medina Sidonia. In Murcia things do not seem to have gone so well for the insurrection: Orihuela, for example, held out, though Murcia itself and Galera fell. What is more, help was arriving from North Africa for the rebels, and Alfonso had to resist a landing in the Guadalquivir estuary (BAE:LXVI, 10).

The Reconquest really had to be undertaken afresh in many places. A full-scale siege, lasting five months, had to be mounted at Jerez, with siege engines to batter down the walls. Alfonso did just manage to subdue Jerez, and from there, one by one, the other centers of rebellion. The aid from Muslims across the sea did not come. The last attempt of the Muslims of Lower Andalusia and of Murcia to recover their ancestral homes failed.

The consequences were, of course, serious. The settlement after this campaign left nothing to the Muslims. In Jerez their mosques became churches. Most of the Muslim population, if they survived, had to leave, and these areas were largely settled by reliable Christians, often from far away.

From this point, the Mudejars of Andalusia, such few as remained, count for very little. The story of the "Mudejars of Castile" becomes almost exclusively the story of the Mudejars of Old and New Castile—those who had wisely not budged when the conspirators rebelled. They knew that Granada could effectively do nothing for them, and that they must work out their own fate.

The year 1264 is also a vital date in the history of Granada. From this point onwards there may be truces and long periods of peace between Castile and Granada, rather empty mention may even be made at times of Granada's vassal status, but nobody is taken in.

We hear very little of the Mudejars of Castile from this time onwards. This community knew very well that its only hope of survival lay in discretion. Cagigas is of the opinion that from this date of 1264 we can begin to speak of *mudejarismo* in Castile. The community sought survival at the price of accepting a limited role and a secondary status in society. As we shall see, they may not have been prominent in society at large, but there are signs of intense intellectual activity within the *aljamas* as these Mudejars grappled with the problems of how to be Muslims within a Christian world.

FOUR

Mudejar Status: The Teachings of the Islamic Lawyers; Christian Attitudes and Doctrines

The Teaching of the Islamic Lawyers: Muslims Should Never Accept Subjugation

The Mudejars posed a series of problems within their own religion. Islam pays great attention to the models of conduct provided by good Muslims of the past, and in particular by the Prophet and his Companions. No direct guidance was forthcoming to Muslims living under Christian rule, for in its early days Islam was a religion always in process of expansion, never of contraction. No Muslim community in the early days ever lived on a permanent basis in the territory of a non-Muslim ruler. (The nearest precedent one might find would be the period spent by some of Muḥammad's flock in the lands of the Christian ruler of Ethiopia, as refugees from the persecution of the Meccan pagan authorities, but those early Muslims returned to Arabia as soon as it was safe to do so—the case is really quite a different one.) When large numbers of Muslims in Spain began to pass under Christian domination, all sorts of doctrinal problems arose, and the pious did what Muslims in doubt about the interpretation of the faith should do: they consulted a *muftī*.

A *muftī* is an Islamic lawyer qualified to provide a formal legal opinion (*fatwā*) on difficult cases referred to him. A particularly valuable source of *fatwās* on the subject of Muslims under Christian rule in Spain is the enormous collection entitled *Kitāb al-Miʿyār* formed by al-Wansharīshī. He was from North Africa (Tlemcen, and he worked mainly in Fez); chronologically he falls towards the end of our period (he died in 1508), so that it might be objected that his opinions do not necessarily reflect the range of experience of the Spanish Muslims. In fact, he seems to have had a special interest in the problems of his brethren across the water, and his compilation gathers together a tradition of jurisprudence which stretches back to the famous twelfth-century Andalusian *qāḍī*, Abūʾl-Walīd Ibn Rushd and beyond. What is particularly valuable is al-Wansharīshī's firmly historical grasp of the context within which the problems he is studying evolved, and his *consulta* fill in at times considerable detail with regard to the general conditions of the Spanish Muslim communities.

The views of al-Wansharīshī on Muslims living under Christian rule are forthright and unambiguous: they all ought to leave the land of unbelief without delay and emigrate to a place where they could live under Muslim rule. He cites with approval the opinion of Ibn Rushd that "the obligation to emigrate from the lands of unbelief will continue right up to Judgment Day" (al-Wansharīshī 1908:196). Al-Wansharīshī, therefore, is not putting forward a narrow personal opinion of his own, but articulating a well-established religious teaching. His is the orthodox view of the Islamic West at this period.

Let us begin with a case that arose in al-Wansharīshī's own day, a case that must have been brought to him direct. It brings out in a particularly clear form the firm conviction that subject Muslim status is not advisable and should be avoided at all costs.

The problem concerns a man who stayed on in Marbella after its conquest, and therefore is chronologically to be situated in the 1480s or even 1490s.

> There is a man from Marbella who enjoys a reputation for his nobility of mind and for his respect for sound religion. He did not go into exile along with his fellow townsmen because he wished to pursue his search for one of his brothers who had earlier gone missing in enemy territory during the fighting. His search has

continued up to the present, but he has abandoned all hope of tracing his brother, and so has decided to depart for exile, but he has been detained for the following reason: he has become the spokesman and the interpreter for the Muslims who have been reduced to tributary status, and they now rely on him heavily, and not just the Muslims of Marbella, but also those of the adjacent western region, who are in a similar plight. When they are in trouble he appears on their behalf before the Christian judges, acts as their advocate and often delivers them from perilous predicaments. If he should leave, few would be able to match his skill. It would be a great loss, and would affect them all adversely.

The question to be decided, therefore, is whether he would be justified to stay on under the rule of the unbelievers, on the grounds that by so doing he affords great assistance to the poor folk of tributary status, even though he himself is in a position to leave for exile whenever he likes.

In the first place, how can it be justifiable for this man to stay on when they [the Mudejars] themselves have no justification for staying under the jurisdiction of unbelievers? There is even less justification, since most of them have permits to leave, and do not lack the means to do so. How could this man possibly find justification for performing his prayers merely as and when the opportunity arises? Especially if we bear in mind that he will never be free from the contamination of the presence of the Christians, with whom he will be in constant contact in the course of his affairs. He will have to sleep in their lodgings, and get up in the mornings in their dwellings while rendering service to his fellow Muslims in the ways stated.

My considered legal opinion [*fatwā*] is accordingly as follows:

God Almighty, the One, the All-Conquering, has created abasement to be inflicted on the accursed unbelievers, fetters and chains for them to drag from one place to the next as a demonstration of his power and of the superiority of Islam, and to honor his chosen Prophet . . . and what is required of the believer is faith in God, in the last day, and an effort to distance oneself from the enemies of God.[1]

1. al-Wansharīshī 1908: 192–93 (= 1981:137–38). I am indebted to Dr. Hossein Bouzineb of the University of Rabat for allowing me to see a draft

Al-Wansharīshī appears to be saying that the obligation to go is a primary one, and he brings out the point that it is on a level with the other primary obligations of the faith, indeed is intertwined with them. Prayer is made impossible because of ritual pollution coming from the Christians. As for alms:

> The collection of alms is a matter for the *imām,* such is one of the basic tenets of Islam, and is laid down for all mankind. But where there is no *imām,* there can be no collection of this tax, for the necessary conditions are absent. As for payment of alms to someone appointed to distribute help to needy Muslims, that is not allowable [as a substitute].
>
> Then there is the fast of Ramadan, the poor man's alms, as it has been called. This has to be celebrated according to the sighting of the new moon as attested to the *imām,* or the Caliph. But where there is no *imām* or caliph, the witnessing of the beginning of the month must remain in doubt. (al-Wansharīshī 1981:138–39)

Al-Wansharīshī goes on to spell out that contact with Christians is a peril; coexistence leads to the erosion of the distinctive features of Muslim life: "One has to beware of the pervasive effect of their way of life, their language, their dress, their objectionable habits, and influence on people living with them over a long period of time, as has occurred in the case of the inhabitants of Ávila and other places, for they have lost their Arabic, and when the Arabic language dies out, so does devotion in it, and there is consequential neglect of worship as expressed in words in all its richness and outstanding virtues."[2]

It is to be noted that living with Christians who are subject to Muslims would not be considered dangerous in the same way; their inferior status makes them safe. "For living with unbelievers, if they are not folk who have protected subject status and a situation of inferiority [*min gayr ahl al-dhimma wa'l-ṣigār*], is not allowable, not for so much as for one hour a day, because of all the dirt and filth involved, and the

of an article, "Respuestas de jurisconsultas magrebíes en torno a la inmigración de musulmanes hispánicos," to appear in *Hespéris-Tamuda.*

2. al-Wansharīshī 1981:141. The place name I have rendered "Ávila" is written "Abulla."

religious as well as secular corruption which continues all the time."[3]

An excellent example of how the sort of teachings set out so forcefully by al-Wansharīshī reached Mudejars is provided by a document from the hoard of books and papers discovered walled up in an old house at Almonacid de la Sierra. (This village is in Aragon, not Castile, but, as will be seen, the document had been addressed to all Mudejars, and it is best considered at this point in connection with al-Wansharīshī's teachings.) The Almonacid document is a copy of a circular sent out by Yūsuf III of Granada (1408?–1417), which was then relayed and copied onwards in Barcelona:

> Praise be to Allah in his Unity! This is a transcript extracted from the original of a letter from ʿAlī al-Barmūnī of Barcelona to the communities of subject Muslims resident in the lands of humiliation.
>
> The sultan of Granada, God grant him succor and victory: to the noble faithful members of the community, our Muslim brethren, loyal companions in the service of God, worshippers of the one true God, God preserve them and raise them up among the saints, and bring us and them together in this victorious city of ours, Granada, over which God watches with his own eyes, from him who is striving to fight the Holy War, God grant him and his servants the Muslims victory in it . . . our lord and master Abū'l-Ḥajjāj Yūsuf [III].
>
> O Brethren, manifest your devotion to the service of God through emigration [*hijra*] as is enjoined on all Muslims by God Almighty. We should flee ourselves and take our families and our wealth with us, for you all know, God bless you, what is to be found in the Holy Koran on the subject of exile. By God, O Muslims, Granada has no equal, and there is nothing like service on the frontier during the Holy War, as the tradition [*ḥadīth*] has it in the words of the Prophet: "Al-Andalus, where the living are happy and the dead martyrs," a city to which, as long as it endures, Christians will be led as prisoners, and where, thanks to God's power, five or six thousand of them and hundreds more are de-

3. al-Wansharīshī 1981:138. ". . . min al-adnās wa 'l-awḍār wa 'l-mafāsid al-dīniyya wa 'l-dunyawiyya ṭūl al-a ʿmār."

> tained. There is no place like it in the East or in the West, thanks be to Him and His bounty. (Ribera and Asín 1912:259–60)

This appeal is based on the authority of the Koran and on tradition. The Koran, of course, does include very many references to *hijra* (exile), but the exile in question is that of the Prophet who left Mecca to take refuge in Medina; so these are not strictly relevant to the exile of Muslims who might think of leaving Christian Spain. As for the *ḥadīth* (tradition) which allegedly praises life in Al-Andalus, that was not a place name that existed in the seventh century. The alleged words of Muḥammad are a fabrication, beyond any shadow of doubt.

Muslims, then, were exhorted in the strongest possible terms to leave Christian Spain and to avoid Mudejar status. Christians, as we will see, were exhorted on the highest authority to cut themselves off from contact with Muslims. Separation of the communities is to be seen as the desire of the religious leadership on both sides of the confessional divide. Christian clergy and Muslim *fuqahāʾ* (jurists) alike called for *apartheid*. Interfaith contact was to be eschewed, if possible banned altogether.

The teachings of the Christian religious hierarchy in practice were ignored by the civil authorities because Christians needed the services of the Muslim inhabitants of the occupied territories. The teachings of the *fuqahāʾ*, such as Abūʾl-Walīd Ibn Rushd, were ignored by many Muslims. Whether the reason was love of the homeland or whether it was poverty and lack of means we do not know, but very many Muslims who in all ways tried to lead pious lives stayed on in spite of the strictures of their leaders. We have seen that the rigorists, such as Al-Wansharīshī, ruled that to be a good Muslim in Christian lands was impossible. What then was the good Muslim there to do if he could not leave or did not wish to do so?

One solution to the problem was to ignore it by simply performing as many of the obligations as possible and replacing those which were impossible with the next best thing. The piety of the Mudejars fell below the standard of the most authoritative teachers, but it was Islamic piety nevertheless. The rigorists, such as al-Wansharīshī, put forward the view that Islamic piety became dangerously weakened by contact with Christians. No doubt many cases would have backed up the view that all contact with a Christian-dominated society was ultimately corrosive, but even the sparse evidence available to us from within Mudejar Islam gives ample proof that Islamic devotion and Islamic virtues could also flourish under the conditions which people like al-Wansharīshī feared so much. Probably the most cogent arguments against him would come from the numerous Morisco documents from the sixteenth century, which show that under conditions of close contact, when Muslims were being forced willy-nilly to attend Christian services, they remained deeply attached to the basic tenets of their faith, and that ignorance of Arabic, cited by him as a sign of spiritual decay, could go along with a stubborn determination to preserve the old religion, even under extremes of persecution. A proper analysis of Morisco devotional literature must be made within the framework of the study of that final Morisco period of Spanish Islam, however, and for our present purposes two documents may serve to demonstrate how in the later Middle Ages Islam did survive among the Mudejars as a structural and organized faith, preserving the essential virtues and pieties in spite of the misgivings expressed so forcefully by *muftīs,* such as al-Wansharīshī.

A number of documents of Mudejar provenance have been published by W. Hoenerbach (1965).[4] One of these is a begging certificate (Madrid B.N. 5324). We know of such documents from Christian sources, of course: a respectable authority provides a piece of paper which a beggar can show in case of need to prove that he is a *bona fide* pauper and a worthy object of charity. Such certificates issued by Muslims and for use in exclusively Muslim circles are, not surprisingly, rare.

After the customary salutations, it is addressed to "the religious lawyers, presiding officers [*umanā*ʾ], *qāḍīs,* judges, elders, and younger men of the community of Muslims and association of worshippers of the one God, wherever they may be, in the regions of Aragon, Valencia and Castile." It then leaves spaces for the name of the authority granting the certificate to be filled in, and then the name of the pauper in question, who is described as: "a poor man from this town of ours, and a neighbor with children to support, indigent, with no property or resources apart from his hope of your charity and what he obtains thanks to your kindness, so that we recommend him to your worships that you may bestow on him your voluntary alms [*ṣadaqāt*]." It then cites verses of the Koran (IX, 60), in which charity is enjoined on the faithful, and it quotes

4. Hoenerbach speaks of the "Naṣrid and Morisco periods" in his title, and under this includes several Mudejar documents.

traditions (*ḥadīth*), such as "the Prophet has said, '*ṣadaqa* is a bridge to Islam'"(Hoenerbach 1965:292–94).

A rigorist taking a position similar to that of al-Wansharīshī might well object that Islam distinguishes between voluntary alms, however laudable, and the formal and canonical requirement to pay *zakāt*. As al-Wansharīshī said in the passage quoted, this has to be done to the duly constituted authority, the *Imām,* so that one type of alms does not make up for absence of the other. However, the existence of certificates of this type does show us that a peninsula-wide network of communities existed, with a hierarchy of officials and with mutually agreed forms of communication.

It will be remembered that al-Wansharīshī specifically mentioned Ávila as a place where in his judgment contact with Christians had led to the loss of the Arabic language, which in turn brought about a decline in religious faith. Our second document is a fifteenth-century *fatwā* emanating from ʿAbdallah b.ʿUthmān b. Aḥmad al-Anṣārī, the minister (*khādim*) of the al-Qibla mosque in Ávila. It concerns the following point of Islamic law: may a man perform the canonical Islamic prayers (*ṣalāt*) on a prayer mat in the form of a sheepskin jacket? The problem arises because *ṣalāt* has to be performed under conditions of ritual purity: tanned leather could not be washed and purified in the prescribed manner, and might be seen as a form of uncooked animal remains (the remains of animals, moreover, which might not have been slaughtered in an acceptable manner).

> May God grant you his recompense in this world and in the next. Since in this famous city there are three *aljamas,* each with its own *alfaquí* [lawyer], and each one of us, insofar as I can understand, is far from following the correct teachings of the religion, we have directed our supplications, first of all to Him and then to yourself, asking that you direct us to the path of obedience to Him, by answering our questions on matters relating to religion over which we disagree.
>
> The first question is whether it is lawful to make the prayer on dead skins in the form known as *zamarra* [a word, probably ultimately of Basque origin, meaning "sheepskin tanned with the wool still on" or "a jacket made of such skin"], either when wearing such a garment or when kneeling on it. In the *Tafrīʿ* [a well-known textbook by Ibn al-Jallāb] the author declared that the use

> of the skins of dead animals was allowable on condition that they were cured, but that it was not allowable to trade in them or to perform the *ṣalāt* on them and this is what we find in the *Risālas* [the *Risāla* of al-Qayrawānī had considerable authority as a summary of Islamic law] and in the *Talqīn*. However, they [presumably the other *alfaquís* from the other Ávila *aljamas*] disagreed with me, and asserted that prayer on a dead skin was lawful, but I repeated my disagreement, and there is divergence of views between us, so I make the declaration that skins before they are cured are impure [*najasa*] and after being cured they are pure [*tahira*] in a special sense: their use when they are dry or if damp with scented water is allowable, though Mālik [i.e., Mālik b. Anas] found objectionable their use if wet with plain water although otherwise he made no restrictions, and he forbade trade in them and prayer on them or on skins of dead animals whether of kinds which may lawfully be eaten or not, they are both treated alike.
>
> We request that you acknowledge in your own handwriting written on the back of this document.

The document is then annotated by two other *alfaquís,* Abū'l-ʿAbbas Aḥmad b. ʿImrān of the *aljama* of the Muslims of Valladolid and Ibrāhīm b. ʿAlī b. Farash (*sic*) of the *aljama* of the Muslims of Burgos, both of whom signify that they agree "that prayer on the skins of dead animals is not lawful" (Fernández y González 1866:393–95).

Thus, presumably, this matter of religious discipline was settled, and settled, be it noted, in a rigorist sense—no relaxation of Mālikī doctrine was to be allowed. Al-Wansharīshī was mistaken in thinking of Ávila as a place where laxity prevailed. This document, like the begging certificate, shows us that the Mudejars of Castile were organized, that there were mechanisms to settle differences of opinion on matters of doctrine, and that the faithful in Castile were far from indifferent where religious faith and practice were concerned.

The Teaching of the Christian Lawyers: Muslims Must Accept Subjugation

The Mudejars not only posed problems for their own jurists within their own system of religious law, but were also an anomaly to Christian lawyers and administrators. True, the theoretical problem was not as grave for Christians. Muslims had somehow to come to terms with the fact that some Muslims were now living on a permanent basis within Christian states in a way never envisaged when Islam was first preached, so that quite fundamental adjustments of attitudes were required. For the Christians, however, there was no theoretical presumption that a Christian state ought to be exclusively Christian or Christian-dominated. Indeed, insofar as the Scriptures provided a model for conduct, the Acts of the Apostles spoke of minority Christian groups living within non-Christian societies. In the Gospels Christ's words about rendering to Caesar the things that are Caesar's, however difficult they might be to interpret, gave a firm basis for a distinction between church and state. Western Christendom had, however, in the past experienced relative religious uniformity within its own borders. Non-Christians were thought of as pagans beyond the outer rim of civilization. When pagans fell under Christian rule they had sooner or later always been converted. The Jews were a problem that Christendom never solved to its own satisfaction, and Christian policy for dealing with them provided no model for dealing with the large numbers of Muslims who came within the confines of Christendom in the thirteenth century. So it was that although Mudejarism did not pose fundamental problems for Christianity as it did for Islam, nevertheless in practice the Christian response to the fresh challenge was muddled and inadequate. The eventual outcome was the Expulsion of 1609–1611, a signal admission of total failure.

As we shall see, there were considerable variations between one Christian kingdom and another where the treatment of subject Muslims was concerned. In the chapter immediately following, Castilian policy and practice is examined, leaving for later sections a survey of the experience of the Aragonese, Valencian, and Navarrese Mudejars.

Castilian Attitudes Towards Subject Muslims

As masters of vast areas recently acquired in the conquests of the mid-thirteenth century, the Castilian authorities governed their Muslim subjects firmly, but such practical administrative documents as survive from the early days show us that they were quite ready to allow them free exercise of their religion. A good example of attitudes at this period is an agreement between Alfonso X's *alcalde* in Morón (fifty kilometers southeast of Seville) and the Muslim inhabitants of that town. The underlying reason for this agreement was no doubt most unwelcome to the Muslims: they were being uprooted and their community being moved and re-established some distance farther south at Siliébar, and an exchange of lands and an enforced sale of property was taking place. But no gratuitously vexatious measures were taken against the Muslims as such:

> Let the aforementioned *alcayad* [*sic;* is "governor" perhaps being confused with *alcalde* 'magistrate'?] Çabah be in judgment over those Moors from Morón who go to live in Siliébar, as befits their religion and their customary law [*fueros*], and let no Christian dwell with them except the tax officer [*almoxerife*] and his men, and no others, and let all those from Morón who wish to settle at Siliébar travel thither safe and sound by any route they desire, together with their wives and families and possessions, without . . . and without hindrance. (Fernández y González 1866: 346–48)

The isolation from the Christians is not something imposed, but is a matter of the free choice and preference of the Muslims.

Royal permission is given for the construction in the new village of baths, shops, bakehouses, mills, and merchants' quarters (*alfóndigas*), all "according to the custom of the Moors," and this grant is made "for all time." Alfonso X's representative is making arrangements for the setting up of a Muslim settlement with all the facilities and institutions one would expect to find in a large Muslim village.

This is one side of Christian policy: acceptance of cultural and religious differences as a permanent feature of the new society. A quite different attitude is apparent in other documents. In 1258, for example, the Cortes of Valladolid sought to impose regulations with regard to Mudejar hairstyles; the Cortes of Jerez in 1268 sought to prohibit residential quarters of mixed races.[5] The sources of such policies are to be found in the teachings of the church. The Lateran Council of 1215, for example, had laid it down:

> Whereas in certain provinces the divers forms of dress serve to distinguish Christians from Jews and Saracens, in others there is such confusion that no difference is apparent, and thus it can occur that the Christians by mistake may mingle with the womenfolk of the Jews or Saracens, or the Jews and Saracens with the Christian

5. For references see Hillgarth (1976:I, 167–69).

women. In order to prevent the continuation, under the cloak of ignorance, of such damnable mixing, and so that there can henceforward be no shadow of an excuse, we hereby decree that such people of both sexes through all Christendom at all times shall be distinguishable by the nature of their clothing in public. (Fernández y González 1866:307)

The church then sought to keep non-Christian subjects of Christian princes separate, and not only separate but also suitably humble, and public opinion gladly accepted this teaching. The royal policy in practice, as at Morón de la Frontera, was tempered both by common sense and by respect.

Alfonso X's great legal code *Las Siete Partidas* gives expression to both these aspects of attitudes towards subject Muslims—the hostility towards them as people who reject Christianity, and yet the desire that they should be dealt with justly:

> *Concerning Moors*
>
> Moors are a sort of people who believe that Mahomat was the prophet or messenger of God. Because the works or actions he performed do not demonstrate any great holiness on his part, such as might justify according to him such holy status, their law is like an insult to God. . . .
>
> And so we say that the Moors should live among the Christians in the same manner as . . . the Jews, observing their own law and causing no offense to ours. But in the Christian towns the Moors may not have mosques, nor may they make public sacrifices before men, and the mosques which formerly were theirs must belong to the king, who may grant them to anybody he wishes. And even though the Moors do not have a good law, nevertheless, so long as they live among the Christians under their protection, they ought not to have their property stolen from them by force, and if anybody should steal from them, he must pay a penalty of twice the amount so taken.[6]

6. Alfonso X 1807:III, 675–76. The Jews were required to live *mansamente et sin bollicio malo* ("quietly/tamely and without evil uproar") (II, 670). On Alfonso's legislation on the Jews, see Dwayne E. Carpenter, *Alfonso X and the*

The *Siete Partidas* are very concerned to set out penalties designed to dissuade any Christian who might contemplate conversion to Islam (he would lose all his rights) and at the same time to punish those who might discriminate against converts from Islam to Christianity (from which it seems fair to conclude that such converts indeed might expect to meet insults and contempt). Alfonso's legislation certainly does not provide any coherent and comprehensive code for the administration of a Mudejar community. No mention is made, for example, of any badge of identification to be imposed on Muslims, although it might be argued that the words which required the Moors to live like the Jews implied such a badge, since one is specified for the Jews.

As is well known, the *Partidas* were not a code actually in force either in Alfonso's day or later; rather, they were an ideal compilation of laws Alfonso would have liked to see in existence, so the code had an exhortatory function. We must not fall into the trap of supposing that Alfonso's ideas were put into practice. (Certainly some mosques continued to exist in Castilian towns in spite of the ban on them.) Nevertheless it is legitimate to consult the text to discover what his attitudes were.

The one action of the *Partidas* that provides unequivocal full protection of Muslims is that on diplomatic representatives:

> Messengers at times come from Moorish territory and elsewhere to the king's court, and although they come from the land of the enemy and on his instructions, it is our pleasure that every messenger coming to our land, whether he be Christian, Moor, or Jew, may come and go safe and sound, throughout our realm, and so do we command. We forbid anybody to dare to harm them, or to commit any offense against them, or any harm, either to them or to their property. (1807:III, 680)

Jews: An Edition of and Commentary on Siete Partidas 7.24 "De los Judíos," Berkeley, 1986, and David Romano, "Alfonso X y los Judíos: Problemática y propuestos de trabajo," in *Anuario de Estudios Medievales,* 15: 151–77.

FIVE

Mudejar Communities: Castile

The subject Muslims of the Christian kingdoms sought to have no history, to live discreetly and unperceived. Both within their own worldwide religious community and within Christendom, publicity was more likely to bring them harm than advantage. Within the Islamic community, as we have seen, the advice that they would receive would be to end their plight by emigration to an Islamic state. Within Christendom, to attract the attention of the enthusiastically pious might bring disastrous consequences. It was prudent to remain inconspicuous, to pay such taxes as were due, and where possible to seek powerful protectors. This they did. Such a community, intent on staying out of the limelight, does not leave many traces of itself, and so its history is hard to write. Yet in recent years much progress has been made in studying the Mudejars. In what follows I am much indebted to Ladero Quesada's studies of the Mudejars of Castile, and to Torres Fontes for those of Murcia (just as I am in later chapters to Boswell on the Muslims of Aragon, to Burns for Valencia, to García-Arenal for Navarre, and to many others). However, in spite of the excellence of recent scholarship, our information on Mudejars in all areas and of all periods is sporadic and incomplete. In general we hear of the Mudejars in the period immediately following the initial conquests, and in the final period after 1492, but almost everywhere there are long gaps in the fourteenth and early fifteenth centuries.

The Mudejars of the Crown of Castile: Old and New Castile

A. Old Castile

The tax returns of 1293–1294 show the Mudejars of Burgos paying 1,092 maravedis, Palencia 5,671, Ávila and Segovia 6,515. These are relatively large sums, and we must assume that the amounts paid are reflections of population figures (Ladero 1981:354). How old were these communities? Ladero takes the view that they did not date back to the earliest times, but were the consequence of immigration into these relatively northerly regions from the region of Toledo, where Muslim settlement was both denser and more ancient. By the end of our period, in 1495, *pechas* (a community-based tax reflecting in some way relative community sizes) were being paid by 251 households in Ávila, 107 in Arévalo, and 103 in Valladolid (Ladero 1981:387). Besides such relatively large *morerías,* medium-sized groups were to be found in Burgos, Barco de Ávila, and Piedrahita, and small numbers in places such as Carrión, Medina del Campo, Palencia, Sahagún, and Sepúlveda.

B. Osma, Calahorra, and Sigüenza

In a zone to the east of Old and New Castile, along the borders with the lands of the Crown of Aragon, Muslim settlement may not have been as dense, but there were a number of *morerías* of note. The largest in 1495 was Agreda, near to Soria, with 122 households contributing to the community tax; others included Cervera with 40, Deza with 47, Aranda with 29, Molina de Aragon (in the province of Guadalajara) with 45, and numerous small groups in places such as Ayllón, Medinaceli, Peñaranda, San Estéban de Gormaz, and Sigüenza (Ladero 1981:387).

C. Toledo and Cuenca

As we move southwards to the dioceses of Toledo and Cuenca, we find less dense settlement in 1495 than we might expect—no *morería* of more than 100 households. The largest group is that in Guadalajara, with only three other places having more than 25 households: Madrid with 50, Talavera with 33, and Toledo with 43. Whether figures were so low in the thirteenth century is not known (Ladero 1981:388).

The Mudejars of Andalusia and Murcia

D. The Guadalquivir Valley

South again from Castile proper, by 1495 only one place in the Guadalquivir valley, Palma del Río near Cordova, was above the 100 mark (126 households). Cordova itself and Seville each had 45, and Archidona and Priego de Cordova very few less (Ladero 1981:388–89). The Guadalquivir valley had been largely cleared of Muslims in the course of the thirteenth-century fighting and the subsequent movement of Muslim population to Granada. These Andalusian Mudejar communities were beyond doubt the consequence of subsequent resettlement, often, as we shall see at Palma del Río, under the patronage of a powerful Christian family.

In all the areas so far mentioned (A–D), the pattern of Muslim settlement in the lands of the Crown of Castile was that the Muslims lived in Moorish quarters in towns or villages. They were everywhere in a minority, and although they often did live by cultivating the soil, that was usually in settlements sponsored by noble Christian families. Extensive tracts of country were not in the hands of a Muslim peasantry.

E. Murcia

The situation in Murcia differed from the other Castilian lands because of the different pattern of conquest. By 1495 there was only one area, "the six villages of the Val de Ricote," which made up an agglomeration of more than 100 families (177 in all). Other places in Murcia with medium-sized Muslim populations were near to the Val de Ricote, so that one can really speak of a Ricote triangle, which has as its base Mula (to the west of Murcia) through Albudeite to Murcia itself. The northwestern side was formed by the Sierra de Ricote, the northeastern by a line from Ricote through Villanueva to Lorquí and Molina de Segura to Murcia. Although in 1495 only seven places had more than 25 families, the whole area was one where Muslims felt secure. It is not by chance that Cervantes chose the name Ricote in *Don Quijote* for an independently minded Morisco. The only group with which the Muslims of the Val de Ricote might be compared were the Hornacheros of Extremadura (see below). Both these groups differ from their coreligionists elsewhere in the lands of Castile because they are not people living in relatively small groups with often restricted horizons, but Muslims often living on their own lands and used to moving about with relative freedom.

F. Extremadura and the West and the Lands of the Military Orders

Apart from the towns and villages held by the military orders, there were in 1495 in Extremadura only two *morerías* of any size: Plasencia (81 contributing households) and Trujillo (71), although there were smaller groups at Medellín and Badajoz (Ladero 1981:388–89).

The military orders naturally held much land in Extremadura. It may seem a contradiction that such Christian bodies, set up in order to combat Islam, should frequently have shown a preference for settling their lands with Muslim tenantry, but that is the case. They sometimes experienced difficulties in attracting Christian settlers (who preferred to have greater protection for their individual rights than was available in the lands of the orders). Muslim cultivators no doubt often accepted work on an estate belonging to one of the orders because nothing better was available, but it would seem that often the Mudejar community got on very well under the rule of the church militant.

The largest single concentration of Muslims in the whole of the lands of the Crown of Castile, apart from Granada in 1495, was at Hornachos (432 households). This is an isolated area, far from any large center of population. There can be no doubt that such a secure area acted as a magnet attracting Muslims from elsewhere. The men of Hornachos were famed for their skill as *arrieros,* organizers of transport by pack animal. Their roving life and the self-reliance it engendered made them a formidable group. In the sixteenth century there was no area where Muslims proved more able to protect themselves. The seeds of that situation were sown in the later Middle Ages, when the tacit understanding between the orders and Mudejar settlers led to the community growing and flourishing.

Palma del Río

The case of the *aljama* of Palma del Río has already been referred to. In a number of respects it is not typical, and yet it does illustrate very well how a regime, which did not seek to be oppressive or in any way destructive of Islamic institutions, nevertheless could eat away at the Islamic code. Palma del Río is an exception because it is a place where a considerable number of Muslims moved back into the cultivated lands of the Guadalquivir valley after the expulsions that followed the conquest. It is an exception even in this area in that the protector and sponsor of the Muslims here was an individual Christian nobleman, and moreover an Italian. The lands of Palma were of the Genoese Bocanegra (Boccanegra) family. The group of Muslim settlers brought in were not local people at all, but from distant Gumiel de Hizán, twelve kilometers north of Aranda de Duero.

The charter granted by Ambrosio Bocanegra to his Muslims in 1371 is extant (Fernández y González 1866:389–92). This document in fact largely repeats the concessions granted to the first settlers a generation earlier by Ambrosio's father, Gil (or Aegidius). The Bocanegras had entered Castilian service in 1341, and the original charter presumably was of about that date (the need for a new charter cannot be unconnected with the fact that Gil left until too late the switching of his allegiance from Peter the Cruel to Henry II, and presumably the family and his tenants needed a more reliable title).

The Palma charter alludes to the fact that the Muslims concerned had first been settled by Gil at Carmona and only subsequently moved to Palma. Henry II had regranted them as vassals to Ambrosio "to be my vassals, as is right and proper, to live in the said township of Palma." Now at the request of his vassals Ambrosio himself grants as a *fuero* and a *privilege:*

1. that so long as they respected the terms agreed they should be free men (*horros*) and should preserve their religion and law (*axara e çumna*), and have their own judges;
2. that civil actions to which Christians were party should be dealt with by the Muslims' judge, criminal actions by the royal justices with ultimate right of appeal to the King (similarly with questions involving tax law);
3. that the Palma Muslims were exempt from providing lodgings "save when the King or other numerous companies pass by, so that it is unavoidable";
4. that they were to be on an equal footing with Christians where import and export taxes were concerned;
5. that they were *to have the same liberties as they have* (my italics);
6. that they were to have their own facilities for butchery of meat, and on the occasion of the *ʿīd,* exemption from the standard taxes on it.

The commercial connections of the Bocanegras are apparent in the provision that the lord was to have a monopoly of selling oil and spices, a concession he would annually auction "to whatsoever Moor of you is the highest bidder." (Stiff penalties were provided for if people sought to shop elsewhere.)

The fact that these "Moors" were by no means all strictly observant Muslims is apparent because they are granted a tavern "for an account for which you will pay me." That this license to sell wine is expected to be profitable is obvious because a fine of sixty maravedis is to be inflicted on those who try to take their custom elsewhere!

The Koranic (*ḥadd*) penalty of stoning is confirmed for the offense of adultery, with an interesting escape clause: any fornicator not wishing to undergo the penalty could opt to become Bocanegra's slave instead. Almost the only discriminatory feature of this charter was a provision that a male Muslim committing adultery with a Christian woman would be put to death by burning. In general the terms of the charter indicate that Bocanegra valued his "vassals" and sought to make the conditions under which they lived attractive. Bocanegra pays lip service to the ideal of allowing his cultivators to live by their law, but in fact the penalties stipulated are not those of the *sharīʿa*. It may well be, however, that that was one of the attractions of this form of settlement. In a true Islamic state, the believer could not pick and choose the legal sanctions of the law; in a Mudejar settlement, the penalties "imposed" by the lord might be more to the liking of his vassals.

In studying the situation of the Muslims of the Crown of Castile, and in particular their religious and juridical status, we are thus concerned with two quite distinct sets of problems. The Christian rulers had to develop their own legal codes and enactments as a framework to permit them to govern their new subject populations, and the Muslims themselves had to discover how to follow the precepts of their faith in the quite new circumstances in which they found themselves.

SIX

Mudejar Legal Codes from Castile

THE LEYES DE MOROS AND THE BREVIARIO SUNNI

The strictures of those rigoristic jurists who demanded that all Muslims should leave Christian territory did not drive Muslims to seek guidance from laxer teachers. Even when they could not manage to observe all the orthodox rules as laid down by the Mālikī school, the Mudejars nevertheless wished to know what the correct doctrine was. Their standard legal textbooks in Arabic were the ones that were most current everywhere in the Mālikī West; a great favorite was the *Risāla* of Ibn Abī Zayd al-Qayrawānī, many Mudejar copies of which have survived.[1] But Arabic texts, even such a straightforward one as this, were not accessible to all the faithful in Castile. Arabic was probably never much spoken in Old Castile (New Castile, and especially the area of Toledo, was a different matter), but it was the Mudejars' language of culture and of religion. It must have been very difficult for them to face up to the fact that lack of Arabic was creating a problem, still more difficult to accept that the only workable solution was for some religious writings to be made available in the vernacular.

We have in fact two vernacular legal codes from the Mudejar period

1. For example, the Biblioteca Nacional, Madrid, has two manuscripts (Guillén Robles 1889 Nos.36 and 42) and one commentary (No.114).

in Castile. The older of them, usually known by the title *Leyes de moros,*[2] is strangely devoid of references to the aspects of Islamic law concerned with religious ritual and practice. The nineteenth-century editor, Pascual de Gayangos, described the *Leyes* as "Civil Code," and he even speculated that "in this form it may have received the sanction of the monarch reigning at the time in Castile, for since the subjects of the Crown were to be judged by it, it is reasonable to suppose that he may have had some means of intervention" (*Mem. Hist. Esp.,* 5:5). It is not, in my opinion, necessary to suppose that there was any attempt by the Castilian kings to modify in any way the Muslims' code, but Gayangos may well be right in supposing that the *Leyes de moros* was a redaction prepared for submission to a Christian ruler.

There were at least two categories of occasion when it was necessary for Christian officials and judges to be informed about Islamic law in this Mudejar society. First and most important, whether the Christian monarch wished to find himself in that position or not, he inevitably came to preside over some cases which had been initiated in lower courts of a purely Islamic nature but which, for whatever reason, were referred to higher authority. Whether the monarch sat in judgment himself or had an official to act for him, it was still necessary for the Christian administration to be reliably informed as to the nature of the offenses under consideration and the penalties available. A second circumstance requiring communication between Muslim and Christian authorities was the provision that where a case involved people of both religions, those involved should each be dealt with by judges of their own religion and in accordance with their own law. That apparently simple arrangement no doubt gave rise to endless complications, and the judges needed to know how their opposite numbers would have to proceed. For these and no doubt for many other purposes, summaries of Islamic law in Castilian must have been required. Possibly, then, the *Leyes de moros* were not primarily intended for use by Muslims at all, but by Christian lawyers.

The other code, Ice de Gebir's *Breviario sunnī* (*Mem. Hist. Esp.,* 5:247–421), was intended for circulation among Muslims, and it contains a full treatment of such specifically religious questions as regula-

2. *Mem. Hist. Esp.,* 5:1–246. The identity of the editor is not stated, but it is Pascual de Gayangos.

tions concerning ritual purity, Islamic prayer, and pilgrimage to the Holy Places in Mecca. There are some areas where the *Leyes de moros* and the *Breviario* intersect. Both works, for example, have full treatment of marriage law, and both deal with the law of contracts (though here the *Leyes de moros* goes into closer detail). Such differences as there are in no way arise from differences of doctrine and probably are simply the consequence of the different purposes for which these legal texts were designed.

It is unfortunate that the original manuscript of the *Leyes de moros* had disappeared already before Gayangos edited it (he worked on a later copy), so that it is not possible to date the code by any of the normal methods. Gayangos, whose authority in such matters was unrivaled, based his dating—"the first third of the fourteenth century"—on an alleged facsimile copy of a six-line passage and on the opinion of an academician who had actually handled the original book in the eighteenth century. Linguistic criteria are not of great use in dating such a text, for the language of the law everywhere tends to archaism and quaintness. Moreover, we are dealing with a text translated from Arabic in a way that copies slavishly the syntax and even other linguistic features of the Arabic original. Similar techniques of translation continued to give very similar "Spanish" results right up into the sixteenth century, so that the language of such translations tells us little about the date at which they were made. Nevertheless, Gayangos' estimate should be accepted; his experience with a wide range of all sorts of manuscripts, especially Mudejar ones, made him an excellent judge.

The evidence of the *Leyes de moros* has to be interpreted with great care, for we do not necessarily find information in this text about life as it was lived among the Muslims of Spain, whether in the thirteenth century or at a later date. A good example of the perilous nature of this material is provided by the section on the law of sales and contracts (Law CL). (An underlying idea necessary to seize here is that uncertainty of outcome is repugnant to the pious Muslim, because it might bring a transaction into the forbidden zone of gambling.) A contract might be unenforceable if the eventual amount of the price and the quantity for sale were uncertain: "De como se a de coger el pan y los dátiles a medias. Non enpesce segar el pan et coger dátiles a medias, et non pasa el segar de un dia, nin coger de un dia a medias" ("Concerning half-shares in the harvesting of corn and dates. There is nothing against harvesting corn or gathering dates by equal shares, but it is not permissible to go halves in harvesting or gathering over the period of a single day"). The legal point established is that since by the time of the harvest accurate estimates of the crops could be made, so that sharecropping whereby the laborer agrees to do all the work for half the produce is quite legitimate, over a single day the unknown factors (weather, terrain, etc.?) were proportionately so much greater that a man might find himself working all day for very little reward.

What is of interest to us here is that the crops mentioned—corn, dates—come straight from the Middle Eastern legal manuals. Some dates were, it is true, produced in restricted areas of the Iberian Peninsula, but in warmer areas than those where Castilian was spoken in the thirteenth century. Dates were not a feature of everyday life, they were discussed because the Arabic texts that were the sources for the *Leyes de moros* discussed them. The code is conservative and archaic.

An even clearer example of how far out of touch with reality the code was is to be found in the section "concerning the oath taken by a woman in a mosque" and other similar solemn oaths (Law CXCVII). This seeks to lay down, inter alia, how Jews and Christians are to take oaths: "Let Jews and Christians swear their oaths in their church near to the altar, and let them not take any oath except in the name of God." The idea that Muslims in the thirteenth century or after could ever be in a position to control Christian oaths is absurd. Law CXCVII is a carry-over from legislation concerning subject Christians in Muslim territory. The regulations with regard to the form a greeting ought to take is equally far removed from social realities. Since the normal form of greeting between Muslims (*ʿalayk al-salām*) implies an exchange of benedictions, it was felt to be inappropriate if directed towards non-Muslims, and the pious lawyers of Islamic countries sought to prevent people of different religions from exchanging the same greeting. "It is forbidden to greet the Jew or the Christian first. If one of them greets us [Muslims], then we should reply 'and upon you'" is how the teaching is phrased in the *Risāla* of al-Qayrawānī.[3] (This is taken up exactly in Law CCCVI: "Who is greeted by a Jew, let him return it saying 'upon you,' and you should not be the first with the greeting.")

3. al-Qayrawānī 1952:312–13. This author does mention one other way out of the difficulty: instead of *salām*, pronounce *silām* (the greeting would then become: "The rock on you!"). Lawyers the world over are fond of their little joke.

To conclude this examination of the anachronism of the *Leyes de moros,* we may take Law CLXI "concerning homicide committed by those living in villages (*aldeas*)." "The blood-price [*omezilla*] of those who commit murder in villages is one hundred camels which are four years old." Gayangos, in editing this passage, was moved to remark that "here we must understand by 'in villages or country places' among Beduin or Arab shepherds who do not live in cities, so that their only property is in their flocks. This disposition was not directly applicable in Spain, where the Arabs and Moors to a certain extent forget their nomadic ways, and where camels, if they existed at all, were never in such numbers as to permit one hundred to be paid for the death of a man." One can only agree with what Gayangos said. Interestingly, the text of these *Leyes de moros* is in a way even more archaic than that of the *Risāla,* which at this point speaks of "people who keep camels" (*ahl al-ibl*) and "people who use gold" or "people who use silver" (al-Qayrawānī 1952:242). Ibn Abī Zayd (ca. 922 A. D.) seems to have felt the need to provide a more up-to-date form of reckoning than did the author or compiler of the *Leyes de moros*!

We must now turn to the second code known to us, the *Breviario sunnī* or Sunni Breviary (*Mem. Hist. Esp.,* 5:247–421). In this case we do know the date of compilation, and not only the name of the compiler, Ice de Gebir, but also quite a lot about him and his other activities. He was, as we will see, a key figure in the final periods of the history of Islam in the Iberian Peninsula.

Ice de Gebir and the Creation of a Vernacular Islamic Literature in Spain

ʿIsā or Ice de Gebir was *alfaquí* and *imām* in Segovia about the middle of the fifteenth century (Cabanelas 1952:145ff.). Although we know more about him than about almost any other Mudejar of the period, there are exasperating gaps; for example, we do not know when he was born or when he died. He demands our attention because he is not only a figure of primary importance in the development of Islamic law in Spain, but also in a number of other areas, including the translation of the Koran.

There are three separate sources of information about Ice. I am indebted to Gerard Wiegers of Leiden University for drawing my attention to what is chronologically the first of these (it is undated but to be placed between 1414 and 1440). Wiegers saw that a document emanating from one Muḥammad Ibn Yūsuf al-Qaysī of Toledo, who was "alcalde mayor de las aljamas de los moros de Castilla" (chief justice of the Moorish communities of Castile) and as such a royal appointee, contained an interesting reference to Ice (the "Icam" of the printed text being a mistaken reading) (Martín Pérez n.d.:534–38). The chief justice bowed to the strongly expressed preference of the Muslims of Sepúlveda to take their lawsuits to be heard by "Don Ice, judge appointed by me in the city of Segovia" and so authorized them to regard the appointment of one Alí de Montejo as *alcalde* of the Muslims of Sepúlveda as being null and void.

The Alí de Montejo in question was clearly well connected; the chief justice had given him the post of Sepúlveda "because of a request made to me by great lords of these realms, Pero Carrillo and others." The chief justice had to promise to compensate him for the loss of the post. He would never have done this if the pressure of opinion among the Muslims had not been very great indeed: "You say in your letter that you have no other judge but me and the one I appointed in Segovia [i.e. Don Ice]" (Martín Pérez n.d.:537).

Standing by itself among the Sepúlveda documents, this text seems to be an unimportant reflection of a provincial wrangle, but if we take into account the other two sources, we can understand why Ice came to be so highly regarded among his coreligionists.

Chronologically the second of these sources is the Latin correspondence and writings of John of Segovia (published by Cabanelas [1952]). Among John of Segovia's many claims to fame is his important role in the intricate web of the ecclesiastical politics of the Conciliar Movement, and the fact that he was given a cardinal's hat by the antipope Felix V in 1440. After the fall of Felix V, John of Segovia spent the closing years of his life in exile in Savoy at Aiton. It is during this period (and not while he was resident in Spain, curiously enough) that we hear of prolonged contact between him and Ice from Segovia, who is clearly our man.

John's project to keep himself busy after he was exiled from the halls of power was to study how the conversion of the Muslims might be effected. As a necessary first step, he judged that future missionaries would need a reliable translation of the Koran, for although he was determined that Muslims should be brought to Christ, that conversion must, in his view, be by gentle persuasion and the force of sweet reason. In those days the Koran was a rare book in Christian Europe, for Islamic scholars operated an effective ban on supplying it to unbelievers (a ban based on their fear that the holy text would not be respected). John of Segovia successfully circumvented the embargo by the ingeniously simple device of importing to Savoy from his home town of Segovia an Islamic scholar who was a *ḥāfiẓ* or memorizer of the Koran. The *ḥāfiẓ* could come to Savoy, write out the text he had by memory, and then help in the labor of translation. John's family ties in Spain meant that he was able to provide the pledge and guarantees which at length, after protracted negotiations, led to the *muftī* and *imām* of the Muslims of Segovia making the long journey in the middle of the winter of 1455 from central Spain to the Alps, and there at the priory of Aiton the work was carried out. The *ḥāfiẓ* in question was Ice de Gebir.

The task of Ice was divided into several stages, which are described by John in his Latin letters to his learned friends and in the Latin introduction to the Koran translation (unfortunately all that is extant, the translation itself having disappeared). John says that his compatriot worked very hard, twelve hours a day (stopping only for the Prophet's birthday), for four months. During the first month he wrote out the consonantal text, during the second he added the vowel signs, during the third he translated it, and in the fourth he checked the translation against the text (Cabanelas 1952:142). It seems fairly obvious that this allocation of time does not correspond exactly to what happened. It may well have taken a month to write the text out, but a month to vocalize that text is rather a long time, even though the vowels were, as John tells us, in inks of different colors (an ancient practice, this). A month to translate the text thus produced seems absurdly little, on the other hand. (It should be explained that Ice was to produce a vernacular Spanish version, which was to serve as an intermediate stage in the making of John's Latin translation.)

Did Ice really bring the Koran only in his memory? Or did he actually bring a written copy? John tells us in any case that he brought many books written without vowels, and above all the books of those Muslim doctors whom he called commentators of the Koran, and these, in case of doubt, he consulted. Now any commentary must contain, cut into short sections, the text being explained, so that the full text would presumably have been available in that way (even though Ice may well have had such a good memory as not to need it).

Did Ice really make a fresh translation at Aiton at John's request, or did he in fact bring with him a version already in existence? I think we may take it that if one had been in existence he would have brought it—nobody undertaking such a mammoth task would fail to make use of any assistance that might be available. Surprisingly, we get a direct answer to this question in the third of the sources. The answer is very explicit, and it was John of Segovia's idea, but let us examine the whole passage in question.

The introduction or preface to the book Ice wrote in 1462 (and so after the strange journey to Savoy), his *Breviario sunnī* (or sometimes *Kitāb Segoviano,* Segovian Book), after a pious invocation of God and his blessed Prophet Muḥammad, begins as follows:

> The honored scholar, *muftī* and *alfaquí* of the *aljama* of the Moors of the noble and loyal city of Segovia, Don Iça Jedih [a footnote by Gayangos says "elsewhere called Gebir"] said, "Compendious causes moved me to interpret the divine grace of the Arabic Koran into Spanish [*aljamía* is the word used], and on this subject some cardinals wrote to me saying that we kept our Koran hidden away as if it were some thing which we dare not bring out in public. For it was not without great cause that I abandoned my native land to go to the East [by which we now know he meant Savoy via France]. For this reason I set about translating it into this Castilian language, spurred on by that lofty authority which commands us and tells us that any creature who knows anything of the law ought to teach it to all the creatures in the world in such language that if possible they may understand it, so as to avoid the doubts and difficulties which lie in our path. God grant that I may do so, with the commentary [*tafsir*] of the Koran open before me, so it may be a guide to those who are ignorant of Arabic, here and abroad. So as to make the explanation even clearer, I will copy out the articles which are to be found in the Koran and in other summaries of the most important of its teachings, under the guidance of which great kings and princes and peoples without number dwell in freedom in the Promised Land and Holy Places at Mecca and in divers other parts of the world where justice and truth are upheld.
>
> And because the Moors [*sic*] of Castile, under such great oppression, subjected to the exaction of tribute, forced labor and

exhaustion, have declined in their wealth and have lost their schools of Arabic, in order to put right all these things which are wrong, many of my friends, and especially the honorable body which is charged with assessing our collective taxes [*repartidores*] have pressed me hard, and have asked me to draw up and to copy out in Romance such an outstanding written work concerning our law and our *sunna:* what every good Muslim should know and have as his normal practice. I could find no way of avoiding the satisfaction of their request, and so trusting firmly in that sovereign good which assists all good desires, and being aware of how easily we fall away from those virtuous objectives which we set ourselves, I have striven hard, and have kept in mind that this compilation is directed to those who succeed us and come after us. I have borne in mind how short our life is, and how this age of ours will come to an end. I have explained chapter by chapter, but only as much as is needed, how we ought to fulfil the commands of our law and *sunna,* so that [my] prolixity may not provide an excuse to those who listen and so that exhaustion may not distract the three capacities of the soul. For long writings are all very well for those who have secure resources on which to maintain themselves, and that is a thing of the past here in Castile. In order to be as brief as possible I have bethought myself of naming in this prologue the books by which this book will be guided, so as not to have to mention them all the time. Noble scholars will find in them the authorities for what is said in this book. They are as follows: thirteen volumes of books of our law and *sunna* from which I compiled sixty chapters summarizing our faith and works such as a man or a woman must observe, and in accordance with what was revealed to our blessed Prophet Muḥammad. This work, I have considered, should be called the *Sunnī Breviary,* and I have put my name to it in order that where I was guilty of ignorance the blame may be attributed to me, for I am the very humblest of the masters of the holy law and *sunna,* and I beseech those scholars to correct this work, bearing in mind that it is only a brief compendium. Wherever they find any lack of sustenance in it, let it be corrected by them as far as is necessary. I pray to God I be granted grace and days that I may finish it, and the other works for His service, and that I may do so in order to be guided straight to everlasting glory. Amen." (*Mem. Hist. Esp.,* 5:247–250)

If we examine this preface with care it turns out to be not one text but two. It is a conflation of the preface to the translation of the Koran (as undertaken at the urging of the "Cardinals") and the preface of the book to be called *Sunnī Breviary* (of which more later).

All the manuscripts of the *Sunnī Breviary* contain this preface. None includes the actual Koran translation mentioned. It may be, however, that the Koran translation is not irretrievably lost. We do have manuscripts of several Koran translations, none of them earlier in date than the Savoy journey (Harvey 1958a:119, 357; López-Morillas 1982:18–24, 42–45). It is very likely that a version deriving from Ice's labors in the Alps is somewhere extant, and it ought to be possible by patient analysis to recognize his handiwork (and possibly even John of Segovia's intervention).

Whether or not we have any part of Ice's actual translation, we can be sure that the innovation of undertaking such a task acted as a vital stimulus to the creation of an Islamic devotional literature in Spanish for Mudejar use and thus led to the whole phenomenon which Hispanist scholars call "*aljamiado* literature." How ironic it is that John of Segovia's importunate insistence that Ice should travel to Savoy to help him with his Koran translation provided the basis on which the new Islamic literature was constructed! John wished to convert Spanish Muslims to Christianity. What he achieved was to demonstrate to Ice that it was feasible to translate the Koran into Spanish. Once the Koran had been so translated, Ice seems to have overcome the misgivings which Muslims had always felt up to then about abandoning Arabic, and he went on to write his all-important *Breviary*.

The influence of Ice de Gebir, and behind him of John of Segovia, is probably to be detected in the manner and technique of translating from Arabic which the Muslims of Spain continued to adopt for their scripture and holy books right up to the end (López-Morillas 1982:33–42). John of Segovia, for reasons that are not altogether clear, was insistent that his translation should imitate as many of the external features of the Arabic original as possible. He was not content to produce a faithful rendering of the *sense;* what he aimed at was a close linguistic calque. One example given by John in his preface must suffice to illustrate the extreme lengths to which he was prepared to go: it concerns the possessives of the third person. Arabic has possessive suffixes which convey the full range of sex and number distinctions, with different words for *his, her,* etc.: *hu* 'his', *hā* 'her', *hum* 'their', and even the dual *humā* 'of them twain'. Now Latin *suus* is variable according to the thing possessed rather than the person possessing. John was not ready to make do with the inadequacies of this aspect of Latin, so he decided to make up a word in Latin: *sussuus* ("where duplication is introduced it indicates plurality in the Arabic"). In other ways, even in the workings of the Arabic case system and questions of agreement he intended to have his "translation" follow the structures of Arabic.[4]

The resultant Latin translation, if ever it was completed, would have been extremely difficult to follow, if not downright incomprehensible. Perhaps it is not surprising that not a single copy has survived! This Latin translation with all its idiosyncrasies was something quite distinct from the working translation into Spanish produced by Ice as a necessary intermediate stage. There is no reason to suppose that that version was marked by the wilder peculiarities John aimed to insert into his Latin text, but Ice would have been encouraged by his paymaster to produce as literal a rendering as possible, one that preserved as many of the features of the original as possible. This turned out to be of the greatest importance.

In the twentieth century we have become accustomed to demand from our translations faithfulness to the sense combined with a style that reads as if it were an original composition in the target language. Any linguistic or stylistic carryovers from the original are felt to be a blemish. Things have not always been thus. At various periods in the past, and in various languages, translators have tried to carry over into their translations not only the sense, but also something of the linguistic texture of the original. Great translations, such as the Vulgate or the King James Bible, or many renderings of Latin texts, have acclimatized in English originally alien structures and features. The translations of Koranic texts which we find in use among the Muslims of Spain in the periods subsequent to this all to some degree inject into Spanish features of the Semitic morphology and syntax of the holy text. A new Arabized Spanish emerged as the literary language of the Muslims; specialists generally refer to it now as *aljamía*. One of the features of *aljamía* is usually that it is written in the Arabic alphabet. Of the manuscripts of Ice de Gebir's *Breviario* that have survived, one is in Arabic characters (No. 1 of the

4. John of Segovia discusses his theory of translation in his *praefatio:* Codex Vaticanus Latinus 2.923, folios 186–96, ed. Cabanelas 1952:279–302, esp. 297.

Almonacid collection) and four in the normal Latin alphabet. We cannot be certain what script was used originally, although Cabanelas found a strong argument in favor of a Latin-character version being the copy-text from which the Almonacid Arabic-character manuscript was transcribed. (The author's name is given as "Ika," inexplicable unless we assume that the name "Iça" was written without a cedilla and then misinterpreted when it was being transliterated from Latin into Arabic characters [Cabanelas 1952:151–52 and pl. 4].) Whatever script Ice used himself in the writing of his *Breviario,* the book became a work of reference to which Muslims in the peninsula subsequently referred frequently, and as such it underpinned the devotional literature in Spanish, the *literatura aljamiada* which became so important as the vehicle through which Islamic culture was transmitted to subsequent generations.

In the history of the Mudejars there took place two developments whereby Arabic retreated and Romance dialects advanced, but we must distinguish between them. One concerned spoken communication, and the other communication in writing. We can obviously know more about the changeover in written communication, because it is there to be seen in such records as have survived. About the spoken language we have only indirect and sporadic evidence. Nothing indicates that Arabic was spoken in Castile much north of Toledo, but Arabic was the written language of the *aljamas* for religious and other purposes. As time passed, Arabic became difficult to sustain even for purely religious purposes, because of the lack of educational facilities. There are many remarks in manuscripts in *aljamía* lamenting the loss of Arabic. If Muslims had simply adopted standard written Castilian as their language of culture, they would have been subjected to all the cultural attraction of the powerful majority.

One of Ice de Gebir's great contributions to the survival of Islam in Spain during the final period of the Middle Ages and in the sixteenth century was that he provided his coreligionists not only with a translation of their scriptures into their vernacular and a textbook of their religious law, but also, and perhaps more important, a language that was theirs in the sense that it was based on their own Castilian, but was also theirs in the sense that it had Islamic roots. As the language of the Muslims evolved in the later period, it did not, as one might have expected, tend to merge with the language of the majority. Instead, it retained and even, in the hands of some writers (notably a curious author known as the Mancebo de Arévalo), accentuated its distinctive features. Now even without Ice, an Islamic literature in one of the Hispanic dialects would probably have arisen, and we cannot ascribe all the credit for the creation of vernacular Islamic literature in Spain to him alone, but there are two strong reasons for regarding his role as crucial. In the first place we find that his *Breviario* is cited by subsequent writers more than any other work, and in the second place we can see that before him datable works written by Spanish Muslims in their own vernacular are extremely rare (if not nonexistent),[5] whereas after him there is a considerable degree of activity. To trace the influence of Ice fully would take us into the field of Morisco studies and would require an exhaustive survey of *aljamiado* writings such as would be out of place here.

In what has been said here of Ice's creative contribution to the culture of his community, stress has naturally been placed on the Islamic dimension of his work. Perhaps mention should be made of one way in which what he was doing in some ways paralleled the major innovative feature of intellectual life in Western Europe at this time. One of the major changes that took place at the end of the Middle Ages was the rise of the various European vernaculars as media not only for lyric poetry and popular narrative, but also for serious intellectual communication. In most parts of Western Europe—notably, of course, in England and Germany, but also in other countries—an essential role in the emergence of the vernacular as a language of culture in its own right was played by the translators of the scriptures. This was the period when great minds turned towards the transposition (I use the word advisedly instead of *translation*) of the scriptures of the Christian tradition into the appropriate local languages. Ice was making his scriptures available in his local language. Islamic resistance to the translation of the scriptures was even deeper than that of the Christian church. It is very

5. Harvey 1958a:357. Whereas the generally accepted view has been that much of *aljamiado* literature is early, a survey of manuscripts that are susceptible to rigorous dating threw up only two or three dubious examples of manuscripts written before 1462. This is certainly very far short of demonstrating that Ice created *aljamía* as a literary medium, but it does place his work in a different perspective. We have no evidence that the Mudejars wrote very much in Spanish in Arabic characters before his days.

difficult (though not impossible) to construct a defense of the position that the Vulgate ought never to be translated (it is, of course, itself a translation), but it is easy to justify the position that if the Koran is the final revelation of God's Word, and it is in Arabic, then no translation can be entirely satisfactory. The Koran is in this sense untranslatable. It can be interpreted, but that is not the same thing. Only in modern times has the provision of Koran translations in a wide range of world languages been undertaken, so that Ice's work to make a version of his scriptures for his community really was a radical departure within the history of Islam in general. As we have seen, we have the most explicit and unambiguous evidence to show us that that innovation was not just the consequence of a general European climate of opinion in favor of vernacular scriptures, but was specifically the result of the direct intervention and even patronage of a Christian scholar. It really is a most curious story.

We can now turn back to Ice's more purely legal and devotional contribution to the life of his community.

Ice de Gebir's Sunnī Breviary

The introduction of this work has already been translated in full above because of the information it contains on his labors as a Koran translator. That part of the introduction which refers specifically to the compilation of a summary of the teachings of the Islamic law makes it quite clear that Ice regards this as something for which he is personally directly responsible: "I have put my name to it in order that where I was guilty of ignorance the blame may be attributed to me, for I am the very humblest. . . . "

It is not until the fourth chapter of the *Breviary* that the legal treatise proper begins (with part of the regulations on ritual purity). The first chapter deals with "principal commandments and prohibitions" (*Mem. Hist. Esp.,* 5:250–53). It is impossible not to see in the way these are formulated some influence flowing from the Ten Commandments, and even from the teachings of the New Testament. In saying that I am in no way implying that Ice's text is unorthodox from the Islamic viewpoint, or syncretistic: the influence is on form rather than on content, and indeed the chapter includes some commandments intended to block the adoption of Christian ways.

This chapter is such a succinct statement of Mudejar beliefs that it will be translated here without any omissions:

Principal Commandments and Prohibitions

Worship the Creator alone, attributing to him neither image nor likeness, and honoring his chosen and blessed Muḥammad.

Desire for your neighbor [*proximo*] that good which you desire for yourself.

Keep constantly pure by means of the minor and major ritual ablutions, and the five prayers.

Be obedient to your father and your mother, even though they be unbelievers.

Do not swear in the name of the Creator in vain.

Do not kill, do not steal, do not commit fornication with any creature.

Pay the canonical alms [*azaque,* i.e., *zakāt*].

Fast during the month of Ramadan.

Make the Pilgrimage [*ḥajj*].

Do not sleep with your wife unless both you and she are in a state of ritual purity.

Honor the day of Assembly [i.e., Friday], above all during the holy times, with all purity and with devout prayers, and with visits to the holy men of the law and to the poor.

Honor the scholars [of the law].

Serve in defense of the law both with your goods and with your person.

Honor your neighbor [*vecino*], whether he be a stranger or a relative or an unbeliever.

Give lodging willingly to the wayfarer and to the poor man.

Do not break your word, your oath, your bond, or your guarantee, unless it be something which be contrary to the law, when you must make an act of expiation.

Be faithful, do not trade in goods which you know to be stolen.

Do not cause sin or consent to sin, for if you do you participate in it.

Do not falsify weights and measures, nor be guilty of deceit or treachery, do not engage in usury.

Do not drink wine or any other intoxicating thing.

Do not eat pork, nor any carrion flesh, nor blood, nor any suspect thing, nor anything which has not been properly slaughtered, nor anything offered on an altar or to a creature [i.e., any sacrifice to a divinity other than God].

When you meet a Muslim, greet him with your *salāms,* and assist him in whatever is to God's service, and visit him when he is sick, and carry out his interment should he die.

Oppose any Muslim who transgresses the law or the *sunna* in any way.

Let anyone who speaks, speak well or keep silent, and let him not speak evil, even if it be the truth.

When you sit in judgment, be a faithful judge; do not take usury; abstain from covetousness; be faithful to your lord, even though he is not a Muslim, because he will become your heir should you have nobody else to inherit from you; pay him his due; honor the rich and do not despise the poor; beware of envy and wrath; be patient; do not follow enchanters nor fortune tellers, nor those who interpret omens, nor astrologers, nor those who cast lots, but your Lord alone.

Do not live in the land of the unbelievers, nor in any land without justice, nor among evil neighbors, nor should you keep company with bad Muslims.

Live among good men, and spend up to a third of your wealth, and more if you can do so without harm, and so long as you have no cause to regret it.

Do not play at draughts [checkers] or any other idle pastime.

Do not take pleasure in what is forbidden, and do not hanker in your heart after that which is not yours.

Beware of the Enemy: forgive him who leads you astray, and ask forgiveness of him whom you lead astray, and avoid overweening pride. Obey those who are older than you, be merciful on those who are younger, and be the brother of those who are the same age as yourself.

Do not be two-faced; be a peace-maker between people; put those who have gone astray back on the right path; calm down those who are angry, and please Allah.

Set the captive free with your wealth; bring aid to the orphan and to the widow, and you will be a neighbor to your Lord.

Learn the law, and teach it to everyone, for on Judgment Day you will be called to account for it, and sent to heaven or the flames of hell.

Stand in the way of those who are disobeying the law or *sunna*, because those who commit the sin and those who stand by and do nothing are equal in sin; strive in this respect, and you will please Allah.

If you are truly repentant, you will deserve everlasting praise.

Hold this world in contempt, and have worthy hope for the future, and you will receive everlasting life and blessings.

Do not employ the practices, uses, or customs of the Christians, nor dress like them, nor should you have their images, nor those of the sinners, and you will be free from infernal sins. [Here the word translated "practices" could possibly mean "conversations," but in the context "practices" is the more likely interpretation.]

You are to carry out and to preserve the sayings, teachings, uses, customs, habits, and way of dress of that excellent and blessed one, Muḥammad, on whom be benediction and peace, and those of his Companions, on whom Providence bestowed such grace, and on Judgment Day you will be one of those who enter paradise without being subjected to the test.

In this remarkable collection of maxims and teachings, some contradict others. "Do not live in the land of the unbelievers . . ." is an expression of the orthodox teaching already discussed as exemplified in the *fatwās* of al-Wansharīshī. Obviously if Ice were to take notice of this doctrine he would not need to write in Castilian! "Be faithful to your lord, even though he is not a Muslim, because he will become your heir, should you have nobody else to inherit from you" appears to be the ultimate refinement of that sort of subservience which in a different context we call Uncle Tomism. How the Muslims of Christian Spain reconciled themselves to the way in which these teachings pulled them in opposite directions we cannot tell from their writings. People the world over and in every age have found ways of juggling with contradictory beliefs. Elements that speak to the revolutionary and to the quietist will be found in most Christian liturgies. The contradictions of Ice's commandments and prohibitions are the product of the stresses of the Mudejar situation. What does shine through in this chapter is the determination of the Muslims of Christian Spain to continue to live in their religion, and their conviction that its most profound message was relevant to them in their specific historical situation because it was relevant to them in their eschatological situation, as they understood it. It is curious that the twentieth century should find it so difficult to come to terms with the eschatological beliefs of earlier ages, for in our own age Last Things are never very far from the front pages of our newspapers. What we need to understand with regard to Ice and his community is that everything was seen and understood in the perspective of an imminent end to the historical process on Judgment Day.

Immediately following on the commandments and prohibitions is a short chapter on "what faith is, and how it is the salvation of the soul" and another on "the articles which the good Muslim is obliged to believe and hold as faith" (*Mem. Hist. Esp.*, 5:253–60; discussed in Harvey 1981). These creedal statements are as orthodoxly Mālikī as any other aspects of Ice's writings. The first of the articles of faith (there are thirteen in all) deals with the oneness of Allah and rejects the Christian teaching with regard to the divine sonship: "he did not engender, nor was he engendered, was not a son and did not have a son."

The second article deals with the importance of the mission of Muḥammad:

> The second article . . . is to believe . . . that Allah at the end of all his prophets sent that excellent, blessed, and chosen Prophet Muḥammad with the holy divine law of the Koran . . . and through it revoked all other laws and brought the people back from the doubts and errors in which they were living, and guided them towards everlasting good. For this reason we are obliged to follow the uses and customs of the said Prophet . . . and of those who were his Companions because he knew our holy law better, and understood it better, so we must abandon all the uses and customs of other nations, past or future. Thus works are testimony to faith, and for them to be acceptable to Allah they must be in conformity to the *sunna*, for faith waxes and wanes according to works.

The teaching here is orthodoxly Islamic, the preoccupation with assessing the relation of works to faith is very much of the European fifteenth century.

The rest of the thirteen articles are concerned with eschatology. Again the theology is orthodox from the Islamic viewpoint, and yet the rendering of this Islamic vision of the end of all things is reminiscent of many aspects of the European intellectual world of the time (Hieronymus Bosch was born the year this was written):

> Hell is the place for [the damned]. It is a fire which burns endlessly, it is a cold and frozen fire, and all in it is stench and poison and infernal corruption, with serpents, and worms, and ravening wild beasts which inflict great and grievous suffering, there the devils torture those who are evil and cause them endless pain. There some are burnt and some are reprieved. Every man should think on this and hold the world in contempt, for such is the way of thought of the men of Allah, exalted be He!

This thirteen-article creed had the widest circulation among the Muslims of Ice's day and after. It is a perplexing document in that it resembles no creedal statement known in Arabic, but is very close indeed to a summary of Islamic belief in twelve articles given by Lull (ca. 1272) in *The Book of the Gentile and the Three Sages*. Ice was certainly not the originator, therefore. We do not know where Lull got his formulation from, and the most acceptable hypothesis is that both Lull and Ice are reproducing a creedal statement with some currency in Spain. However, we cannot altogether exclude the possibility that Ice did derive his creed from Lull. If John of Segovia was studying the problems of attempting to convert Muslims, he can hardly have failed to look at the writings of his predecessor Ramón Lull. Can *The Book of the Gentile and the Three Sages* have been on the shelf in the priory of Aiton when Ice went there? It is surely more likely than not that it was.

Linked with the problem of the origins of the creed of Chapter III is another posed by Chapter LX: "Concerning the doctrine and degrees in which the world is governed" (Harvey 1981:23–29). This last chapter of the *Breviary* is so different in tone from the rest of the work that one might be tempted to suppose that this was simply a text copied out at the end of the book, in which Ice had no hand. Ice announced in his introduction that his book had sixty chapters, so if the "Degrees in which the world is governed" is not by Ice, then his last chapter is missing. All of the manuscripts of the *Breviary* give this as the sixtieth chapter, and just before a colophon in which he is named. The section is therefore almost certainly by Ice. And yet it turns out to be an Islamized version of a passage that occurs in Enrique de Villena's *The Twelve Labors of Hercules,* a work written first in Catalan in 1417 and subsequently translated into Castilian by the author (who died in 1434).

Villena's text gives a list of twelve estates from the peak of the social pyramid to the base. Ice also lists twelve social classes in virtually the same order as Villena, but where necessary he transposes the specifically Christian terms used by Villena into Islamic equivalents:

Villena	*Ice*
1. prince	caliph (*alkhalīfa*)
2. prelate	mufti
3. knight	military leader (*caudillo*)
4. religious	religious
5. citizen (or perhaps "burgess")	citizen
6. merchant	merchant

At this point, whereas Villena has in seventh place *labradores* (farmers), Ice consigns them to tenth place, and goes on to craftsmen (*menestrales*), Villena's eighth category. After craftsmen both have schoolmasters and then students (*disipulos*). Villena next has hermits, who do not figure in Ice's list. Ice in eleventh place has "idle fellows" (*baldíos*), of which the equivalent in Villena is an unnumbered class of "people who live like pirates" to be found at the end. Both agree in placing women at the bottom of their table!

Villena	*Ice*
7. farmer	craftsman
8. craftsman	schoolmaster
9. schoolmaster	student
10. student	farmer
11. hermit	idle fellow
12. woman	woman
—pirates, etc.	

A picture is emerging of Ice de Gebir as a pious Islamic scholar who is in contact with Christian writings and who is prepared to modify and Islamize any item he thinks can be turned to advantage. Why he was attracted to Villena's "twelve estates" it is difficult to say. A view of society as hierarchical is not common in Islamic writings, which usually stress the equally base status of all men as compared with God Almighty. In the fifteenth century Christian literature and art was much obsessed with the depiction of a hierarchical society which yet was rendered equal in the face of death. The *danse macabre,* in which all classes from the Emperor downwards are led away by Death the great leveler, is one of the major artistic themes of the fifteenth century, and one can understand how Ice may have thought (mistakenly in my view) that it could be turned to account as a finale to his treatise.

In concentrating on these aspects of Ice's book which can be traced to Christian antecedents, we run the risk of giving the false impression that the bulk of the contents of the *Breviary* is, in some way, of mixed origin, whereas most of the work is conservative, traditional, and purely and orthodoxly Islamic. The legal requirements for valid prayer are set out in careful detail, and, after faith and prayer, the other "pillars of Islam" are examined: fasting, canonical alms, and pilgrimage. Food regulations are detailed, there are provisions for oath-taking, there is a summary of marriage law and of the law of inheritance, there are details of the regulations for the settling of blood feuds and for the punishment of adultery.

The tariff of punishments is a fierce one, and Ice shows no sign of advocating any relaxation. Heresy ("to go against the law or the *sunna*") is to be punished as follows: the offender has three days in which to repent, and if he does not, he is put to death and his estate is forfeited to the *aljama.*

A Muslim living secretly according to another religion "so that he is neither Moor nor Christian" is to be put to death, and if he denies that he had committed the offense, "let him not be believed." "If he says he wishes to repent, let his word not be accepted, and let him die, and let his Muslim heirs inherit from him." Anyone who rails against God is to be put to death by stoning.

"He who drinks wine in Ramadan, let him receive the punishment for wine, which is 80 lashes, and if he should eat and refuse to keep the fast, without legitimate cause, let him die. If he denies that there is an obligation to prayer or alms or pilgrimage, let him die" (*Mem. Hist. Esp.,* 5:383–85).

It will be seen that Ice's readiness to absorb Christian material and adapt it in no way betokened a desire to modify the *sharīʿa:* the penalty for adultery (duly witnessed) was death by stoning, and for fornication between an unmarried couple, 100 lashes and exile for one year for the man, who is to be kept in prison in his place of exile. The woman has to be lashed exactly the same as the man, although she is to remain clothed, whereas he is to be naked. Her clothing, however, is to be such "that it does not save her from the pain."

Perhaps under the influence of Gide and other such writers, it is sometimes thought that Muslim attitudes towards homosexuality are essentially less hostile or vindictive than those of Christians. There is nothing in Ice's code that suggests any degree of laxity in this matter. The penalty for sodomy is death by stoning "if they are married men or not," and the only glimmer of mercy is shown where there is a large age difference between the offenders: the older man is to be put to death but not the younger (*Mem. Hist. Esp.,* 5:388). The strong disapproval felt within the community for homosexuality is reflected in the very heavy penalty visited on anybody uttering "sodomite" as an insult or taunt: 80 lashes (*Mem. Hist. Esp.,* 5:386). It must have been considered to be almost the worst of all possible insults.

Penalties for theft followed the Koranic precept contained in Sūra V.38: "As for the thief, male or female, cut off their hands." Ice stipulates the limits below which the punishment does *not* apply as "a quarter of a gold *dobla* or three silver *adarmes*." The word *dobla* makes it look as if perhaps we have a code evolved for medieval Castile, but that is not the case. The Arabic legal manuals study the problem of *niṣāb* or minimum limits for the penalty, and speak of a quarter of a gold dinar, so that here too Ice is following authority (*Mem. Hist. Esp.,* 5:392; cf. Doi 1984:256–57).

Mercy is to be shown to anybody driven to crime by hunger: "If a man is very poor, with no means of sustenance, and if he steals one portion to eat, or one meal only, then he and a man who steals to the value of less than three *adarmes* do not deserve to have their hands cut off." The manuals of law, besides setting minimum limits, specify that the object stolen must actually be in the custody of somebody, and the thief must be adult, in his right mind, and not under duress or under such pressure as compelling hunger. All this comes out in Ice's formulation:

> They should not cut off [the hand] of anybody out of his mind, nor of a man who takes an animal running loose, nor of sons or daughters who steal from the parents or from grandparents who live in the same house, nor if a wife steals from her husband, nor

> a husband from his wife, if they are living together. Nor anybody who plucks a fruit without climbing the tree, so long as he does not trespass to pick the fruit up, and does not climb up on something high in order to reach it. The penalty should not be inflicted for the theft of vegetables from an unfenced garden which is not locked and is left unguarded, nor any wayfarer who cuts something to eat. [This last provision is reminiscent of the deeply ingrained popular conviction which exists in most parts of Spain to the effect that out of towns it is *not* theft to pick fruit growing within reach of the public footpath.] (*Mem. Hist. Esp.*, 5:393)

When in Chapter XV we come across a section on "the responsibilities of the *alfaquí*," we might reasonably infer that here we have a reflection of Ice's personal experience as *alfaquí* of Segovia, but not so—he renders the contents of an Arabic source. Perhaps there is one even closer than the *Risāla* of al-Qayrawānī, but that text is substantially identical. Chapter XI of the *Risāla* deals with "the office of *imām* and those worshippers who pray behind him." This equivalence shows us how Mudejars used the word *alfaquí* (Arabic *faqīh* 'Islamic jurist') in a much broader sense, as a title for the local religious leader or *imām*. (There could be no better example of how in Islamic Spain the men of the Law came to be the general leaders of the community.)

There is little in Ice's text at this point which is not derived from the *Risāla*, unless it be the formula setting out the conditions under which two ritual prayers might be run together (i.e., one missed out). Ice's phrase seems to reflect the harsh realities of winter up on the Meseta Central: "For any one of six reasons prayers may be run together: for darkness, or for rainstorms, or for mud, or for snow, or for enemies, or for fear" (*por escuridad, por llubia, por lodos, por niebes, por enemigos y por temor*) (*Mem. Hist. Esp.*, 5:288).

We have seen that this manual by Ice de Gebir may not have been the first such text (*Leyes de moros* being earlier), but Ice did provide a comprehensive work of instruction giving essential details to enable Muslims to fulfil all the requirements of their religion throughout their life. Life was seen not so much under the shadow of death as looking forward to it. At the end of the section on the Law there are texts on "the signs of Judgment Day and the end of the present age." Life was lived by these Muslims in expectation of the imminent blast on Isrāfīl's trumpet, which would mark "the bringing to an end of this present age" (*el afinamento deste presente siglo*). Thus, Ice words his colophon as follows:

> The book entitled *Sunnī Breviary* which was compiled by the honored scholar, Don Ice de Chebir, *muftī*, principal *alfaquí* of the Muslims of Castile, *imām* of the honored *aljama* of Segovia, was completed in the mosque of the said city in the year 1462, may the Sovereign place him in His Glory. Amen, O Lord of this world and of the next. (*Mem. Hist. Esp.*, 5:416–17)

The earnest hope of glory was not just an item of pious rhetoric, it was the expression of how Ice saw his situation in a world perched on the brink of the end of days.

Ice's date of death is unknown, although if, as we have seen, he was already an honored judge in 1440 or earlier, he can hardly have lived to see the end of the century. There is no trace of him in the records after 1462. His story does not bring that of the Castilian Mudejars to an end, but he was beyond doubt the most influential individual in this community.

SEVEN

Mudejar Communities: Aragon

The lands of the Crown of Aragon in the Middle Ages comprised a number of distinct component parts. There were more marked differences between its various regions and linguistic and cultural communities than existed within the lands of León and Castile, and yet, paradoxically, Aragon suffered less from internally generated forces of dissension and disorder than did the rival bloc. Besides the Aragonese-speaking lands of the Ebro basin, which gave the name to the kingdom, we have the Catalan-speaking country of Barcelona, early a preferred seat of the court. The regime thus became bilingual, with Catalan predominating in literature and commerce, but never threatening to oust Aragonese from its heartlands. (If Aragonese has retreated to become by the twentieth century a rural dialect of a few hill-farmers in the Pyrenees, that is in the main because of the pressure of Castilian from the east, not of Catalan from the west.) By and large it was Catalan which the Aragonese empire bore to its overseas Mediterranean dominions, and Catalan extended ever farther southwards in the course of the Middle Ages to form a populous, albeit narrow, seaboard strip eventually reaching as far as Alicante and beyond. Overseas, but more directly linked to the homeland than the distant colonies and outposts, were the Balearic Islands, incorporated into the crown by James the Conqueror. How Valencia came to enter the crown of Aragon as a kingdom with an immense Muslim population is discussed in the following chapter. The Muslim communities that lived in these distinct political units (they all owed independent allegiance to the Aragonese crown) were also distinct.

We get a vivid picture of the Muslim communities of the upper Ebro valley and of its tributary the Jalón (Salón in medieval texts) in the *Poema de Mio Cid.* (The text is, of course, of a considerably earlier period; it was probably written in the early thirteenth century and narrates events of the late eleventh.) Since the distribution of Muslim villages remained remarkably unchanged right up to the final expulsion of 1609, we may reasonably infer that what the *Poema* tells us about the region bears some relevance to the state of affairs ca. 1250. The Cid is depicted as making his way over the rugged watershed between the tributaries of the Duero and those of the Ebro. He emerges into prosperous cultivated lands down the banks of the Jalón, where a string of Muslim villages offered tempting pickings to the freebooter: Ariza, Cetina, Alhama, Bubierca, Ateca, Terrer, and the township of Calatayud. Settlement was in relatively small groupings and did not constitute blanket occupation over a whole area, as was the case near Valencia, nor yet was it of isolated *morerías* in the pattern to be found in Castile. The *Poema de Mio Cid* depicts these settlements as combining for certain purposes (as for example to negotiate mass ransoms), but ready to feud and maneuver for advantage at the slightest excuse. This loose structure must have given the Muslims great flexibility of response and power to survive the adversities of life in an environment that was by no means an easy one. The speciality of these Muslims seems to have been intensive settled agriculture, and through the interstices of the web of their villages moved Christian stockmen with their sometimes transhumant flocks.

One thing the *Poema de Mio Cid* does not tell us is what was the language of these Muslim Aragonese cultivators. That Arabic was their language of culture, the language of their religion and of their legal documents, goes without saying, but was this a bilingual community with Romance the language of the family and everyday life? Documents in Arabic from this period are not conclusive proof at all. In very many other parts of the Islamic world at this period (Berber North Africa, for example), two languages coexisted. The absence of Arabic from the area in later periods when documentation is fuller (the fifteenth and sixteenth centuries) and the survival in Morisco speech of deeply embedded Romance archaisms of pure local provenance seem to indicate that these folk may never have possessed Arabic, even at the beginning of our period, as their spoken language.

In Cataluña the Catalan-speaking Muslim community lived as a small, largely urban minority among the Christian majority, although usually in *morerías*—a pattern of living that must have owed more to their need for certain community services, such as a butcher capable of providing *ḥalāl* meat, than to any policy of exclusion on the part of the Christians.

In the Balearics the conquests seem to have destroyed the community; at least we do not hear of the Christian authorities dealing with whole congregations (*aljamas,* etc.) of Muslims, but with individuals and small groups. They seem to have been Arabic speakers, and the market in Muslim slaves for North Africa meant that there was an inflow of captive Arabic speakers as well as the outflow of those who could take advantage of the islands' position to escape.

In Valencia and the surrounding lands the pattern was different again. Here Muslims had created the irrigated landscape, and Muslims were at first needed to make that productive agricultural machine work. From the studies of Burns we can trace how the Catalan-speaking invaders who arrived in 1238 came in the course of the later Middle Ages to take over these rich lands, but that did not occur at the outset of our period. Valencia had been the final refuge for many Muslim families who had constituted the aristocracy of the sword and the pen in other regions, and who had in the face of the rising Christian tide felt the need to move to places where the exercise of their religion was freely permitted. Valencia thus constituted a more self-confident and self-assertive Muslim community than the others outside Granada. It was to Valencia that Aragonese Muslims sent the young men who needed to be trained in Arabic. Arabic was the first language of the Muslim peasantry, and many of them spoke no other tongue. Across the seas they knew were Arabic-speaking coreligionists in North Africa, and they did not feel isolated.

One of the bitterly contested issues of Hispanic historical dialectology is whether an aboriginal native Romance was spoken in Islamic Valencia before Catalan arrived there. As with almost all linguistic questions relating to Valencia, this is debated mainly as a way of making coded statements about twentieth-century Valencian politics. The Romance in question is usually denominated Valencian Mozarabic. The use of the term *Mozarabic* leads to an easy assumption that those who spoke this language were Christians—since the "Mozarabs" were Christians. In my view, there is no more reason to suppose that all Valencian Romance speakers (if there were any) were Christians than to make that assumption for Aragonese Romance speakers. However this may be, the vast majority of Valencian Muslims clearly had Arabic as their first and usually only language. Valencia was one of the most populous centers of Muslim Arabic speakers in the peninsula, second only to the independent kingdom of Granada.

Mudejars in the Kingdom of Aragon Proper

It was the opinion of Macho y Ortega (1923) that subject Muslims first occur in Aragon in 1096 after the conquest of Huesca. There was considerable diversity of status, ranging from entirely free Muslims who accepted Christian rule to those of near servile status, cultivators attached to the soil (*adscriptos a la gleba*), and obliged to work a particular piece of land. The term *exaricos* occurs in some documents to describe one class of cultivators. The word derives from Arabic *sharīk* 'sharer', and in this context 'sharecropper' (elsewhere it can mean one who "associates" other divinities with Allah, i.e., a polytheist). The status of the sharecropper might under some circumstances be a relatively desirable one, and at all events higher than that of the completely landless man or the serf, but in the usage of the times the *exarico* was undoubtedly perceived as a person of low status, and it is difficult to distinguish *exaricos* at times from *adscriptos a la gleba*. It would be wrong to see the situation of the *exaricos* as without its advantages. As J. M. Lacarra has put it: "The *exarico* did not wish to be separated from the excellent land which he cultivated, land which he was entitled by law to hand on to his sons for them to cultivate. The owner, for his part, could not expel him, even if another cultivator offered more profitable terms" (1981:23). It is at the bottom of the social ladder that we find most of Aragon's subject Muslims, but there is another side to their servitude. All Mudejars were to the kings of Aragon *servi camare nostri,* and as Boswell encapsulated it in the title of his detailed study of them in the mid-fourteenth century, they constituted *The Royal Treasure*. As he puts it, "All Muslims were in a sense royal Muslims: the Crown of Aragon claimed ultimate jurisdiction over every Muslim living in lands under its rule" (1977:30). One might add that this attitude ought to be understood against the broader European background as an extension to Muslims of a constitutional device first developed in order to find a place for Jews within a predominantly feudal order. In a society of which the only full members could be the faithful of the majority religion, Christianity, a society often engaged in crusading warfare under the banner of the cross, the position of any non-Christian monotheist was anomalous. Just as the special status accorded to Jews ("the emperor's Jews" in German lands, or Jews such as Raquel and Vidas living in the protective shelter of the royal castle of Burgos in Castile) had two contradictory aspects, so did that of Aragon's protected Muslims. On the one hand there was a positive protection of those who might otherwise be subjected to persecution or vexatious treatment by the majority, on the other hand there was confirmation of the exclusion of such groups from the society of the majority. Such men were outside the nexus of obligations and rights which bound the king's (or emperor's) Christian subjects into one polity. The device of deeming the Mudejars a special royal treasure was a protection against the worst abuses, but that device was necessary because they were excluded from full participation in society, and not included in those complex networks of protection which guarded (and oppressed) the Christian majority.

The bulk of the Mudejar population could obviously not look for the same level of interested protection as was enjoyed by a minority of Jewish financiers or professional men, or indeed by the upper echelons of their own community. As in most societies, proximity to power meant political protection. However, the king did have a special interest in all Muslims (although it would be argued that slaves or those specially imported by a lord from areas outside crown jurisdiction by law belonged to the lord and his family). Access to royal justice must have been of inestimable value to those oppressed by a bad lord, and at times some Christians must have envied the anomalous status enjoyed by their Muslim neighbors.

As in Castile there was a conflict which arose out of the administration of Islamic law within the community of Muslims under the aegis of the crown. The Muslims were to live "according to their own law" (*secundum zunam et xaram eorum*), but for this to take place there had to be in position a range of office-holders, justices, and so forth. Whereas in an Islamic society such offices would be filled by the Islamic authority, in Mudejar Aragon such places might be filled by men nominated by Christian authorities, perhaps on the grounds that the nominees were politically acceptable or safe, perhaps because a favor had to be returned, perhaps because of considerations of profit and gain. It is in no way surprising that the same practices should apply in the distribution of offices within the Muslim community as were current among Christians. In some cases (at relatively later dates) we even find Christians appointed to specifically Muslim posts. It is not clear whether a Christian who was a *qāḍī* would exercise the functions of the office himself or, as is altogether more probable, put in his own nominee to do the work, contenting himself with a proportion of the emoluments. There is no doubt that in Islamic law such a Christian *qāḍī* would be totally unacceptable. But protected Muslim favorites appointed by the king to positions of power would also have been unacceptable to the faithful. What are we to make, for example, of Faraig (Faraj) de Bellvís? (Boswell 1977:43–49; Febrer Romaguera 1986:esp. 281). In the 1360s, he was *qāḍī* of the whole kingdom (*alcaydus totius regni Aragoniae*) as well as *qāḍī* of Valencia and Játiva and *faqīh* and notary of Borja, Huesca, and other places, most of these offices held for life. Clearly this plurality of benefices betrays corruption, and even if the letter of the Islamic law had been carried out by such an office-holder, such arrangements would have been offensive.

The Aragonese crown needed loyal and tame Muslims to man its administration. There are indications that something by way of an Aragonese professional class grew up, and indeed this class seems to have extended its activities across state boundaries. The brother of Faraj de Bellvís, Yahya by name, was a Mudejar of substance in Castile. Faraj's son Ovechar (Abū Bakr?) was a member of the household of Peter the Ceremonious in Aragon. Through his second wife, Fatima, Faraj was related to the Fuster family of merchants in Valencia. We cannot tell what were Faraj's principal sources of income, and what came to him from his judicial offices may have been subsidiary to the fruits of the administration of his own estates, or his activities as a lender of money to the crown. The combination of the activities of Islamic judge and usurer is not exactly orthodox.

The Christian Law as It Affected Muslims

If Muslims were guaranteed that they would be judged according to their own law, that did not mean that they did not figure in the Aragonese codes for Christians. The legal system of Aragon was complex in the extreme, certainly no less so than other systems of other parts of the peninsula, so that any exhaustive treatment would be quite impossible here. A sound basis for a summary of characteristic legislation as it affected Muslims is provided by the compilation of *Fueros* (laws) made in 1247 by Bishop Vidal de Carnellas of Huesca (Tilander 1937: 1–197). This was promulgated by James I, and although all sorts of exceptions and saving clauses need to be introduced when speaking of this, as of any other medieval code, it does serve as a clear illustration of the position of the Muslim in Christian Aragon: on the margins of society and in a position of inferiority.

Tithes. "All Jews and Muslims are obliged to pay tithes and to give first fruits on all their possessions except in the case of land which never within human memory has been in Christian possession." It is obvious that in the long term the impact of this clause will have been to reinforce the conservatism and immobility of the Muslim cultivators (Tilander 1937:11 [No. 4]).

Oaths and Evidence. These sections confront the problems that arose when conflicting evidence was adduced in court. In suits between Christians alone there were various mechanisms, such as oath taking and trial by battle. Trial by battle was not available to Moors, but the pattern of oaths required is strictly fair and symmetrical: "a Christian must back up assertions which he made which were denied by Muslims by finding a Christian and a Moor ready to depose on his behalf, whereas the Moor must find a Moor and a Christian." The principle seems to have been that it was not sufficient to bring evidence from one's own religious community.

Similar fairness is to be observed where written evidence has to be attested by a notary: the notary should be of the religion of the person deposing, with witnesses from both faiths.

Where exaction of debts was being demanded, and the alleged debtor contested his indebtedness, a scale of oaths was set up: debts below six dineros could be "on any Christian's head," up to twelve dineros "on the head of his grandfather," above that "on the book and the cross," whereas from Muslims "*bell ylle ha ylle hu*" ("By Allah, there is no god but He"?) suffices in all cases. Here is admirable respect for the non-Christian system, and no desire to force Muslims artificially into a pattern parallel with that of the Christians (Tilander 1937:53 [No. 107], 59 [No. 121], 65 [No. 134]).

Offenses of Violence by Captives. "If any man's captive wounds any person or any person's beast and the Moor denies it, proof must be adduced by two loyal Christian witnesses, and if such proof is lacking, the Moor's owner must swear that he did not commit the offense" (Tilander 1937:82 [No. 161]).

Here there is no symmetry, and the scales of justice are weighted against the Muslim. It should be noted that this does not affect Mudejars at all. In general, legislation with regard to captives was harsh (Law No. 152 [1937:79], for example, punishes severely anyone giving assistance to fugitives).

Limits on Rates of Interest. Members of all three religions are forbidden to charge interest above 100 percent under any circumstances (Tilander 1937:95 [No. 189]).

Religious Conversion. Any Muslim wishing to be converted to Christianity should be allowed to do so without penalty. While he was alive his children could make no demands on him, although after his death they might ask for what they would have received from his estate if he had remained a Muslim.

When preachers wished to preach, the Muslims must all attend and listen patiently, and if they would not attend of their own free will, the officers of justice could compel them. This enactment, dating from 1242, is a clear infringement of Muslim religious rights (Tilander 1937:160 [No. 271]).

Blood Price. The penalty for wounding a Moor so as to draw blood is set at five hundred sueldos, or fifty if the wound is quite superficial. (Direct comparison is not simple. In the case of a commoner or of a villein who was a Christian and who struck another of similar status so as to knock him to the ground, two hundred fifty sueldos was payable. Five hundred sueldos was the penalty for killing a foreigner (*omne estranio*). It would seem that Muslims were given a fairly high level of protection (Tilander 1937:162 [No. 273]).

Property Sales. A Moor might not sell his real estate to a Christian without royal approval, and if approval were given, one-third of the price went to the crown (Tilander 1937:162 [No. 274]). However, Moors are quite free to sell to other Moors. The policy seems to have been one of separate development.

Disputes over Cattle. Where disputes arose over beasts being grazed for their owners, the oath of a Muslim in his mosque should be sufficient to establish ownership (Tilander 1937:163 [No. 275]).

Aiding Escaped Muslims. The penalty for helping a Muslim escape was confiscation of goods (Tilander 1937:163 [No. 276]).

Change of Residence. "Moors, both men and women, who dwell on the king's estates are, if they move to live on the estates of nobles [*infançones*], and are detained while moving, to become the property of the king and his officers, and suffer confiscation of all their goods, both what they had brought with them and all real estate or goods or chattels left behind on the king's domains, but once they reach the boundary of the estate of the noble, they may not be detained, nor may anything which they have with them." The noble has the same rights, neither more nor less, over Moors, whether male or female, who move to the estates of the king, or to the estates of other nobles in order to live there. "However, the persons of the Moors, male or female, may not in any of the circumstances set out here be detained by any noble or any other man against the king's will or that of the ministers of his justice, because it is quite certain [*cosa es cierta*] that all Moors, male or female, wherever they live, belong to the king, with the exception of prisoners and those imported by the noble to settle on his estates from places beyond the frontiers of the kingdom. In that case all those Moors and their descendants belong legally to the nobles" (Tilander 1937:164 [No. 277]).

This somewhat confused enactment sheds much light on the condition of the Muslim cultivator. On the one hand we see that he was regarded as a resource to be exploited: he did not enjoy full protection *in his own right* away from the land of his lord or master. On the other hand he did, within certain limits, seem to have possessed some freedom to change his lord, so that under certain conditions he may have been able to bargain for better terms. In general, though, this law gives us a picture of the Muslim as a member of an oppressed class exposed to the dangerous rivalries of those who maneuvered for the chance to profit from its labor.

The situation of the Moors within the king's realms is well conveyed when, in one text, various classes of society are mentioned. They do not figure with "citizens, townspeople, and our men" but with "widows, orphans, all penurious folk, Jews, Moors" (Tilander 1937:150 [No. 262]). At the bottom of the social pile, then, there is a protected place for these necessary cultivators.

Islamic Law in Aragon

In Aragon as everywhere else in the Christian lands there was a tension between the rigorist call for the Muslim to emigrate to a country where he could lead a true Islamic way of life and the desire of the plain man to live a decent life on the land that had been occupied by his forefathers for generations.

It has been seen that in Castile there eventually emerged a code in the Romance vernacular. No such code appeared in Aragon until the sixteenth century, and, when it did, the committee of "the nobility of this kingdom of Aragon" (meaning, of course, the Muslim nobility) presided over by the *imām* of Cadrete, had to call in the assistance of a Muslim from Castile, the Mancebo de Arévalo (see p. 86 above). The volume they produced, entitled *The Brief Compendium of Our Holy Law and Sunna,* incorporated important sections of the *Sunnī Breviary* of Ice de Gebir. If an Aragonese code had been available already, this group of scholars, who in several ways display local pride in quite an exaggerated form, would probably have made use of it (Harvey 1958a:esp. 65).

One may speculate that the Aragonese Muslims lagged behind their Castilian coreligionists in producing a code in their own variety of Romance because it was not necessary: their Islamic lawyers seem to have maintained a reasonable standard of competence in Arabic. It was possible to send young men for training in Arabic in the Valencian region without excessive difficulty. The Aragonese do seem to have produced their own abridged summaries of *fiqh,* but even in the fifteenth century these were being copied and used in Arabic, at a time when that language was not in everyday use.

Examples of this sort of work are to be found in Ms. XLV of the Almonacid hoard (Ribera and Asín 1912:158–75). This manuscript contains three legal treatises together with notes on a number of *fatwās* and other legal matters, and the second of the treatises (*kitāb fīhi maʾānī ʾl-aḥkām wa ʾl-sunan muʾallafa min kutub jumma* . . . 'Book containing the senses of legal judgments and established practices compiled from a number of volumes . . . ' by the *qāḍi* of Tortosa, Abūʾ l-ʿAbbās Aḥmad b. Khayr al-Saraqusṭī) had been specified in A.H. 834 (1431 A.D.) by one Muḥammad b. ʿAlī from Cosuenda. Presumably of this date too is the scale of punishments specified at the end of the text:

Arguing with the qāḍī about a penalty, 30 lashes
Insulting the qāḍī, 39 lashes
False witness, 49 lashes
Riding a horse without the owner's permission, 4 lashes

Casting dirt in the qāḍī's face, 9 lashes
Calling somebody son of an adultress without proof, 80 lashes
Entering a house without permission, 20 lashes.
(Ribera and Asín 1912:173)

A certain preoccupation with the fragile status of the *qāḍī* is obvious here. According to Macho y Ortega the office of chief *qāḍī* for the lands of the Crown of Aragon (including Valencia) was located in Saragossa. This assertion should be accepted with caution; Febrer Romaguera says that Faraj de Bellvís appeared to combine the office of chief *qāḍī* of Aragon and of Valencia ca. 1355 (Febrer Romaguera 1986:281). What we do not know is the sort of relations that existed between such Islamic lawyers who were the appointees of the Christian monarchs and the general community of pious believers. The Bellvís family for generations controlled the office of chief *qāḍī*, but that name does not turn up once in the Almonacid hoard of manuscripts and documents. It would be unwise to argue from silence when the selection of material that has survived is so restricted. Probably in Aragon as in Castile such Mudejar lawyers managed the difficult balancing act of providing the religious guidance their fellow Muslims required while serving the administrative purposes of their Christian masters.

The Muslims on the Estates of Nobles

In the *Fueros de Aragón* we have come across the distinction between Muslims living on royal estates and those on lands belonging to nobles. It might at first sight seem that the situation of such Muslims would be much worse. Since the noble might well wish to dispose of his estates in normal commercial transactions, and since it was the practice on change of ownership for the officials and dignitaries of the local communities to be deprived of office in order that the incoming owner might exercise his full rights and power, it might appear that such Muslims enjoyed only a precarious status, and that their institutions were weak and vulnerable. Yet if we try to read between the lines of such documents as survive from *morerías* situated on estates other than those of the crown, we often intuit a state of relative content with a system which seems to have contained a number of human checks and balances to limit the untrammeled exercise of a lord's power. And for the Muslim on the estate of a noble, if an intolerable situation did arise, it was always possible for him to appeal over the head of his lord to the protection of the king, because of the doctrine already mentioned that all Muslims belonged to the king.

As illustrating life on an estate outside crown domains we may examine a transfer of lordship which took place on July 27, 1454. This date is, of course, relatively late, but it is clear that those participating in what is evidently a ritualized enactment were preserving customs from their past. Obviously earlier evidence would be preferable, if available, but the documents in question appear to preserve a record of a well-established and traditional pattern of relationships.

The document is a written account of the transfer of the lordship of the village of Mediana to one Lope de Viniés, drawn up by a notary. It was the custom for this to be done as part of the formal transfer of title. On the appointed day the village crier (*pregón*) summoned the whole village to witness the occasion. The council (*concello*) and the Muslim congregation (*aljama*) came together in the village square in the presence of Lope's lawyer, Pedro de Esera, and of all persons of note in Mediana: Ibraym de Brea, the *alamín* or village administrator, his relative Abdallah de Brea, and one Mahome Xadret deputizing for Brahem de Exea and Ali Mohip, both members of the council. With them came "the whole council and *aljama* of the said place" (some twenty names are listed). The assembled persons then resolved as follows: "We name as procurators of this council and *aljama* Miguel de Ayesa, governor of the town of Fuentes, Francisco Cuevas and Mahoma el Jacho . . . so that they may on behalf of the said council resolve whatsoever differences may arise, and in the name of which they may as required make an oath of fealty to whatsoever persons."

And then, the notary tells us, "before the gates of the castle of the village of Mediana there was inducted in person Luís (*sic*) Viniés, gentleman and lord of the said place, who affirmed that he did indeed make his entry into the said castle and take possession of it in my presence."

The next day there was a formal ceremony of homage and a little piece of street theater was played out to convey in dramatic form what was happening. First the representatives of Christian and Moorish inhabitants came to do homage, Mahoma el Jacho on behalf of the latter. The Christian did obeisance "*de manos y boca,*" i.e., with a kiss, but the Muslim "*besando en el hombro*" 'kissing on the shoulder'. (This Muslim reluctance to adopt the offensive Christian custom of kissing on the mouth is already recorded for us in the *Poema de Mio Cid,* where it is the way of, for example, Abengalbón, the Cid's *amigo de paz* from Albarracín.) "After which in the said village of Mediana and in the said castle Francisco de Cuevas [i.e., one of the procurators] appeared in the presence of Lope de Viniés, lord, and stated that Ibrahim de Xabe had given him a punch for no good reason, and straightaway Lope de Viniés gave orders for the said Ibrahim to be detained and put in the stocks [*cepo*], and we were witnesses to his detention."

After a space of time had passed, at the request of "good persons," Lope de Viniés released Ibrahim de Xabe on recognisances of good behavior "into the hands of Miguel de Ayesa, and the said Miguel accepted him" (Macho y Ortega 1923).

If this were an isolated document we would wonder whether this little affair were to be taken at its face value or not, but over and over in such deeds of transfer we find that the incoming lord exercises his right to execute summary justice in some such way. There can be no proof, but it is reasonable to suppose that the incident of the punch and the short spell in the stocks was a prearranged charade, no more than the dramatization of the powers of a lord over his vassals, and of his determination to keep the peace. It would be surprising if the parties did not laugh over their parts in it all during the ensuing festivities. In other cases the incoming lord marked his assumption of power by having a gallows raised and ordering a bird, often a partridge, to be strung up. As in the case of this Mediana document, Moorish vassals swear their fealty with an oath written down by the notary in a form very similar to that recorded in the *Fueros: Bille ille alladi ille hua.* It is dangerous to allow one's imagination to breathe life into the notary's dry account, but the impression which I gain is one of rustic good humor and human understanding in a community where everybody knew everybody else—something very far from a regime of heartless oppression.

The principal difference in terms of taxation between Muslims on crown lands (*moros de realengo*) and others was that the former had to pay a levy usually called the *peyta* (Cast. *pecha*) *ordinaria* together with a number of other occasional obligations, such as that of providing entertainment for their royal master (*cena*) on specified occasions. As compared with the bewildering plurality of obligations which fell on the shoulders of Muslims on lands of individual nobles, the *peyta* does not seem onerous; it seems to have been levied at a rate of one maravedi a head. In principle a poll tax, the *peyta* was unpopular in part because the king had the disconcerting way of rewarding those who served him well by exempting them from it. However, since the tax was assessed as a global sum due from each village, and since that sum was not reduced when a tax exemption was granted, the net effect was simply to increase the payments due from each inhabitant. Moreover as cultivators slipped away from *realengo* lands to other estates, the *peyta* payments also rose.

The crown soon became aware of the dangers in the flight of population from its estates. In 1387 John I decreed that the *peyta* would be paid by all Moors, whatever their personal status (Macho y Ortega 1923:182–83). This led to some individuals paying both royal dues and those payable to the lord. In a further round of this complicated set of maneuvers, we find some lords, when entering into engagements with Muslim cultivators whom they wished to attract, promising to pay their *peyta* for them. Clearly there was something approaching a competitive labor market, with conditions varying considerably from one place to another.

Illustrations of the complexities arising from the differences between *realengo* and other tenants are provided by two documents referred to by Lacarra (1981:26). In 1282 the Muslims of Cadrete complained to the crown because those of them on royal land paid the *peyta* and others in the same village but on Hospitaler land did not. Cadrete, in fact, because of the two different tax regimes, had to duplicate its *aljama*, with parallel sets of officials for each regime, right up to the top level of *amín*. The case the *realengo* tenants tried to make was that "since the persons of the said Moors belonged to the King" they ought all to pay on the same basis. The argument, based on the doctrine of the "royal treasure," is ingenious, but it was thrown out by the courts. They had no more luck when they objected to contributing to the king's *cena*. The differential system was affirmed: *realengo* Moors paid on one basis, tenants of the Hospital on another.

In 1306 Muslims in Coglar requested a declaration that their lord was Jaime of Jérica and not the Order of St. John. What they objected to were the dues such as the *sofra* (forced labor) being demanded.

It is to be noted that in the first pair of cases, *realengo* Moors envy the lot of fellow Muslims on church land, in the second, Moors on church land wish to pass into the hands of a well-connected noble. There is a tendency to assume that Mudejars on the lands of the orders were invariably better off. No doubt sometimes they were, but we are dealing with a shifting situation. Generalizations certainly cannot be expected to hold over two centuries. What some nobles collected from some *exaricos* certainly makes a frightening list. From crops of cereals (*panes*), one-half; from flax and similar crops, including saffron, one-seventh; from vegetables, one-sixth; from irrigated lands, one-quarter; from woodland, one-eighth; from dark woods (? *monte oscuro*), one-ninth; and so the list went on (Macho y Ortega 1923:173).

It is not surprising that in the face of such exactions *morerías* sometimes found themselves in financial difficulties and became indebted to meet their dues. Then, if there was a bad harvest or some other disaster, they sometimes found themselves unable to pay, so that lords had to declare a tax holiday (*carta de gracias*), such as that conceded in 1446 to the Moors of Alfajarón by one Juan de Mur (Macho y Ortega 1923:151).

One sidelight on the muddled complexity of the financial regime to which the *aljamas* were subject is provided by the *ḥalāl* butchers. *Morerías* were normally permitted to operate their own butchers, where animals would be slaughtered in accordance with the requirements of their religion in conditions of ritual purity. In return for this privilege, a special due, often called the *sisa,* was collected. And of course to defray the *sisa* higher prices were charged for the meat, generally amounting to one penny (*dinero*) per pound. But some Christians preferred to buy *ḥalāl* meat and objected to paying what they perceived as a tax intended only for non-Christians. Some butchers did not charge them the *sisa.* Then some Muslims asked their Christian friends to buy their *ḥalāl* meat for them, and in consequence the *sisa* had to be raised on the rest of the meat purchases effected.

Such tales of petty tax dodging show how dangerous it is to imagine the Aragonese *morerías* as in any sense hermetically sealed settlements. Even where Muslims had their own clearly defined quarter or street—and this was not always the case—people seem to have come and gone. That the Christians should have traveled out of their way to patronize Muslim shops may be surprising, but even more surprising is the ability of the butchers to operate a dual price scale according to the religion of their customers (Macho y Ortega 1923:151).

Within this society the king's Moors could at times hope for energetic royal protection. Alfonso V's wife, María, had a reputation as champion of Muslims who were oppressed. Here she is writing, in 1399, to Juan Martínez de Luna:

> We have once more heard that without due cause you have a great hatred for ʿAbd al-ʿAzīz, the Moor who is *amīn* of Arandiga . . . and that you seek to do him harm. We are most amazed to hear this, if it is true, and greatly displeased, for it is your obligation not only to refrain from such insolent and accursed actions, but also to treat all our subjects with benignity and to their advantage. . . . For the which reason we do ask and require of you that you should do no harm to the said *amīn,* nor do him any offense, otherwise, so sure as death, it will not pass without firm and harsh [*dura e aspra*] correction. (Macho y Ortega 1923:167)

But even where the Christian authorities gave such protection—and it was not always forthcoming, of course—there were factors at work which tended to undermine the Islamic law and its officers. One such factor on occasion was the simple preferences of the Muslims themselves. Families might prefer their disputes to go before a Christian tribunal. Such cases might in theory be tried according to Islamic law, but presumably the parties preferred to avoid the rigors of some of the *ḥadd* punishments.

That some cases should be resolved by the use of arbitrators rather than going to court is, of course, a practice with many antecedents in Islamic societies. But when we learn that a favorite nominee as arbitrator at Saragossa was the archbishop, we can see that *convivencia* had indeed led to change. The principal factor undermining the *sharīʿa,* the Islamic law, was, however, the functioning of the mechanism of appeal. In the final instance cases went before the king. That the code was the *sharīʿa,* was of less concern than the fact that the case was decided outside the Muslim community. This was an aspect of Mudejar status which the *fuqahāʾ*, the Islamic jurists, must have found distasteful.

Disapproval of people living as Mudejars seems to have been of small effect. The strings of villages along the Ebro and its tributaries, such as the Jalón, depicted as densely populated with Muslims in the *Poema de Mio Cid,* were as densely populated at the final expulsion of 1611. Aragon as a kingdom had found an accommodation with its Muslim inhabitants which somehow worked.

It would be misleading to close by painting an entirely rosy picture.

The tensions of this society of three religions show through, for example, in the frequency with which there occur in the records prosecutions of Muslims for having carnal knowledge of a Christian female (Macho y Ortega 1923:193; Ferrer i Mallol 1987:28–32). At this distance in time it would be idle to attempt to ascertain whether Muslim males really did have any tendency to behave badly towards Christian female neighbors. One cannot help suspecting that the scales of justice in this respect were not even, and that, as in the Deep South in the days when white supremacy was being maintained, prosecutions of this kind were a means of maintaining control over a subject community perceived as dangerously insubordinate and in need of periodic correction.

In the ceremonies that marked the entry of Lope de Viniés into enjoyment of his new estate at Mediana in 1454, we may guess that the brief sojourn in the stocks which was visited on Ibrahim de Xabe (a Muslim) for punching a Christian notable was play-acting taken in good part, and not a harsh reality. Still, the subtext of this drama was a serious one: the authorities were there to punish Muslims if they should overstep the mark, and those authorities had ample powers to repress their subjects, should they wish to do so.

The Balearics

The persistence of a Muslim population in the Balearic Islands after the Christian conquest was studied by Elena Lourie (1970). She was able to show that the pattern in the archipelago was, not surprisingly, different from that to be observed in the mainland domains of the Crown of Aragon. The factors governing the Aragonese-Catalan policy towards *Mudéjares* were in the first place the islands' vulnerability to seaborne attack, and in the second shortage of manpower. Exclusive concern with the first factor might well have led to the elimination of Muslims, but the second factor meant that the conquerors were obliged to allow some Muslims to stay and even meant that some new settlements were made. Majorca was invaded by James I in 1229 (it had been held by Ibn Yaḥyā, who was captured in the siege of Palma) and the conquest completed the following year. This was not the first time that Catalans had made a successful raid on the island, but now they were there to stay, and James proceeded to a *Repartiment,* a division of territories among his men. His inability to settle the island intensively led to a trial policy of holding key castles and leaving Muslims still in occupation of large areas.

The Muslims of Minorca signed a document of surrender at Cap de

Pera in 1231, whereby they became tributaries of the kings of Aragon. In circumstances by no means clear the Catalans undertook a second conquest in 1287. Alfonso III of Aragon sent a large expedition from the mainland in 1286, and from their base in Majorca these forces summoned the ruler of Minorca to surrender. This Abū ʿUmar b. Ḥakam refused to do, but he was defeated, and the terms of surrender (June 21, 1287) largely eliminated the Muslim population. Ibiza was also conquered in 1231, and the terms granted to Muslims by Pedro of Portugal are of some interest. Pedro grants to a number of named Saracens, Muqatil, Ibn David, Muḥammad, "and to all our Saracens from Ibiza" at certain named settlements (*alcherias*) in the place called Exarq (i.e., the East) the right to cultivate and exploit, in return for which the Muslims engaged themselves to pay one-half of their crops and produce of all sorts to him as their lord. In addition they engaged themselves to have no other lord but him and his successors, to pay his *baile,* and to provide service to him when needed (*cum opus fuerit*), but for this service they would be paid maintenance (*faciemus vobis expensas dum in nostro servitio fueritis*). This was not a particularly servile contract. To hold land *a medias* in this way was, and apparently still is, a widespread form of tenure. The Muslims were clearly people whom Pedro wished to have in occupation on his land (Mas Latrie 1866:185–86).

Lourie also draws attention to the presence of Muslim craftsmen in the towns. These are blacksmiths, dyers, shoemakers, swordsmiths, bakers, tanners, silversmiths, and weavers. Because they were subject to the institution of debt slavery, debtors became the property of those to whom the debt was owing while the money was outstanding. They could be sold by their owner, and might become outright slaves if the debt was not met. The existence of these contracts is recorded by the crown, because as protector of all Mudejars, it did not wish to have formerly free Muslims becoming permanent slaves (with consequent loss of taxes by the government). One is tempted to assume that the number of such cases must indicate a degree of economic exploitation. Types of debt slavery exist in many societies, and the institution, while perhaps less degrading than outright plantation slavery, in some ways puts the slave in a more depressed economic condition. However, Lourie points out that one of the blacksmiths who sold himself into slavery in 1271 turned up in the documentation twelve years later, selling his workshop, and presumably therefore not in a state of destitution. One might comment that in the harshest of economic climates there are always a few determined lucky winners (Lourie 1970:635). Slavery of any sort is not accepted unless the alternatives are very harsh indeed.

The Muslims in the islands were of several kinds. Besides the debt slaves already mentioned, there were slaves imported as captives, and these might well seek to earn their own manumission if they had no hope of remittance to them of a ransom payment from overseas. This institution was, of course, an effective means of assuring that slaves worked hard and did not need close and expensive supervision. But besides slaves, there were certainly still free Muslim residents after the conquest, some craftsmen. These Muslims had to pay a special poll tax not dissimilar to the poll tax on Christian *dhimmīs* in Muslim lands. Confusingly, some debt slaves bind themselves to continue to pay poll tax. Presumably this is as a result of pressure from the royal authorities, anxious to maintain the level of tax income, though one may suppose that for the debt slave it may have had the advantage of keeping it on record that he was really of free status. When the debt slave redeemed his debt he might well be allowed to continue as a free tenant. Thus the categories of "slave" and "free" were not watertight ones, and "there was a steady trickle of Moslems from the status of slaves, whether of pre-conquest Mallorcan stock or imported, into the class of free tenant-farmers whose conditions of tenure were far from being uniformly harsh, and who, despite papal disapproval, contributed to the settlement of the island" (Lourie 1970:631).

Another important aspect of the life of the Mudejars in the Balearics which marked it off from the life of their coreligionists in mainland Aragonese territories was that they do not seem to have been organized in *aljamas*. They paid their taxes, even the *morabetins* which entitled them to be resident on the islands, as private individuals (Lourie 1970:645). However, as Lourie says, they must have had some community officials, even if only in the mosques, and there is positive mention of the existence of a mosque as late as 1327.

What we do not know is the length of time that the old native Muslim population continued in existence. The fact that community bonds seem to have been weaker than elsewhere may be of relevance here. Isolated and scattered Muslims will have been under greater pressure to convert than close-knit communities, and the process of acculturation will have gone ahead more rapidly. There can have been no possibility of Muslims ceasing to exist in Majorca, Minorca, and Ibiza, however, for all the time the seaborne trade of the islands, and in particular the operations of the pirates and freebooters, would have brought fresh slaves to Majorca and elsewhere. Other Muslim populations, notably that of Valencia, continued to receive fresh blood from overseas too, but in the Balearics the number of recent arrivals was always greater in proportion to the rest of the Muslim populations.

EIGHT

Mudejar Communities: Valencia

More is known in detail about the Mudejar population of Valencia than about that of any other region. This is in the first place because the Christian archival materials are so much richer for Valencia than for any other region. Not only did the Aragonese and Catalan invaders who took over the kingdom in the mid-thirteenth century have administrative procedures which consigned most of what was done to some written record, but also a very high proportion of what was recorded has survived. What is more, these excellent source materials have attracted the devoted scholarship of many historians, among whom one cannot fail to mention R. I. Burns. Such is the profusion of detail that we are in danger of being crushed by it. The Arabic side to Valencian documentation is, however, disappointing. Primary documents are sparse,[1] and in contrast with Naṣrid Granada, Mudejar Valencia attracted little attention from Arabic chroniclers or writers.

There is a paradox about sources for the study of the Mudejars of Valencia. In so many ways we know much more about this region, than about, say, Castile, but, as we have seen, for Castile we have in parallel with the Christian documentation some writings of the Mudejars themselves, especially from the fifteenth century, and are able to see the Castilian Mudejar situation to a certain extent from inside. The Valencians continued to speak Arabic, and to write it for administrative purposes, but they do not seem to have participated in the interchange of intellectual life of the Islamic world as a whole, and they produce no writers of

1. Barceló Torres (1984) publishes many documents, mainly domestic, both from the Mudejar period and from the sixteenth century. See also her survey of other materials available (1984:42–45).

any note after the conquest. The explanation for this is presumably that Muslims with talent emigrated to Granada, if not farther afield.[2] Valencian documentation gives us nothing to match the sometimes brilliant Arabic writings from Granada; rarely do we get more than an ill-spelled receipt for a brace of chickens. One could say that the great cultural innovation of the Valencians was to begin to write their own Arabic vernacular rather than attempting to write "correct" Arabic, but this written version of vernacular Arabic did not release any great creative drive among Valencia's Arabic speakers, and our knowledge of how the Valencians thought about their own condition remains sketchy.

The general pattern of the Christian conquest in most areas of the Iberian Peninsula was for the military defeat of the Muslims to be followed by the colonization of the conquered lands by settlers who received land grants. As time went by the proportion of Christians to Muslims rose, and the Muslims became a minority community in lands they had once dominated.[3] Valencia was different. The great number of Muslims who remained behind at the conquest and the small number of Christian settlers at first willing to come live in such an alien land meant that for most of the period under examination the Muslims were still the majority community in many areas, and the outward and visible signs of Islamic civilization were much more numerous. They were even much in evidence in the sixteenth century (and shocked François I of France when he was held prisoner there after his defeat at Pavia in 1524).

The survival in Valencia of so much from the Islamic past does not mean that the civilization of Islam was conserved unmodified. If one looks at the language of a Valencian Arabic text one is faced with the curious phenomenon of a language incontestably Arabic and yet suffused at many linguistic levels by the incoming Romance speech of the conquerors. Arabic survived but did not live on unchanged.[4] Similarly institutions and social organization survived, so that it might appear that Valencia preserved most features of the Islamic state, but the fact that at the head of the social pyramid was not a *sulṭān* or an *imām* but a

2. The most outstanding of the Valencian men of letters who departed because of the conquest of 1238 was the historian Ibn al-Abbār.

3. For the fourteenth century, see Ferrer i Mallol 1988:1–15.

4. Harvey (1971) makes the point in relation to a late (1595) document. See now Barceló Torres (1984).

king who was Christian altered the balance of everything. As the years and the centuries passed, the surviving Islamic elements shifted in their function and their sense within the Christian context against which they now had to be read. There is a medieval doctrinal controversy in Islam as to whether it is possible to have a religious society without an *imām* (Lambton 1974:esp. 406 and 416). The history of Valencia after the mid-thirteenth century is almost the working out under laboratory conditions of that problem. And what answer came from the Valencian experience? An ambiguous one. Islam did survive without an *imām,* and Christian missionaries were never able to make inroads in the Muslim masses. But true Islam suffered where the learned classes were not so much members of the worldwide community of Islamic scholars as local officials helping to keep the Christian kings' peace.

The city of Valencia fell to Christian invaders in 1238–1239, but that event, momentous as it was, by no means signaled the end of Muslim resistance. We can say that the conquest of the kingdom did not come until the castle of Biar surrendered in 1245. As the *Chronicle of James I* puts it: "To cut matters short, when it came to the last, the Kaid of Biar whose name is Muzalmoravit surrendered the castle to me. I left the Saracens in the town, and granted them a charter for their 'zunes', and that they should for all time remain under me and my descendants."[5] This Muslim leader is Mūsā al-Murābiṭ, and he is, of course, being guaranteed his law and *sunna.* But this final stage of conquest is hardly to be disentangled from the beginning of dissidence. And the centers of that dissidence are the Mudejar petty states of the region.

MONTESA AND THE BANŪ ʿĪSĀ

The rulers of the Islamic enclave at Montesa were the Banū ʿĪsā clan, who had first been established at Játiva, and who had been moved to Montesa by James I. In his chronicle, Desclot described the pomp of this local ruler as follows: "He looked in truth to be a noble, for he came riding upon a splendid horse and his saddle and harness were inlaid with foil of gold." His bridle and reins were "of silken cord, and studded with precious stones and pearls," while he "was clad in scarlet embellished with golden fringes, and bore no arms save only a sword that hung about his neck, and was of great price and richly jeweled." Perhaps most

5. Soldevila 1983:134 (Jaume I No.359). The translation here is that of J. Forster, London, 1883:II, 437.

significantly, "he brought with him four hundred Saracen horsemen" (Burns 1973:304). This was Yaḥyā b. Muḥammad b. ʿĪsā. James attempted to win him over by overwhelming him with generosity, offering him "ten times more than his dynasty ever had" when he assented to be moved from Játiva in 1246 (Burns 1973:167). Montesa, whither he was transferred, was no small castle but "an awesome stronghold which had not been conquered in the winning of the kingdom of Valencia: in fact the Saracens had held it since olden times" (Burns 1973:344 [*Crónica de S. Juan de la Peña,* cap. 36, trans. Burns]).

In troubled times Montesa served its purpose of offering to the Muslims some security. In 1255 when all Valencia was in uproar in a general Mudejar revolt, we are told that those unable to secure their own strongholds betook themselves to Montesa. We do not hear of the place being captured in the Christian repression that ensued, and Yaḥyā in fact continued to be courted by James, who showered marks of his favor on him. In 1257 James granted him the right to levy six lambs from every thousand transhumant sheep to pass that way, the same percentage of goats, and numerous grants of land. This Mudejar grandee continued to enjoy such state all his life, and in the early 1270s handed on his petty realm to his son Abū Bakr. James did try to turn him out of this fief, eventually by a solemn deed of expulsion in 1275. Abū Bakr ignored him and was still in possession when James died in 1276 (Burns 1973:345).

At this point the affairs of this small stronghold in Valencia almost enmeshed with the affairs of Granada. The new king on the Granadan throne, Muḥammad II, seemed perhaps likely to be able to summon North African aid, and preoccupation of the Christians with Granada would have relieved pressure on Montesa. The hoped-for relief did not come. Peter, when he succeeded to the throne of Aragon, began to prepare outright war on a large scale; victory came only after a massive deployment of military might, with levies summoned from all points of the kingdom. The siege went on for two and a half months, and although for the hapless common folk the Christian victory meant they were sold into slavery, for Abū Bakr and seven companions it brought the opportunity to travel to a Muslim country. The great castle was taken over by Bernard de Bellvís, and was soon to become the headquarters of the order of Bellvís (Burns 1973:348–51).

Between Muḥammad Ibn al-Aḥmar, rebellious vassal of Alfonso X, and Yaḥyā b. Muḥammad Ibn ʿĪsā there was a difference of scale in the lands they controlled, but the Banū ʿĪsā were rulers of their enclave for some thirty years. The space given to them by Desclot and other chroniclers in the description of the final battle shows that this episode was recognized as an event of prime importance.

Al-Azraq

The Banū ʿĪsā were not the only Muslim dissidents with whom the Christians had to deal. Perhaps even more famous was al-Azraq. There must be a suspicion that the name al-Azraq (cf. Castilian *zarco* 'blue-eyed') was a name rather like Ibn al-Aḥmar. There survives a deed of 1244 (or possibly 1245) whereby Abū ʿAbdallah Muḥammad b. Hudhayl al-Azraq declared himself vassal of Alfonso, James I's son, keeping his castles of Alcalá and Perpunchent as his *eredat* "to do with as I please," and many others on which his tenure was limited in some way (Burns 1973:325, 326). We can see that here was almost a *ṭāʾifa* prince. Al-Azraq went into revolt in 1243. What relation this campaign had with a better attested campaign in 1258 is not clear (Burns speaks of "chronological data difficult to reconcile" [1973:327]). In fighting over the years we find him now fending off an army of three thousand men, now ambushing King James, now negotiating with King Alfonso the Wise. His was a clan with a firm hold on their little upland territory, well able to exploit the rifts between Castile and Aragon. He was forced to withdraw from the scene himself, but his family retained their firm hold over the castles (Burns 1973:329). The Aragonese policy was to place in key castles a small number of retainers. Gallinera, one of the most powerful of the castles, went to the Infante Peter, Pego to Arnold of Romaní (Burns 1973:330). For a time the planting of military outposts sufficed, but in 1276 there was an upsurge of dissidence in other parts of Valencia, and an incursion from across the Granadan border. Al-Azraq judged it was his moment to return. He did, and found wide support, but near Alcoy in April 1276 he was killed, and the tiny state seems to have been eclipsed (Burns 1973:331).

Muntaner tells us that old King James was still alive when news of al-Azraq's return reached the court, but he was extremely sick and confined to bed: "Bring me my horse straight away, and prepare my arms for I wish to sally against these treasonable Moors who imagine I am dead! Well, it is not so! And I will wipe them all out!" he thundered (Soldevila 1983:689 [Muntaner]). He struggled to raise himself from his bed, but was unable to do so. Unwilling to accept that he could not confront his old enemy, James had himself borne out on a litter, confident that if the Muslims saw him they would surrender. Peter, his son and heir, was, fortunately for the Christians, able to engage al-Azraq first. Peter had two horses killed under him before the battle was won. Thus it was that al-Azraq kept James on the field of battle at the very end of his days. His war standard flew over his litter, and from the battlefield he was carried to Játiva and to Valencia, where his Christian subjects gave him a triumphal entry. There in 1276 he died, perhaps the greatest enemy of the Muslims of the eastern regions of the peninsula (Soldevila 1983:689–90 [Muntaner]).

The Banū ʿĪsā and al-Azraq were not the only Muslim insurgents in Valencia at this period. We hear of one Abrahim (i.e., Ibrāhīm) Abū Isḥāq al-Asqarī, who actually held out after the surrender of most of his followers in 1276, although only until February 1277. Peter rid himself of him by the well-tried device of offering him and his retinue good transport facilities to take them to Muslim territory (Burns 1973:333–34).

One Muḥammad, operating partly in territory which had been Ibrāhīm's, based himself on the village of Orcheta, sufficiently near to the coast for him to be able to ship in supplies and to move his forces about. The fighting against the Mudejars at this point included a number of maritime actions, but Muḥammad was expelled too by 1278. Peter provided a Genoese merchant ship (carrack), chartered to transport the rebels to Tlemcen (Burns 1973:333–34).

A chancery document of 1276 gives a whole list of Mudejar rebels granted pardons by Peter (Burns 1973:335). Desclot mentions a rebel called Albacor, a shepherd who was a negro (Soldevila 1983:444 [Desclot]). (Burns speculates that Albacor may be a garbling of *baqqār,* Arabic for "cowherd," but the Touareg Berber version of Abū Bakr was Búcar, and this would seem an equally plausible explanation. The Touareg then as now made use of associated negro castes, the *haratīn.*) He is described as a "very valiant man" who had "strong castles in the mountains of Alcoy and Albaida, and many mounted troops and foot soldiers." This King Albacor inflicted great harm on the Christians, and when he was finally taken in an ambush, a particularly unpleasant punishment was found for him: "For this reason they inflicted on him the best justice in the world—for they sent him to every locality in the kingdom of Valencia, where people dealt him whatever kind of justice they liked, until he was dead. He was then dragged behind nags through the whole country."

Dissidence thus at this period was endemic, and it is surprising that such small numbers of Christian settlers (no more than 30,000) could hold down so many determined rebels. The explanation appears to be that the Muslims were never able to coordinate their opposition to the Christian occupation. To determine in detail what was going on is very difficult. As Burns put it, "The revolts themselves are so tangled in subsequent myth and canonized conjecture that they cannot be briefly recounted. King Jaime (in his *chronicle*) telescopes more than a decade's sporadic variously local and eventually general fighting into a few chapters" (Burns 1980:218).

What we can perceive by stepping back and ignoring the detail is that the policy of the victors was at first to hold and occupy only a small number of important centers, leaving some towns and wide tracts of countryside in the hands of Mudejar lords, who enjoyed a considerable measure of autonomy and often lived in considerable pomp. This state of affairs continued until about the time of James's death. Peter implemented the second stage of the Aragonese-Catalan takeover of the kingdom. Some of the isolated areas left undisturbed up to that point had Christian governors introduced: "The king razed the castles, and everything connected with them, and garrisoned them with Christian knights and foot soldiers, but with the Muslim cultivators remaining in the valleys and low-lying areas to cultivate the land and pay their taxes to the king" (Soldevila 1983:444 [Desclot]).

The mention of independent petty principalities in the region of Valencia ought logically to close with the eclipse of the last of them, Crevillente, in 1318: but as it in part fell within the Castilian orbit, this has been treated with the enclaves in Castilian territory.

Peter's policy of eliminating the semi-independent Muslim rulers left in position by James was an important stage in the history of Valencia. From this point Muslims no longer exercise military and political power. Peter initiated a process that certainly left in being a large Muslim population in Valencian lands, but as the years passed by these Muslims became increasingly enmeshed and entrapped in Christian society. The economic exploitation to which they were subject might seem a price which was prudently paid to secure relative religious freedom;

their political subservience to a Christian land-owning class might seem a reasonable bargain because Christian lords often proved effective advocates of the interests of "their" Moors. It was a symbiosis which produced a relatively stable society.

Mudejars of Valencia Under Christian Law

In the year 1250 James I granted to the Muslims of the Uxó valley when they surrendered to him a charter[6] (in fact the second they had been given), which included the following clauses:

> 3. We desire that all Muslims should continue under their *sunna* in their marriages as in all other matters. They may give public expression to their *sunna* in their prayers, and public instruction to their sons in the reading of the Koran, without suffering any prejudice from so doing. They may travel about their business through all the lands of our realm and not be hindered by any man.
>
> 8. They may appoint a judge [*alcadi,* i.e., *qāḍī*] and a superintendent [*alamí,* i.e., *amīn*] of their own accord; they may apportion water rights among themselves as was the custom in the days of the Moors as set out in their ancient privileges. The rents of the mosques are to be applied to the purposes of the said mosques as hitherto.
>
> 9. No Christian nor any baptized person may establish residence with them if they do not so wish, nor may we, nor any person acting in our name on behalf of the Kingdom of Valencia, oblige them to accept such settlement ever.
>
> 11. Any person wishing to depart from the Uxó valley to go to Moorish territory may do so, and this is permitted even though no truce be in force. Moors may sell their property and their goods exclusively to Moors, and never to Christians.
>
> 17. We declare that Moors both now and in the future will pay over one-eighth of all produce to us or to our nominee, and they will not be constrained to make any other payments on their produce. Exempt from this tax are fruit on trees and fresh vegetables.

6. I have used the texts in Fernández y González (1886:322–24). Burns (1973:121–22) discusses the charter.

So long as the eighth is paid, no other demands on the said produce will be made, with the sole exception of the *peyta* when raised from the Moors of the Lieutenancy of Valencia, to which they will be obliged to contribute according to our assessment.

18. Let the Moors remain as they were wont in the time of the Moors, before they departed from the land.

The only clause that is really restrictive is quite reasonable:

14. They may not go to any places with which we are at war, nor may they supply provisions or anything else to them [unspecified]. They must protect our land and serve our vassals loyally.

It will be noted here, as in so many other places, separation of residential areas is something desired by the Muslims themselves. There were considerable variations in the surrender terms negotiated from one place to another, but in general one may say that at the moment of conquest no attempt was made to impose conversion, and that usually a wide range of reassuring promises was made. It may be of interest to note that seventy-two years after this agreement, the first mass was celebrated in a church constructed in the valley,[7] and that thereafter tithes were collected in spite of the promises made.

The Uxó valley was a rural area. As a specimen of arrangements for the administration of an occupied urban area, we have a charter of 1251 in which James lays down how the Muslim quarter of Játiva is to be governed (Fernández y González 1886:324–27; see also Burns 1973:123n.9). The Muslims were to appoint their own *qāḍī* and four *adelantados,* while the crown would appoint an *amīn* (supervisor) to raise taxes and a *ṣāḥib al-madīna* (city chief), no doubt for police purposes. This type of administration seems to have continued for so long as there were Muslim inhabitants there. Other places with Moorish quarters (Montforte, Segorbe, Cocentaina, Chelva, Orihuela, Gandía, etc.) show the same basic pattern, though with minor variations in terminology. Any listing of community officials must therefore be offered on the understanding that from place to place and from time to time differences both of terminology and of function will occur. Still, it is worth attempting a survey of some of the administrative terms.

7. Barceló Torres 1984:101 (citing a publication by Pierre Guichard not accessible to me: *Nuestra Historia,* Valencia, 1980:III, 67).

Amīn. The *amīn* (superintent, agent, etc.) might be an administrator put in by the Christians, sometimes to control a wide area, but in some cases Muslims might themselves (*d'ells matexs*) appoint the *amīn*. One of his functions was to raise dues; he would be paid for his services and usually enjoyed a number of privileges and perquisites, so that such an officeholder might amass considerable wealth.

Qāḍī. The *qāḍī* (judge) ought to concern himself with strictly Islamic jurisdiction, but at times as principal magistrate he appears to have wider powers. (One suspects that non-Arabic-speaking administrators dealing with Muslim officials may sometimes have confused the *qāḍī* 'judge' with the *qā'id* 'governor', 'commander'.)

It is significant that the Aragonese royal house when appointing *qāḍīs* in Valencia frequently had recourse to the same Bellvís family we have already encountered in royal service in the same capacity in Saragossa. Of the *qāḍīs* listed by Barceló we find in 1365 Faraig de Belvís; 1412–1447, Alí de Bellvís; 1448–1484, Mahomat Bellvís; 1484–1495, Alí de Bellvís; 1495–1511, Çahat Bellvís (all serving in Valencia city itself) (Barceló Torres 1984:62,147).

There are obviously two sides to this office. In some ways the *qāḍī* is the principal official through whom the Aragonese-Catalan regime controlled its Muslims, but the *qāḍī* was also a bastion of Islamic religion and culture. Tulio Halperin-Donghi was writing of the early sixteenth century when he said, "Here is an official of the *aljama,* the *alcadí* . . . a functionary who plays his part, however minor, in the machinery whereby Morisco Valencia was governed by the Old Christians; this official is at the same time the director of Muslim religious life" (1980:97), but these words are perhaps even more applicable to the Mudejar period. One might add that even in an Islamic state the *qāḍī* can feel himself to be subjected to the conflicting claims of his loyalty to the ruler, the sultan, and to his religion. In Umayyad times al-Khushānī's *History of the Judges of Cordova* (1966:3–8) records cases of pious men who, to the displeasure of the ruler, refused to accept appointment to the office of chief *qāḍī* because of the risk that they would be involved in actions not provided for in the *sharīʿa* (*ẓulm* 'injustice').

It is noteworthy that nowhere in the literature analyzed by Burns does the important term *muftī* surface. We have seen that in Castile the *muftī* did fill an important slot in the Islamic community. In normal

Arabic usage the *muftī* is the "jurisconsult" prepared to deliver a considered legal opinion (*fatwā*) when consulted. Gibb and Bowen[8] were speaking of Ottoman society when they made the point that "the fact that the office of *muftī* carried with it no salary as such emphasized, in the eyes of the religious, its superiority to that of the *qāḍī*." In Valencia the *qāḍī* was paid by the Christian state, and we might well have expected the authority of the independent *muftī* to act as a check on the activities of the royal appointees. If any such development occurred, we hear nothing of it in the record. There appears to have been a similar difference of usage with regard to the *alfaquí* (*faqīh*). We have seen that in Castile and elsewhere this term comes to be applied to an *aljama* official. In Valencia the *alfaquí* might be little more than a local schoolmaster and teacher.

As an illustration of how much the Christians appreciated the tough way in which the Valencian *qāḍīs* meted out their justice, one cannot do better than to quote the *Regiment de la cosa publica* (Rule for the Common Weal) by Eiximenis (writing in the fourteenth century):

> The Saracens have another procedure which is very speedy, and which does not call for lawyers. It is as follows: the *qāḍī*, who is the one who administers justice, sits in a particular place in the town, together with a number of officials. If you wish to bring a suit against anybody, you must address him thus: "Behold, I wish to raise a complaint against you [you being presumably the accused]." They are so ashamed if they are ever summoned to court, they will ask you straightaway to withdraw your complaint, and reach a compromise settlement instead. If you are deaf to the entreaties, and say you wish to bring the case, the man will have no alternative but to follow you before the judge, because if he failed to accompany you and the case were found proven, he would immediately be flogged. When you get before the judge to make your complaint, he will ask the man you are accusing whether what you say is true. If the accused man denies what is true, and it can ever be subsequently proved, he will be terribly flogged: he

8. Gibb and Bowen 1957:II, 137. I have taken the liberty of replacing their system of transliteration by my own in this and subsequent quotations.

> will be stripped naked and thrown face down on the ground, and given a number of heavy blows with dried ox sinews in public. If he admits the truth of your accusation, and you are unwilling to await [payment], if the sum in question is due immediately, he is obliged to pay up on the spot, or to stay in detention while his goods are distrained upon. If the possessions are insufficient, his flesh has to pay (*parar-s'hi ha la sua carn*) [presumably these last words mean that he is flogged]. (Eiximenis 1927:154–55)

Eiximenis was no expert in Islamic law, and although he explicitly uses the word *qāḍī* (*cadí*) in this passage, one wonders whether the sort of jurisdiction which so excited his admiration was not that discussed in the following paragraph, the *Muḥtasib*. Barceló has found documentary evidence for quite fierce floggings: twenty-five lashes for a stabbing inflicted by one minor on another, two hundred for the theft of "two swords, two trumpets and one long Moorish horn" (1984:60). It is hardly surprising that cases are reported of communities being unwilling to accept the punishment handed down.

Muḥtasib. Alongside the *qāḍī's* jurisdiction, and complementary to it, is that of *ḥisba* or *iḥtisāb*. This may in some contexts be rendered "market inspection," but the *muḥtasib* is something more than an inspector of weights and measures, although he is that. The *muḥtasib's* responsibilities extended to construction work and to manufacturing processes. He was responsible for good order in the markets and public places, and his summary jurisdiction empowered him to inflict physical punishments of a relatively minor kind, so his was a wide-ranging and effective office, the practical usefulness of which led the Christians to take it over and develop it, garbling the name by the way. In Catalan the *muḥtasib* became a *mustasaf* and in Castilian an *almotacén*. Another name for the same official in Arabic was *ṣāḥib al-sūq* (this time garbled in Castilian to *zabazoque*). It is in the code of *ḥisba* that we can find part of the customary practice and law (Arabic *ʿurf*) otherwise absent from our written sources. The *muḥtasib* provides us with a good example of how an official's function can change and evolve because the framework within which that function is exercised itself changes. The *muḥtasib* in Islamic society is a fairly humble official, kept in subordination to legal functionaries working within the more prestigious *sharīʿa* system. Then, as Glick put it, "The tighter organization of urban life in Christian society transformed into a very effective instrument of municipal government an area of law which in the Islamic world was amorphous, ambivalent and not highly regarded" (1979:123).

Zabalmadina. Not to be confused with the *zabazoque* is the *zabalmadina* or "master of the city." It is rarely possible to distinguish this official from *ṣāḥib al-shurṭa* or "head of police," and in all probability the two terms were interchangeable. The *ṣāḥib al-madīna* had under him in Valencia what in the Latin sources are called the *exortivi* (from Arabic *shurṭī* 'policemen'), the gendarmes. Here again some observations which Gibb and Bowen made about the evolution of Islamic institutions in Ottoman Turkey are illuminating. Speaking of the *muḥtasib* and of the *shurṭa* (police) and other allied jurisdictions, they said, "None of these institutions was extra-legal *per se*. The *sharīʿa* itself leaves, in respect of criminal justice, a wide field to the discretion of the sovereign, or of the *qāḍī* acting upon the sovereign's direction, and in the *maẓālim* court the Caliph or his representative, usually sitting with a senior *qāḍī* in attendance, exercised his discretionary powers to award discretionary punishments" (1957:II, 116). In the functioning of an Islamic state, at least after the earliest days of the Caliphate, the system of law in practice was not a matter of pure *sharīʿa* and *sunna*. These superior parts of the system required to be complemented by other more flexible jurisdictions. In conquered Valencia, however, that complementation could no longer come from an Islamic ruler, and so it came from power stemming from a Christian monarch.

The *maẓālim* (grievance) court to which Gibb and Bowen were referring was "a court of superior instance set up to deal with the more serious civil and criminal cases, especially when they involved administrative and military officers" (Gibb and Bowen 1957:II, 116). This provides the model for the kings of Aragon assuming the role of judge of the court of ultimate appeal. There was even in Islamic constitutional thought weighty and authoritative support for the exercise of such a function by some authority who fell below the highest religious standards, the justification being that thereby the greater good of public order was sustained. As al-Gazzālī put it, "An evil-doing and barbarous sultan, so long as he is supported by military force, so that he can only with difficulty be deposed, and that the attempt to depose him would cause unendurable civil strife, must of necessity be left in possession, and obedience must be rendered to him, exactly as obedience must be rendered to emirs."[9] What al-Gazzālī did not have in mind when he wrote those words was that the "evil-doing and barbarous sultan" should not be even nominally a Muslim. Yet, as Burns neatly put it, "King James easily, if illogically in the Islamic context, stepped into the judicial shoes of Valencia's Abū Zayd; the *aljamas* without further ado took their more intractable cases to him on appeal" (1973:249). Burns reports on the king reviewing death sentences, commuting them to other punishments such as enslavement, or acquitting the murderer outright where the king was convinced that the death in question was an accident. This all shows us James I exercising his prerogative of mercy as any true Christian monarch should; what was so decided had little contact with Islamic law. In Islamic law the focus in murder cases is on compensation due to the family of the victim, on blood money, and we have seen that the Mudejars of Castile were well aware of this. In Valencia (as, of course, in the other kingdoms of the crown), Muslims had their own cases tried by their own law in their own courts, and then those cases passed on appeal before the Christian king himself, or a tribunal acting on his behalf—a curious situation. Even if all due respect were paid in such a tribunal to the *sharīʿa* and the *sunna,* the *ḥadd,* the prescribed Islamic penalty, was unlikely to be exacted.

A case reported by Burns will serve to illustrate the profound complications that result when a Christian government is superimposed on a Muslim population, and an attempt is made to preserve some aspects of Islamic law. In the case in question the sentence of the king reads as follows (my translation):

> Know ye that we have granted to Azmet [?Aḥmad], a Saracen belonging to Berenguer Andrew, citizen of Valencia in the parish of St. Katherine, a pardon from all penalties both civil and criminal which might have been carried out or imposed on him arising from the death of Zahit [?Saʿīd], a Saracen belonging to Berenguer, resident in Valencia, of which the said Azmet had stood accused. We have done this because we have established by good men worthy of trust that he did not kill him wittingly [*scienter*], but as a result of the chance way a javelin fell when he was out throwing javelins together with other Saracens. The said Azmet

9. Gibb and Bowen 1957:I, 31 (translating al-Gazzālī, *Iḥyāʾ ʿulūm al-dīn,* II, 124).

> threw the javelin and the said Zahit caught it in his hand before it touched the ground . . . and the said javelin wounded him in the throat and killed him. (Burns 1973:252 n.12, my translation)

James I's decision was certainly eminently wise and showed justice tempered with mercy and common sense. Burns commented approvingly, "Though only a relatively minor affair of one slave accidentally causing the death of another, he [James] demonstrated the royal concern for a humble Mudejar" (1973:252). There may be more to the case than that, and indeed we must ask why such a simple and noncontentious matter needed to be tried in such a high court.

Accidental and unintentional homicide is ruled on explicitly in the Koran (IV.92): "And it does not behove a believer to kill a believer except by mistake, and whoever kills a believer by mistake, he should free a believing slave, and the blood money should be paid to his people, unless they remit it as alms" (Doi 1984:234).

This, though, is not a case of homicide of a free Muslim, but of a slave by a slave. In such cases, "if one slave kill another, the owner of the latter may demand the life of the former, or the value of his own slave, or the owner of the former may surrender his slave in compensation."[10] However, what complicated this affair still further was that both slaves belonged to the same master, and he, to judge from his name, was a Christian. It is at this point that Islamic law becomes impossible to administer in the context—and that, no doubt, is why the apparently straightforward case found its way into the king's court. No provision is made in the *sharīʿa* for a Muslim to be owned by a Christian (even though doubtless the circumstance did arise: Ibn Naqqāsh (d. 1362) lays it down that a Christian purchaser of a Muslim slave should be punished.[11] There can have been no Islamic precedent available to the Islamic judges of lower courts or to James himself. From the point of view of Berenguer, the owner, it must have been a difficult situation too. Neither his material self-interest, nor his Christian conscience, can have prompted him to seek to have a penalty inflicted on his slave Azmet. In effect James was reduced to improvising his way out of a legal impasse, and he did so in a statesmanlike way.

10. *Shorter Encyclopaedia of Islam,* London, 1953, s.v. *diya.*

11. Ye'or 1985:184. Ibn Naqqash was an Egyptian *muftī.*

It was not only at the royal pinnacle of the legal pyramid that conflicts arose because Islamic justice was in the hands of non-Muslims, or because the Islamic judge sat under a Christian judge, the bailiff (*batle*) general. As time passed, local jurisdictions fell increasingly into the hands of nobles; a Muslim living on a noble's estates would find himself answerable in the court presided over by that noble. In such circumstances the fact that the code in use was allegedly "Islamic" might be of secondary importance. The Muslims nominally retained their own system of justice and yet they did not.

Mudejars in a Feudal and Christian Society

The Feudal Order

The constitutional terminology employed by the Christian rulers of Valencia was from the outset a feudal one, as was that of the Christians elsewhere in the Iberian Peninsula. The Aragonese monarchy demanded oaths of vassalage: "All nobles, all knights, citizens and other inhabitants of the kingdom of Valencia must . . . swear . . . fealty to us and to our lawful heirs" (Burns 1973:280 n. 8). As the Mudejars fell under Christian rule they became "our men and vassals" (*homens nostres e vassals*). This was a formula of incorporation. The lord offered his protection, including protection of the vassals' religion, and in return the vassals provided their profitable labor: "Whoso has Moors, has wealth" (*Quien tiene Moro, tiene oro*). The greatest test of Mudejar loyalty to Christian lords came shortly after the end of our period, in the 1520s, when, in the turmoil of the *germanía,* Valencian Muslim loyalty to Christian nobles (and opposition and in places military resistance to the rebellious Christian lower orders), was a major factor in the collapse of the revolutionary movement in Valencia. There was a symbiosis in Valencia between Mudejars and the feudal aristocracy.

This, of course, leaves on one side the question of whether such terms as *vassal* or *feudal* are properly to be applied in conditions such as those of Valencia. Burns concludes, "Clearly this was feudalism with a difference, displaying a concomitant countervailing trend towards assimilation of status among lords, landlords and farmer-proprietors" (1973:277). I would agree, and indeed go further. "Classical" feudalism is that which existed in Northern France at this general period, but the feudal political vocabulary becomes the political vocabulary of the age and of lands where conditions differed widely from those of France and England. To quote Burns again: "In some ways the use of 'vassal' and 'man', sometimes in conjunction with the technical 'fidelis', not only betrayed a mentality but exercised causal activity. . . . Some might prefer to minimize or dismiss the feudalistic style of these words, taking them as bold variants for subject or citizen, and refusing to credit the residual original meaning of words in shaping reality; even at that extreme, however, the terminology still reveals that Muslims high and low entered the Christian political order, becoming an accepted, integral element equal in some way with the other components of the Arago-Catalan feudal state" (1973:282–83).

The Church

If the policy of the incorporation of the Islamic masses into the feudal order was on the whole successful, grave problems arose where the church was concerned. The church seems to have had two major aims here, themselves in conflict with each other: to convert the heathen and to preserve the faithful from contamination. In its crusading zeal the church had contributed financial resources "towards the expulsion of the Saracens from the kingdom of Valencia (*ad expulsionem sarracenorum de regno Valentiae*)." It can hardly have pleased all ecclesiastical opinion that the result of the Valencian "crusade" was the creation of a permanently entrenched Muslim population under Christian rule. In 1266 Clement IV pointed out to James the peril of allowing Muslims to stay in his realms (Barceló 1984:100), and this was a constant theme of the papacy in its relations with the Aragonese (and other Hispanic) rulers. And so when it became clear that the slogan of *expulsio sarracenorum* was not going to mean ridding Christendom of unbelievers, the church pressed for the achievement of more modest objectives at least: limitations on the preaching of Islam (in spite of earlier promises of freedom to teach the Koran) and limitations on Christians and Muslims living in close proximity (on this the two religions were in agreement). In 1311 at the Council of Vienne there were objections to the cry of the muezzin: "The priests of these people in their temples or mosques at certain hours of every day invoke and cry out from some high place" (Burns 1973:187). Two years later James II followed up this lead with legislation against the public recitation of prayers, legislation clearly of limited effect because in 1331 and 1340 the bishop of Valencia had cause to complain at the invocation "of the name of perfidious Muḥammad" (Burns 1973:188).

Against such a background it is easy to understand how popular resentment against Muslims arose among the Christian lower classes. Barceló found riots and disorders directed at the Muslim communities of the following places between 1276 and 1291: Valencia, Chelva Alzira, Lliria, Onda, Murviedro, Játiva, Benissanó, Castellnou, Orpesa, Fortaleny, Gandient, Picassent, Alberic, Onil, Sollana (1984:64–65). For the fourteenth century we have the very complete study of Ferrer i Mallol of "attacks on Moorish quarters" (1988:21–29), with some details for the thirteenth and fifteenth centuries as well. Not surprisingly, in the face of such insecurity many Muslims left for North Africa or for Granada, but on the subject of emigration Christian policy was as contradictory and as muddled as on many other subjects. The Muslim was perceived sometimes as a dangerous Moor, sometimes as a useful and necessary laborer without whose presence profits would diminish and perhaps even society grind to a halt.

We have seen that surrender documents from the time of the arrival of the Christians usually include some guarantee that the Muslims shall be free to travel, and Peter IV in the *Aureum opus* (1515:fol. 120r) asserts that the right of the Muslims to emigrate was long established and should continue (1338 repeated in 1351). On the other hand the Cortes of 1370 voiced alarm at "the great number of Moors departing and emptying the land." "If the said Moors go abroad, you, my Lord, will receive no service from the said estates at all, for if [the Moors] go, the bishops, knights, men of noble birth, burgesses and townsfolk will lack the wherewithal to live, nor will they be able to serve you" (Barceló 1984:67). Between 1382 and 1408 Martin I included in the *Furs* an enactment against Muslims crossing into "Moorish territory or other places outside our realms," even though they bore a permit to do so! (Barceló 1984:67) No doubt this desire to keep Muslim cultivators was exacerbated by the population losses caused by the Black Death. Various regulations of this period seek to keep Muslims on the land and to prevent them from moving about. As in Aragon, they did in fact move in search of better conditions, and new settlements were being set up in all periods, not only by enterprising nobles but by the king himself. Alfonso V set up a new *aljama* at Castellón in 1428. The king's policy met with obstructionism. Some of the Muslims who did move there were harassed. The legal repercussions still occupied the courts more than thirty years later: in 1459 the lord of a locality, Borriol, whence a group of twenty or thirty had been brought to Castellón, brought a successful action against the municipality of Castellón, and was paid compensation for the losses he had sustained as a result of the departure of his "twenty or thirty Moorish dogs." The municipality for its part was prepared to have its lawyers argue that "freedom to come and go as they please" was the right of all the king's vassals and all the inhabitants of the kingdom, but at the same time made sure that those Mudejars required to give evidence in court in this case were sent back just as soon as possible, because it was the season for sowing (Barceló 1984:71). The labor of the Mudejars was valued, they themselves and their religion were not.

To sum up, Christian legislation with regard to Muslims in Valencia had tolerant and intolerant aspects, it sought to drive Muslims out and to keep them confined, it guaranteed free exercise of the religion of Islam and sought to stamp it out. These same contradictions existed elsewhere, but the presence of greater numbers of Muslims in Valencia meant that the veering policies of the Christians led to more violence and bloodshed in Valencia than elsewhere. The penalty paid by the Christians for the uncertainties of their policies, uncertainties already obvious in 1250, was still being paid in 1500 and long after.

The church sought to end by conversion what it thought of as the problem of the Muslims of Valencia. From time to time missions forced themselves on the attention of the Muslims. With the masses these campaigns always failed. There were individual cases of conversion, from the ruler of Valencia, Abu Zayd, onwards.[12] In 1413 the *alfaquí* Azmet Hannaxa from Vall d'Alfandec was converted, and perhaps the best-known case was the *alfaquí* Juan Andrés of Játiva in 1487. It was not until the 1520s that the masses were converted, and the campaign of mob violence which achieved that result simply left Valencia with a community of crypto-Muslims rather than open Muslims. The Final Expulsion of 1609–1611 was an enormous manifestation of the inability of the Christian authorities to persuade those under their jurisdiction to become Christians. It would be wrong to suggest that the terrible tensions of the sixteenth century were exclusively the product of the conditions of that age. Already from the thirteenth century onwards we have seen relations between the two faiths characterized by distrust and profound misunderstanding.

The depth of the incomprehension which existed is well conveyed by the alleged words of James I at the end of his life, as reported in the

12. Ferrer i Mallol (1987:66) characterizes conversions as sporadic.

Libre dels Feyts: "He should expel all the Moors of the Kingdom of Valencia, because they are all traitors, and have often made us understand that whereas we treat them well, they are ever seeking to do us harm."[13] That James could apparently think quite sincerely that his record was such that he deserved the Muslims' gratitude is an indicator of the abyss of misunderstanding that separated the two communities. That abyss was as great or greater at the end of our period, in 1500, as it had been in the mid-thirteenth century.

13. Soldevila 1983:189. "Que gitàs tots los moros del dit Regne de València per ço com eren tots traïdors e havien-nos-ho donat a conèixer moltes vegades que, nós faent bé a ells, punyaren tots temps de fer a nós greuge."

NINE

Mudejar Communities: Navarre

It may come as a surprise to many of those otherwise well informed about Islam in the Iberian Peninsula at the end of the Middle Ages to be told that there was an important Muslim community in the Pyrenean Kingdom of Navarre. Navarre as an independent political entity was, of course, poised geographically and historically astride the Pyrenees, teetering between a French destiny to the north and a Hispanic one to the south. A Muslim presence in such a relatively northerly kingdom must seem anomalous if we fail to bear in mind that Tudela, second city of that part of Navarre which lay to the south of the mountains, had been founded by the Arab invaders in the eighth century. The Navarrese Muslims were not really an isolated enclave: their territory was a northward extension of the lowland Muslim settlements of the Ebro valley within the Kingdom of Aragon. The renown of the Blind Poet of Tudela (al-Aʿmā al-Tuṭīlī), one of the best-known of the Hispano-Arabic poets who cultivated the strophic *muwashshaḥ* form, had made the name of this little city familiar in the farthest corners of the Arabic-speaking world. Tudela continued to possess an important although not large Muslim community throughout the period 1250–1500, and it was the focal point for a number of flourishing agricultural settlements in the district known as La Ribera.

That the Muslims of Navarre should often be overlooked is easy to comprehend: Navarre itself is often forgotten, because it lost its independent status and had its Hispanic lands merged into the Crown of Castile in 1512. A minority community within a now defunct state is doubly marginal. Yet this Mudejar community left abundant traces of itself in the written records, and its distinctive experience throws much light on what happened to the other Muslim communities elsewhere. There is, fortunately, an exemplary monographic study by Mercedes García-Arenal[1] on the Muslims of Navarre (to which further details can be added, especially on economic aspects, from a study by the Japanese scholar Ikio Ozaki [1986]). García-Arenal's work forms the basis of most of this chapter (although she is in no way to be held responsible for any of my views).

The relative prosperity of the Navarrese Mudejars, the absence of religious persecution in Navarre, the fact that Navarrese Mudejars held high office under the crown and served in the army with distinction—all make this community an invaluable test group to place in contrast with other Muslim communities elsewhere in the peninsula. Yet if the experience of the Navarrese Muslims was relatively happy during our period, we ought not to forget the violent haste of the spasm of events which led to all Muslims being eliminated from Navarre in 1516 in the immediate aftermath of the incorporation of Navarre into Castile. How and why Islam was brought to such a sudden end in Navarre takes us outside our appointed period, but since those events cast into such sharp relief the limits of the toleration of the medieval period, some reference will be made to the ultimate fate of this interesting community.

When Alfonso I had captured Tudela from the Muslims in 1119, he had conceded terms of surrender which clearly were intended to persuade the Muslim population to stay. By and large this policy was successful. Although many of the Muslim ruling class did leave, many men of substance remained. Terms of surrender as generous as those of 1119 can be found elsewhere, what was exceptional about the treatment accorded to the Navarrese Muslims was that the spirit of the early capitulations was sustained throughout their history under Navarrese rule. Elsewhere toleration fades away, here it does not. García-Arenal argues convincingly that the policy of the Navarrese Christians was in part the consequence of demography: in those villages where they lived the Muslims formed a not inconsiderable proportion of the population (in places more than 50 percent), but in the region as a whole they were some 17 percent (1984:63 and 17). There was also the consideration that Navarre had no frontiers with any Islamic state (and no seacoast open to

1. García-Arenal 1984 (references are given in this form; the monograph is the first part of García-Arenal and Leroy 1984).

raiders from across the Mediterranean). The Navarrese Muslims were not likely to be accused of treason. Navarre was a small state conscious of the need to make full use of its limited human resources, and so saw its Muslims as a benefit rather than a threat (García-Arenal 1984:62).

These Muslims were concentrated in an area where the soil and their skill in irrigation permitted them to aspire to success and material reward within the larger community. There were enough of them to preserve their distinctive customs and ways, not so many of them that the majority community was ever likely to feel threatened. A significant number of them became identified with service to the royal house of Navarre. Whereas in all other areas of the peninsula Muslims ran the risk of being thought of as dangerous potential allies of the state's enemies, these Muslims must have appeared to the ruling family as invaluably loyal retainers, and to their Christian fellow subjects as fellow Navarrese ready to serve bravely in defense of the homeland.

The most northerly of the villages with a significant Muslim element in its population was Cadreita in the valley of the Ebro itself; from there southwards down that valley we find Ribaforada and, on the extreme southern border of Navarre, Cortes. In the side valley of the Alhama, a tributary of the Ebro, lay Fitero and Corella, and near the River Queiles were Monteagudo, Barillas, Tulebras, Pedriz, Ablitas, Cascante, Urzante, and Murchante. There were perhaps a dozen Mudejar villages, and throughout its history Navarrese Islam was firmly rooted in the rural areas, but what gave Navarrese Islam its special character was the important *aljama* of the city of Tudela.

By the terms of the original surrender (Fernández y González 1886: 286–87), Muslims had been moved out of the old center of the city to make way for Christians; they were given a clearly defined Muslim quarter at the confluence of the streams of the Mediavilla and the Queiles, in the twin suburbs of Velilla and Beoxo. They were thus thrust out in the twelfth century, but were effectively gathered in again in the fourteenth. This happened because the Muslim suburbs had become, with the passage of time, essential parts of the city, so that when the defenses of Tudela came to be reexamined in the light of the defensive needs of those days, it was realized that the unfortified Muslim quarters were a strategic liability as they stood. In 1365 Charles III of Navarre, perilously involved in the war between Castile and Aragon, ordered the walls of Muslim quarters to be brought up to the best standards of that age of siege warfare, with "a good strong construction capable of resisting siege engines" (García-Arenal 1984:84). The cost of such works was enormous, and was borne by the Muslims themselves; the *aljama* had to be granted an exemption from the general *pecha* tax for three whole years in compensation. Thus the *morería* of Tudela was firmly enclosed, with the object not of shutting Muslims off from Christians, but of integrating the community safely within the general defensive works of Tudela as a whole.

The Tudela *morería* was self-contained in the sense that it had all the facilities that a Muslim needed to feel safely in control of his own life, including its own slaughterhouse, butchers shops, and public ovens. It also had its own shops or markets for cobblers, harnessmakers, mat-makers, potters, tile-makers, and weavers. It was not, however, by any means a closed ghetto. Muslims could and did live outside it, Christians lived inside it. And written into the original terms of surrender was the right of the well-to-do to have their own country retreats (*almunias*) in the country round about ("Whoever wishes to be in his own garden and his own *almunia* outside the city may not be prohibited from going") (Fernández y González 1886:287).

Perhaps the advantages enjoyed by this group of Mudejars, their freedom of movement and their closeness to the Navarrese crown, are best illustrated by two documents. The first is from the Aragonese archives, and is a safe conduct granted in 1357 by Peter IV of Aragon but in fact made at the request of Charles II of Navarre. After the usual fulsome salutations, this laissez-passer goes on to state that the travelers "Mahoma Alcordoveri and Abdalla Tunici, Saracens of Tudela in the kingdom of Navarre, were, together with their wives, children and family to the number of nine, traveling overseas to visit Mecca." The document took the whole group "under our royal safe-conduct, protection and custody," together with their goods and animals, and allowed them to travel out and return homewards, safe and sound "through all places under our dominion, by land and by sea, without let or hindrance," and ordered officials to provide for them and look after them (Boswell 1977:446).

Now it is true that this party of pilgrims belonged to the specially privileged élite of the Navarrese court. The name Alcordoveri must be a variant of "el Cortovi," which occurs with frequency in the Navarrese documentation: a Muza el Cortoví turns up in 1433 as a *jurado* of the Moorish quarter of Tudela, then as the queen's physician, then as *qāḍī*. From 1441 he was entitled to receive 300 (Navarrese) pounds a year from the local taxes. He signed his receipts in Arabic. Even though the 1357 travel document may be a royal favor to a loyal retainer, it is still not without significance that the Navarrese crown was willing to request Aragonese assistance to secure protection for its Muslim pilgrims. One cannot but be surprised to find Peter the Ceremonious—one of the victors, after all, of the battle of Río Salado—granting a passport for the *ḥajj*.

Perhaps even more striking, because it betokens protective concern for the generality of the Muslim population, is a document of 1341 (García-Arenal 1984:43). In this year Philip of Evreux (the Navarrese ruling house) set out on a crusading expedition to assist Alfonso XI of Castile in his attack on Algeciras. With his companies of crusaders from the Evreux dominions in the north of France, it was natural that he should wish to break the long southward journey in Tudela. Prudently the authorities anticipated that the men-at-arms who were full of zeal to vanquish the Moors at Algeciras might give trouble to local Muslims in Tudela. The royal treasury responded to Evreux crusading enthusiasm by making financial resources available to help them fight the Muslim enemy, but it also paid for twenty men to guard the Moorish quarter of Tudela for twelve days "so that the crusaders traveling to the frontier against the Moors should do no harm to the Moors of Tudela." The guard was kept in place until the danger had passed, and any hotheads incapable of distinguishing good Moors from bad Moors had gone on their way.

If the *morería* of Tudela was the vital center of this community, the majority of Navarrese Muslims were cultivators, above all cultivators of the irrigated lands. García-Arenal's studies show Muslims participating fully in the rural economy at all levels. They exercised their rights to buy and sell land of all kinds, they leased land from the crown. That they entered into sharecropping arrangements with feudal lords is not surprising. Such arrangements can be documented in many areas, and the sharecropper (*aparcero, xarico,* i.e., Arabic *sharīk*) could easily decline into being little better than a serf. Here in Navarre, however, we find Muslims granting their land to Christians working as sharecroppers, or paying them as day laborers (García-Arenal cites a contract between one Aly Alquanillo from Cortes and a Christian cowherd [1984:121]).

The Muslims produced a wide range of crops: cereals; fibers, such as hemp, flax, and esparto; fresh vegetables and other market garden produce. Their great speciality appears to have been fruit, and in the fourteenth century one meets Amet el Deentón, appointed by royal warrant "fruiterer to the Queen" (García-Arenal 1984:21). Nor did their religion prevent them from producing good quality wine: the Alpelmi family was in 1405 awarded a contract to send a quantity of the wine from the southern part of the kingdom across the Pyrenees to Jeanne of Navarre on the "French" side of the mountains (García-Arenal 1984:21).

Too idyllic a picture of the life of Navarrese Muslims must not be painted. On this agricultural produce they paid a crushing range of feudal dues, levies, and taxes (Ozaki 1986:344–55; García-Arenal 1984:51–56). Crops on marginal land paid at a rate of 20 percent, whereas on the very best lands 25 percent was collected, so that the records speak of "one-fifth grapes" or "one-quarter land." The tax records are full of complaints against the burden this represented.

The taxes and dues levied are bewildering in their confusion, so that generalization is difficult. The range of charges is well brought out in the studies of Ikio Ozaki; dues varied from one village to the next. If they were working lands owned by individual lords, they might well have a duty to carry out work for him for a certain period of days (*azofra*), and there were dues on each head of livestock kept, for irrigation water supplied. Particularly vexatious must have been the due called *aldacas* whereby from every lamb slaughtered the lord could collect one shoulder (Ozaki 1986:367). The villagers of Ribaforada supplied three eggs from each household each Saturday, two hens on each Shrove Tuesday, two more at Advent, the milk of all the ewes one day a week from Easter until Midsummer's Day (Ozaki 1986:366). Some of these obligations to hand over produce were outright payments in kind, others were obligations to supply goods to be paid for at a fixed rate. The duchess of Villahermosa was entitled to her quarter on lands near Cortes, also two brace of chickens from each of her Mudejar tenants, but for these birds she paid nine dineros each.

A most important aspect of the rural activities of the Navarrese Muslims was their work as muleteers and providers of pack horses. Transport by land in almost all parts of the peninsula meant pack animals. Although the Navarrese Muslims did not enjoy the sort of near monopoly of transport which was possessed by the Mudejars of Hornachos in Andalusia, they did secure many profitable contracts. If the royal family took to the road, their removal men were usually Muslims. It was Mahoma Albigeo who transported the queen's saddles, personal baggage, and jewelry from Saragossa in 1450 (García-Arenal 1984:22). Some Muslims also moved goods in bulk: Zalema el Oyo in 1436 delivered a consignment of white candle wax to Tudela from Saragossa. Two loads of spices originally from Gandía (and so overseas) were freighted from Tudela on to Tafalla, sixty kilometers north, for thirty-six sueldos in 1444 (García-Arenal 1984:22 n. 36). Muslims provided the muscle power but also the organization and the expert knowledge of the markets.

There are many examples of Muslims being given missions to purchase horses and mules, and in consequence there were Mudejar horse-doctors, half veterinary specialists, half shoeing smiths. One of them, Zalema Madexa, was in the 1380s rewarded for his services to the king by being granted one of the best-sited blacksmith's forges in the Tudela market (García-Arenal 1984:23).

No doubt from this same family came that Ibrahim Madexa who was rewarded in the same way in 1401 because he had been kept away from home for six years on royal service as blacksmith in the royal castle of Cherbourg, facing the cold waters of the English Channel (García-Arenal 1984:30). Probably the same man is the Abrahim who was veterinary surgeon to the queen's stables and entrusted with a purchasing mission in Castile, selecting mules for royal use. His expense account on this journey was one hundred florins, no paltry sum; he signed the receipt in Arabic (García-Arenal 1984:23 and n. 43).

Everything to do with horseflesh was the special province of these Navarrese Muslims, and so besides the provisioning of the animals themselves, they became involved in the manufacture and maintenance of harness and saddles (García-Arenal 1984:22–24; Ozaki 1986:337). Not only riding tackle of all sorts formed their stock in trade, but all the accouterment of the medieval knight also: spurs, armor, and weapons (including lances and swords, crossbows and bolts, then guns). And being involved in this way in arms manufacture, they found themselves in the forefront of new technologies then evolving with great rapidity (García-Arenal 1984:28–31; Ozaki 1986:330–34).

The preeminence of Muslims in the forging of fine steel in Tudela is well brought out by the handling of a case of murder in 1348. Two Muslims called Juce and Muça were condemned to a financial penalty of 25 pounds for a murder they had committed outside the city. To avoid the heavy fine, they fled, but the penalty was then reduced to 10 pounds to tempt them back because these men were "subtle masters in forging steel and were sorely missed in the town" (García-Arenal 1984:31).

Amet Alhudaly (Ahmad al-Hudhaylí) was in the 1360s "master crossbowman to the king, and master of the ordnance of his castles." During this period artillery passes from crossbows and *ballistae* to cannons and cast-iron cannon balls. Artillery was constantly being redesigned and improved. The house of Navarre, heavily involved as it was in the French wars, needed the best equipment, and for this equipment they relied largely on their faithful Muslim military experts. As experts and skilled artificers these men received high pay and public honors. Ali, the son of the Ahmad just mentioned, was on a pay scale of six florins a month in 1368. He was soon to be put in charge of all the artillery of the castle of Estella, and one of his rewards was exemption from the *pecha* tax. This dynasty of military experts was continued into the third generation in 1388 when young Ahmad took over from Ali, because of his father's advanced age. (Ali was a sprightly old man who was still collecting his pension in 1391 [García-Arenal 1984:30–31]).

The Navarrese Muslims showed in this way that they could participate in the technological changes of their age, and stay at the forefront. We find them being appointed to the royal household (*mesnaderos del rey*) and in receipt of favors of all kinds (García-Arenal 1984:58). In a most literal sense their liberties sprang from the barrel of a gun. It was a gun they had cast and forged themselves. In the capitulations of 1119 Alfonso *el Batallador* had promised "he would not force any Moor in any summons to arms to go to war either against Moors or Christians."[2] There seems to be little indication that the Muslims were forced to fight for their royal masters; they served as well-paid soldiers. It is ironic that military service, something against which they sought to protect themselves in the terms of surrender, turned out to be one of the principal factors protecting them and assuring that they were well treated. "*Non devetet nullus homo ad illos moros lures armas,*" "Let nobody ban the Moors from possessing arms" (Fernández y González 1886:287) was perhaps the most important clause in the whole document (and is perhaps reminiscent of the second of the ten original amendments to the U.S. Constitution).

2. Fernández y González 1886:286. "Non faciat exire moro in apellito per forza in guerra de moros nec de christianos."

Navarre and Islamic Law (*Fiqh*)

The capitulations had included assurance that law should be administered "just as in the days of the Moors" (Fernández y González 1886:286). We must ask whether these crucial promises were kept. Any answer must be complex, for the Islamic code was both respected and subverted, and among those seeking to subvert Islamic justice were many of the Muslims themselves.

The Muslims had been told they would be "in the hand of their *qāḍī*" (*in manu lure alcadio*), and legal officials were confirmed in exercise of their functions. This provided for the situation at the moment of conquest, but made no provision for the future. And as time went by, the Navarrese crown sought to influence and control appointments to high office within the Muslim community. In doing so it was behaving towards Islam as it behaved towards Christianity. A situation developed whereby the kings of Navarre expected to appoint to the principal Islamic offices (*qāḍī*, etc.). As García-Arenal put it, "The *qāḍī* finished up by being more like a royal agent within the Moorish quarter than an authentic Islamic authority" (1984:36).

There could be no better illustration of the dilemma of the Mudejar situation. On the one hand the Islamic purists, such as al-Wansharīshī, called on Muslims in conquered territories to emigrate to avoid the dangers of life under Christian rule. This position abandons those poor Muslims devoid of the means to emigrate to an uncomfortable life without protection. The Islam of the poor under such circumstances is likely to wither away. The opposite course is that of those Muslim communities which sought to secure the best terms possible in order to preserve the right to keep their own mosques, schools, and legal officials. Under such a dispensation the law and its officers may themselves become instruments for the modification of Islamic faith and practice.

How the Islamic law may be eroded is well illustrated by the way a case of adultery was dealt with in 1416 in the village of Ablitas. Axa the wife of Mahoma Matarran had committed adultery with a Christian and "on the supplication of her husband and for certain reasons which moved us thereto" was fined sixty florins by the king, and then released. But after release she was again accused by her husband of adultery with Antonico, son of a Navarrese Christian, resident in Ablitas. This time there was a criminal charge—theft of goods from the marital home—

and for this she was arrested by the lieutenant of the district of Tudela. "And notwithstanding that for the offenses proved against her merited whipping according to the *sunna* of the Muslims, and stoning, and being put to death, because the said offenses are obscure and unclear [*no bien claros*] and on the entreaty of her father and of her husband, we desire that, provided she pay as a fine in respect of these most recent offenses the sum of 110 florins, she is to be released from prison, and no further enquiries are to be made, and her goods or her person are to be subject to no further distraint." The king orders that the case shall be closed.[3]

There are a number of observations to be made. In the first place the proof required in Islamic law to secure conviction in such a matter has not been adduced (there is no mention of four reliable Muslim witnesses), so that there could be no question of applying the extreme penalty of stoning. Pleas for mercy by interested parties would be irrelevant. And Islamic law provides for no substitution of a fine, certainly not a fine collectable by a Christian official. Second, those requesting that the Islamic law be ignored in this way are the Muslims themselves. In almost all countries that seek to apply Islamic law, the severity of the penalties is such that devices are developed to avoid some of the rigors of the code. Here the Muslims, including the aggrieved parties, are taking their case before a Christian judge to avoid penalties they do not find acceptable. It would be wrong to accuse the Navarrese authorities of bad faith in failing to respect their promises about preserving Islamic justice, but it would be idle to pretend that the legal system as it evolved in Navarre was the *sharīʿa*.

Not only the judges (*qāḍīs*) were appointed by the crown. The important magistrates who supervised public order at markets (*zalmedina*) were royal appointees, and such offices were often rewards for services rendered (García-Arenal 1984:36–37). Thus although Muslims continued to have their own officials to regulate their own affairs, these officials were usually royal appointees, men with "sound" reputations, and to function they had to enjoy the support of "responsible" opinion in their district.

Royal control extended down as far as the office of notary public (*escribano y notario de los moros*), who drew up contracts, above all mar-

3. García-Arenal (1984:108) gives the complete document; see also 62 c.

riage contracts (García-Arenal 1984:37–38). The following is the royal deed of appointment of one Ali Serrano to be notary in Tudela in 1391.

> We, because of good and laudable testimony which we have received concerning the aforementioned Ali Serrano, trusting in his loyalty, hereby institute and create him in virtue of our royal authority as notary public of our community [*aljama*] of Moors in the said city of Tudela, and of all other *aljamas* of our kingdom with the customary emoluments thereto appertaining, and we have granted to him and we do so grant power and authority to perform and to receive all manner of contracts between Moors or between a Moor and a Christian and also between a Jew and a Moor as befits a notary public appointed by our royal authority according to the *sunna* [*çunia*] of the Moors. And from the said Ali Serrano we have taken an oath sworn on the book called the Koran [*clamado l'alcoran*] in accordance with the aforesaid *sunna* that he will rightly and truly administer the said office of notary, and will draw up the contracts in due legal form, truthfully and in accordance with what the contracting parties state in his presence, and will maintain a register where he will set down all notes by him received, and that he will uphold our rights and preserve our secrets. (García-Arenal 1984:100–101)

From the point of view of the Mudejar community, the unstated but crucial role of the notary was to defend the status of the Arabic language, which was until the end in Navarre acceptable for all official purposes. Officials would sign receipts in the language, and they would authenticate documents with the customary *ṣaḥḥa* ("this is correct"). In Navarre Arabic never came to be a symbol of political subversion.

Not controlled by royal nominations were the physicians and other medical men. The royal family frequently did have recourse to their services. At the end of the fourteenth century Mahoma Almonahar earned royal gratitude because he had been able to cure the sickness of the royal falconer. His reward was to be excused payments of the *pecha*. Besides doctors there were also midwives, who seem to have been in demand outside their own community as well as inside it. Leonor de Trastámara employed one Marién, paying her 150 florins and presenting her with a gift of cloth (García-Arenal 1984:32).

Leonor also made use of Muslims in her palace building schemes.

The Muslim she appointed to supervise her construction projects at Olite, one Lope Barbicano, was sent by her to look at what was being done at Segovia. Lope made extensive use of Muslim craftsmen, who provided the ornamental tiles, the pipe work, the fitted rush matting, the ornamental stucco, even, surprisingly perhaps, the paintings (executed by Muça Alpelmi and his apprentice Jucefico). The master carpenter was a Muslim. The kitchen installation was done by a Muslim (Audilla), and so on. For the royal family the prestige environment created was largely a Mudejar one (García-Arenal 1984:25–26).

One curious institution of Muslim Navarre was the official state gambling casino (*tafurería*) situated in the Muslim quarter of Tudela, and sometimes referred to as "the King's gambling table."[4] Gambling was banned by the church, so the king, who found the casino a source of income (the right to run the place was sold to the highest bidder), avoided conflict with the Christian authorities by placing his "table" in the Moorish quarter. Koranic strictures against gambling are, of course, quite unambiguous (see Koran II, 219 and V, 93), but presumably the Muslims had no say in the matter.

What then brought such a well-established community to an end? This is no place to enter into the background to the rapid occupation of the kingdom in 1512 by Castilian troops commanded by Fadrique de Toledo, Duke of Alba. Navarre was unable to resist superior force. The only quarter from which it might have hoped for help was France, but Louis XII was too preoccupied by the direct threat to his own territory arising from the presence in the area of an English expeditionary force (ten thousand men under the Earl of Dorset) for him to be prepared to run the risk of defending his neighbor.

Ferdinand assumed the title of King of Navarre in 1512, but there appears to have been no immediate change in the situation of the Muslims of Tudela. Among the documents published by García-Arenal is one dated January 1513 (i.e., after the Castilian invasion) dealing with a case of robbery in the *morería* there. The depositions make it quite clear that the old Mudejar ruling class had been left in power by Ferdinand: Jayel Cortobi is named as the *qāḍī,* Mahoma al Cortobi is his lieutenant, Mahoma Cetillo is the *çalmedina* (police chief). The old ways

4. García-Arenal 1984:47. It was officially only for Moors and Jews, but García-Arenal remarks that Christians "apparently normally participated."

continue unchanged too: an oath is taken "as a Moor ought to do" (*segunt moro deue hazer*), and people append their signatures in Arabic.

Disaster struck when, in 1515, the decision was made to attach Navarre to the Crown of Castile (rather than leaving it as a free-standing entity, or linking it with Aragon). The Cortes of Burgos in that year opted for a triumphalist Castilian formula of incorporation: all the laws and *pragmáticas* of Castile were extended to Navarre. Among the Castilian legislation so extended was the *pragmática* that had in 1502 presented the Muslims of all parts of the Crown of Castile with the stark alternatives of conversion to Christianity or expulsion. So it was that in 1516, and at one month's notice, the hitherto secure and even privileged loyal Navarrese *aljamas* had to decide where their future lay. Many Muslims preferred to avoid forcible conversion by moving across the border into Aragon, where the *pragmática* of 1502 did not apply.

The Muslims of La Ribera in Navarre had entrusted themselves entirely to the protection of their rulers, whom they had served both diligently and courageously. For almost four centuries their secure and often enviable way of life seemed to demonstrate that Mudejar status under Christian rule was acceptable. Navarre seemed to disprove the teachings of the more rigorist Muslim religious teachers. The Duke of Alba changed all that. Suddenly Castilian attitudes prevailed, a Castilian policy governed relationships between Christians and Muslims.

The way in which Castile swallowed Navarre and imposed its destiny on a state with very different traditions is still in some way a live political issue in the twentieth century, but, if the issue does remain alive, it is because of Basque nationalism. In the northern *merindades* of the old kingdom thoughts of what was lost so long ago are still capable of causing disaffection. La Ribera's lost Muslims (and Jews) disappeared too long ago for them to figure on the agenda of any modern political party. The Muslims' existence is a forgotten fact of history. It is necessary to call the way of life of these Muslims to mind, for what they were is a direct challenge to the stereotypes concerning subject Muslims everywhere.

TEN

Muḥammad II (1273–1302)

After the death of his father, Muḥammad I of Granada, in an accident, Muḥammad II took over the reins of power without problems, but he had to face up to a continuing crisis at home which had serious repercussions on Granada's relations with its neighbors. The dissidence of the Banū Ashqilūla in no way diminished after the death of Muḥammad I, whose decision to exclude them from power had been the cause of the feud. Complicating this feud was the presence in Granadan territory at the time of Muḥammad I's death of a considerable contingent of Castilian nobles, of whom the most powerful was Nuño González de Lara; these *Ricos Hombres* had been welcomed by Muḥammad I, and used as a countervailing force to set against Ashqilūla rebellion. Could these foreign men-at-arms expect to receive the same backing from the new king? Some of them decided that the time had come to negotiate their return, and Alfonso X for his part was most anxious to bring their disaffection to an end.

Muḥammad II thus found himself in danger of losing a contingent of supporters which had been doubly useful, because it had both enabled the Ashqilūla rebels to be held in check and reinforced the Naṣrids' ability to resist Castilian aspirations to hegemony. The countermove he found was brilliantly simple: he himself entered into talks with Alfonso X. In this way he sought an effective replacement for the support of the *Ricos Hombres,* but such was the turmoil within the Christian camp that he must have calculated that Alfonso would be in no position to exact any great price from him by way of surrender of territory or tribute. What Alfonso X was seeking in these negotiations was that the ports of Tarifa and Algeciras should be handed over to him. (As we will see, the question of who was to control the principal ports on the Spanish shore of the Straits of Gibraltar obsessed the Christian and Muslim powers of the region for a century and more.) What Muḥammad II wanted from Alfonso X was that he should cease to support the Banū Ashqilūla against him. Each side was being asked for what it did not wish to give.

In late 1273 Muḥammad II made the journey to Alfonso X's court at Seville in the company of some of the *Ricos Hombres* who had found refuge in Granada. *The Chronicle of Alfonso X* narrates these events as follows:

> There came [to Seville] with them the king of Granada and Prince Felipe and Don Nuño and all the other nobles who had been in Granada, and the king received them well, and did them great honor, especially the king of Granada, and on this visit he knighted him. The king of Granada pledged him his friendship as firmly as could be, as had already been agreed in negotiations with Don Fernando and the queen, and promised to be Alfonso's vassal for all time, and to pay to him from his revenues 300,000 maravedis in Castilian money. All through his stay in Seville, Alfonso did great honor to the king of Granada.
>
> Once the agreements were concluded, and the settlements signed, the master of Calatrava handed over to the king the money he was holding on trust, and had the letter containing the agreement between the king of Granada and Don Felipe and Don Nuño [i.e., the *Ricos Hombres*] torn up. As soon as all this was concluded, the queen and Don Fernando addressed themselves to the king of Granada, giving him to understand that Alfonso [X] did not know that they were doing so. Into these talks they called Don Nuño and Felipe and they all pressed the king of Granada very hard to grant a truce to the *arrayaces* [i.e., the Banū Ashqilūla].
>
> The king of Granada was much grieved at this, for he could see that what they wanted was to protect the *arrayaces,* whereas they had already taken his money, paid over to them on the understanding that they would abandon that cause. The queen and the prince were so persistent that he had to grant this truce for one year. The queen and the prince sent to inform them immediately so they would know they were protected by a truce. The king of

> Granada then set out from Seville, and King Alfonso and all those with him escorted him to the city limits in order to honor him. (BAE:LXVI, 46–47)

Such honor was all very well, but Muḥammad II will have learned how dangerous it was to trust too much in the Castilians. Alfonso X had been on the point of seeking an alliance with the Marīnids against the Naṣrids, but with an income from Granada assured, he decided against calling in North Africa. Now Muḥammad II had his opportunity to turn the tables by looking across the seas.

Al-Dhakhīra al-saniyya is a Marīnid chronicle, which includes what purports to be Muḥammad's missive to the Marīnid emir "concerning the parlous state of al-Andalus, the frequent incursions of the enemy, and the great terror which reigns there" (*Dhakhīra* 1920:160–61) (there is another version of this text in another Marīnid history, the *Rawḍ al-qirṭās*). We can have no confidence that these sources record the actual words of the diplomatic contacts between the Naṣrids and the Marīnids at this period, but the inclusion of the text in both works would seem to indicate that Marīnid historiography was anxious to depict Muḥammad II as a supplicant desirous of entering the Marīnid sphere of influence. After the collapse of the Caliphate of Cordova in the eleventh century, the pattern of Spanish Islam seeking military support against the Christians had been established (under the Almoravids, under the Almohads). Hitherto military support had always been changed eventually into military domination. Thus it was that to call in North Africans in 1273 was a step the potential consequences of which were clear to all. Solidarity between Muslims on both sides of the straits was likely to lead sooner or later to the eclipse of the Naṣrid dynasty; Granada would become a northward extension of the Marīnid empire. We ought not to underestimate the skill with which Muḥammad II and his successors carried forward the project initiated by Muḥammad I of creating in the mountainous redoubts of southern Spain a country that Andalusi Muslims could call their own. An essential element in the defense of that state was the military assistance generously provided by North Africans. We will see that the flow of aid became institutionalized, and that command over the Volunteers for the Faith became one of the great offices of state, for long in the hands of a Marīnid, but we will also see how through a hundred crises, and thanks to countless shifts and maneuvers, the Naṣrids did manage to retain their essential independence.

The circumstances surrounding the first Marīnid intervention are thus of importance because precedents were set, a pattern of North African support-short-of-domination which was to last a long time.

The Marīnid *Al-Dhakhīra al-saniyya* presents the intervention as follows:

> After messengers and despatches reached the emir of the Muslims [i.e., Abū Yūsuf] from Ibn al-Aḥmar [i.e., Muḥammad II] and from Ibn Ashqilūla requesting assistance, and urging him to cross the sea and join in the Holy War, in response to their summons he left Fez in the middle of Ramadan 637 [April 1275] . . . and appointed Abū Zayyān to command a body of five thousand of the finest Marīnid cavalry, awarding him the drum and banner of his command, and providing him with all necessary financial and material resources, and handing to him his own personal pennant to bear victoriously in his own hands. He enjoined on him fear of God Almighty in both public and private, and so admonished, the emir made his way from Tangier to Qaṣr al-Mujāz ["the castle on the strait"], where he found that al-ʿAzafī [the ruler of Ceuta] had already assembled twenty vessels for him, with attendant lighters, and with crew and archers ready to transport the troops on their way to the Holy War across the narrow seas. So the emir sailed with all his army, and landed at Tarifa on the Spanish shore. This crossing was effected in Dhū'l-Ḥijja of the above-mentioned year. The emir remained in Tarifa three days, to give both troops and their mounts time to recover from the buffeting of the waves, and then set out for al-Buḥayra which he sacked, sending the booty back to Algeciras. He pushed onwards through enemy territory until he reached Jerez, killing his enemies or taking them prisoner, and laying waste all in his path, whether in the villages or in the castles and strong points, destroying crops, cutting down fruit trees, leaving behind him a trail of destruction. None of the Christians was able to withstand him, or to cause him to deviate from his objectives. He then transported booty and prisoners to Algeciras, where he made a triumphal entry accompanied by manacled and shackled Christian prisoners, the women and children

> being tied with ropes. This gave the inhabitants of Algeciras great cause for rejoicing, and their religious faith was confirmed. From the date of Las Navas de Tolosa in 609 [= 1212 A.D.], when the Almohad Emir had been routed, up to that point, there had been no Muslim victory comparable to this triumph of Abū Yūsuf. The people of al-Andalus had been overcome with fear of the Christians, and quite unable to put up effective resistance, and the Christians had been able to occupy most of their territory, their chief towns, castles and strongholds. When the emir brought over his father's victorious standard, Islam was given cause to rejoice once more, and the worshippers of idols and graven images were immediately humbled. (*Dhakhīra* 1920:163–65)

Thus Abū Yūsuf had Abū Zayyān carry out a successful reconnaissance in strength for him. He negotiated with Yagmurasān, ruler of Tlemcen, an accord which freed him of the fear of having to fight on two fronts, and he then called up his tribes, the Masmūda, the Jalūla, the Gumāra, the Zanāta, to the Holy War.

> In the year 674 [1275] on the 1st of Muharram [June 27] Abū Yūsuf arrived at the straits and began to embark those who were crossing to fight the Holy War, transporting with them mounts, arms and equipment. Each day a whole tribe of the Banū Marīn was ferried across, together with detachments of Volunteers for the Faith and tribes of Arabs: Sufyān, Khalat, ʿĀsim, Banū Jābir, Athbaj, Banū Hassan, Riyāh, and Shabbanāt. When he had completed the transfer of the Banū Marīn and of the Arabs, he went on to send his personal retinue across, and his household troops. And so they crossed in waves, tribe after tribe, contingent after contingent, by night and by day, from the castle on the straits to Tarifa packed so close together that:
>
> They crossed morning and evening to assault the foe
> As if the ocean were a pavement for their steeds,
> With the seaweed bearing the chargers up
> As if the two shores were joined together,
> And all had become a single causeway to tread.

When the troops were all across, and a firm base was established in al-Andalus, the armies stretched all the way from Tarifa

> to Algeciras, and then the emir crossed with the members of his council, his ministers and officials, accompanied by many of the holy men (*ṣāliḥ*) of the Magrib.
>
> He made the crossing on the afternoon of Thursday Safar 21 674 [= August 17, 1275] at a time people did not expect, so nobody was aware until the vessel came in sight: God granted him a smooth passage. He disembarked at Stag Rock on the Spanish shore. Those well versed in the ways of fortune declared that Islam was to come to triumph in al-Andalus by the hand of a king from across the sea who would come ashore by a stag rock unsought and unseen. This was a wondrous occurrence. From Stag Rock he went to Tarifa to perform his evening prayer, and that same day traveled on towards al-Latīna [?] where he met both Ibn al-Aḥmar and the Banū Ashqilūla *raʾīses,* who were waiting for him with their armies. They rallied round and greeted him and all the land of al-Andalus was much moved.
>
> Now between Ibn al-Aḥmar and the Banū Ashqilūla discord, strife, rancor and enmity had prevailed, but they laid this aside, and thanks to the power of God Almighty's word they came together in concord, desirous to prosecute the war against those who worship idols. They came to the parley as good Muslims, and remained with Abū Yūsuf three days. Ibn al-Aḥmar then departed for Granada none too pleased, while the Banū Ashqilūla went to Malaga, and, last of all, Abū Yūsuf set out together with his ministers and his retinue and with the holy men of the Magrib. (*Dhakhīra* 1920:166–67)

We can see in this account a desire to create a myth of a divinely guided Marīnid successful intervention in al-Andalus. The text is stylistically quite elaborate, with in the Arabic duplicate versions of various incidents, now in rhymed prose, now in fully metrical verse. The *Dhakhīra* does not pretend that Abū Yūsuf was able to unite the factions, and Muḥammad II goes back "none too pleased" (*gayr rāḍin*) at being dealt with on an even footing with his Banū Ashqilūla subjects.

One of the strange reversals effected by the Marīnid intervention was that although the Banū Ashqilūla were now still fighting Nuño González de Lara and his men as before, Nuño was Alfonso's man, and the Banū Ashqilūla were Alfonso's enemies. At Ecija Abū Zayyān fought a great battle against the Castilians. The Marīnid chronicle gives a gruesome account of the piles of Christian corpses left on the battlefield:

> [The Muslim commander] gave orders that all the Christian dead were to have their heads cut off and counted, so they were cut off and collected together, and they totaled eighteen thousand and more. The heads were piled high, and then the muezzins clambered up, and made the call to the prayer of *al- ʿaṣr* from the top. After the prayer, the emir reviewed his troops, and ascertained how many of his men had died a martyr's death and gone to Paradise: 6 of the Banū Marīn; 7 Arabs; 3 Andalusi Muslims; 8 Volunteers for the Faith, making 24 in all. He ordered the Muslims to be buried. This raid was a great victory for Islam, a great reverse for the idol-worshippers. The date was Rabīʿu al-awwal 15 674 [May 1275]. (*Dhakhīra* 1920:173)

Immediately following this passage, the Marīnid chronicler notes: "In this campaign there were present the *ra'īs* Abū Muḥammad Ibn Ashqilūla together with his son and his brother and their confederates [*jamaʿātuhu*], all of whom gave a good account of themselves in the fighting" (*Dhakhīra* 1920:174).

In the eyes of the Marīnids, the Banū Ashqilūla were reliable allies. Muḥammad II and his men, who had gone off in a huff after the landing at Algeciras, contributed proportionately little to the fighting.

In the victory celebrations in Algeciras, Abū Zayyān had the captured Christian nobles paraded into his presence whilst he was waving "the head of the accursed Don Nuño on a stake so that the people could see it." He then had the head sent to Muḥammad II in Granada, who had it preserved in musk and camphor and sent on to the accursed Alfonso "in order to court his friendship and ingratiate himself with him" (*Dhakhīra* 1920:174).

Whether Alfonso would have been pleased to receive the pickled head and regarded it as a mark of favor we may doubt, but we can see that the Marīnid chronicler is attempting to link Muḥammad with Alfonso: the North Africans are presented as fighting the Holy War, the Naṣrids as people of dubious loyalty to their own cause. One might have expected that the star of the Banū Ashqilūla would be in the ascendant since the Banū Marīn were now the most powerful military force in Islamic Spain and were well disposed towards them, but when in 1278 the Banū Ashqilūla governor of Malaga handed his city over to the

Marīnids (the new governor being ʿUmar b. Yaḥyā b. Maḥallī), the Banū Ashqilūla lost their securest base, and Malaga's period under a Marīnid governor proved little more than a transitional interim. By February 1279 Malaga was delivered by ʿUmar into Naṣrid hands (Ibn al-Khaṭīb 1934:289 [*Aʿmāl*]). As so often before and after this, the Naṣrids had successfully used their enemies to eliminate their enemies. How had they managed to persuade ʿUmar to relinquish Malaga? By the expedient of encouraging Yagmurasān of Tlemcen to break his truce with Abū Yūsuf, by cultivating the friendship of the Aragonese, but above all by playing the Castilian card and encouraging Alfonso X to besiege Algeciras (in Marīnid hands, of course). Thus did Muḥammad succeed in converting the Marīnids from being a dominant power exercising hegemony on both sides of the Mediterranean into an overstretched force whose troops in Spain were in danger of being cut off, whose Banū Ashqilūla allies had been outmaneuvered, and who wisely opted to fall back on their North African heartland.

To occupy and to exercise control in the second city of the kingdom, Malaga, and to gain the access to the Mediterranean world which it ensured, were vital, but until the end Malaga was a place where internal dissidents tended to establish themselves. Without Malaga, Granada was no more than an isolated mountain-girt city. With it, Granada was a viable, if vulnerable, independent state. The year 1279 was thus a triumph of considerable magnitude for the Banū'l-Aḥmar, and none the less important because it was achieved at very small cost: allegedly the castle of Salobreña for ʿUmar, together with a bribe of fifty thousand dinars (Arié 1973:73n. 1).

The next move in the game of changing patterns of alliances is astounding even by the kaleidoscopic standards of the period. Muḥammad II, having obtained Malaga, no longer needed his Castilian alliance; he made a deal whereby his ships joined those of the Marīnids which were harassing the Castilians besieging Algeciras. The Castilians had to make a precipitate withdrawal: "The Christians who were in the [sailing] ships saw that the galleys had been overwhelmed and burned, realized they could mount no effective defense, but could do nothing as there was no wind to permit them to move: most scuttled their vessels and fled in small boats" (BAE:LXVI, 56). The remaining Christian ships were attacked, and with the hand-to-hand combat still in progress they drifted, impelled by the current, towards Tangier. Abū Yūsuf, on the North African shore, offered a truce, and some of the Christians landed to negotiate terms. At this point a great gale sprang up, and the Castilian ships all dragged their anchors; the sailors were so afraid their vessels would be smashed that they ran with the wind and finished up in Cartagena. The negotiating party of Castilians was left on shore cut off from its fleet; Abū Yūsuf not unreasonably took them all prisoner (and it was two years before they were released) (BAE:LXVI, 57).

The Castilian narrative of this episode does not seem to be aware that any forces other than those of the Marīnids were involved, but Ibn Khaldūn tells us that "Ibn al-Aḥmar was grieved by the state of the Muslims shut up in Algeciras, and was ashamed of his part in their suffering (because of his alliance with the Christian king). To make amends, he tore up the treaty which bound him to the unbelievers, and fitted out vessels in Almuñecar, Malaga, and Almería to bring assistance to the believers" (Ibn Khaldūn 1969:IV, 101 [*Berbères*]).

Perhaps at this point Muḥammad II was just too clever and unscrupulous. Far from winning Marīnid gratitude (gratitude was never an emotion much in currency in these wars), Muḥammad suddenly found himself facing three enemies at once. The Marīnids instructed Abū Zayyān to open hostilities against him, with the objective to regain Malaga; the Castilians resented the way they had been left in the lurch at Algeciras; as for the Banū Ashqilūla, they no longer needed a motive for hostility, the two Arjona clans were now locked in a self-perpetuating feud. All three enemies attacked Granada in 1280: from May 1280 until April 1281 the little state had to face warfare on two fronts.

It was fortunate indeed for Muḥammad II of Granada that although the Marīnids were operating against him in the region of Marbella, North African Volunteers under Ibn Maḥallī and Tashufīn Ibn Muʿṭī could still be relied on to keep the Castilians at bay on the northern front. Quite how the Volunteers were so successfully integrated into the Naṣrid fighting machine is by no means clear, but some of the North Africans do seem to have identified themselves with the Granadan cause. Another piece of fortune for Muḥammad II was the rifts among the Castilians between Alfonso X's men and those of Sancho. In perhaps the most unexpected and outrageous of all the switches of loyalty of all these campaigns, Alfonso X himself now in desperation sought to counterbalance the onslaught of his own son Sancho by allying himself with the Marīnids! (Ibn Khaldūn 1969:IV, 106–7 [*Berbères*]) The consequence was that Sancho became the ally of Granada, and since Sancho was the more dangerous of the two Castilian rulers, Muḥammad II found that his new alliance brought him great relief. When Alfonso X died in 1284, Sancho remained well disposed towards Muḥammad II.

Thus it was that the enemy Muḥammad II had to face in 1285 was a Marīnid force sent to give support to the Banū Ashqilūla. Once in the peninsula the Marīnids became embroiled with the forces of Sancho (allies of Muḥammad, enemies of the Banū Ashqilūla), and Sancho quickly realized that Granadan politics were bringing him risks and small possibility of advantage. Suddenly, the situation was simplified, although we cannot understand the motives of all the parties to the conflict. At one and the same time Sancho pulled out of the Granadan imbroglio, and (a development that could never have been foreseen) the Banū Ashqilūla left Granada altogether. The Marīnids, by now led by Abū Yaʿqūb, who had succeeded to the throne in 1286, offered them estates in North Africa, and almost all the clan crossed the straits in 1288.[1] The Marīnids also largely abandoned their own positions on the Spanish side of the water.

In place of a complicated ballet for five dancers—Granada, Castile, the Banū Marīn, the Banū Ashqilūla, and the rebellious Castilians—there begins a much simpler piece of choreography for three participants, Castile, Granada, Banū Marīn. What is more, both Castile and the Banū Marīn were anxious to disengage.

So delicate was the balance of power that Granada could not risk stasis. The year 1290 saw Muḥammad engaged in the dangerous game of encouraging enemies to fight each other (BAE:LXVI, 85–86). Castile was to attack the Marīnid position at Tarifa (one of the few remaining North African outposts on the Spanish shore), and by a secret agreement, once captured, the town would be handed to the Granadans, who would pay for it by handing over six fortresses on the northern frontier (Ibn al-Khaṭīb 1934:291; Ibn Khaldūn 1969:VII, 218). This may seem like a continuation of the sort of Machiavellian negotiating that had been going on for years, but now, with the Banū Ashqilūla eliminated, the game was a different one.

Control of the Straits

The North African impulse to intervene in Spain had, as we have seen, a religious dimension: many of the Volunteers for the Faith conceived

1. Ibn al-Khaṭīb, *Aʿmāl al-aʿlām,* trans. I. S. Allouche, *Hespéris,* 25 (1938):9. See also Rubiera 1983:93.

of their actions as sacred duties. If pursued consistently and successfully, North African action in Spain would have had an economic consequence. Granada would have been kept in the Islamic Mediterranean sphere to which it had always belonged. North African intervention would have served to put a brake on the expansion of trade between Granada and the Christian lands of the western Mediterranean. This was partly in Catalan and Aragonese hands, but it was above all controlled by Italian merchant venturers from Genoa and Pisa. Castile and Granada might be the principal protagonists, but the Italians were everywhere. Their ships carried trade goods and troops alike. Italian mariners provided entrepreneurial skills and also naval leadership. They took profits, and not only from the trade of the ports of Granada but also from the Castilian acquisitions in the Guadalquivir valley (where we have seen a Boccanegra recolonizing Palma del Río). The constant commercial enterprise of the Genoese, Pisans, and others is the counterpart to the constant diplomatic efforts of the Naṣrids. And if until the end of the fifteenth century the Naṣrids were successful in their maneuvers to keep Granada a Muslim state, the Italian merchants—the Centurioni, the Pallavicini, the Datini, the Vivaldi, and others—were successful in detaching much of Granadan trade from the Islamic orbit and capturing it for Europe. This economic struggle underlies the political and military one.[2]

Tarifa was taken by Castile from the Marīnids (BAE:LXVI, 86; Ibn Khaldūn 1969:IV, 131–32). An essential element in the campaign was the naval assistance provided by Aragon. At Montegudo, Castile and Aragon had signed a treaty by which they agreed to separate spheres of influence for themselves in North Africa, the dividing line to run up the Mulawiya River to the west of Tlemcen, more or less at the modern frontier between Morocco and Algeria. Moreover, Tlemcen was brought into this anti-Marīnid consortium, so that Abū Yaʿqūb was hampered by a threat on land as well as on the water. When the Castilians took Tarifa they also took the six border fortresses which Granada had thought of exchanging for Tarifa. Granada felt cheated and rushed into the arms of Abū Yaʿqūb (Ibn Khaldūn 1969:IV, 133), who in 1294 came to besiege the Castilians in Tarifa, where what Castilian historiography depicts as one of the great heroic deeds of the war, in-

2. See R. S. López, *Storie delle colonie genovese nel Mediterraneo,* Bologna, 1938.

deed of the whole series of campaigns, took place. Alfonso Pérez de Guzmán, the Christian commander, confronted with the terrible choice of saving his son's life (his son was a prisoner of the Muslims) by surrendering the vital stronghold, or holding out knowing his son would be put to death, unhesitatingly decided to resist (BAE:LXVI, 87). The Marīnids failed to recapture the port, and blamed not Guzmán but the Granadans, allegedly lukewarm in their attacks (Ibn al-Khaṭīb 1934:292).

The Marīnids once more withdrew to Africa; the Naṣrids thought to occupy the areas which the Marīnids were relinquishing, but they found that in some places it was not easy to do so. In Ronda and the western zone in general the Granadans had tended to encourage North African Volunteers to set up bases—well away from Granada itself. The local Muslim population did not always appreciate the sacrifices being made on their behalf by these warriors of the holy war. Like good folk almost everywhere, they resented having rough soldiery billeted on them. Under the Banū'l-Ḥākim they set up their own petty state round Ronda. The terrain, and the determination of the local people, kept this enclave in being for a year, and when the Naṣrids did enter, it was on terms: none of the Naṣrid family was to live in the area, none of the Volunteers would be lodged in the town (Ibn al-Khaṭīb 1934:292 [= Allouche 111]). It is interesting to see how for the inhabitants of this mountainous area the Volunteers and the Naṣrids had come to be the enemy.

The final year of Muḥammad II's reign saw a renewal of hostilities on the Castilian frontiers. When Sancho IV died in 1295, Ferdinand IV was a minor. The absence of strong central government once again gave rebels their chance, and the Aragonese could intervene by backing a rival claimant to the throne. Christian divisions were Granada's opportunity. Attacks were launched all along the frontier, and a notable victory was the capture of Quesada. The grand master of Calatrava attempted a counterattack and was routed at Iznalloz.

Castile's time of weakness was a time of opportunity for both Granada and Aragon. The two states reached an outline agreement in 1296 whereby, to simplify matters, one might say that Aragon was to get Murcia and Granada was to be given a free hand in Andalusia.[3]

3. The treaty of 1296 between Granada and Aragon (Alarcón and García de Linares 1940:1–3) is almost exclusively concerned with commercial matters.

Granada set its price high, though, and insisted on getting, *inter alia,* Alcalá, Tarifa, and Castile. When Alfonso de la Cerda, acting on behalf of Aragon, vacillated, the Castilians must have got wind of what was happening. The tutor to the young Castilian King, Don Enrique, made the journey to Granada to make the counteroffer of Tarifa in return for Granadan support. That deal broke down too. In a confused situation the Aragonese were pushing ahead with their plans to enter Murcia. Granada did nothing to hinder them, and at the same time struck at the Castilians.

Granada continued to profit from the weakness of Castile during the period before Ferdinand IV came of age, and successfully retook border fortresses such as Alcaudete, even raided as far as Jaén and Andújar. In September 1301 Muḥammad had just concluded negotiations in Saragossa whereby Tarifa was to become Granadan again. The agreement, ratified in January 1302 (Alarcón and García de Linares 1940:7–10), was never put to the test, for in April 1302 Muḥammad II died. A story was put about that he had been poisoned by a sweetmeat administered by his heir.[4] We have no means of telling what really happened. Reports of extreme cruelty inflicted on others by Muḥammad III do indicate that his was an abnormal psychological make-up.

Muḥammad II had in the final quarter of the thirteenth century been able to build on the foundations created by Muḥammad I. Ibn Khaldūn's assessment of Muḥammad II's achievements in his *History of the Banūʾl-Aḥmar* is an interesting one. Ibn Khaldūn clearly perceived the Naṣrids as calling in question his theory of the decisive role of tribal solidarity as the necessary cement to bind regimes together:

> He [Muḥammad II] had no tribal or clan leader on whom to rely, all he had were the exiled Zanāta troops and members of the Marīnid family who probably came in the hope of booty, but of whom it could be said in their favor that they had courage and élan. What happened is to be ascribed, as we have said, to the complete disappearance of tribes and clans in Spain. At the outset Ibn al-Aḥmar [Muḥammad I] had been able to count on his own clan and the Banū Ashqilūla and Banū'l-Mawl with such of their clients as followed them to war. These forces were just sufficient,

4. Ibn al-Khaṭīb 1973:I, 566 (*Iḥāṭa*). "A cake made specially for him in the house of the crown prince, but Allah knows best."

> thanks to assistance received from the Castilian king against Ibn Hūd, assistance from the ruler of Morocco against the Castilian king, thanks too to the advantage of having members of the Marīnid family in his service. Later on it is understandable that both people of power and influence and also the lower orders should have been united by a common hatred of the Christian king, whom they feared as the enemy of their religion. All felt the same fear, so all had the same desire to fight. To a certain extent this bond came to replace tribal bonds which had been lost. (Ibn Khaldūn 1898:409)

Ibn Khaldūn was describing the coming into existence of a state that for him was strange. It was a state that possessed many of the characteristics of a modern European nation. The bonds holding society together were not those of tribe but of a single religion (Islam in this case), a single universal language (Arabic), and an awareness of the profound difference between loyal subjects and the Other beyond the frontiers. The Other was Romance-speaking Christian people, ever ready to encroach.

The obligation to fight on the frontier (*ribāṭ*) was, of course, a religious one; the essentially *defensive* nature of this frontier warfare (could Granadans ever hope realistically to expand their territory very much?) gave a very sharp definition to what it meant to be a Granadan. Muḥammad II's reign was a vital stage in the formation of a Granadan identity.

ELEVEN

Muḥammad III (1302–1309)

The first two monarchs of the Naṣrid line certainly did not enjoy easy reigns: the kingdom had to be created by boldness, by unceasing effort, both military and diplomatic. Theirs were long reigns by any standard of comparison, and Muḥammad II ruled for twenty-nine years. From this point onwards such stability is difficult to find. Muḥammad III did indeed succeed his father, but in the most dubious circumstances, and his kingdom was relatively soon lost, so that he ended his days in a sort of internal exile at Almuñécar, and is usually identified as *al-makhlūʿ* (deposed). (It may seem that he scarcely deserves to be singled out to enjoy exclusive use of an epithet to which many of his successors were to have equal claim.) With Muḥammad III the pattern of more than half a century of stability was broken. But there is a paradox here. The Naṣrid kingdom of Granada was the invention and the creation of the first two kings of the line, and they had to struggle to establish the regime; after them, the state's survival became a matter of concern not only to the Naṣrid family, but also to a complex of interest groups, both inside Granada and outside it. The new state began as the domain of one warlord among many, it became heir to the loyalties of all Spanish Muslims who earnestly desired to live under Muslim rule in their homeland, and as such it acquired legitimacy. It became at the same time a key element in that Castilian policy which preferred dealing with a client state, however refractory, to the risk of seeing a foreign power, whether Muslim or Christian, being tempted to intervene. The inability of Castilians, or indeed any other Christian power, as yet to dominate the considerable area of difficult terrain in which the remnants of the Muslim population of al-Andalus had taken refuge created a vacuum of power.

The idea that rule should necessarily be handed down from father to son is not enshrined in Islamic statecraft. Legitimate succession would be assured when the most powerful or most acceptable male available at the time of the demise of the previous ruler took over from him. The history of the Umayyad emirate and Caliphate in the early Middle Ages in Spain shows how a tendency towards succession within a narrow ruling family, and even to something approaching straightforward primogeniture, can evolve within the looser and more primitive system. We have seen that the Naṣrid regime may have begun with ideas of power sharing between two related clans, the Banū Naṣr and the Banū Ashqilūla, and how the Banū Ashqilūla were eventually deprived of their share in the state.

If the story (related in the preceding chapter) that Muḥammad III killed his own father is correct, was he overcome with an impatient desire to assume power? Ibn al-Khaṭīb depicts a personality schizophrenically dominated by conflicting traits. He sets out in full "what is related concerning his brutishness and cruelty":

> At the outset of his reign, he had a group of his father's household troops, about whom he had formed an adverse judgment, arrested in a sudden swoop. He had them imprisoned in the dungeons of the Alhambra and he kept the key, threatening with death anybody who threw them food; there they remained for days, raising their voices in the agony of their hunger, and those who died first were eaten by those left alive: finally from sheer weakness and exhaustion all fell silent. One of the guards set to watch at the mouth of the dungeon, moved by compassion, threw down to them a small leftover crust of bread. Somebody reported on the guard, and orders were given for his throat to be cut on the brink of the top of the pit, so his blood would flow out onto them [the prisoners]. (1973:I, 547–48)

If this horrific account is to be believed, Muḥammad was indeed a sadistic brute, but he was not that alone. A complex character in very many ways, he would sit up all night reading by the light of immense candles (and this may have been the cause of his defective eyesight). Perhaps the most attractive anecdote told about him is that when a poet was reciting verses to celebrate his ascension to the throne:

For whom are the banners today unfurled?
For whom do the troops 'neath their standards march?

Muḥammad added, "For this fool you can see before you all" (Rubiera 1969:110; Ibn al-Khaṭīb A.H. 1347:47 [*Lamḥa*]).

This dangerous, superstitious, unpredictable, and disconcerting man took over power at a time when Muḥammad II had created a situation of military advantage. Only two weeks after his accession, the fortress of Bedmar near Jaén was taken by troops under the Berber Ḥammū b. ʿAbd al-Ḥaqq b. Raḥḥū. Muḥammad III did not push ahead, but entered into negotiations with the Castilians. Fernando IV's chancellor, Fernando Gómez de Toledo, accompanied by a Jewish official of his court called Samuel, who was acting as interpreter, came in 1303 (BAE:LXVI, 133), and was prepared to offer a good deal, in fact almost all of Granada's war aims: Bedmar, Alcaudete, Quesada, although he was not prepared to yield Tarifa. In return, Granada would have to acknowledge that it was Castile's vassal. The agreement was to stand for three years. To the settlement Aragon also added its assent in 1304. The Marīnids were left isolated. Politically this peace settlement, signed in April 1304, was doubtless wise and, as we shall see, gave Granada a dominant position in the straits, but that did not mean that the Granadan people would necessarily welcome it, still less those North African Volunteers for the Faith whose reason for coming to Granada had been to continue the war on the frontier. The unpopularity that led to Muḥammad III's eventual deposition may have arisen from his brutal cruelty, but how many of his subjects would know about what went on inside the Alhambra? A more likely motive for dissatisfaction was that he appeared unduly precipitate in seeking peace with the Christians, and thus deprived Muslims of the fruits of their struggles.

The reaction of neighboring powers to the peace was scarcely more enthusiastic. Neither Aragon nor Fez had reason to welcome a settlement that tended to stabilize the center of the peninsula and might even have led to the blocking of the straits. Aragon, for all its readiness to employ the rhetoric of crusading fraternalism, had, in terms of Mediterranean power politics, a firm grasp on the advantages that would flow to it from freedom of navigation through the straits for its own shipping. For Granada to be securely attached to Castile did not fit into that pattern. The alliance can hardly have commended itself to the Marīnids, who sought to prevent the Castilians and Granadans from establishing any stranglehold on the Gibraltar area.

Aragon and Fez therefore had a certain community of interest at this point, and yet the problems experienced in their negotiations bring out clearly the nature of this power struggle, and the limitations experienced by the protagonists. The envoy whom James II of Aragon sent to Fez, Bernat de Sarrià, realized that to make too much of the community of interests which had arisen between his master and Abū Yaʿqūb might drive the Granadans into permanent alliance with Castile. Nor was Granada free to push too far, for if Aragon, worried by the formation of a Castilian-Granadan bloc which weakened its position in the peninsula, should decide that pursuit of its overseas policy objectives ought to be subordinated to safety at home, then Granada might once more be placed under threat from Valencia. The Granadan vizir al-Dānī took the trouble to assure Bernat de Sarrià that Granada's understanding with Castile did not preclude good relations with Aragon (Arié 1973:86). Aragon does not seem to have been mollified, and looked for better relations with Castile. A settlement of differences, facilitated by the arbitration of Dinis of Portugal, the Infante Juan, and the bishop of Saragossa, was concluded between Castile and Aragon at Agreda in 1304. James II of Aragon gained Alicante, Elche, Orihuela, and the north bank of the Orihuela River in exchange for promises to help Castile and the abandonment of support for the claims of Alfonso de la Cerda. The 1304 accord was witnessed by Granada as Castile's vassal, but in the treaty of Alcalá de Henares, concluded between James II and Ferdinand IV in 1308, Castile gave a promise that Almería and one-sixth of the Kingdom of Granada would eventually fall as Aragon's share, so that the agreement between the Christian powers took an anti-Granadan flavor. For such concord to exist between the two major Christian states was already bad enough for Granada, but events took an adverse turn in North Africa as well. The problems centered on the port of Ceuta.

The reasoning of Muḥammad III with regard to Ceuta may have been understandable, but the consequences of his policy were disastrous. Direct control by Granada of the straits must have seemed highly desirable, for this was the route for essential supplies and reinforcements. To be cut off altogether from North Africa must have been one of the nightmares of any Granadan policymaker at any period. The paradox, which Muḥammad III does not seem to have grasped, was that by securing firm control over part of the North African shore, the Granadans might be able to count on a port, but they also would alienate North African allies. This was what made Muḥammad III's Ceuta policy his major political error.

Muḥammad III exploited rifts within the Marīnid state, and in 1304, egged on by Granadan emissaries, the inhabitants of Ceuta had declared themselves independent of the Marīnid sultan. In the confused events of Ceutí politics at this period, one may distinguish various rival factions and interest groups, and on these Muḥammad III's agents (notably his governor of Malaga, Abū Saʿīd Faraj) played with some skill. The Banū'l-ʿAzafī were a family with claims to regard themselves as lords of Ceuta, and so it was easy to exploit their anti-Marīnid sentiments. Another key figure was a potential rebel Marīnid who had seen service in Spain, ʿUthmān Ibn Abī-l-ʿUlā Ibn ʿAbd al-Ḥaqq, whose dissidence reached the point in 1307 of him declaring himself *amīr al-muslimīn* and occupying territory in the hills (Arié 1973:87). He appears to have enjoyed Naṣrid support, and naval raiding pinned down Marīnid forces in various ports.

Initially there could not be any firm Marīnid response to these confused events, for the war against Tlemcen was a constant drain on their resources. In 1307 the Marīnid sultan was assassinated outside that city: the wise action of his successor, Abū Thābit, was to pull out of this disastrous commitment and to return to Fez. The evident Marīnid determination to secure a firm control of their Moroccan territories might well have served as a warning to the Naṣrids, who in 1307 had assumed the title of lords of Ceuta. They had sought to eliminate opposition in Ceuta by shifting the Banū'l-ʿAzafī clan across the straits to Granadan territory (Ibn Khaldūn 1969:IV, 160–61), an action that cannot have failed to create resentment.

The evolution of the relations between Aragon and Castile interacted with what was in Ceuta a very small-scale rivalry. The alliance which surprisingly had brought Aragon and Castile together in order to press ahead with the Reconquest also had a North African dimension, whereby the Marīnids of Fez were partners in a tripartite anti-Granadan alliance. The advantages of such an arrangement to the Christian states are obvious: faced with a concerted Christian attack, Granada would certainly seek help in Fez, and the tripartite agreement forestalled such an attempt. What was in it for Fez was quite simply a promise that Ceuta would be restored to it.

In Granada the immediate effect of the emergence of such a devastating line-up of enemies was the fall of the government. Muḥammad III had begun his reign by entering, in 1304, into a tripartite alliance against the Marīnids. He was now outmaneuvered, and the tripartite alliance was against him. In such a situation the reigning monarch might well have feared that his political opponents at home would make sure that the change of policy would be put into effect through the simple expedient of assassinating him. In the palace revolution of March 14, 1309, however, it was not Muḥammad who died but his chief minister, Ibn al-Ḥakīm al-Rundī. Muḥammad was replaced by his brother Naṣr, but was allowed to depart to take up residence at Almuñécar.

The anger of the mob in 1309 was directed at Ibn al-Ḥakīm, no doubt because he was perceived by many as holding the keys to real power in the state. We have seen that his family had at one time in the 1280s and 1290s made itself almost independent in the region of Ronda, but by negotiation this dissident area had been absorbed by Muḥammad II. Ibn al-Ḥakīm had entered Muḥammad II's service as secretary, and he rose to the highest rank in the chancery. When Muḥammad III came to power he kept the services of Ibn al-Ḥakīm who, by 1303 already, was styled *dhū'l-wizāratayn* 'charged with a double ministry'. The power the minister wielded was no doubt reinforced by the king's poor sight.

Ibn al-Ḥakīm's wealth and the sumptuous life-style he enjoyed in his palace were well known. It was against Ibn al-Ḥakīm that the people, outraged by the failure of a foreign policy which had managed to alienate both Christians and North Africans, directed its anger. The minister's palace was sacked, the minister himself was killed by ʿĀṭiq b. al-Mawl, his would-be ministerial rival. Ibn al-Ḥakīm's corpse got into the hands of the crowd, who subjected it to such indignities that it was lost, and he never could be buried. As "one of the outstanding men of the period" (who can al-Maqqarī have wished to cloak in anonymity in this way?) laments, "Unjustly they killed you, transgressing all decent bounds, / and your battered corpse they cast away, but such was your hidden fate, / and if, my Lord, you have no grave, still your tomb is in our hearts" (Rubiera 1969; al-Maqqarī 1940:II, 344–45). A strange period this, in which the most brutal of realities went together with the most mannered and delicate literary culture!

TWELVE

Naṣr (1309–1314); Ismāʿīl (1314–1325); Muḥammad IV (1325–1333)

Naṣr, 1309–1314

When Naṣr took over from Muḥammad III, Granada was engaged in an ill-advised overseas adventure in Ceuta, and in addition to the hostility of the Marīnids, faced that of the Castilians and of the Aragonese, united in a crusading drive in which, after a half century and more of pause, they were determined to bring the Reconquest to an end. Thus it was that Granada found itself in the situation it had always sought to avoid: fighting both its major Hispanic enemies and the principal power in North Africa. By the end of Naṣr's five-year reign, of the three enemies, Aragon had had inflicted on it such a crushing defeat at Almería that never after did the Aragonese realm seek to take war into Granadan territory; the Castilians had made one important gain—Gibraltar—but had suffered a terrible and disgraceful defeat at Algeciras (more at the hand of the Marīnids than of the Granadans, it is true); and as for the Marīnids, they had, as we shall see, not only pushed the Granadans from the bridgehead in Ceuta that Muḥammad III had unwisely thought of securing, but had also reoccupied much territory on the northern shore of the Mediterranean at the expense of Granada. It might be said that Naṣr had to face one of the most dangerous crises which ever threatened the existence of his state, and that he emerged from these testing times in general triumphant. The defeat inflicted on the flower of the Aragonese chivalry, the elite troops who had demonstrated their power to operate far from their home base at so many other maritime cities round the Mediterranean, was decisive, and Granada continued to benefit for a century and a half from the lesson it had taught its enemies. Thus it might be assumed that Naṣr would have enjoyed a reputation as almost a savior of his people. Not at all. Naṣr was to be relieved of power, and although he did not give up his pretensions to royal authority, he lived out the final eight years of his life exiled from Granada in Guadix, plotting unsuccessfully against his cousin Ismāʿīl, who had replaced him on the throne in 1314.

At the beginning of Naṣr's reign Muḥammad III's policies aimed at securing Granadan control over the Straits of Gibraltar by securing the port of Ceuta had so antagonized the Marīnids that they were willing to enter into an alliance with Aragon and Castile. Aragonese naval support was promised to the Marīnid land forces, and a curious deal had been struck whereby after allied victory the Marīnids were to take over the territory, but the Aragonese were to have the booty arising from sacking the port. Clearly it had been anticipated that the Aragonese would enter the territory, and then hand it over after removing objects of value. The agreement broke down when some of the people of Ceuta allowed the Marīnids to enter first.

Naṣr hastened to reach an accord with the Marīnids (now under Abūʾl-Rabīʿ). He reversed Muḥammad III's policy, and far from trying to hold his own bridgehead in Africa, he allowed the Marīnids back into his territory, allocating them Algeciras and lands as far as Ronda. The Marīnids had withdrawn from the peninsula in 1294, and now in 1309 they returned.

Algeciras had been one of the objectives of the tripartite alliance (Aragon, Castile, the Marīnids), and in the middle of the siege the Castilians found themselves facing a garrison now fighting on behalf of one of their erstwhile allies. The naval assistance Aragon was providing was not very effective, but probably the major cause of the collapse of the Castilian assault was the fact that the great Castilian noble of the royal blood, Juan Manuel (author of several works on the duties of a Christian knight) led five hundred knights from the field of battle in November 1309[1] and inflicted a great blow on Castilian morale.

1. BAE:LXVI, 163. For his treatises on chivalry, see Juan Manuel 1982 and BAE:LI (*Libro del caualllero et del escudero; Libro de las armas; Libro de los Estados*).

The most serious Granadan loss of 1309 was Gibraltar: it was in fact only to remain in Castilian hands twenty-four years, for it was to be recaptured in 1333 and not then occupied by Castilians until 1464. It was taken by conquest, and Muslims residing there had to leave, most for North Africa. The *Chronicle of Ferdinand IV* tells us that

> The total of those who left in this way was 1,125, and amongst them was an old man who said to the king [Ferdinand IV]: "Sire, what have you against me to drive me out in this way? When your great-grandfather took Seville [i.e., A.D. 1248] he drove me out, and I went to live at Jerez; then when your grandfather took Jerez he expelled me, and I went to live in Tarifa where I thought I might dwell in peace, but your father Sancho came and took Tarifa, so I came here to Gibraltar, judging that in no place in all the lands of the Muslims on this side of the water could I live more secure. Now I see that I can live in none of these places: I will depart beyond the sea and settle in a place where I can live in safety for the rest of my days. (BAE:LXVI, 163)

Whether this little incident did in fact occur (and it does read rather like a propagandist's celebration of the relentless advance of the Castilians under their kings), it summarizes for us the experience of many Muslims in this period. And if the story was intended as Castilian propaganda, it might well have served Naṣrid purposes as well. The old man, starting from his original home in Seville, had kept as far west as possible in his choice of where to live. If he had opted at the outset for one of the more central Granadan provinces, he would have stood a better chance of living undisturbed. The continual activity on the Granadan frontiers and overseas tends to divert our attention from the great success of the Muslims in their mountain redoubts in organizing profitable areas of intensive agriculture which not only fed the vastly increased population of this refuge for all the Muslims of Andalusia, but also produced sufficient surplus value to enable the Granadan state to organize an efficient military machine, and in addition to build solid castles and examples of delicate domestic and civil architecture.

Probably the greatest triumph of Granadan arms in this eventful reign was the successful defense of Almería from an assault which was mounted as part of a concerted Aragonese and Castilian campaign (although on this sector of the front, as we would expect, Aragonese participation was predominant). The Aragonese entered the campaign with some enthusiasm, for the joint Castilian-Aragonese offensive was based on the understanding that if the allies succeeded in conquering Granada one-sixth of the lands would be given to the Aragonese. (One can see that the Aragonese would have been attracted not only by the new lands in the south, but by the fact that they would no longer be blocked off at the south of Valencia. The Murcian question would by implication be reopened.)

The fundamental flaw in the Aragonese campaign was that it started so late in the year. It was mid-August before Aragonese forces appeared off the coast at Almería. Such a season of the year was quite suitable for the initiation of campaigns of frontier skirmishing, but the organized siege of a major city was another matter. Of course Almería's climate is a clement one, but mid-winter is no time to be out in the field. By starting late the Aragonese put themselves in a position whereby the rigors of the siege began to be greater for the besiegers than for the besieged as the months went by.

In anticipation of an attack, Almería had built up its grain stocks, and this must have had an important impact on the outcome: "One of the signs of Allah's protection of the city's inhabitants was that great quantities of barley were in the storehouses at the beginning of the siege. The ration was one pound a person distributed to all at a price of one *qirāṭ* a pound. The highest price reached by bread made from wheaten flour was three *dirhams,* and ten ounces of wheaten bread cost two *dirhams.*" The supply of basic food was assured inside the city. Outside, the attackers were themselves suffering from lack of supplies. "Allah caused a wind to blow from the west for two months, which prevented Christian merchant ships from sailing, cutting off supplies to such an extent that they all went hungry." These were the logistical problems of a campaign insufficiently well prepared by the attackers. The defenders, on the other hand, were ready to meet the onslaught. For this, credit must go to the governor Abū Maydān Shuʿayb and his naval commander Abūʾl-Ḥasan al-Randāḥī. The walls had been strengthened, potentially dangerous chinks in the defenses had been sealed, buildings near the ramparts which might have been made use of by the attackers had been knocked down. The Aragonese forces might have been poorly organized, but they did not lack in courage, dash, élan. As narrated by Aḥmad Ibn al-Qāḍī in his *Durrat al-Ḥijāl,* the siege was full of incident (Sánchez-Albornoz 1946:II, 386–92; Ibn al-Qāḍī 1907:279–88).

He comments on how the Christians were "decked in fine clothing" as they disembarked and to the sound of martial instruments advanced towards the walls. The colorful caparisons and the general high standard of turnout of this army taking the field at the peak of the period of ostentatious heraldic display was to be a factor in one of the most memorable incidents in the fighting.

Immediately after the landing, the sheer numbers of the attackers demoralized the townsfolk, but as days and weeks went by they became more confident: "After they had experience of a few attacks, they realized war has its ups and its downs, and they took courage and committed themselves boldly to the fray. Their archers became more audacious, the defenders, heartened by their successes, struck out without fear."

Ibn al-Qāḍī gives a vivid description of the besieging army making one of its periodic assaults:

> On Saturday Rabīʿal-awwal 21, the Christians had a great bell sounded, as they do when the king mounts his horse. All took up arms and advanced all round the city. They had got ready high wooden siege towers on wheels permitting them to be moved forward. These they manned with troops, and they brought up scaling ladders and set them against the walls. Their foot soldiers and archers advanced ahead of the cavalry all round the city. The Muslims, in the lively resistance they put up, poured boiling oil and other flammable substances on them so they were obliged to retreat, leaving many of their number behind as prisoners.

An event of considerable significance was the arrival of a contingent from Granada, who could not break in to relieve the besieged city, but who, by encamping at Marchena, hampered the attackers greatly, and harassed the foraging parties. The Christian side began to need a quick decision.

> When the Christians began to grow impatient, and when they realized how many of them had died, they decided to have recourse to a strategem. A group of riders slipped through the lines by night, and went out into the country, and next day they came back into view, but all of them dressed in burnouses, so they seemed to be Muslims. The Christian knights [in the city] then pretended to rush out to head them off, leaving their tents unpro-

> tected so as to tempt the Muslims to pillage them. Near to these tents they had set up ambushes, with soldiers in position and traps dug. The Muslims were taken in: all unaware of the trick, they sounded the alarm in the marketplaces, and led by many of their nobles under the commander of the fleet they rode out, making first for the tents to pillage them. Allah, however, put it in their mind to deviate and make first for some tents on high ground because the Christians encamped there were particularly bitter enemies of theirs. When the men posted in the ambushes saw the Muslims receding, they thought they were going that way because the traps had been discovered, and so they emerged into the open, because they wanted to cut the Muslims off from the city. The Muslims had reason to regret their failure to grasp the situation, and it was fortunate for them that a postern gate on that side of the city had been made ready to open only the day before: they managed to rush in through it. Others who were separated from the main body had to take shelter at the foot of the walls. The defenders threw down planks for them to use to take shelter, and they kept up a hail of covering fire. When fighting died down they were able to slip back in. (Ibn al-Qāḍī 1907:283)

Finally, a month later, the Christians launched a great attack: they brought up siege engines which the Muslims burned down; they brought up ladders, and out to sea the Christian ships went into action.

> The Muslims were in dire straits, but then the cry went up, "Empty the cesspits on them, nothing will humiliate them so much!" So people began to extract excrement from the cesspits and hoist it up to the battlements so as to cast it down on the attackers. This was a great success because it brought together two things of the same sort. The stratagem is infallible. The knights in their fine array were covered in filth, and were mocked by their companions. This device proved more effective than combat, and Allah by this means brought a respite to the Muslims. (Ibn al-Qāḍī 1907:284)

The respite was only short-lived. On Rajab 22 a whole section of the battlements collapsed, and the Christians rushed into the breach, but the defenders managed to hold firm, the Christian impetus faded. Disappointed at their lack of success even after breaching the wall, the Christians had to accept overtures for peace.

Muntaner in his account of the fighting at Almería includes a relatively minor incident, one which, moreover, he almost certainly misplaces chronologically, but one which ought to be recalled because it conveys something of the way that some of the principal actors thought of their roles in these great events, conscious of the epic behavior that was expected of them.

The incident in question is dated by Muntaner as having occurred on St. Bartholomew's Day, i.e., August 23, and towards the end of the campaign, but that did not come until December:

> When my lord the king [James] was ready with all his host to attack the enemy [in this case not the Almerians themselves, but the Granadan contingent outside the walls], there emerged from inside the city over the spur which runs down to sea by the cliffs the son of the king of Guadix with four hundred mounted men and many foot soldiers. Alarm was sounded through the tents, and the prince, fully armed, rode out with his knights in due array. When the Moors had all crossed the obstacle, this son of the king of Guadix, who was a skilled horseman, one of the best in the world, and very strong, charged out first, with his javelin in his hand, shouting: "*Ani ben e soltan*" [a not unreasonable representation of the vernacular pronunciation of *Ana ibn al-sulṭān* 'I am the Sultan's son'].
>
> He kept saying the same thing, and Prince Ferdinand asked, "What is he saying?"
>
> The interpreters he had with him replied, "Sire, he says he is a king's son."
>
> The prince then said, "I too am a king's son!" and as he attempted to reach him he killed more than six knights with his lance, which then broke, so he drew his sword, and brandishing it in his hand he forced a way through to where the man was shouting he was a king's son. When the Moor saw the prince coming, he rode up to him and dealt him such a blow that it cut off the top quarter of his shield, which fell to the ground, such an unusual blow it was. And he cried out, "*Ani ben e soltan!*"
>
> The prince then struck him with his sword such a blow to the head that he split it open to the teeth, and the Moor fell dead to

> the ground. Thereupon the Saracens all acknowledged they were beaten, those that could climbed up the way they had come down, and the rest all died. (Soldevila 1983:887–88)

The aristocracy on both sides may have liked to see warfare as essentially conflict between great heroes. Ibn al-Qāḍī makes it clear, however, that the fighting at Almería was quite largely an affair of artillery. Artillery, of course, at this point in the history of warfare meant siege engines, catapults, and *ballistae,* and not yet cannons and gunpowder, though they were soon to come (and since cannons often took over the old names for types of *ballistae,* it is surprisingly difficult at times to know exactly when the new technology arrived).

> All round the city they [the Christians] set up eleven catapults and mobile engines. Some cast rocks at the battlements, others into the city, others at the main keep of the fortress. The Christians directed their main efforts against the ramparts on the hill dominating the city, and there the fighting was intense. During the course of the siege the catapults projected 22,000 rocks. Consider, O Reader! what divine wisdom! The number of casualties was several times greater than that of rocks projected. Each one weighed twenty-five to thirty pounds. Inside the city they had only one catapult, but it could be used to throw stones in a landward direction or out to sea as the need arose. When it was put out of action by a hit from a rock launched from the Christian camp they constructed three others. (Ibn al-Qāḍī 1907:286)

With winter coming on in December, with no hope of taking the city, and with the danger that Juan Manuel's desertion at Algeciras would so relieve pressure on the Granadans that they could redeploy their forces eastward, the Aragonese must have decided to pull out on the best terms available. A truce was concluded in a parley held at the Aragonese camp at the end of December (and the news was conveyed back instantly by a carrier pigeon) (Ibn al-Qāḍī 1907:286). Muntaner almost managed to present the defeat as a victory, and blames the winter and "the disloyal way in which the Castilians had behaved."[2] "Thus agreement was reached, a truce concluded, and my Lord King gave

2. Soldevila 1983:888. "La gran desconeixença que els castellans li havien feta."

orders that all his men with all their belongings should be embarked, and they returned, some by land, some by sea, to the Kingdom of Valencia" (Soldevila 1983:888). The logical muddle of that last sentence reflects the logistical muddle of the arrangements for the evacuation. Not all the Castilian and Aragonese troops could be crammed onto the vessels available, and a number had to be left behind under promise of Muslim protection! When this rump of an army left in Almería realized that the authorities were doing little to bring them out, some decided to fight their own way back home across country. As they struggled back they were ambushed and picked off. From Lorca on the frontier the *Concejo* was moved to write to James II warning him of the dangers created by this situation: "You should know that some of the foot soldiers from the army sent against Almería are daring to make their own way home by land. Most have perished on the way, as they are being slaughtered and made captive by Granadan troops who attack them as they journey. This gives great encouragement to the Moors when they get to hear of it."[3] (The date of the document is January 30, 1310, which would seem to indicate that the troops left behind had not waited very long for their transport to arrive.)

Ignominiously, many of those who had not struck out on their own were put into confinement in Almería because they were causing trouble: "We have assigned them a house and given them food at our own expense because some of them were starving. This we did out of respect for you. As soon as you send the ships we will give orders for them to be released," says a letter from Naṣr in response to Aragonese complaints.

Meanwhile, "because of a rumor that the King of Aragon was coming again" (Sánchez-Albornoz 1946:II, 392), the inhabitants of the city turned out to clear away the abandoned Aragonese siege works outside their walls. It was no doubt necessary to have the city's defenses back in order, but they need not have feared that James II would return. The Aragonese had been taught a lesson.

The defense of Almería as also that of Algeciras, were major triumphs for the Muslims. The advance of the Christian Reconquest was put back many decades. Castile and Aragon had concerted their efforts to crush Granada, and they had failed. But from the Granadan point of view there was little cause for rejoicing. Ceuta on the African shore and Gibraltar had been lost. The Marīnids were in Algeciras. A number of

3. Tapia 1986:225 (for the whole siege, 171–232).

frontier towns (Quesada, Bedmar) had been taken by the Castilians. Even the Aragonese had been able to negotiate a face-saving release of prisoners.

Exactly why Naṣr fell is not clear. Ibn Khaldūn gives the explanation that he and his minister Ibn al-Ḥājj "displayed tendencies towards violence and injustice" and says he was unworthy to exercise power because of "his own wickedness and the stupidity of his family and of the court circle" (1898:411). Such hostile propaganda tells us little. Malaga, governed by Abū Saʿīd Faraj, seems to have been a hotbed of disaffection. In Malaga the Marīnid garrison under ʿUthmān b. Abīʾl-ʿUlā sided with the rebels against Naṣr, and was one of the supporters of Abū Saʿīd Faraj's son, Ismāʿīl, when he made his bid for the throne. On the other hand Naṣr's North African militias under the Zanāta princes ʿAbd al-Ḥaqq b. ʿUthmān and Ḥammū b. ʿAbd al-Ḥaqq b. Raḥḥū were faithful to him to the end. When Naṣr finally in 1314 had to abdicate in favor of Ismāʿīl, the Zanāta princes accompanied him to Guadix, where he still maintained his claim to power. Naṣr died leaving no heirs, fortunately perhaps for the unity of Granada.

Ismāʿīl, 1314–1325

With Ismāʿīl there came to power a distinct collateral branch of the Banūʾl-Aḥmar. (Naṣr was the last of the direct line going back to Muḥammad I.) We have seen that Naṣr was blamed (perhaps unfairly) for the insufficient energy which he brought to the conflict with the Christians. Ismāʿīl made it clear that he would undertake energetic campaigns on all fronts. His relative success is the more surprising because at this juncture he could not count on the assistance of the Marīnids, who were preoccupied elsewhere.

Naṣr in Guadix was being besieged by Ismāʿīl when the Castilians under the Infante Peter decided to stage a spectacular campaign against Ismāʿīl the troublemaker, demonstrating Castile's ability to support its allies. A great supply train of provisions with a powerful escort under the master of Calatrava, Garci López de Padilla, set out in the spring of 1316 to fight its way through to Naṣr in Guadix. It was intercepted by Granadan forces under ʿUthmān b. Abīʾl-ʿUlā, commander of the frontier volunteers (*ṣāḥib al-guzāt*). That a thrilling battle ensued seems to be agreed by all sources, Christian and Muslim, but the Castilians claim a great victory, with 1,540 killed on the Muslim side, whereas Arabic sources speak in glowing terms of Muslim heroism (BAE:LXVI, 180; *La Gran Crónica de Alfonso XI* 1976:297; Ibn al-Khaṭīb 1973:I, 379; Ibn Khaldūn 1961:VII, 183). Perhaps one may presume that the Christians did get the better of their adversaries, for they continued operations ever nearer to Granada, capturing castles, Cambil, and Algavardo, and even burning the outskirts of Iznalloz and laying siege to Belmez; no doubt some of the mobile column got through.

The outcome of another battle fought in 1319 leaves no room for doubt. The Castilians suffered a crushing defeat. The boldness of the Castilian military activities was such that the city of Granada itself was besieged by both Peter and John, regents of Castile during Alfonso XI's minority, and from the rashness of these forays the Castilian disaster of the Battle of the Vega stemmed.

> They went very close to Granada and they stayed there the next day, which was Midsummer's Day (1319) and a Sunday. Prince Peter wanted to go on farther, but Prince John did not, and on the Monday they had to turn back. Prince John was left to bring up the rear. He found himself so hard pressed by the Moors that he had to send to Prince Peter, who was leading the columns, to ask him for assistance. Peter turned back to help him immediately, and when he reached the place where John was, he tried to halt his knights and soldiery so as to make a charge against the enemy, but he was never able to do so, and on that day his men were so out of control [*mal mandados*] that he was never able to bring them into action against the Moors. The knights on that day were so disobedient and overawed [? *embazados*] that they could not handle their weapons. Prince Peter set his hand on his sword to lead them, but was able to do nothing. He was struck down by blows, and was left speechless, and fell from his horse dead on the ground. Only a few of the cavalry with him knew what had happened, and they immediately went to tell Prince John who was straightaway so overwhelmed by grief that he was deprived of his understanding and his speech. They kept him in this condition from midday till the evening, neither dead nor alive. The masters of Santiago, of Calatrava, of Alcántara, the archbishops of Toledo, and the men from Cordova who had all been traveling at the head of the column, were about half a league away waiting for Prince John and

> Prince Peter to catch up with them. When they heard that Prince Peter was dead they were all overcome by such terror [*desmayamiento*] that they all ran away.
>
> The Moors, who saw the cavalry grouped together and remaining still, did not know that Peter was dead, and John had lost use of his senses, so came to the conclusion they wanted to do battle. They then charged the Christian camp, pillaged it, and took everything they could lay hands on, and carried it back to Granada.
>
> As soon as the Christians saw this, they lifted Prince John, who was not yet dead, and set him on a horse, and they put Prince Peter across a mule, sideways, and began their journey. At nightfall Prince John died. They led his horse, but it became lost and remained behind in Moorish territory. The men bringing Prince Peter reached Priego, and thence made their way to Baena and Arjona. (BAE:LXVI, 183–84)

The discomfiture of the Christians at their defeat in what was called the Battle of the Vega was no doubt complete when Ismāʿīl had to be asked to institute a search for John's corpse. When it did eventually come to light, he had it kept in state in Granada, and sent it back with a large escort to Cordova (it was eventually interred at Burgos). One must add that even this chapter of disasters may be no more than a face-saving fiction of the Castilian chroniclers, and Muslim sources speak of an even more shameful end for the Prince's corpse. Al-ʿUmarī, writing in 1337 and so near enough to events, had it that "Peter's corpse is still in a coffin hung up in the Alhambra" (Arié 1973:97n3). By the seventeenth century al-Maqqarī claimed that "his skin was stuffed with cotton and hung up at the Alhambra gate, where it remained for several years" (1949:I, 425). In this way, and in one passage of arms, many of the leaders of Castilian society were wiped out, others overawed and demoralized. It was a major success for Ismāʿīl and his aggressive policies. As Ibn Khaldūn put it, "This was one of the most marvelous of God's interventions in favor of the true faith" (1898:412).

Ismāʿīl was able to pass over to the offensive, and he recaptured a string of frontier posts, Huéscar, Orce, Galera, Martos. For their part the Castilians were glad enough to be able to conclude long-term truces: in Andalusia one was settled for eight years (Tapia 1986:238). Castile was unlikely to cause trouble; quite apart from the losses inflicted in the

Battle of the Vega, it was torn apart by strife between factions of nobles during the minority of Alfonso XI.

If relations between Granada and Castile were characterized by such dramatic hostilities, those between Granada and Aragon seem to have been warm and friendly, and the disaster of Almería seems almost to have served to clear the air. A number of documents survive from the Aragonese diplomatic interchanges at this period (enough to make us realize what has been lost by the disappearance of the Granadan state archives). There is, for example, a curious short missive from Ismāʿīl's *wazīr* ʿUthmān b. Idrīs b. ʿAbdallah (Alarcón and García de Linares 1940:41–42). Apparently an ambassador from Granada to Egypt, al-Ḥājj Aḥmad b. ʿAbd al-Salām by name, had returned from Alexandria to Barcelona (or possibly Valencia), and while in Christian territory was liberally entertained by James II and assigned a house in which to reside. When he was on his way back to Granada, Aḥmad was to discover to his horror that he had left behind him in the house a big wooden document box containing the official correspondence from the sultan of Egypt! The *wazīr* wrote requesting that a search be made and the box sent on. The story sounds scarcely credible (unless the Granadans *wanted* the Aragonese to read the Egyptian documents). We unfortunately hear no more of the incident, but good relations do not seem to have been interrupted.

Many of the diplomatic missives are concerned with the cases of prisoners being held by the other side. In some, the prisoners are returned, in some the authorities on the other side say they know nothing of the people in question, or they deny that the prisoners are being detained illegally. Relations, then, were sometimes tense, but the channels of communication were open, negotiations were going on. It is too easy to assume that at all times Granada's relations with the other states of the peninsula were hostile. For long periods of time Granada conducted foreign relations with its peninsular neighbors in exactly the same way as relations might be carried on between any pair of sovereign states.

It is towards the end of Ismāʿīl's reign that we begin to hear of one Yūsuf b. Muḥammad Ibn Kumāsha (or Aben Comixa in the Castilian-style spelling which renders faithfully the typical Andalusian pronunciation of *a* as *i*). He was then governor of Vera, the outpost of the kingdom which lay farthest to the north and east. On its security clearly depended the whole hinterland of Almería. The family were to produce leaders and statesmen in Granadan service right up to 1492. The Banū Kumāsha were one of the great dynasties of public servants and military men on whom Granada depended.

In 1323, when the truces between Granada and Castile ran out, both sides became active again on the frontiers. The Granadans suffered a defeat at sea, for the Castilian admiral Jofre Tenorio, who had experienced such a reverse at Algeciras, routed a Granadan fleet, and allegedly shipped twelve hundred captives (the figure seems very high) to Seville (BAE:LXVI, 202–7).

One curious detail that emerges from the confused frontier skirmishes is that the Muslims appear to have made use of a cannon for the first time in warfare in the peninsula in an attack on Huéscar in 1324. It may seem strange that there is any doubt as to whether a cannon was used or not, but it was Ibn al-Khaṭīb who recorded the event (1955:398 or 1973:392), and his allusive and metaphorical style leaves the way open to more than one interpretation. A great deal turns on how we read one key word: *nafṭ*. In Arabic this term is applied to various flammable substances (in the modern world it is "petroleum"). Arié (173:261) very reasonably takes it as "Greek fire." However, in the Arabic of Spain in the fifteenth century it could also mean "gunpowder" and "cannon." It is perhaps in one of these senses that it occurs here (see Dozy 1927 s.v. *nafṭ* for reference to early discussion of this very passage). What may help to decide against Greek fire is that both Ibn al-Khaṭīb and another eyewitness stress the thunderous noise made by the device as it projected its iron ball (*kurra ḥadīdin*). If this interpretation is correct, Granada must have been in the forefront of technical innovation in the world at this time. The new weapon was a success, for Huéscar hastened to surrender, but there is nothing to indicate that it had any more general impact on the fighting.

It might have seemed after the triumph of the Battle of the Vega that Ismāʿīl was destined to enjoy a long and successful reign. The circumstances that led to his violent death arose as an indirect consequence of one of his successful frontier raids. From the victory at Martos a cousin of Ismāʿīl called, somewhat confusingly, Muḥammad b. Ismāʿīl took as a captive a Christian woman. According to the *Chronicle of Alfonso XI,* "the king sent and required him to hand the woman over, and when he did not wish to do so, spoke harshly to him. ʿUthmān then conferred with this Muḥammad, cousin of Ismāʿīl, and with this Muḥammad's brother and his son, and they agreed to kill the king because he had spoken to him without respect, and ʿUthmān agreed to provide assistance" (BAE:LXVI, 206).

This ʿUthmān is none other than ʿUthmān b. Abīʾl-ʿUlā, commander of the Volunteers of the Faith. The Castilian chronicle goes into great detail on how the plot was put into effect. How a Castilian historian could have secured access to eyewitnesses of these events is not clear, and we may well have reservations about accepting this account of what went on behind closed doors in the palace.

> Thirteen days after the raid on Martos, when the king was in the Alhambra, Muḥammad, son of the governor of Algeciras, with his brother and his son, came to see him. They had each secreted a dagger in the sleeve of their gown [*aljuba*] and told the king they wished to speak to him. He went to one side with them, taking with him his chief minister [the minister is not named in the Castilian sources, it was Ibn al-Maḥrūq]. As they made their way from one chamber to another down a narrow passage, two of the men went ahead of the king, and he came behind with the third, having the minister at his back. In this passage Muḥammad and his son turned on the king, and with the knives in their hands wounded him about the head. The minister drew his sword and began to strike out in the king's defense at those who sought to kill him. Muḥammad's brother, the one who remained behind, struck out at the minister, but he, outraged at the assault on his master, interposed himself to ward off the blows they were raining on him, and did not look round at the man who was attacking him. With his sword the minister was able to drive the two out of the passage, and shut the door against them. Meanwhile Muḥammad's brother managed to reach the king, and clutched him to himself, driving a pointed dagger into his back through his shoulder, and from that the king subsequently died.
>
> When the minister got back to the king, he found him wounded, and immediately rushed at the man who had inflicted the wound and put him to flight. The man fled into a chamber in which the minister shut him, and then he returned to the king, to find him fainting from his wounds, principally from the one he had received in the shoulder. He picked him up in his arms, and attempting to bring him round, he bore him to a chamber where his mother, the queen, was. There he had the wounds bound and

sent for surgeons. He told the king to be of good courage and said that he would go to mete out justice to those who had done that thing.

He immediately went out to the courtyard of the Alhambra, where he found the people in an uproar, for there were some there privy to the plot to kill the king. They asked him how the king was, and he told them he was alive and well. He called on some of those on whom he knew he could rely for help, and told them to go into the Alhambra, and with them went to the rooms in which the attackers had been shut, and he cut off their heads. He then returned to the king, who was being examined by the surgeons, and saw him very much weakened.

He went to the gate of the Alhambra, where he found ʿUthmān [b. Abīʾl-ʿUlā] and all the mounted guard. ʿUthmān asked him how the king was. "Alive and well," the minister answered, and he said that he had given orders to arrest some of those who were in the plot to kill him. ʿUthmān, in order to give the impression that he was not privy to the plot, and also because he had been told the king was alive and well, agreed to go and help. The minister left careful instructions on how he was to be received when he returned to the Alhambra, and went down to the city accompanied by ʿUthmān, and arrested all those who were relatives of Muḥammad, son of the governor of Algeciras, and all their friends whom he suspected of having joined in the plot. He then returned to the Alhambra and killed them all, then went to the chamber where the king was, and found him about to die. He remained with him comforting him till he died.

As soon as King Ismāʿīl was dead, the minister sent word to ʿUthmān and the mounted guard to come there because the king wished to speak with them. ʿUthmān was afraid that the king was still alive, and that he knew how he had been in the plot to kill him, so he called his sons and grandsons and relatives, and all his friends, and they all came to the gate of the Alhambra armed.

Once they had assembled, the minister came out, bearing the eldest of the king's three sons in his arms, a young boy called Muḥammad. The minister told ʿUthmān and all the mounted guard that the king was dead, and that he had given orders that they should accept this son of his as king. ʿUthmān, because of the suspicions he held, and also because he thought he might do better

> under a boy king than under his father, was much pleased and began to shout aloud, "We have a king!" All the people who had come did the same, and went through the town shouting, "We have a king. Muḥammad son of Ismāʿīl is our lord." (BAE:LXVI, 206–7)

As we might expect in such a shady affair, accounts of what happened do not coincide at all. Ibn Khaldūn (*History of the Banūʾ l Aḥmar*) says that the anti-Ismāʿīl plot was instigated by "one of his relatives of the Banū Naṣr family" and that the assassin, after taking refuge in ʿUthmān's house, was "killed by him immediately, and the black guard and the army straightaway put to death all those suspected of siding with the assassin" (1898:413). One narrative is designed to exonorate Ibn al-Maḥrūq and the other to perform the same function for ʿUthmān b. Abīʾl-ʿUlā!

Muḥammad IV, 1325–1333

As might have been expected, rivalries between ʿUthmān and Ibn al-Maḥrūq characterized the early years of Muḥammad IV's reign. In 1328, three years after he was proclaimed, the young king himself brought the dissensions to an end by having Ibn al-Maḥrūq assassinated: "At his [Muḥammad's] order, the foreign guard put him to death by the scimitar, and the king took control of the government himself, ʿUthmān becoming once more commander of the frontier warriors, and of the North African troops, with his son Abū Thābit nominated as his successor" (Ibn Khaldūn 1898:413–14).

In the same year Alfonso XI had come of age. The dissensions within Granada emboldened the Castilians to resume hostilities which had remained largely in suspense after the disaster of the Battle of the Vega in 1319. A great international crusade was planned, with participation from France and Navarre, from England and Bohemia, not to mention Aragon. The very diversity of this army was its downfall. Castile hesitated to assign garrison towns to these foreign troops. The Castilians and the church wrangled over the degree of financial support that could be accorded. The international crusade came to nothing.

The Christian forces that did take the field against Granada in 1330 were Castilian, and they were not unsuccessful: they took Teba (to the west of Antequera) (BAE:LXVI, 256–57). Faced with this renewed danger from the north, Muḥammad IV decided to call in North African help, and himself crossed to Morocco to negotiate direct with the Marīnid sultan. The request came at a difficult moment, as the sultan was dealing with a rebellion led by his brother ʿUmar, but some aid was spared (and despatched, it might be added, in Genoese ships). In 1333 a five-month siege yielded the prize of Gibraltar (BAE:LXVI, 248; Ibn Khaldūn 1969:IV, 216–18), which was taken from the Castilians by Marīnid forces. Alfonso XI hastened to sign a truce (BAE:LXVI, 257) in August of that same year (the Aragonese had done the same a month earlier).

It is strange that discontent in Granada with the decision once again to call in North African help should have been led by the chief of the existing North African militias, ʿUthmān b. Abīʾl-ʿUlā.

Ibn Khaldūn puts it as follows: "The Banū Abīʾl-ʿUlā had not looked kindly on the alliance of the king [Muḥammad IV] with Abūʾl-Ḥasan [the Marīnid], and entered into a plot which brought about the king's death, pierced with lance thrusts as he was returning to Granada from Gibraltar" (1898:414).

The Castilian chronicle presents things from a Castilian viewpoint. Ibn Khaldūn sees the rebels as troubled by Muḥammad's Marīnid contacts, whereas the Castilian chronicle explains his downfall as due to his Castilian contacts. Just before his death, Muḥammad had been in negotiation with Alfonso XI, and they had banqueted together, and exchanged presents.

> Because at the meeting which the king of Granada had with the king of Castile they stayed talking with each other a long time, the Banū Abīʾl-ʿUlā [the Castilian text calls them *fijos de Ozmín*], who had been there, thought the talk must have been to their disadvantage. When the king of Granada had pitched his camp by the River Guadiaro, he sent for his chief minister to determine with him the route they were to take to Malaga, and also how he was to route various people he had brought with him so they might reach their destinations. The king had put on a garment [*crocha*] that had been presented to him by the king of Castile: it was of very fine cloth, and superbly ornamented. The sons of ʿUthmān [*fijos de Ozmín*], Abotebe [Abū Thābit] and Ibrāhīm, wishing to kill their king, said that because he had eaten with the king of Castile and because he was wearing his clothes, he was a Christian. This they recounted to those on whom they counted for

> assistance. They all went to the tent where their king was, and once there they unsheathed their swords and killed him. This was on August 25.
>
> A Moor called Riḍwān, son of a Christian man and a Christian woman, a person in whom the king always placed great trust, was there with the king, although not in his tent. As soon as he learned his master was dead, he left the camp, and, riding as fast as he was able, he reached Granada, entered the Alhambra, and of the king's two brothers, Faraj and Yūsuf, he proclaimed the younger, Yūsuf, as king. And the Banū'l-ʿUthmān and all the rest of the people in the kingdom accepted him as their king. (BAE:LXVI, 258)

The bloody pattern of Granadan politics had thus been confirmed. After the relative stability of the long reigns of Muḥammad I and Muḥammad II, and the relative restraint of the way in which both Muḥammad III and Naṣr were allowed to live on after being deposed, both Ismāʿīl (in 1325) and Muḥammad IV (in 1333) met their end in treacherous attacks. The two stories recounted about the death of Muḥammad IV point in the two directions from which stress was being exerted in this regime. Placed uneasily between Castile and North Africa, Granada could ignore neither. A Granadan ruler needed North African aid, but he might displease his own troops by relying too much on outside help. A Granadan king needed an understanding with Castile, but his people might hate him if they thought he was being too pro-Castilian. To maintain some equilibrium between these two forces was virtually impossible, and it must have seemed at this point that Granada could scarcely hope to last for long and would soon be swallowed by Castile or the Marīnids. That Granada was to last a century and a half more was due to the genius of a very great ruler, Yūsuf I. Up to this point Granada is remarkable because it survived against all probabilities. From this point onwards, there begins the creation of the edifice of an Islamic culture which makes the kingdom not merely a political curiosity but a lively center of artistic and literary creativity which could not be omitted from any survey of the achievements of Islamic culture worldwide.

Not that Yūsuf's achievements were to save him from being caught up ultimately in the terrible pattern of bloodshed and violent death.

THIRTEEN

Yūsuf I

(1333–1354)

The solidity of Yūsuf I's contribution to Granadan life and culture is made apparent to any visitor to the Alhambra nowadays: an inscription records his construction of the Puerta de la Justicia, the massive gateway permitting access to the palace complex. No longer in existence is his major creation, the monumental *madrasa* or college for the city. Yūsuf presided over the beginning of what was undoubtedly the Golden Age of Granadan cultural achievements, but he was also ruler at the time of the greatest single reverse suffered by the Muslim cause in Spain until the final loss of Granada in 1492: the Christian victory of Salado in 1340. Yūsuf does not appear to have had blame imputed to him for Salado. As a leader he appears to have enjoyed the trust of his subjects.

We are told by Ibn Khaldūn that "as soon as Abū Ḥajjāj Yūsuf [Yūsuf I] came to power, he hastened to take revenge for his brother [Muḥammad IV], drove out the Banū Abī 'l-ʿUlā into exile in Tunisia, and appointed Yaḥyā b. ʿUmar b. Raḥḥū, one of the Banū Raḥḥū b. ʿAbd al-Ḥaqq, as commander of those fighting on the frontier in the holy war, in the place of Abū Thābit" (1898:414). By the standard of acts of revenge in those days, it must be said that this was quite restrained, but it will be recalled that in the version recorded by Ibn Khaldūn, ʿUthmān was claiming that far from being the assassin, he was the assassin's executioner.

Yūsuf could not risk alienating North African sympathies: he needed an inflow of Volunteers, and in fact his next action was to cross the straits and seek from Abū'l-Ḥasan further military assistance (Ibn Khaldūn 1898:414). Abū'l-Ḥasan sent his son Abū Mālik, who in 1339 would meet his death at the hands of a Castilian raiding party.

The Muslim states of the west and the Christian kingdoms of the peninsula, above all Castile, had all been locked in a succession of combats for more than half a century, disputing the mastery of the Straits of Gibraltar. Associated with this conflict was the question of the extent to which the Marīnids (or other North African powers) might establish control in the peninsula similar to that enjoyed in earlier ages by Almoravids or Almohads. That conflict over the straits was about to be resolved in favor of the Castilians, and as for the Marīnids, they were to become less and less interested in peninsular affairs. It might seem likely that the new situation would create insuperable problems for the Naṣrids, but Yūsuf and his successors proved able to accommodate themselves to the new power balance.

Yūsuf had made truces with Castile after his accession, and then entered into a formal tripartite peace with Castile and with the Marīnids. The Castilian chronicle presents the negotiations as initially taking place between the Marīnids and Castile, with Yūsuf being brought in only at a later stage:

> Albohasan [Abū ʾl-Ḥasan], king of the lands beyond the sea [*allén mar,* i.e., North Africa] ordered King Abū Mālik, his son, to despatch two of his knights to the king of Castile with letters and a message to say that he desired a truce for some period of time. Abū Mālik was told that if he were asked whether King Abū ʾl-Ḥasan and his army would be included in the truce, he should reply that he did not know, but if the king of Castile were to send emissaries to enquire, he did not doubt but that he would receive a satisfactory reply. . . .
>
> The king of Castile, . . . seeing it suited him to have a truce of some length with the Moors, sent as his emissary Gonzalo García de Gallegos, alcalde mayor of Seville, to Abū ʾl-Ḥasan to invite him to have Abū Mālik request a truce, and to this Abū ʾl-Ḥasan agreed, but he added that since the newly appointed king of Granada had only just sent him an embassy asking to be placed under his protection, he asked that the king of Granada be allowed to enter the negotiations as liege man [*ome*] of King Abū ʾl-Ḥasan, and that out of respect for King Abū ʾl-Ḥasan the king of Castile should do away with the tribute payments [*parias*] which the kings of Granada had paid in times of truce. . . .
>
> The king of Castile, seeing he had no alternative to concluding a truce and peace with the Moors for some period of time, because he needed to bring peace to his own realms, sent to tell Gonzalo

> García to sign for four years on the conditions described. This the envoy did, bringing the documents containing the terms back sealed with King Abū'l-Ḥasan's gold seal. (BAE:LXVI, 259–60)

It will be seen that this account places Granada as a pawn between the two great powers, and shows that Castile was willing formally to renounce its right to *parias*.

Castile was seeking peace because of its own grave internal problems with rebellious nobles. Both sides still had their attention very much concentrated on the straits, where each side was building up naval strength. Quite why the Castilian admiral Alfonso Jofre Tenorio should in 1340 have allowed his ships to become committed to battle is not clear, for they were much outnumbered. It would seem that he had been criticized for his over-prudent avoidance of combat, and perhaps he allowed himself to be trapped in a battle in which his forces were weaker than those of the Muslims because he felt he had to show his readiness to fight.

When he sailed into an attack on the combined Granadan and Marīnid fleets, very few of his ships responded to his trumpet and drum summons to battle. His ships met with disaster. Jofre himself, clutching his battle standard, had one leg cut from under him and then died from a blow to the head from an iron bar.

> And the Christians in the other galleys and sailing ships who had not wished to join in the battle, as soon as they saw the battle standard lowered, and the other galleys lost, abandoned the galleys in which they were, and took refuge in the sailing ships. In the slight breeze which arose they made off towards Cartagena, leaving their galleys abandoned in the water. The Moors, seeing them make off like this, went to the galleys and captured them intact, with all their oars, sails, and equipment, so that of all the fleet which the king of Castile had there, not more than five galleys escaped. (BAE:LXVI, 307–8; *La Gran Crónica de Alfonso XI* 1977: II, 318, esp. 324)

It is not surprising that Abū'l-Ḥasan saw this Castilian naval disaster as a great opportunity. He crossed the straits not only with his troops but with his court, his wives, and all his entourage, and he besieged Tarifa, having brought with him at least twenty siege engines. When Alfonso XI decided to send a relief column to Tarifa, many thought

Tarifa not worth defending. Thanks to Alfonso XI's marriage to a Portuguese princess, his relations with Portugal were good, and the king of Portugal himself came to lead his troops (BAE:LXVI, 324). The combined Christian troops stood firm in the battle of Salado, the Muslims broke and fled in what was obviously a confused rout:

> Although the Moors suffered heavy casualties, things would have gone much worse for them if the Christians had not stopped at the Moorish camp to kill and capture the Moors of Abū᾿l-Ḥasan's household, his wives and little children, and to loot the gold and silver objects there. Amongst the womenfolk were Fāṭima, wife of Abū᾿l-Ḥasan, and daughter of the king of Tunis, the most honored wife he had, also one of his sisters called Umm al-Fatā, and three other freeborn wives of the king. Other women, Christian and Muslim, belonging to the king were killed, or captured and enslaved. The victor of this battle was God, who granted that not more than fifteen or twenty of the knights on the Christian side should be killed, whereas on the Muslim side very many were killed or captured. (BAE:LXVI, 327; also *La Gran Crónica de Alfonso XI* 1977:II, 433–34)

Why did Yūsuf and his North African allies meet with such a crushing defeat at Salado? Huici in the most authoritative study (1956:342–77) of the battle gives the number of Granadan troops as seven thousand and the North Africans as sixty thousand. On the Christian side, besides Alfonso XI's twelve thousand infantry and eight thousand cavalry, there were the thousand Portuguese knights with Alfonso IV, and in addition there were many urban militias and even men from as far away as the Basque provinces and Asturias. The Muslims probably had superior numbers, but the crucial factor was the Christian use of the highly-developed heavy cavalry charge. This was a form of fighting to which the aristocratic society of Western Europe had a heavy ideological commitment. Muslim cavalry, on the other hand, was lightly armed, and in conditions of open warfare often left the Christian knights with their heavy armor floundering and helpless. On the relatively constricted Tarifa battlefield, however, the ability of the Christian battle line to smash in a disciplined way through their enemy's ranks gave them superiority. Abū᾿l-Ḥasan had brought his forces to fight on the terrain best suited to the Castilians.

For Abū᾿l-Ḥasan the reverse might well have brought him trouble at home, and his immediate reaction was to cross the straits as soon as possible so as to take a firm grip on events in Morocco. Yūsuf fled to Granada (BAE:LXVI, 327–28).

Such was the quantity of precious metal taken by the Christians that although Alfonso XI strove to control the situation, the bullion markets in Paris, Avignon, Valencia, Barcelona, Pamplona, and Estella saw the price fall by one-sixth! (BAE:LXVI, 330)

Alfonso's prime objective was now Algeciras, the port with the best harbor facilities near the straits, but in the aftermath of Salado he set in train a number of other attacks at points on the frontier, such as Alcalá de Benzaide, Priego, and Benamejí. Although the fighting at Alcalá (Alcalá la Real on modern maps) was on a relatively small scale, the accounts which we have of the siege do serve to convey very graphically the nature of frontier warfare at this period, and it is worth our while to examine some of the principal stages of the assault. Our account will follow *La Gran Crónica de Alfonso XI* (cap. cclvii; BAE:LXVI, 332–4).

The Siege of Alcalá de Benzaide

Alfonso's besieging forces at first encamped round the town in such a way as to leave gaps through which the townsfolk could easily slip in and out with supplies. This initial error was soon corrected, and the besieging forces settled down to wait. As they waited, their own food supplies ran low, and they could only be revictualed from Jaén, at least seventy kilometers away, or from Cordova, even farther. What is more, the castle of Locubín, some ten kilometers to the north, was still in Muslim hands, and Castilian pack trains were being picked off by raiders from Locubín. This led to a decision to besiege that castle too, and one siege engine and two catapults had to be diverted from Alcalá for the purpose. After the Muslims in Locubín had been pinned down, supplies got through more regularly to the besiegers at Alcalá.

The initial onslaught on Alcalá had enabled the Christians to penetrate outer defenses, but the main city wall had held. Eight catapults were in use, launching stones at a tower believed to contain a well, the stronghold's only supply of water. This was a solid structure, and the stones made very little impression on it, so there was nothing for it but to begin sapping. Tunnels were started at some distance away, the aim being to undermine the tower and leave it resting on an underground scaffold of pit props, which could then be removed suddenly, causing the tower to fall and thus depriving the defenders of their water. This task was considered so important that members of the king's household were assigned to supervise the work and ensure it was progressing satisfactorily. While the attackers were waiting for the underground sap to be constructed, raiding parties were sent off to loot the countryside. Such activity no doubt had the attraction that it permitted those taking part to indulge in authorized theft, violence, and destruction, but there was a strategic justification in that it created round the town a zone deprived of its own food, and thus unable to supply those besieged. In this case there was obviously ill-will involved, for the looters not only took grain and vegetables but also cut out vines—an act of destruction that did them no good, but would affect the area over several years.

After the king had completed his forays, he returned to supervise the work of his engineers, not only at Alcalá but at Locubín. At this point in the action, news came that Yūsuf I had moved up his troops to Pinos on the Granada road, presumably because the Granadans feared that Alfonso would extend his raids into the rich *vega* of Granada itself. Should the Castilians take this opportunity to come to battle with the Granadans, normally so elusive? Alfonso decided against any such course, because the Granadan army was situated in a tactically strong position, protected by irrigation ditches, so that the Castilians would be fighting at a disadvantage. The Castilians determined to extend the zone they were pillaging and burning towards Locubín, another rich and productive region, in hope that the Granadans would be tempted to leave their excellent defensive position at Pinos to protect the poor farmers of Locubín. It was felt they would almost certainly do this, and ambushes were set up to trap them, but the Muslims were not so foolish, and the main Granadan army remained in its post. The Castilians' response was to extend the area of devastation towards Illora.

Meanwhile at Locubín the commander of the attackers, Alfonso Ferrández Coronel, had kept up such a rain of missiles day and night from his two catapults that the defenders sued for peace, offering to hand over the castle with all its supplies if only they were allowed to march out alive. The king accepted the offer and redoubled the attack on Alcalá, and above all the tower containing the well. Before long the tower was resting only on wooden scaffold poles. The plan was to set these ablaze, and to make the consequent collapse of the tower coincide with an all-out assault on the city walls, so that if Muslim reinforcements managed to plug the gap where the tower collapsed, there was a good chance of entering elsewhere on the perimeter. The carpenters and other specialists who had constructed the scaffolding set it alight during one night, and well before dawn the whole structure fell in. There had been four guards on duty on the top of the tower. Two of these fell to their deaths, but in the confusion the two others scrambled to safety.

When dawn came Alfonso inspected what his engineers had achieved. The well was completely blocked, but such was the strength of the natural situation of the town, protected by a sheer slope, that the ring of defenses was in fact still intact, so that he did not after all order an assault.

The king thought he had cut off the only water supply, so presumably he judged that before long Alcalá would be reduced by thirst into suing for surrender, but from Martos to the north, on the road to Jaén, came bad news. The military order of Calatrava held the castle there, and one of their Muslim captives, a man born and brought up in Alcalá, revealed that there was an alternative water supply. He knew of a well the existence of which few people suspected: it was actually outside Alcalá, but could be reached from inside the town by an underground flight of steps. If the king would free him, he promised to show where the well was.

Naturally the king had the Muslim prisoner brought up to the front, and when the location of the well was identified, the Christians began with great enthusiasm to dig towards the water from the outside. They made rapid progress, and came across a great vault full of an abundant supply of excellent water, but as they broke in, they found the vault occupied by Muslim guards who attempted to keep them out with their spears and crossbows. The Christians were, however, able to drive the Muslims back, and from that time onwards they had to post their own guards underground night and day to keep the Muslims from returning. This underground warfare went on several days, with the Christians at times being driven out, only to return.

While all this was going on under the surface, aboveground the Castilians were extending the zone they were devastating in the direction of Pliego, and this meant bringing into the picture Juan Manuel, who was entrusted with the execution of some of the scorched earth policy. The king was not pleased with the way the task was carried out, and said that he would have to do the job again himself. It is obviously impossible to guess what lay behind this wrangle, which may have stemmed in the main from a clash of personalities, but one has to bear in mind that Juan Manuel may have been avoiding an over-zealous elimination of agricultural resources because he would need to bring the land back into production in the future, whereas the king would have had as his priority starving the local Muslims into surrender.

The king had to turn aside from the burning of Muslim crops because an important visitor arrived. To replace the admiral Jofre Tenorio, who had died so courageously, and so unsuccessfully, off Algeciras, Alfonso XI had appointed a Genoese naval expert, Egidio (Gil) Boccanegra, and he came to report for duty. Boccanegra was to play an important part in Spanish history and incidentally in that of the Mudejars; he has already been mentioned in relation to the establishment of a new Mudejar community in Palma del Río.

Since Boccanegra had brought fifteen galleys to serve in the Castilian navy, and they were lying at anchor in the Guadalquivir, the king's first concern had to be to get them into effective use, and he had to turn aside from the small-scale fighting round Alcalá. Hardly had Boccanegra been attended to when there appeared on the scene at Alcalá a youth who was a Christian, but who said he had been sent by Yūsuf I with despatches for Alcalá; he had been told he could expect to bring back a reply.

Our source does not tell us whether this mysterious Christian messenger working for Yūsuf I fell into Alfonso's hand as a prisoner, or whether he traveled openly. Alfonso naturally took the letters, read them—or rather had them read, as they were presumably in Arabic—and then handed them back. The boy was told to enter the town by night, and to bring the reply back to the king. In order to make sure this happened, a special watch was kept.

At dawn the next day the boy emerged, and took the despatches which had been entrusted to him by the people of Alcalá. When they were read, the king deduced that Alcalá was very short indeed of food and water, for the townsfolk were appealing urgently for assistance. He was, however, suspicious, and kept Alcalá under close observation, abandoning his program of laying further cultivated areas waste, and meanwhile encouraging the siege artillery to keep up their hail of rocks.

When the king of Granada had news of the dire straits of the Muslims of Alcalá, he decided to send to Algeciras to request more aid from his North African allies. The chronicle tells us that he was sent a thousand mounted troops in return, but this seems an extraordinarily large number. With the reinforcements, Yūsuf moved forward to Moclín, a place some ten kilometers ahead of the position at Pinos. Such an advance implied exposing the Granadan forces considerably. Alfonso left all the siege operations in the hands of others, and moved out to set up an ambush. The master of Santiago, Alfonso Méndez, was then sent to patrol near the Granadan position, no doubt with the object of tempting the Granadan army to break ranks and attack him, but Granadan discipline must have been good, for although the master tried all day, nothing happened. On the following day the same tactic was repeated, and this time a few Muslims did take up the challenge, but then desisted. That night Alfonso returned from his ambush to the Castilian camp, and Yūsuf remained in occupation of Moclín.

At this juncture the Muslims of Alcalá concluded that relief was not going to reach them, and they offered to surrender the castle with all its grain store and weapons in exchange for a safe conduct. Alfonso considered the bargain a good one, for he was not certain of being able to take Alcalá by storm, and if he accepted Alcalá in this way, there would still be time for him to undertake further operations that summer. The Muslims were accordingly given safe conduct to Moclín, and not one of them came to harm.

When Alfonso had occupied Alcalá, Yūsuf sent offering a period of truce, and even to renew his payments of *parias* and to be his vassal, so long as the Marīnid Abū'l-Ḥasan would join in the agreement. Alfonso said that he was willing to accept the truce and the *parias* and the vassalage, but that Yūsuf would have to break with the North Africans. This Yūsuf refused to do, negotiations failed, and Yūsuf returned to his capital.

Although relatively inconclusive, this minor incident of the border wars brings home the varied scale of the hostilities: at one moment the protagonists would have been concerned with a handful of men locked in hand-to-hand combat down a pit, at another, with negotiations involving forces from Spain, Italy, and North Africa, and large-scale, almost geopolitical calculations. In this kind of fighting, personal courage was always required, but so were alertness, intelligence, and the ability to grasp complex strategic issues. The Castilian account has shown us, from a Castilian vantage point, Yūsuf with great wisdom refusing to be tempted to expose his vital home territory, the *vega* of Granada, to the danger of attack, even when his Muslim subjects in an outlying stronghold were being pressed beyond endurance.

The major engagement for which Yūsuf I had to prepare was Alfonso XI's assault on Algeciras. Salado had been a victory that had weakened the Muslim hold in the hinterland; a Christian attempt to take the great port through which North African troops and supplies passed so easily was inevitable. But neither Granadans nor Moroccans were prepared to give up such a vital facility easily. When the siege began in 1342–1343, the Castilian army was reinforced with contingents large and small from all over Western Europe, even from England, whence came two great nobles described as "the Count of Arbi and the Count of Solusber," along with their own companies. Solusber is not hard to identify as the earl of Salisbury, but if it were not for the fact that he is described in the chronicle as "of highest birth, and of the lineage of kings" one might fail to perceive behind Arbi, Henry, from 1352 duke of Lancaster, but from 1337 earl of Derby (d'Arbi) (BAE:LXVI, 360). Both, we are told, came for the salvation of their souls and also to get to know the king. At this point in the struggle, with the Christian army poised to take the great port facing Africa, and with the glory of the victory of Tarifa very fresh in Christians' minds, the spirit of the crusade came to be a factor in the situation. Many bulls of crusade had been granted by popes before, and were to be granted in the future before the final victory of 1492, but rarely did a crusading enterprise so catch the imagination of Christendom. The attack on Algeciras did bring men together from all over the West.

In the history of warfare it is surprising that the siege of Algeciras has not attracted more attention from those interested in the development of weapons and tactics. It is a key battle in a period of rapid change and transition in techniques and in the design of equipment. It was fought with an array of mechanical devices, ranging from bows and arrows to catapults and other stone-projecting engines of war, but it is as the first major engagement in the Iberian Peninsula at which cannon were used that it is really memorable. It is, in fact, one of the earliest of such engagements anywhere (Crécy, 1346, has been much cited).

A widespread mistaken interpretation of the text of the Castilian chronicle has led to the innovation being ascribed to the Castilians, but there can be no doubt that what the chronicle says is that the Muslim defenders brought the new weapons into use at Algeciras (they did not assure them of victory, as we shall see). Although cannon at Algeciras had no decisive influence on the outcome of the battle, it is a matter of some interest to determine under what circumstances cannon-like devices came to be employed. The chronicler is concerned to stress the difficulties experienced by those constructing the siege works, such as trenches and assault towers, outside the city walls: a rain of missiles from the defenders on the walls fell on the engineers exposed on the half-finished military structures. Among the hazards to be endured by these engineers were cannonballs:

> The work on the assault platforms [*bastidas*] and the need to assure their protection lasted for several days. Because this was so close to the city, the Christians suffered greatly, for they needed to wear their armor day and night, as they were taking casualties from arrows, stones, and spears. They were also shooting stones at them with siege engines [*engeños*] and with catapults [*cabritas*], and also many iron balls which they projected by bombards [*truenos*, lit., "thunders"], of which the men were much afraid, for if anybody were hit in a limb by them, it was cut clean off, as if by a knife, and if a man were only very slightly wounded by them, he would die straight away, and no surgery was of any avail. This was in part because the iron balls came burning hot like fire, and partly because the powder with which they were shot was of such a nature, that whatever wound they caused, a man would die of it immediately. They were shot so hard that they went straight through a man with all his armor. But the siege platforms were completed, even though many Christians died, both from among the construction workers and among those on guard duty. . . .
>
> The worst casualties were suffered by the Christians up on the platform. While on guard duty one day on these siege towers, a gentleman called Beltrán Duque, who had lived with the king for some time, and who was from Majorca, was hit in the arm by a ball from one of the bombards, and it cut it off, and he died on the very next day. The same thing happened to all those wounded by the bombards. (BAE:LXVI, 359)

Although the Spanish text is most erratic in its use of pronouns, so that on grammatical grounds it might be possible to argue that in the third sentence quoted above, "they" refers to the Christians firing against the Muslims, this interpretation is not possible if one reads the passage as a whole, and particularly if one bears in mind that the only named casualty of the bombardment was Beltrán Duque of the Castilian king's own household. The Muslim defenders of Algeciras were firing iron cannonballs down on the assault troops from the battlements of the town, and there is no indication that the Christians were able to reply in kind.

One curious aspect of the account of the wounds inflicted by these early guns is the stress on their lethal nature even when they were quite superficial. One cannot exclude the possibility that there may have been a psychological effect at work: the terror created by the bombardment is explicitly mentioned, so perhaps we have here an early account of an extreme form of shellshock, or simply exaggeration. The chronicle itself may be correct, though, in pointing to the nature of the gunpowder itself as a cause. Early gunpowder incorporated saltpeter, and although pure mineral saltpeter might have been available in southern Spain, a far more likely source of supply at this time would be the scraping of crust deposits from the walls of stables and similar farm buildings, so that the risk from tetanus may have been high.

The Castilian attempts to penetrate the defenses of Algeciras failed, but somehow the Castilian forces were kept in the field in spite of all the difficulties. The foreign contingents, however enthusiastic, did not always remain: the English nobles excused themselves on the grounds that a diplomatic mission had to be executed at the papal court (BAE:LXVI, 370); the count of Foix pleaded business back home (though he let it be known that if payment were forthcoming he might stay on), the king of Navarre fell mortally ill and had to leave, but perhaps worst of all Alfonso XI had no confidence in the Genoese ships which formed such an important part of his naval forces, especially after the defeat of Jofre Tenorio. It was at root a question of finance, and the king had to scrape together what resources he could. "He took all the silver plate off which he ate, and the drinking vessels of his household, and also all the plate of those nobles and prelates who were present there with him, and all that of the officials of his household, and collected together whatever he could, and with this, and such money as he could borrow, here and there, he made a payment to them" (BAE:LXVI, 379).

If the Castilian ability to sustain their campaign was very much in doubt, so that possibly if it had not been for the stubborn determination of Alfonso XI the siege would have collapsed, on the Granadan side the ability to resist was also weak, and the long campaign was bringing a desire to seek a negotiated peace. But in the diplomatic maze of international relations there could be many obstacles to achieving peace, and the principal parties on each side, Yūsuf and Alfonso, had to reckon with problems created by allies (Alfonso found the Genoese particularly difficult). Yūsuf knew how Alfonso's allies were evaporating, and he sensed the moment was propitious:

> The king of Granada thought that he might be able to liberate Algeciras by making a payment in cash [*doblas*] to Alfonso, for he was very reluctant to come to battle. He knew that the king of Navarre had left, and the counts, so he thought the king of Castile might more readily open negotiations. As his emissaries, Yūsuf sent the honored *alcaides* he had employed on former occasions, Abomayn Roduan [his *ḥājib* Riḍwān] and Hasan Algarrafa. When the emissaries had delivered their message to Alfonso, he sent them to their lodgings and told them he would let them have his reply, and when he had settled on what it would be, he called them back, and said he was pleased that the king of Morocco and the king of Granada should make peace and have a truce with him, and that the king of Granada should be his vassal. He would raise the siege of Algeciras. Because of the expenses he had incurred they must pay him 300,000 *doblas,* and the king of Granada should pay him annual tribute [*parias*] as before, to him and to all kings of Castile, and he wished to have a meeting with the king of Granada." (BAE:LXVI, 379)

The chronicle is quite frank about Alfonso's motive in asking for this meeting: "He asked for this because it would have one of two consequences. Either he might win over the king of Granada to his side, or [if not] he might be able to create such an atmosphere of suspicion between the king of Granada and Abū'l-Ḥasan of Morocco that they would never trust each other or help each other again" (BAE:LXVI, 379).

Alfonso's plotting was almost frustrated by the treachery of his Italian admiral. Boccanegra had been informed that the Granadans had been offered a safe-conduct to cross to North Africa to seek the finance needed to make the payments required in the settlement. As the Granadan ship was returning, a Genoese galley commanded by one Valentín de Lorax came alongside and attached itself to the Granadan ship by grappling irons. The Granadans fought back, and as a wind was blowing and the sails of the Granadan ship were still set, the two interlocked vessels began to drift downwind towards Gibraltar. When the Genoese perceived what was happening, Valentín had his ship cut loose, and prudently sailed away not to return. As soon as the Granadan ship landed, Yūsuf entered a complaint, saying that the Genoese were failing to respect Alfonso's safe-conduct. Alfonso XI was beside himself with rage. He sent to Yūsuf to tell him that if he could capture Valentín, he hoped he would send him his head, but he was really able to take no effective action because he needed the help of the Genoese (BAE:LXVI, 380).

Ibn Khaldūn does not present quite the same picture of what happened in this incident. He says that the ship of a messenger sent by Yūsuf "was treacherously attacked by several Christian ships sent by the king [of Castile]" (1969:IV, 235).

Not surprisingly, nothing came of these particular negotiations. The siege of Algeciras continued, with the suffering and hardships of the besiegers outside the port as acute as those of the defenders. Skirmishing of an inconclusive kind went on. What seems to have obliged Yūsuf to yield was that the Castilians managed to prevent boats running supplies in under cover of darkness by patrolling the waterfront in small boats. The Muslims used their cannon (*bombardas*) to fire at these patrol boats, and "the noise was very great, particularly from the bombards" (BAE:LXVI, 384). Across the waters of the bay in Gibraltar the Granadan garrison heard the explosions and concluded the Christians must have made an all-out assault. From Gibraltar Yūsuf's forces hastened out to the assistance of their beleaguered brethren, and a series of confused and bloody mêlées continued well into the night (BAE:LXVI, 384). Whether the Castilians were correct in claiming the outcome of this skirmishing as a victory is dubious, but it was the case that Granadan troops were not capable of forcing the Castilians to leave the siege, and when the Castilian naval patrols found a way of making it even more difficult for the supply boats to slip in by constructing a floating barrage made up of barrels lashed together (BAE:LXVI, 388), Yūsuf decided to come to a settlement.

Hasan Algarrafa was sent on March 22, 1344, to negotiate (BAE:LXVI, 388). The terms he offered were surrender of Algeciras if the inhabitants could leave with their personal possessions, a truce for fifteen years, and payment of annual tribute of twelve thousand *doblas*. Alfonso realized that if he persisted in his attack success was by no means certain. There was always the risk that the Genoese might, if paid enough, undertake to convey a few cargoes of supplies to the town, and that would mean all his hopes would vanish. So he accepted Yūsuf's offer, stipulating a truce of ten rather than fifteen years. The siege ended on March 26, 1344 (BAE:LXVI, 389).

The troops of the Algeciras garrison were not Granadans, and Ibn Khaldūn tells us that the Marīnids received them well when they returned home to North Africa, with the sole exception of the commandant ʿAskar b. Tahadrīt, who was imprisoned for his failure to drive off the attackers (1969:IV, 236).

Why Alfonso insisted on cutting down the fifteen-year truce to ten years is clear enough: in fact within five years he was back in action against the Granadans, this time attempting to take Gibraltar. What Alfonso did not reckon with was the Black Death (*llamada mortandad grande*) (BAE:LXVI, 390). Troops on campaign at this period were always exposed to dangerous infections, but the plague was a quite exceptional menace. That Alfonso in a stubborn and foolhardy way persisted with his attack is no doubt due to the guilt he felt at Gibraltar having been lost to the Muslims at the beginning of his reign. Alfonso XI died on Good Friday 1350, and his Castilian forces could then at last withdraw.

As soon as Alfonso XI's successor Peter I came to the throne, an accord was concluded between him and Yūsuf. Peter was often criticized by his Castilian enemies for being too friendly to Muslims. In this accord he agreed to accept as a refugee at his court one of the Marīnid princes in rebellion against the sultan of Morocco, Abū ʿInān Fāris. Yūsuf was being accused by the Marīnids of allowing Granada to be used as a haven for malcontents such as this prince, and Peter was no doubt pleased to be of assistance. (Whether Abū ʿInān in fact was mollified when he heard that Peter provided the prince with transport to Tunisia, whence he proceeded to mount a campaign, is another matter.)

Yūsuf's Reign

Yūsuf's reign was brought to an abrupt end in 1354 when an assassin stabbed him to death in the Great Mosque in Granada as he was completing his prayers. The Arabic sources seem to indicate that this was an attack by a madman: "a crazy man [*mamrūr*]," says Ibn al-Khaṭīb (1934:352); "a low-class fellow," says Ibn Khaldūn (1969:IV, 392), and it may be so. Ibn al-Khaṭīb tells us the culprit was interrogated and could "only mumble confused words," which is hardly surprising, as he must have known what fate awaited him, although here too there is confusion. "Put to death and burned in the fire," says Ibn al-Khaṭīb (or is it hell-fire he has in mind?); "cut into a thousand pieces by the guard," says Ibn Khaldūn. The element of overkill in these reports, and the lack of any explanation as to the motive, fill one with suspicion, although it is obvious that we will never know why Yūsuf died.

As a ruler his achievements were considerable. He had had to withstand the onslaught of Alfonso XI's attacks, and although he had suffered defeat along with the Marīnids at Salado and at Algeciras, thus losing the strategically important westward shoreline facing on to the Straits of Gibraltar, and had to the north lost Alcalá la Real, he was trusted by his people as a reliable custodian of their interests. Under him the city of Granada flourished, the arts were cultivated, and his court was ornamented by some of the finest writers of the day. He steered his country through a period when dependence on the Marīnids was perforce almost complete, and towards the end of his reign, when Marīnid commitment to Spain was waning, was able to find a way of preserving Granadan independence with minimal help from across the sea. His was a key contribution in the history of this little state.

FOURTEEN

Muḥammad V (1354–1391): A Reign Interrupted by Those of Ismāʾīl II and Muḥammad VI

With Muḥammad V, who came to rule in 1354, we have the first example of a phenomenon which was repeated several times in the history of the Naṣrid dynasty: the interrupted reign. Muḥammad V was only sixteen when his reign began; by the age of twenty-one he had already been replaced by another Naṣrid prince (who himself was to be replaced by a third member of the royal family). Then, at the age of twenty-four, he was to return to power and rule without further interruption till he was fifty-three. Such a pattern gives an impression of great instability, and one feels sometimes there is almost an element of moral censure present in the way some modern historians report such constitutional arrangements. How can we take seriously a dynasty which has its rulers playing Box and Cox in this fashion? When in a twentieth-century state a ruler, whether president or prime minister, is replaced by a rival, and then eventually finds his way back into power, this is not taken as an indication of the instability of the system, indeed the fact that the constitutional system in question makes room for adjustment and change is regarded as one of its desirable features. It would seem illogical for us to interpret the interrupted reigns of the Naṣrid constitution[1] as being necessarily a sign of weakness and decadence. A change at the top may indicate instability, or it may on occasion show the system responding to change and serve as a demonstration of the ability of the Naṣrid clan as a whole to keep a firm grip on power. If any member of the family appeared weak or vulnerable, there was always a faction waiting to unseat him and set somebody else, also a Naṣrid, in his place. The system was not perfect, and at times led to a great deal of bloodshed, especially inside the ruling elites, but it is not to be seen as inherently inferior to, say, the principle of primogeniture (which caused endless problems for the Christian states of the peninsula all through our period).

The first period of Muḥammad V's rule was very much the regime of his chief minister (*ḥājib*) Riḍwān,[2] who, after all, had been one of the king-makers who placed young Muḥammad where he was. Riḍwān was in charge of the administration, he commanded the army, and as tutor of Muḥammad and other royal princes he had special authority. Under him, and in charge of the North African contingents in the army, was Yaḥyā b.ʿUmar b. Raḥḥū. With him in the secretariat served such gifted young men as Ibn al-Khaṭīb. The Arabic sources speak of this as a well-administered time of prosperity (Alarcón and García de Linares 1940:66–67, 72–73, 92–93; Ibn al-Khaṭīb 1973:I, 516). In foreign relations Muḥammad made peace with Peter I of Castile, who had come to the throne in 1350, also at the age of sixteen. (Peter I was to rule in all not quite as long as Muḥammad—until 1369.) One of the criticisms leveled at Peter by some of his rebellious Christian subjects was that he was too friendly towards Muslims, too fond of Muslim ways; these accusations smell of rabble-rousing propaganda, and it is difficult to evaluate them, but certainly during much of Peter's reign relations be-

1. I am, of course, using the word *constitution* in the more general sense which it has in expressions such as "the British Constitution" ("the sum of governmental arrangements, conventions, and practices which exist") rather than in the more specific Franco-American sense ("document setting out how a state is to be governed"). It goes without saying that Granada had no written constitution.

2. al- ʿAbbādī (1973:22) gives him the surname Venegas. Seco de Lucena (1956) gives the full name as Abū'l-nu'aym Riḍwān Ibn ʿAbdallah al-Naṣrī.

tween Castile and Granada were good and at times cordial, though at others soaked in blood.

Peace with Castile did not, of course, imply peace with Aragon. When the boy-king came to the throne in Granada, Peter IV of Aragon began military operations on his frontiers. Riḍwān's policy was to secure a peace negotiated if possible with all parties. Peace was sought with Morocco too, and Ibn al-Khaṭīb was sent on a mission to Fez which did bring some amelioration in relations. (The Marīnids saw Granada at this period as a state too ready to provide a base for malcontent members of the Marīnid family; tensions sprang as much as anything from the weakness of the crumbling North African state.)

The readiness of Muḥammad V to seek good relations all round is brought out by an Arabic letter dated September 9, 1354, in the Aragonese archives. Muḥammad V addressed Peter IV's lieutenant in the following terms:

> Know, O honored *infante* [the word is used in the Arabic] that good relations [*ṣuḥba*] have from early times existed between this royal house and that of Aragon, and that our late lamented father [Yūsuf I] made a peace settlement with the king which was negotiated by Abū ʾl-Ḥasan b. Kumāsha, and that, from that time to this peace, has been faithfully respected in all particulars, until Ibiza, and Majorca and the islands broke the truce, and the islanders carried out several reprehensible attacks, behaving themselves as if they were combatants in an all-out war, carrying Muslims off as captives and transporting them with goods and other things back to their own land.
>
> The sultan [Muḥammad V] and you were apprised of this, and you replied that the only persons carried off to the islands were people speaking different languages such as people from North Africa [*al-ʿadwa* 'the far shore']. A letter was sent to you pointing out that North Africans and others were covered by the truce as concluded, and that the same obligations had been incurred with respect to them as with respect to the people of our country, so that Christians ought not to be presenting Muslims for sale in Valencia and elsewhere openly and before witnesses, something which has been going on right up to the present.
>
> If the king [Peter IV] has empowered you to put a stop to

> these reprehensible practices in all his Christian territories, and if you are indeed able to proceed against such abuses, and find a remedy, inform us, so that we may act in accordance with our established good relations and friendship, and in a way fitting to a person as distinguished as yourself. This is what we wish to communicate to you. (Alarcón and García de Linares 1940:135–37)

Such firm diplomacy obviously paid off. Good relations developed, and by July 1367 an accord was signed between the two states (somewhat to Castile's discomfiture). In 1359 Abū Sālim came to the throne in Fez. He had spent some time as an exile in Granada, and Fez and Granada also moved into a period of good relations. However, in 1358 Aragon and Castile had gone to war, and Muḥammad V, as vassal of Castile, became involved in the conflict. It was particularly Granada's naval assistance which was requested—use of Malaga as a friendly port, some reinforcements (three galleys), and even financial support. Clearly the war was incompatible with the policy that was being implemented, and against this background the palace revolution took place which replaced Muḥammad V by Ismāʿīl II.

Ismāʿīl II

The coup that unseated Muḥammad V in August 1359 had features we find repeated many times in subsequent history. As we have seen, the background to the revolution was the involvement of Granada in the turbulent relations between her Christian neighbors, but a more proximate cause was intrigue within the Alhambra palace in which the ladies of the court circle played their part. Maryam had borne Yūsuf I several children, of whom Ismāʿīl was one and Qays another; of her daughters, one was married to the son of Yūsuf I's brother, Abū ʿAbdallah Muḥammad (*el Bermejo* in the Christian chronicles). Ismāʿīl, and hence his mother Maryam, had been disappointed when Riḍwān proclaimed Muḥammad king, but Muḥammad had nevertheless allowed Ismāʿīl to continue to live in the Alhambra, which became a hotbed of disaffection, especially after Granada entered Castile's war against Aragon. With *el Bermejo* also in the plot, and with finance from Maryam's resources, a group of one hundred conspirators was found to scale the heights of the Alhambra and take the royal palace by surprise in Ramadan of 1359 (Ibn al-Khaṭīb A. H. 1347:108). Riḍwān was the individual the plotters most wished to eliminate; his accumulated wealth was their reward. The raid found Muḥammad V outside the Alhambra precinct; he tried to fight his way in, failed, and fled, managing to reach Guadix. There the commander of the North African volunteer garrison, ʿAlī b. Badr al-Dīn b. Mūsā Ibn Raḥḥū still sided with him, and so Granada as a kingdom was split. Muḥammad V tried to rally his other supporters, but with little success: Almería refused to back him. Worst of all, Peter I, who might have been thought to have an obligation to him, could spare no forces to help (he was too deeply involved in the early stages of the Trastamaran revolution which was eventually to be his downfall). What saved Muḥammad was the fact that Abū Sālim in Fez offered him asylum, and so Muḥammad sailed into exile from Marbella in November 1359 (Ibn al-Khaṭīb 1974:II, 18). The Marīnids had often been irked by members of their family who from safe exile in Granada had been able to plot against the ruler of Fez. Now the Marīnids could play the same game against Granada, and Muḥammad V was a convenient king-across-the-water.

Ismā ʿīl, placed so suddenly on the throne by Maryam's plot, did not manage to retain power very long. He had the misfortune to have been opposed by no less a propagandist than Ibn al-Khaṭīb (Ibn al-Khaṭīb A. H. 1347:114–15). He portrays the ruler as indolent and given to effeminate dress, his hair plaited with silk down to his waist (as cited by al-ʿAbbādī 1973:33), for example, but one must ask whether this is not studied character assassination. Even while Ismā ʿīl II was still alive, *el Bermejo* was much in control. In June 1360 a new plot saw the assassination not only of Ismāʿīl II but also of Qays and most of their court circle. *El Bermejo* became king, Muḥammad VI in our modern regnal numbering, *al-Gālib billah* in his own boastful style.

Muḥammad VI

In contrast with Ismā ʿīl, his manner of dressing was allegedly rough and ready, and he was blamed for a lack of a sense of what was required by the dignity of his office. He would roll up his sleeves and go about bareheaded. The court found him rather a laughingstock with his coarse manners, unstylish garb, and, what was worse, an uncontrollable tic: he constantly moved his head from side to side (al-ʿAbbādī 1973:33; Arié 1973:110 and n.4 for further references).

With Muḥammad VI, Peter I of Castile was as ready to reach an accommodation as he had been with Muḥammad V. The *Chronicle of Peter I* (an anti-Petrine compilation put together by Pedro López de Ayala) summarized the situation as follows:

> When King Peter was in Seville this same year [1360], he received news of how a *raʾīs* [leader], a Moor of Granada called the Red King [*el rey Bermejo,* Muḥammad VI], had driven Muḥammad [V] from his kingdom, and taken it for himself. They said he was a partisan of the king of Aragon, and wanted to make war on the king of Castile. King Peter then ordered military preparations to be made throughout Andalusia, and sent back to Castile for companies of troops, but he then heard that the Red King wanted to make peace, which he was pleased to accept, for he had already begun his war with Aragon. So Muḥammad [VI] negotiated with Peter [I], and agreed to become his friend, and Peter agreed to stir up no trouble for him with [Muḥammad V] his enemy. But Peter remained full of anger against Muḥammad [VI], because at such a juncture he had presented him with a threat of war, and never after that did he forget it, as you will hear. (BAE:LXVI, 51)

When three chapters later the chronicle picks up the thread of its narrative concerned with the affairs of Granada, it places Muḥammad V back on Granadan soil, but in Ronda. What it omitted was the diplomatic moves initiated by Peter which led to that return. When Muḥammad V crossed the straits he was invited by Peter to Seville, where Peter put on for him a most lavish display of hospitality. A large subvention (30,000 dinars) was made to Muḥammad V to enable him to set up a government based in Ronda in opposition to that of Muḥammad VI. It was an administration not lacking in talents. The military forces were under ʿUthmān b. Yaḥyā b. Raḥḥū, the administration was headed by Abūʾl-Ḥasan ʿAlī Ibn Kumāsha, the poet Ibn Zamrak was a member of the secretariat (Arié 1973:111). Ibn al-Khaṭīb, meanwhile, remained in Morocco looking after Muḥammad V's family interests.

The *Chronicle of Peter I* picks up the thread as follows:

> As soon as the king arrived at Seville he sent for the lords and the knights of his kingdom, for he resolved to make war on the king of Granada known as *el Bermejo,* because he was angry with him for making war against him at a time when he was engaged in

> conflict with the king of Aragon. That had forced him to enter into negotiations with Aragon when he would have preferred not to do so, and in consequence he had had to hand back many townships and castles which he had won in Aragon. What especially rankled with him was that he had had to hand back Ariza, because that is such a good castle on the Castilian frontier.
>
> King Peter told all his men that he had an obligation to help Muḥammad [V] of Granada because he was his vassal and paid him tribute, and had been driven out of his kingdom against all right and justice by *el Bermejo*. So the war began, and King Muḥammad [V] who was in Ronda, a place held by the Marīnid king, came to King Peter with four hundred mounted Moors. The king of Castile provided assistance with money he had to borrow. They had an agreement that once hostilities commenced, all places captured by Peter should belong to him, but those places which chose to obey Muḥammad and to yield to him should be his, and King Peter would not make war on them. (BAE:LXVI, 513)

The allies at first had little success: "The king of Castile did win some places in the Kingdom of Granada, but no place surrendered to Muḥammad" (BAE:LXVI, 513). After Peter failed to capture Antequera, "he ordered his men to make an incursion into the *vega* of Granada, and with him went King Muḥammad, thinking that if he made an appearance, many of the nobility would come over to him" (BAE:LXVI, 514). The chronicle gives a long list of the principal Castilians taking part: there were six thousand horse in all. They were met at the bridge at Pinos by the Granadan army, which seems to have had the worst of some ensuing skirmishes, but which certainly refused to come over to Muḥammad V as hoped. Nor was the alliance any more successful at Guadix in 1362 (BAE:LXVI, 515), and in fact many Christians were taken prisoner in fighting there, including the master of Calatrava, Diego García Padilla. Muḥammad VI, finding himself in possession of such a valuable prisoner, tried to make use of him to persuade Peter to desist, but Muḥammad VI badly misread Peter's strange psychology. To Peter, the master of Calatrava laden with Muḥammad VI's lavish gifts was a bitter reminder of the chaos and lack of success at Guadix: the master was blamed for that defeat (BAE:LXVI, 516), and Muḥammad VI earned no gratitude.

In February 1362 Peter began an energetic campaign on the frontiers, and took a number of fortresses, notably Iznájar southeast of Rute. The fortunes of war then changed—why it is not at all clear. Muḥammad V was able to take Malaga in a campaign in which we hear of no Castilian participation. The Castilian chronicle tells the gruesome final act of the drama as follows:

> As the king [Peter] won more territory from the Moors, the Moors began to complain that since *el Bermejo* had been king of Granada, the land of the Moors and the Kingdom of Granada was being lost as a result of the quarrel he had with King Muḥammad [V]. *El Bermejo* was much perturbed at these words, which were being uttered all over the kingdom, and he thought that he could not hold out, nor continue what he had begun. He took counsel from a great gentleman who was one of his supporters, Don Idrīs Abenbulula [b. Abī ʾl-ʿUlā] son of Don Hozmin [ʿUthmān] and others of his household in whom he placed much trust, for they had been with him since he decided to take Muḥammad [V]'s kingdom from him. When they perceived how day by day things were getting worse, and that Muḥammad [VI] could not sustain the war against the king of Castile, and also took into account the discord between the Moors, they all agreed that *el Bermejo* should throw himself on the mercy of the king of Castile, and place himself in his power. They said as soon as he saw him he would have mercy, and even perhaps prefer him to the other King Muḥammad, because *el Bermejo* was physically a fine horseman, who could be of service to the king wherever he sent him in any war. So *el Bermejo* decided to go to King Peter, taking with him the finest of his jewels, those of the House of Granada, to use them in case of need. With three hundred horse and two hundred foot soldiers he put the plan into effect, and went to Baena, which belonged to the [Castilian] king, where he was well received. (BAE:LXVI, 517)

Why Muḥammad VI decided to place himself in the power of Peter I in this way is difficult to understand. Little in Peter's record would have given Muḥammad cause to believe he would be merciful. If it was a courageous gamble, it did not come off. Peter feasted his unexpected guests in Seville, then, as they were sitting at the table after their meal, the Granadans were all arrested, and stripped of their valuables. Two days later Peter had Muḥammad VI led out to "a great field in Seville near the castle called Tablada, mounted on an ass and clad in a scarlet robe which he had, and with him were thirty-six of his Moors." King Peter it was who dealt the first blow with his lance, saying, "Take that for causing me to get a bad deal from the king of Aragon and lose the castle of Ariza" (BAE:LXVI, 519).

When Muḥammad was struck, the chronicle tells us, he said in Arabic, "What a little deed of chivalry!" ["*O que caballería feciste.*"] (BAE:LXVI, 519). The thirty-six strong escort were despatched on the spot. Idrīs and the rest of the party were first consigned to prison, where they were later poisoned.

> King Muḥammad [V], as soon as he learned that the king *el Bermejo* had been taken into captivity, went to Granada, where he was acknowledged as king, and all the kingdom obeyed him. King Peter sent to him *el Bermejo*'s head with those of others who died with him, and King Muḥammad V sent King Peter some prisoners who had been captured during the fighting at Guadix. (BAE:LXVI, 519)

Thus it was that in 1362 Muḥammad V entered for the second time into possession of his kingdom, after a harsh and bloody initiation into the realities of Granada's brutal politics.

As soon as he assumed power, he had to face a major international crisis which arose from the revolt of the Trastamaran faction, led by the future Henry II, against Peter I of Castile. Muḥammad V sided with Peter, and provided him with military support: six hundred mounted troops commanded by Faraj Ibn Riḍwān (BAE:LXVI, 526) who helped Peter to take Teruel in 1363. Muḥammad's outright support of Peter placed him in an exposed position, for Henry, with the assistance of Bertrand du Guesclin and the mercenary companies, was proclaimed king in 1366. Even in Seville, his much-loved city, Peter was no longer in control. According to one of the redactions of the *Chronicle of King Peter,* people there were openly identifying him with the Granadans: "The word ran through the city that even when everybody else abandoned him, the Moors would not let him down, especially King Muḥammad of Granada, whom he had caused to recover his kingdom. And there were some who did not wish to serve him, and who said the Moors were coming, and the king wanted to welcome them into the city" (BAE:LXVI, 542).

Henry's anti-Petrine propaganda made much use of the accusation that Peter was really a lover of Moors, so we must beware of taking this statement at its face value. What is clear is that Granada was in great peril, and any one of its enemies might have made use of the crisis as an opportunity to grab Granadan territory; in particular an Aragonese attack on Almería seemed imminent. Granada thus became once more a supplicant for North African aid.

When Henry II began active military operations in Andalusia, Muḥammad feared that his home territory would be devastated (as so much Christian territory had been already). Muḥammad accordingly rapidly changed camps, abandoned Peter, acknowledged Henry II (BAE:LXVI, 545), and even followed this up by a treaty with the Aragonese in 1367 (Alarcón and García de Linares 1940:146–49). The successful recovery which Peter I was able to stage later that year, thanks in part to the English intervention under the Black Prince, led Muḥammad to change sides yet again! Jaén, a city which had come out against Peter, was struck by a devastating raid, as were Ubeda and Baeza. Muḥammad was able to take home many prisoners.

The final act of the dramatic civil war in Castile has no direct bearing on Granadan history, but it is as well to recall it, for it provides us with a point of comparison with the brutality of much of the strife within the Naṣrid royal house. Peter I met his end after defeat on the field of battle at Montiel, allegedly at the hands of his own half-brother Henry. When the two finally came face to face in Bertrand du Guesclin's tent, Henry at first did not recognize Peter "for it was so long since he had seen him."

> And they say that King Peter twice said, "It is I, it is I." Then King Henry did recognize him, and struck him in the face with a dagger, and they say that both Peter and Henry fell to the ground, and Henry caused him several further wounds while they were on the ground, and there King Peter died. (BAE:LXVI, 592)

For Muḥammad V the troubles through which Castile was passing provided an opportunity to regain lost territory, not only a string of frontier posts—Cambril, Haver, Rute—but Algeciras itself in 1369 (Ibn al Khaṭīb 1974:II, 59). He even raided towards Seville and took much booty.

It is perhaps in relation to the capture of Algeciras that the statesmanship of Muḥammad V emerges most clearly. The response of all those who had taken this key port up to this time had been to strengthen its defenses. It is not clear whether Muḥammad's decision to *destroy* its defenses was made immediately (as the Castilian chronicle of Henry II suggests [BAE:LXVIII, 4], or somewhat later, as Ibn Khaldūn states (1969:IV, 381), but what matters is that the original decision was made and carried out. To be understood, the dismantling of the massive Algeciras fortifications must be linked with the break with North African support which he made after 1372.

The North African Volunteers for the Faith had by long-established custom been commanded by members of the Marīnid royal family, the Banū ʿAbd al-Ḥaqq, but from 1372 the Volunteers were under direct Naṣrid command. There is no doubt that the rather peculiar custom of having such direct foreign participation in the running of the Granadan army had in the past helped the state to survive. Here was an acceptable form of aid which did not constitute a serious threat of becoming a form of foreign military occupation. For the Volunteers themselves the arrangement had the advantage that their commanding officer was from their own background, whereas a Granadan would have been a man from a very different culture. The arrangements, therefore, had served very well for a long time, but Muḥammad V, in a radical reappraisal, decided to dispense with the North African member of his military staff.

His opportunity came when the accession of al-Ṣāliḥ in Fez at the age of only seven created an atmosphere of weakness and uncertainty. Far from being a puppet state itself manipulated by the Marīnids, Granada was becoming one of the powers most actively engaged in manipulating the politics of Fez. When Abū'l-ʿAbbās ascended the Marīnid throne in 1374, he did so already heavily obligated to Muḥammad V. From being a powerless refugee at the court of Abū Sālim, Muḥammad V had moved to the opposite position of being something of a king-maker.

Muḥammad V must have realized that by striking at Algeciras immediately after Henry II so brutally took over from his half-brother Peter, he was running the risk that he might provoke an indignant military response from Castile. He was correct in assuming that Henry would be too preoccupied to do anything. The skill and success of Granadan diplomacy at this period is remarkable. The question of who should control the Straits of Gibraltar could never cease to preoccupy all the powers in the region, but the intensity of the rivalry of Aragon and Castile, of the North African states, and of Granada itself, had created instability, and Granada had suffered. Now the decline of Marīnid power and the exhaustion of Castile after the civil wars gave Muḥammad V an opportunity to move the question of the straits away from the center of international concern. His imaginative dismantling of much of the defensive complex at Algeciras was an element in this policy.

Perhaps another element was the strange incident of the judicial murder of Ibn al-Khaṭīb in Tlemcen. The statesman-historian had, for reasons which are not altogether clear, taken refuge in North Africa. Muḥammad V's new minister, Ibn al-Khaṭīb's former protégé, Ibn Zamrak, sought to have him extradited. The rulers of Tlemcen refused to release him but, curiously, allowed a Granadan tribunal to try him in a Tlemcen prison. The charge was heresy. He was condemned and put to death in his cell in 1374. This was a murky affair (bringing small credit on Ibn Zamrak), about which we can only speculate.

On May 31, 1370, Henry II was prepared to sign a truce for eight years; in 1375 the truce was renewed. Relations were tense in 1378, but when John I came to the throne in 1379 there was once again a truce, and yet again in 1390. Granada could adopt a policy of peace because it was so clear that the desire for peace did not spring from weakness. The series of truces negotiated by Muḥammad V was probably the longest period of peace enjoyed by Granada in all its history. Rulers are often praised when they perceive an opportunity for action and take it. He, on the contrary, perceived an opportunity for peace, and took it—peace in all directions, north, east, and south. In the earlier days of the development of his policy he benefited from the brilliant members of his government service, such as Ibn al-Khaṭīb; he later was quite ruthless in disposing of the services of such advisors (and even brutally ending their lives) when he judged that reasons of state so demanded. As he must bear the responsibility for the blood of those of his ministers who died, it is only just that the avoidance of war in his times should stand to his credit.

Peace with Castile was not the only concern of Muḥammad, of course. Good relations with Aragon, which had begun with the peace of March 1367, were continued. In 1377 Peter IV and Muḥammad V renewed their truce for a further three years as from Midsummer Day (*al-ʿanṣara*). An exchange of prisoners was arranged, and security of navigation for merchants and seafarers guaranteed. There was even provision made for the services of Granadan mercenaries to be made available to the Aragonese, with rates of pay specified (seven gold dinars a month to knights, forty to the commander), all on condition the troops were not used against Granada's allies. In return Aragon promised to provide ships equipped and manned to agreed levels at a rate of nine hundred dinars a month for each vessel (Alarcón and García de Linares 1940:409–15).

One clause shows Muḥammad V conscious of a role as general protector of all Muslims in the peninsula, even those in Christian territory:

> Neither you nor any of your servants [*nās*] will at any time prevent those Muslims resident [*sākinīn*] in your country from leaving for Muslim countries [*arḍ al-muslimīn*] in complete security, with their family and possessions, whether by land or by sea at any time, without the imposition of any taxes other than those established by custom. It will not be permitted that any of your officials exact anything from their possessions, or submit them to constraints of any kind.

This treaty shows Muhammad V fulfilling the function of the *amīr al-muslimīn,* and the Aragonese authorities acquiescing in the exercise of such a general protectorate.

Henry II died in 1379. His reign had not proved to be the period of danger for Spanish Islam that might have been feared, given the anti-Islamic tone of some of the anti-Petrine propaganda. Castile under Henry had turned away from the enterprise of the Reconquest, and the agenda of the Christian states in the peninsula at this period seems to have been laid down in France and even in England. Castilian monarchs were content from time to time to receive Granadan emissaries and to sign extensions of truces, and for their part the Granadans paid tribute (*parias*) and lived in peace. The febrile dance of ever-changing alliances of the first part of the century was replaced by the relative stability of a situation in which in general neither North Africa nor Castile sought actively to intervene, and naval squadrons no longer maneuvered to control the Straits of Gibraltar. Perhaps the terrible impact of the Black Death on both shores of the Mediterranean had something to do with the relative calm that prevailed. But Granada had demonstrated that it was no easy prey to any power. The Christian kingdoms were content to leave the Granadans in their mountain kingdom, and in that mountain fastness Granada flourished both materially and culturally.

Muḥammad V's chief minister, after Ibn al-Khaṭīb had fled to North Africa, was Ibn Zamrak, the poet whose verses adorn so many of the walls of the Alhambra. Rarely can a civilization anywhere in the world have found a more sumptuous setting for its court poetry. It would be pleasant to record that the creator of this poetry was as admirable as the verses themselves, but that is not the case. Ibn Zamrak was behind the charges of heresy leveled against Ibn al-Khaṭīb, and he was as devious an intriguer as was to be found in this age. He wrote verse of great delicacy, not only in the eulogistic mode, which he certainly did cultivate, but also in celebration of the natural beauty of Granada, conveyed in the following lines in which he employs the imagery of a wedding banquet:

Stay awhile here on the terrace of the Sabīka [i.e., the Alhambra] and look about you.
This city is a wife, whose husband is the hill:
Girt she is by water and by flowers,
Which glisten at her throat,
Ringed with streams; and behold the groves of trees which are the wedding guests, whose thirst is being assuaged by the water-channels.
The Sabīka hill sits like a garland on Granada's brow,
In which the stars would be entwined,
And the Alhambra (God preserve it)
Is the ruby set above that garland.
Granada is a bride whose headdress is the Sabīka, and whose jewels and adornments are its flowers.[3]

Much of the Alhambra as we know it today is the work of the craftsmen and architects of the days of Muḥammad V. To him are to be ascribed, above all, the Patio de los Leones and the neighboring halls and chambers. What we admire in the architecture of the Alhambra in general is its lightness, its delicacy, its wonderful combination of geometrical composition with imaginative freedom. The Patio de los Leones has all these characteristics but combines them with a certain monumental dignity which never becomes heavy. This style of making royal buildings has never been equaled anywhere.

Muḥammad V died on January 16, 1391.

3. Ibn Zamrak, freely translated from al-Maqqarī 1949:X, 30–31. Cf. García Gómez 1944:246.

F I F T E E N

Yūsuf II (Abū˒l-Ḥajjāj) (1391–1392); Muḥammad VII (1392–1408); Yūsuf III (1408–1417)

Yūsuf II (Abū˒ l-Ḥajjāj), 1391–1392

Yūsuf II succeeded his father Muḥammad V without violence and without rebellion, but this reign follows an unpleasant pattern of Naṣrid government which has already been encountered more than once: a king begins under the domination of a faithful servant of his father's household, and that domination is only brought to an end with the killing of the faithful tyrant servant. In the case of Yūsuf II the process was accelerated, and within the space of one year the servant-minister Khālid went from all-powerful tyrant to victim of a cruel execution: Yūsuf had him tied up and hacked to death by swords as he watched. The Jewish doctor whom Yūsuf suspected of having joined with Khālid in a plot to poison him was poisoned. Before Yūsuf disposed in this way of his father's retainers, three of his brothers, Saʿd, Muḥammad, and Naṣr, had also met their death. As for Ibn Zamrak, chief minister under Muḥammad V, he was transported off to a dungeon in Almería, although left alive.

Such a regime must surely have crippled the state: it was fortunate for Granada that neither Aragon nor Castile represented any threat at this time. Yūsuf II died before reactions began. The equilibrium and stability achieved at the cost of so much effort in the days of Muḥammad V was now lost. The fighting was about to begin again.

There is an incidental mention of Yūsuf II's death in a curious missive allegedly sent to Ferdinand of Antequera from one Fernán Sanchez by way of warning to beware of presents sent by Yūsuf III. Fernán Sanchez was an ambiguous figure who had lived as a Christian at Carmona, and after the Muslim recapture of Priego in 1403 had passed back into Muslim-held territory. He allegedly sent his warning to Ferdinand in writing, and claimed that "I saw with my own eyes in Granada that the King of Fez [presumably Abū'l-ʿAbbās] sent a tunic [*aljuba*] of gold to King Yūsuf [II] father of the king of Granada reigning now [Yūsuf III], and as soon as he had put it on he felt he was poisoned, and died within thirty days, with his flesh coming off in pieces." Fernán Sanchez has so many stories of similar assassination attempts using poisoned garments that without confirmation one is reluctant to accept the report as true (*Crónica de Juan II* 1982:269–70).

Muḥammad VII, 1392–1408

The succession on the death of Yūsuf II was from father to son, but Muḥammad VII was the younger son: Yūsuf the elder son was shut away in the castle of Salobreña as a result of a palace plot. The poet Ibn Zamrak was brought back from the prison to which Yūsuf II had condemned him, and was made *kātib,* but did not survive long. He was assassinated in 1393, and Abū Bakr Muḥammad Ibn ʿĀsim appointed in his place. The *wazīr* of this dangerous king was Muḥammad al-Ḥammāmī (Arié 1973:122).

Bloodshed and violence in the palace was reflected now in bloodshed and violence on the frontiers. Peace, which had prevailed for much of the second half of the fourteenth century and had permitted Islamic culture to flourish in Granada, was abruptly abandoned as a policy. Muḥammad VII led a raid into Murcian territory in the Lorca region. Alfonso Yáñez Fajardo, the governor of the province (*adelantado*), was able to take revenge for the losses inflicted when he caught the Granadan raiding party in the pass at Nogalete.

There thus begins a period of foolhardy and courageous raiding from both sides of the frontier. This is the heroic period of the frontier war as recorded in the incomparable Castilian frontier ballads (*romances fronterizos*)—a period in which noble leaders, Muslim and Christian, matched their strength, cunning, and valor, riding on faithful steeds, serving beautiful ladies, and achieving really rather little for one side or the other, apart from disrupting the long frontier truces which had allowed the region to recover its prosperity. Warfare might be seen quite sincerely by those taking part on both sides as loyal service performed for one's God and one's ruler, but the objective was frequently a herd of cattle, or a harvest recently gathered. These frontiersmen were developing a way of life that was to be borne across to the New World, where riding hard and raiding for cattle were to form the basis of the myth of "how the West was won," and to provide the plot outline for so many films. There is a profound difference, though, between the myth of the frontier as presented in the cinema and the myth that underlies the literature of the Granadan wars. One of the attractions of the celluloid western is the ease with which the good guys may be distinguished from the bad, whereas in the Castilian ballads both sides are presented as imbued with the same admirable moral qualities, both respect the same chivalric code of conduct. What marks off the one group of men from the other is a purely superficial set of differences of dress and language. Villains are absent from this frontier literature, as are weak men and cowards. The literary stereotypes undoubtedly color the historical record and our interpretation of it. Behind the authentically splendid heroism of the poems, and largely ignored even in the historical record, were the disrupted lives and the misery created by the reversion of much of the Granadan frontier to anarchy and chaos.

The Jews in 1391

It may seem that relations between Christians and Jews in Castile are irrelevant to a study of the Muslims of the Iberian Peninsula. That is in a strict sense true, but any shift in relations between two of the monotheist religions in the peninsula was likely to have repercussions on the status of the third. At the outset of our period, Jews in Castile enjoyed a position not dissimilar to that which they had had all through the Middle Ages: condemned to a lowly position, subject to sporadic persecution, but tolerated. A change seems to have taken place in the fourteenth century, and that change was not unrelated to the Trastamaran revolution. Trastamaran propaganda that Peter I was the son of a Jewess is one aspect of the general anti-Jewish sentiment of the new regime. The use made by Peter of Jewish administrators was resented. In various ways and in various places the anti-Jewish current manifested itself in

Castile during the century (for example, in 1366 in Burgos and Toledo, in 1369 again in Toledo, Jews had to pay a ransom or accept conversion).

That the anti-Jewish agitation came to the boil in Andalusia is perhaps not a matter of chance. Resentment in the lower strata of society at the unwillingness of rulers to take what were felt to be necessary steps to protect poor Christians was one of the factors in the situation. A principal agitator and instigator of anti-Jewish campaigns was the archdeacon of Écija, Fernando Martínez, and one of the issues on which he campaigned was usury. He demanded strong legal action to stop usury, but the royal authorities refused. The confusion and the weakness of central government provided the opportunities needed by this movement of a populist and racialist tone, and in 1391 riots in Seville culminated in the sacking of the Jewish quarter. A wave of similar acts of violence occurred in other Andalusian towns, including Écija and Carmona, before the pogroms spread to the rest of Christian Spain.

This is not the place to enter in detail into the far-reaching effects of the pogroms of 1391 on the history of Spanish Jewry, and indeed of Spanish culture in general. Many Jews were forced to accept conversion, others in panic "chose" conversion, and from this time onwards there was a considerable contingent of *conversos,* converts from Judaism. Not accepted fully by either community, this group included a disproportionately great number of writers and thinkers. What is of relevance to the history of the Muslims in the peninsula is the clear evidence which the pogroms supply of a frustrated current of lower-class Christian resentment at what was perceived as the failure of the authorities to defend the interests of Christians and of Christianity.

The Crusade of Martín Yáñez de Barbudo

The crusade of Martín Yáñez de Barbudo[1] against Granada is by no means unknown, but it has received far less attention than the 1391 pogroms; it clearly arises from the same current of intolerant populist religiosity. As we read in the *Chronicle of Henry III:*

> *Chapter Eight*
>
> While the King [Henry III] was in Madrid, there reached him a messenger of Don Martín Yáñez de Barbudo, a man born in Por-

1. Tapia (1986:295) gives the name as Yáñez de la Barbuda.

tugal whom King John had made master of the order of Alcántara. The messenger delivered letters of credence from the master, and told the king that the master wished to inform him that for the faith of Jesus Christ, and out of love for Him, he had sent a challenge to the king of Granada which was as follows:

He affirmed that the faith of Jesus Christ was holy and good, and that the faith of Muḥammad was false and deceitful, and if the king of Granada objected, the master would have him know that he would fight against him and anyone he liked to name, giving him the advantage of one half more, so that if the Moors were two hundred, he would take one hundred, and so on up to the figure of one thousand, or any number he liked, whether mounted or on foot. The master had sent two of his squires to the king of Granada with his request, and the king of Granada had had the squires arrested and had much dishonored them, so that for that reason the master had decided to set out immediately for Alcántara, and go directly to Granada, where he would attend to the challenge he had issued.

When the king [of Castile] and those of his court heard of the challenge which the master of Alcántara had issued, they judged it did no service to the king, because he had signed a truce with the king of Granada but a short while before, and also because the master was the king's vassal, so that if he went in person and with his companies into the Kingdom of Granada, the truce arrangements would be broken, which would not be to the interest of the king. What is more the king could see that the master was putting himself into great danger, for he had no more than three hundred lances with him, and inconsiderable companies of foot soldiers, so that it was impossible for him to come to battle with the forces of the king of Granada, and they agreed to send letters and a messenger to the master of Alcántara to divert him from his course, and this they did.

Chapter Nine

When the messengers and letter reached the master, they found him on his way from Alcántara to Cordova with three hundred lances and a thousand foot. He had hoisted a cross up on a pole, with his pennant close to the cross, and when he saw the king's letters he said he obeyed the king's letters because he was his lord, but that this was an affair of the Faith, and that it would be a great dishonor for him to turn the cross back, instead of bearing it forwards, and not to complete what he had started; he did not stop.

When he reached Cordova, the gentlemen and the officers of the city did not wish to allow him to pass over the bridge, but there was so much disturbance and complaining among the common people of the city, who sided with the master, and said he was traveling in the service of God and for the Faith of Jesus Christ, that the gentlemen were not able to prevent him, so the master crossed the bridge at Cordova, and many people on foot from the city and the country round about joined up with him, and thence he made his way to Alcalá la Real.

Chapter Ten

When he reached Alcalá la Real Don Alfonso Fernández, lord of Aguilar, and in command of Alcalá, and his brother Diego Fernández, marshal of Castile, came out to speak with him. What they said is as follows:

"My Lord:

We know that you have undertaken this exploit with sound intentions and out of great devotion to the Faith of Jesus Christ, but here are some things which you ought to know, if you will, such that should make you desist from this incursion which you wish to make into Granadan territory. Firstly, my lord, you should know that the king has signed a truce with the king of Granada, and given his oath thereto but a few days ago. You will also know now what befits our lord king, bearing in mind his tender age, is peace and quiet. If the king of Granada sees a man of your status, master of Alcántara too, making an incursion into his kingdom with armed men, the truce will be broken, and war will return. The region of Andalusia is not prepared in any way, and there are no ships at sea. From this there could result great harm to the king and his kingdom, especially in Andalusia.

Also, my lord, as we understand it, and we have taken advice too from others more experienced than we are, you are not equipped, nor have you sufficient forces, to mount an effective attack in the Kingdom of Granada. What you should know is that the city of Granada is less than six leagues away, and the king of Granada is there with his whole army, two hundred thousand foot

> soldiers, five thousand horse, while you, my lord, have three hundred lances and five thousand foot who have just joined you, so that we do not understand how you could undertake a battle." (BAE:LXVIII, 221–22)

Alfonso Fernández continued with great tact to point out that others who had made unsuccessful attacks in Granada—Alfonso X, Prince John and Prince Peter, Peter I, and Muhammad V—had all had bigger armies. Realizing that the master of Alcántara's pride was the greatest obstacle, he tried to persuade him to go as far as the border, at the Río de Azores, so that if the king of Granada did not come there after a day or two, the master could go away with his honor intact. The master's reply was that "until he could see the Elvira Gate [one of the gates of Granada] or came to battle he would not turn back." "But," as the chronicler continues, "for one thing the master was a man with his own ideas, and for another he attended to astrology and to fortune-tellers, and had with him a hermit called Juan del Sayo [John in the Cape] who was telling him he was to conquer all the Moors [*la Morería*]. Also the foot soldiers who had joined him were common folk, and all they cared about was saying, 'We are on the way in the Faith of Jesus Christ' " ("Con la Fe de Jesu-Christo imos"; BAE:LXVIII, 222–23).

Nothing would dissuade the master from his enterprise, of course, and on April 26, 1394, he crossed over the Azores stream into Granadan territory.

> He found a tower which is immediately on the way into Granada which is called the Exea tower. There is usually a Moor there to look after the trains of pack animals and the merchandise belonging to the Christians when they go into Granada. As soon as the master pitched his camp there he had an attack mounted against the tower. He was wounded in his hand, and three of his men at arms were killed. The master summoned Juan del Sayo and said to him, "My friend, did you not say that of this company who are with me not one would die?" "Master," he replied, "the truth is what I am telling you, and I will add that as I understand it, that was to be in the battle." The master said that they should all go and eat, and after their meal they could burn the door of the tower down, for they had collected a great deal of firewood. The master went to eat, and halfway through the meal, while he was at table,

> the Moors appeared. As far as one can ascertain, there were one hundred twenty thousand foot soldiers, five thousand horse, for the king of Granada had called up his forces all over his kingdom, all men between sixteen and eighty were to come there, for that was the only frontier post under attack. (BAE:LXVIII, 223)

The Christian forces, when attacked, were quite outclassed and outmaneuvered. The master's own men were surrounded and fired at by "arrows and canonballs and slingshots and darts until they were all killed" (BAE:LXVIII, 223). The body of irregulars recruited on the way suffered heavy losses, but fifteen hundred got away and arrived in Alcalá la Real. And twelve hundred were taken captive. "And thus did this raid, which had been begun with such scant preparation, come to an end."

Of course matters did not end there, and what is reported about the repercussions gives us a good idea of the mechanisms for preserving the peace, and also the pressures which could drive the two societies into conflict. Henry III sent to Muḥammad VII to say "that he could be quite certain that the master had carried out that raid without his permission, so that if he had come to no good in it, that was what he deserved" (BAE:LXVIII, 223). As new master of Alcántara, the king nominated the treasurer of the rival order of Calatrava, obviously as a reproof, "and the friars of Alcántara took it as a great insult." The reaction of another order, that of Santiago, was interesting. The master of Santiago granted that the Alcántara adventure had been ill prepared and ill advised, but to teach the Moors a lesson he was now prepared to take part in a massive expedition. However, if the king of Granada really did wish to preserve the truce, his advice was for Castile to agree to peace (BAE:LXVIII, 224). The general feeling seems to have been that a war would ensue, but then news came to the king that Granada did indeed wish to continue the truce, and so Henry III decided to "cross the passes into Castile" and leave these Andalusian problems behind him (BAE:LXVIII, 224). Henry III did not wish to become entangled in a Granadan campaign, he had sufficient problems elsewhere.

Yet it was becoming increasingly difficult to maintain the peace. Raids came from the Muslim side of the frontier, and in one raid the Granadans penetrated as far as Cartagena.

Muḥammad VII sought, alongside his policy of peace with Castile, to have peace with the Aragonese crown, and in 1404–1405, while negotiations were going on in Barcelona, we find Henry III attempting, behind Muḥammad's back, to persuade Aragon into an anti-Granadan alliance instead (Arié 1973:123).

At this point a new potential ally for Granada arises where one might least expect it: in Navarre. What has been said about the Navarrese Mudejars and the friendly attitude of the kings of Navarre towards their Muslim community make it perhaps understandable that Charles III of Navarre should have had the idea of seeking in Granada a countervailing force to that of the Trastamarans, but inevitably the obstacle in the way of such an alliance was the distance that separated the two tiny kingdoms, and negotiations foundered when a Navarrese emissary was intercepted at Alcalá la Real (HEMP:XIV, 374). It was Granada that was ready to strike out in 1405, again on the eastern front. Raids towards Vera and Lorca were repulsed with heavy losses, but on the western front, to the north of Ronda, Ayamonte did fall to them (CCE:IX, 11). Just as Muḥammad VII had had to protest to Henry III in 1394 at the spectacular border infraction of the master of Alcántara, so Henry protested in 1405, sending Gutierre Díaz to the Granadan court. The long years of peace were coming to an end. It was becoming increasingly difficult on each side for the authorities to restrain hotheads and to patch up a peace without loss of face after a raid had taken place. Ayamonte's loss in particular seems to have been felt by the Castilians as a humiliation which they were called on to avenge.

In order to arrive at a two-year truce in 1406 difficult negotiations dragged on for a long time, with the Castilians insisting that all hostages should be released before they would sit down and talk (HEMP:XIV, 374). An agreement was finally reached, with commercial exchanges guaranteed, and provision for ad hoc frontier judges to bridge the gap between the incompatible Christian and Islamic legal codes.

As the Christians saw it, these negotiations were used as a cloak behind which the Granadans hid while preparing a massive attack on Quesada and Jaén. We do not have the Muslim side of this story, so it is impossible to judge if Muḥammad VII was guilty of misleading his interlocutors. In all probability it was as difficult for the Granadan crown to keep its belligerent military on a short leash as it was for Henry III to do the same. The Castilians long remembered and resented the fighting of 1406. Pedro Manrique acting in defense of Jaén took his troops up into the passes near Quesada to head off the invading troops, and there was cut to pieces by superior forces at the battle of Collejares (October 1406) (CCE:VIII, 11–12).

An accommodation was not now possible. For the first time for a very long while the Castilian king laid his plans to summon up popular support and a broad base of finance for a campaign; he placed the matter before a Cortes summoned at Toledo in late 1406 (Arié 1973:123). A new chapter was opening in the fighting between Castile and Granada.

At this very point, on Christmas Day, 1406, in fact, Henry III died and John II, who was a child in arms, succeeded him. In the past the death of a monarch had often been enough to lead to the suspension of a planned campaign. It is indicative of the very different mood in Castile that the Cortes went ahead and voted money for a campaign which was undertaken by the regents Ferdinand and Catherine of Lancaster. Castile was growing stronger. It had recovered from the demographic setback of the Black Death, which had struck in the middle of the fourteenth century. Castile was developing that formidable strength which was to take it into a position of dominance over Europe, America, the known world. Little Granada had never possessed the power to stand in Castile's path, and had survived by astute diplomacy as well as courage. Castile, conscious of its superiority, was ever less ready to accept easy negotiated settlements.

It is unfortunate that the relatively good sources available in Arabic for the fourteenth century are not matched by any Arabic work conveying the Muslim viewpoint on events in the fifteenth. Castilian historiography is particularly rich for this period, so we are by no means ignorant of the details of the fighting, but inevitably we lack perspective. Why Muslims did what they did is too often a subject of speculation. Whether the somewhat foolhardy campaigns sometimes undertaken were the result of desperation, and whether there were voices speaking for restraint and compromise, we cannot know. The way that the fighting developed suggests that the Granadans had little hope of achieving a satisfactory long-term truce or peace, and so a policy of vigorous responses to Castilian aggression and all-out resistance imposed itself as the only one that presented any hope of slowing or stopping the Castilian advance. One great difference between the fighting of the fifteenth century and that of the early fourteenth is that Granada in general had to rely on its own resources and was not able to import North African troops. Clearly some individuals came to fulfill a religious obligation to defend the frontiers of Islam—such outside help continued to arrive until the very end (and even into the Morisco period)—but organized bodies of troops no longer crossed the straits. Muḥammad V's policy of breaking loose from North African tutelage had had its advantages, but Granada was now paying the price.

Changes in Warfare

Warfare was changing in other ways, too. Above all artillery was beginning to play a greater role. For almost a century forms of artillery based on the use of gunpowder to project large stones had been known in the peninsula together with all the other engines of war, but they had not proved to be of decisive importance in the fighting. The first use of such artillery at Huéscar in 1325, and the much more important use of it at the siege of Algeciras in 1342–1344, were both examples of Muslim technical innovation. It was not an innovation that the Muslim side seems to have known how to exploit in the conditions of warfare of those days. This is readily comprehensible.

The new cannons were essentially instruments of offense, not defense. They battered down walls, and so could tip the balance in favor of those attacking a fortress. Now, attacks on fortresses were essentially of two kinds—either attacks mounted by rapidly moving groups of relatively lightly armed troops relying on surprise and/or stealth, or else siege operations bringing to bear large and slow-moving bodies of troops deploying the heavy engines of war of the day. Both sides made use of the tactics of rapid surprise raids, penetrating deep into enemy territory. Such tactics were felt to be of Muslim origin, and the Christians called the lightly armed horsemen who carried out these raids *zanātas* (*jinetes*). The heavy cannon had no place in such operations. Where the cannon came into their own was in set-piece sieges of fortified towns and cities. Since the Granadans were on the defensive and besieged very few Christian towns in this period, clearly the Christians had an incentive to develop and perfect the new weapon, while for the Muslims the cannon was a military toy of dubious use, as was demonstrated at Algeciras in 1342–1344.

In Ferdinand's campaigns during his regency we find that artillery has become not just one of many alternative forms of siege devices, but the principal weapon available to breach castle walls. Arrangements for bringing the guns to bear, for protecting the gunners, transporting the guns, supplying them with explosives and with cannonballs, become a major element in military planning. Ferdinand did not get his expedition into the field until very late in the season of 1407, in September, and he was in no position to attack Ronda itself, but he launched successful assaults on several strong points.

A good example of this stage in the fighting was the siege of Zahara, a naturally very strong castle where the inhabitants had had sufficient warning to strengthen their defenses by last-minute additional building works, sealing up with mortar possible means of ingress. In earlier times they might have felt secure, but Ferdinand brought up three mighty bombards. In this type of fighting holders of great military offices, such as the master of the order of Santiago and the *adelantado mayor* of Andalusia, were given the important, but inevitably subordinate, role of guarding the gunners, creating the conditions that enabled them to operate effectively. At first the inhabitants must have been able to congratulate themselves, for several days went by with all the shots going wide. The gunners were no seasoned experts, were in fact quite new to their task, but they quickly learned. The bombard set facing the main gate hit the gate post, and the stone projectile lodged there. Another hit knocked a corner out of the main tower, and a whole section of the wall fell. Yet another shot hit the gate and left the structure about to collapse. Meanwhile all round the ring of the ramparts the other guns were knocking holes in the defenses. All the Muslims had with which to reply were crossbows. These did great execution among the besiegers, but the weight of the bombardment was too much. "When the Muslims saw the stone which the cannon shot at the gate, they were amazed at the stone and at the impact, and they immediately began to sue for terms" (*Crónica de Juan II* 1982:136).

With all possible ways in and out blocked, four of the chief among the men of Zahara were lowered on ropes and spoke with Ferdinand, negotiating terms: the inhabitants were to be allowed to leave, but must surrender the fortress. It was only when they occupied the place that the Castilians realized how strong the defenses in fact were, and how well prepared Zahara had been for warfare of the old style; it was still stocked with grain and with projectiles for the crossbows. All this was left behind when the Muslims rode out on animals lent to them for the occasion by Ferdinand (*Crónica de Juan II* 1982:141).

Thus we can see that already by this stage the Castilians were beginning to pull ahead of the Granadans in their ability to mount a campaign. At Algeciras in 1342–1344 neither side had had a monopoly of the knowledge of technological skills required, but the superior economic and hence logistic strength of the Castilians was by the early fifteenth century enabling them to deploy the new arm effectively, and to blast open defenses which had hitherto been thought impregnable.

The cost of such a campaign was enormous. We are fortunate to have a complete breakdown of the personnel required to keep the Castilian siege artillery in the field in this campaign (*Crónica de Juan II* 1982:143–81 [*Ordenanza y reparto de los pertrechos de guerra*]). Of the three bombards already mentioned, we know that the biggest required a crew of two hundred men, the two others fifty each—and this does not take into account crews for lighter pieces—eighty men to provide the gunpowder, one hundred fifty men to procure and shape the stone projectiles, thirty men to maintain supplies of charcoal, and numerous others to look after transport and repair of carts, blacksmiths to make and repair tools and weapons, the list seems never to end. We can see in this campaign a different kind of fighting force emerging. The knights and the mounted fighting men, elite of so many armies, become auxiliaries to enable the effective weapon, the gun, to be brought to bear by sweating dirty artillerymen. When, after the victory at Zahara, the Castilians moved on to nearby Setenil, they began to run out of rocks, and the knights were given what must surely have been the somewhat inglorious task of finding more:

> With the agreement of the king's council, [Ferdinand] issued orders that each knight and nobleman, both those in the council and those in the camp, should transport eight rocks each in his carts. And he commanded Pedro Fernández de Sover, deputy accountant to the king, that each day he should allocate duties among the gentlemen so that they should each bring forty stones daily, and send out five knights for stones, so that the bombards should have an adequate supply. (*Crónica de Juan II* 1982:156)

Organized in this way the cannon fired "all day and even part of the night." The Muslims were not slow to react, and we hear of them reinforcing their structures to stand up to the cannonades, but it is obvious that in those places where the Castilians could deploy their new weapons they had an enormous superiority. Victory was not automatic, however, and this should be stressed. Even after the great gun with its two-hundred-man crew was brought up, Setenil still held out, and by the end of October Ferdinand decided that he would have to withdraw before winter came on. The withdrawal was obviously executed in some haste. As they were burning down their scaffolding (so the Muslims would not profit from it), the flames got out of control, and Ferdinand had to flee "as fast as he could to escape the fire," and the besiegers left most of their food stocks behind for lack of transport (*Crónica de Juan II* 1982:180).

The final incident of this attack on Setenil is of no consequence to the outcome, and yet it conveys the nature of this campaigning very well, and deserves quoting:

> The constable [of Castile, the great Ruy López Davalos] had remained with the rear guard, and he saw that the men with the equipment were scattered and badly led. The Infante Ferdinand had put him in charge, and he went down there, and had several carts containing equipment brought up and told them to keep together. But some of the men were turning back to collect an iron-bound ramrod for the big cannon which had been left behind in a cart. The constable went with this man but they could not find it, so the constable told him, "You wait here. I will go up to the town [of Setenil] and will see if it is still there. If they see one man they will not shoot or do anything, but if they see more, they will realize that we are looking for something."
>
> The constable did what he said, and as he arrived the people in the town began to call out insults. So he replied in Arabic, "Do not be rude!" Also a convert from Islam whom he had with him told them to keep quiet. Whereupon the governor of the fortress recognized the constable and said, "My lord Constable, what is it? Have you not had enough of doing us harm?" He replied, "All I am doing is looking for a ramrod and some pieces of iron which were left behind." And they replied, "Do not go on looking, we have got them up here to make horseshoes and billhooks." (*Crónica de Juan II* 1982:181–82)

On his journey down from Setenil the constable had a report of three thousand Granadans massed at Ronda to fall upon the Castilian artillery train and baggage:

> After a while the mounted Moors came to a place near to the transport columns, and they sent out a Moor to find out what

> escort there was with the transport column. The man they sent had been a Christian, and was nephew of Juana Martínez, a member of the Infante Ferdinand's household staff, who was married to Pero García, a notary. From the way he enquired after her, he was much attached to her. He went back to the Moors who sent him, and told them that the escort must be three thousand lances and many foot soldiers, and for that reason the Moors turned back to Ronda. The Moor who was Juana Martínez's nephew crossed over to join Prince Ferdinand that very day in Olvera. (*Crónica de Juan II* 1982:182–83)

Here we see how the constable of Castile knew quite enough Arabic to understand insults and to reply. We also see what an important role is played by converts, from Islam to Christianity and from Christianity to Islam. According to the theology of each side, such converts should not exist, but we constantly hear of converts on each side of the frontier. The renegade, the *tornadizo,* the *elche* might be regarded as suspect by both sides, but they provided an essential channel of communication between these two warring societies.

After failure at Setenil, Ferdinand had to pull back, and he returned to Seville itself. In spite of his success at Zahara, the Granadans had had sufficient success against the new Castilian offensive to encourage them. They struck back in the east, towards Jaén, in a raid that demonstrated that if Ferdinand and his cumbrous expeditionary force had to pull back into winter quarters, they—using *jinete* tactics, exploiting their superior knowledge of the terrain—could with their tough, more lightly armed cavalry still move, and even initiate a siege, in mid-winter. The fort at Alcaudete (north of Alcalá la Real) almost fell to them in February 1408. The Castilians needed a propaganda victory, and in what was a pointless incursion Fernán de Arias de Sayavedra forced his way right up to the outskirts of Ronda.

At this point what both sides needed was to regroup and lick their wounds. A truce was negotiated in April 1408. It might seem that the old pattern of truces was being resumed, but not so. This was a truce for seven months only. From now onwards truces were not, as they had been in the later fourteenth century, another way of describing an uneasy peace. During much of the fifteenth century truces were more or less short pauses in an incessant war.

In May 1408 Muḥammad VII died. It will be remembered that at his accession he had taken the place his elder brother Yūsuf might have expected to occupy, and had then consigned Yūsuf to captivity in Salobreña. There, during his whole reign, Yūsuf remained. A story exists which has every appearance of being a fiction, but which yet must be recorded. Allegedly on his deathbed Muḥammad bethought himself of his brother, and decided to do what he had refrained from doing all through his reign: have him killed. The order went out, and Yūsuf was about to be put to death, when he asked to play one last game of chess. This he managed to draw out for such a long time that his partisans were able to rally and to reach Salobreña in order to free him and place him at last on the throne (Lafuente y Alcántara 1859:41).

Yūsuf III, 1408–1417

Muḥammad VII had chosen constant activity and attack as the basis of his relationship with Castile, and at the end of his reign had come into conflict with Ferdinand who, as regent, had succeeded in putting into the field considerable forces. Yūsuf III, who for so long had languished as his brother's prisoner in Salobreña, began his reign by suing for peace. A skilled negotiator, ʿAbdallah al-Amīn, was despatched to the Castilian court, and a truce was obtained to last until April 1409 (later it was to be extended to the beginning of April 1410). Whatever were Yūsuf's true wishes, he now had to contend with Ferdinand's belligerent policies. The Granadans themselves were often only too ready to begin hostilities. On the Zahara front in particular the loss of that strongpoint as a result of the intense artillery bombardment was still resented. Four days only after the expiry of the truce, Granadans scaled the walls of Zahara and took it by surprise. In all, 140 men were killed, and 61 women and 122 children were taken off as captives, and the town itself was pillaged. No attempt appears to have been made to hold it. The loss in this way of what had been won with such effort rankled with Ferdinand. He had the town's governor (*alcaide*), who had been absent from his post at the time of the attack, arrested and accused him of treason. The charge had to be dropped, and another, less powerfully connected scapegoat was found for the defeat, but Ferdinand's fury was patent to all (BAE:LXVIII, 316). What he wanted was revenge, and the battlefield on which he chose to fight for that revenge was Antequera.

Up to this point Ferdinand's campaigns had not been directed seriously against any major town. Antequera was (and is) a prosperous agricultural center. The capture of Antequera, if it could be achieved, would represent an important step forward in the Castilian advance. If it could be held, then sooner or later Ronda, probably Ferdinand's real objective, could be picked off.

When Ferdinand first took up positions implying a siege of Antequera, in April 1410, the Granadan response was determined and vigorous. Yūsuf III's brothers ʿAlī and Aḥmad led an expedition from Archidona to break through the Castilian lines. The Muslim troops were led into battle by "a Moor who is said to have been their *alfaquí,* who kept saying: 'Charge, you poor ones [*mezquinos*], and you will not die!' " (BAE:LXVIII, 319; *Crónica de Juan II* 1982:306). (Why the Muslims should have been addressed as *mezquinos* is not clear.) A battle was fought and won by the Christians, who pursued the Muslims to where the Muslim camp had been pitched, at Boca del Asno.

The failure of the relieving forces left the field clear for Ferdinand to bring up his heavy train of siege equipment. Artillery was important, but here Ferdinand seems to have placed special reliance on an enormous siege ladder. The attempt was a ludicrous failure. All the men involved had been carefully trained, and they all knew in exactly what order they should make the assault: "who was to go first, who next."

It was a question of bringing the ladder sufficiently close to the walls and then dropping it into place. "They all said, 'My lord, it is near enough.' The infante thought it was not quite near enough, but they were all in such a hurry, and shouting it was in place, that he gave orders to have it lowered on the tower, but when it dropped down it fell short by at least one pace. As soon as the Moors saw the ladder had fallen short they rushed up onto the tower and began emptying burning pitch on it, and tow, so they set the ladder alight, and although the Christians put vinegar on the ladder, they could not put the fire out" (BAE:LXVIII, 323; *Crónica de Juan II* 1982:318–20). That was on June 27.

Ferdinand, who had a choleric temperament, was very angry indeed. Perhaps his anger explained the rather puzzling fact that in spite of Granadan attempts to negotiate an end to the siege on terms advantageous to the Christians, Ferdinand insisted on fighting on.

In the *Chronicle of John II* (BAE:LXVIII, 330–43), there is an account of these negotiations in 1410, which consists largely of quotations from letters allegedly exchanged between Yūsuf and Ferdinand—correspondence which is most illuminating both for the information it provides on the long-term evolution of relations between the kingdoms (on the questions of whether Granada was or was not "vassal" to Castile and whether it regularly paid tribute), and also on the immediate motivation of Ferdinand and of Yūsuf in the flare-up of fighting in this period. It is, for this reason, worth examining in some detail.

In general, of course, we need to be highly suspicious of "documents," or purported extracts from documents, incorporated into chronicles. Even if it is genuine, a single document out of its sequence and out of its context may give a misleading impression. The archives of Granada have long since disappeared, so that we have imperfect information on the characteristics of genuine documents of this type (although some do survive, as for example in the archive of the Kingdom of Aragon). Nevertheless, there are strong reasons in this case for accepting the "letters" as a reasonably faithful reflection of the negotiations which undoubtedly took place. Reasons for accepting the information contained in chapters 156 and 157 of this chronicle are both internal and external to the text. Insofar as internal evidence is concerned, these letters allegedly translated from Arabic to Castilian do bear all the hallmarks of such documents, down to a certain degree of syntactic incoherence, such as often results when translators grapple with the near-impossible task of rendering the flowery formulae of Arabic diplomatic usage into another tongue. A would-be forger could have counterfeited such formulae as the initial *en el nombre de Dios, piadoso apiador* or the final authenticating words *Cierto es esto* (Ar. *ṣaḥḥa*), but it would have been difficult to counterfeit the general style. A forger would have tended to produce better Castilian, and less clumsy calques on Arabic usage.

This argument based on language and style would be of little weight if the other characteristics of the chapters did not also suggest that they contain texts of genuine Granadan provenience. The correspondence presents the Granadan case in a forceful and cogent way. To many readers it will seem that Yūsuf rather than Ferdinand gets the better of the argument, although the chronicler presumably would not have agreed, since he presented these documents to illustrate what was from his point of view Ferdinand's admirably firm way of handling such negotiations.

A very brief account indeed of negotiations that end nowhere is all we find in Galíndez's version of the *Chronicle* (BAE:LXVIII, 332), but it is placed after the capture of Antequera, not before:

> [After capturing Antequera the Infante Fernando left it and proceeded to marshal his forces.] And to see the infante there came Diego Hernández Abenzacin [?] and Zayde Alemin, and he told them to travel with him to Alhonoz, and he would there attend to the business they brought. On the following day he went to a river called Alhonoz, and was there with Zayde Alemin, who spoke to him on behalf of the king of Granada in order to arrange a truce, but one could not be arranged.

The longer account of why these negotiations failed (in the text edited by Carriazo in 1982) places them before the main battle, and shows us Yūsuf III reproaching Ferdinand for having felt inhibitions (*sufre verguença*) about allowing his negotiator Saʿd al-Amīn to enter his camp (although he did eventually let him in to do honor to Yūsuf). "Allowing negotiators [*alaqueques*] access to towns and camps is not to be denied whether in time of peace or war, and we allowed Diego Fernández into our court, our Alhambra and our own palace, and even our own presence [*fasta entre nuestras manos*]."[2]

Yūsuf III states his objective as follows:

> What we want is to remove the harm which results to both Christians and Muslims from the slaughter and captivity and the pointless loss of life and property inflicted upon great knights and good men on both sides, so that what is lost in a day could not be replaced in many years, or will never be replaced, for when a great knight or some well-known leader dies on either side, time does not bring another such: what we are asking for is of common benefit to both sides. (*Crónica de Juan II* 1982:332)

Ferdinand's blunt answer to this plea was: "If the king wanted a truce, let him pay the tribute which they used to give to the kings, and pay to the king his lord and his nephew what they used to give to King

2. *Crónica de Juan II* 1982:332. Yūsuf's view of the function of the *alfaqueque* corresponds to that set out by Alfonso X in *Las Siete Partidas* (1807:336–39).

Alfonso [the Wise], son of King Ferdinand, who conquered Seville, and let vassalage be sworn."

The arguments by which Yūsuf rejects Ferdinand's demands are perhaps the most interesting part of the exchange: "He said he would behave towards him and towards his king as his brother the king of Granada [i.e., Muḥammad VII] had done towards him, and as the king his father [i.e., Yūsuf II] had done to his father [i.e., John I], and as his grandfather [i.e., Muḥammad V] had behaved towards his [i.e., Henry II]" (*Crónica de Juan II* 1982:333).

This is a crushing argument. For three generations, since the 1370s, no tribute had been paid, no vassalage sworn, so why should he start to do so in 1410? Ferdinand's arguments are based on the original Alfonsine dispensation which had fallen into desuetude. As for the period of interruption, that is not denied, it is simply blamed on the Castilian king's preoccupations:

> Prince Ferdinand replied that it was not right, for the three kings, his grandfather, his father, and his brother, had lived in times when, if tribute was not paid, and vassalage not sworn, this was because they had not asked for them when due, through being occupied with their own subjects, and for that reason there arose the practice of not paying them. The truce had been broken [by the Castilian] because Muḥammad VII had not kept his word and had taken the castle of Ayamonte by stealth.

Ferdinand's last word was that if the king would not pay the tribute and hand over all the Christian captives whom he held in his country, and hand over certain towns to be held as a security to guarantee payment of the tribute, he could in no way assume the responsibility of stopping a war which had been begun.

Each side was unwilling to yield. Ferdinand insisted on the rights of Castile as established in the mid-thirteenth century. Yūsuf saw no reason to resume the tribute payments so long interrupted in the fourteenth.

At this point the *Chronicle* interjects a story of a plot to burn down Ferdinand's camp, a conspiracy allegedly launched by the ambassador Çayde Alemin, and which was to have been put into effect by a number of converts from Islam who were serving in the Castilian forces (*Crónica de Juan II* 1982:336–43). There would seem to be no reason to accept that this plot ever existed except as a propaganda exercise aimed at discrediting Saʿd al-Amīn and his embassy. It would seem incredible that a conspiracy of this nature should be planned well in advance and yet depend, as the account has it, on little boxes looking like ointment boxes but containing pitch, and a fire to be fanned by the evening breeze so as to set the camp ablaze!

What is of interest in this farrago is that the plot is said to depend on six men in the camp of Muslim descent, the chief of whom is Rodrigo de Vélez, "son of Abdarrahamel, grandson of Don Abdallah" (*Crónica de Juan II* 1982:337). Men of such origin were clearly not unknown in the Christian forces, and the picture of a purely Christian army facing a purely Muslim one turns out to be too simple. On both sides we find some people who are bilingual, some people brought up on the other side of the frontier, some people whose loyalties were divided. The states of the Iberian Peninsula had lived with this situation all through the Middle Ages, and it had presented no special problem. We have seen that the Kingdom of Navarre developed a corps of military specialists who were Muslims, and who were clearly felt particularly loyal to the house of Evreux and to the kingdom. What we can see in the alleged incident in the camp of Ferdinand at Antequera was how in the fifteenth century the old ways were under strain, old bases of trust and loyalty were about to be destroyed. The pogroms directed at the Jews twenty years or so before in Castile may not have been without effect on what was happening between Christians and Muslims. The Christian kingdoms, in particular, were beginning to perceive members of non-Christian religious communities as dangerous. The rather fantastic circumstances of the alleged plot may bear little resemblance to what went on in Ferdinand's camp at Antequera, but this story reveals a great deal about the forms of the popular imagination of this period. The nasty incident ended with the agent provocateur Rodrigo de Vélez being paid handsomely to send him on his way, and eventually rewarded with a state pension, and with the five others allegedly implicated being tortured, executed, quartered, and the quarters strung up on a gibbet (*Crónica de Juan II* 1982:343).

Meanwhile fighting continued all round the walls. It is interesting that at this stage the chronicler notes that the weapons the Christians had that were able to inflict the heaviest casualties on the Muslims were two heavy windlass crossbows (*ballestas de garrocha*), which the Castilians managed to position very high on the siege scaffolding they had constructed (*Crónica de Juan II* 1982:376). From this vantage point they could shoot down on the Muslims inside the town "and the shots went straight through them, and the armor and shields, and came out the other side. However heavily protected they came, nothing could stop the crossbow bolts."

Against the Christian crossbows the Muslims did deploy a cannon, showing that they possessed such weapons. "For this reason they shot at the firing platforms from the towers with a cannon [*trueno*]. It had often shot at them and done no damage, but on September 12 they scored a hit on the middle of the platform where the two crossbowmen were, and killed one of them immediately" (*Crónica de Juan II* 1982:377).

It was a group of men with a scaling ladder who finally took the defenses unawares on September 16, and although there was some continuing resistance in the castle keep, Antequera had to surrender on terms that simply allowed the inhabitants to leave with transportable property. The author of the *Chronicle of John II* claims to have counted them himself: fighting men, 895; women 770; children, 863: total, 2,528. Fifty of these died as they waited for transport "and on the road to Archidona many more of them died for there were sick and old people among them" (1982:390).

Ferdinand had secured the victory on which he had staked so much. Granada had lost not only a fine town but a fertile region. What was worse, the fact that a large army led with determination could take not just a border fortress but a populous town in the Muslim heartland exposed to the Castilians the fact that the military balance now favored the aggressor. The Christian victory was indeed an important one, and Ferdinand is always after this referred to as *el de Antequera*. He might well have hoped to have other Granadan battle honors attached to his name, but, to the great good fortune of Granada, in 1412 he became king of Aragon, and was absorbed by other preoccupations. Even as king of Aragon he represented a threat to Granada, and he opposed maritime commerce between Granada and his new kingdom. His death in 1416 removed Yūsuf III's most dangerous enemy.

Thus it was that from November 1410 a new period of peace began. John II's new regent Henry (later Henry IV) was content to negotiate a truce between 1412 and 1415. The renewal of the truce concluded in 1417 was negotiated with Catherine of Lancaster. The Granadans, emboldened by the disappearance from the scene of their great enemy Ferdinand, refused to give formal tribute (*parias*), and a diplomatic face-saving formula was accepted by the Castilians: "the king of Granada would give her *by way of a present* 100 Christian captives, that should not appear as if they were given as tribute" (BAE:LXVIII, 373).

Once again we see that wherever they could the Granadans escaped from the burden of paying tribute, and that Castile was by no means always able to impose its will on the neighboring state.

In 1416 Ferdinand had died, in 1417 Yūsuf III died too, and in 1418 Catherine of Lancaster also passed away. With the new Granadan monarch Muḥammad VIII there began a very different period of Granadan-Castilian relations.

SIXTEEN

The Interlocking Reigns of Muḥammad VIII, Muḥammad IX, Muḥammad X, Muḥammad XI, Yūsuf IV, and Yūsuf V (1417–1452)

The period that followed the death of Yūsuf III provides an extreme example of the Granadan phenomenon of multiple interlocking reigns. The days of Muḥammad V seem in contrast a model of stability and of continuity. Underlying causes for the many changes in government of this period were the interference in Granadan affairs emanating from Castile (and, to a lesser extent, from North Africa), but an important new factor in the situation was the bitterness of the fighting between factions within Granada. Of course this clan warfare was frequently manipulated by the Castilians (or other foreign powers), but, as in other parts of the world, the feuding at times got out of hand and was self-perpetuating. After 1410, or perhaps we should say after 1417, the drive to complete the conquest of Granada, which had been so in evidence when Ferdinand "of Antequera" was in command, became lost, and the mountain kingdom gained yet another half-century of respite. It was, however, a sad half-century, during which the Arabic-speaking nation the early Naṣrids had created was in process of bleeding to death from internal wounds. From the high point of Granadan culture achieved at the end of the fourteenth century, Granada declined rapidly.

When simply listed, the many changes of monarch are confusing. The underlying stability of the Naṣrid system even in this period is best grasped visually (see Figure 1). To say that over thirty-five years five monarchs ruled for varying periods of time gives the impression of bewildering inconsequentiality. But to describe the same period as one during which one monarch reigned for twenty-seven years, another for four, with three others reigning for less than a year apiece both sounds and is far less chaotic. A far greater degree of continuity underlay this regime than would be found in many others subjected to similar stresses and strains.

Upon the death of Yūsuf III rule passed direct and by primogeniture to the eight-year-old Muḥammad VIII, known as *al-sagīr* (*el pequeño,* "the little one"). In the circumstances, it is not surprising that Yūsuf's *wazīr* ʿAlī al-Amīn continued in office. The al-Amīn family had filled many senior posts under Yūsuf, and appear to have made enemies of a powerful clan, the Banū Sarrāj from Guadix and from Illora, which was to continue to be prominent in Granadan affairs until the very end. The Banū Sarrāj made their mark in 1419 when young Muḥammad VIII was ousted by a pretender who was the Banū Sarrāj nominee, Muḥammad IX *al-aysar* (*el zurdo,* "left-handed"). ʿAlī al-Amīn was executed and Abūʾl-Hajjāj Yūsuf b. al-Sarrāj took over from him.

The feuding of the Banū Sarrāj (Abencerrajes) captured the imagination of the Castilians, and already in the literature of the sixteenth century the Abencerraje was a romantic figure. The legend continued to flourish and proliferate inside Spain and outside it too: Chateaubriand gave us his *dernier Abencérage,* and Washington Irving found a place for the clan in his colorful tales and histories.[1] The literary dimension of the Abencerraje legend often stands in the way of our understanding the nature of political struggle in this period, although the earlier Castilian tales do serve to remind us of the importance of lineage (*linage*) in this society (Caro Baroja 1957:39–53).

1. There are many excellent studies of this literary dimension; see *El Abencerraje* (1983) and Carrasco Urgoiti (1956) for further bibliographical orientation.

FIGURE 1. The Kings of Granada, 1417-1454

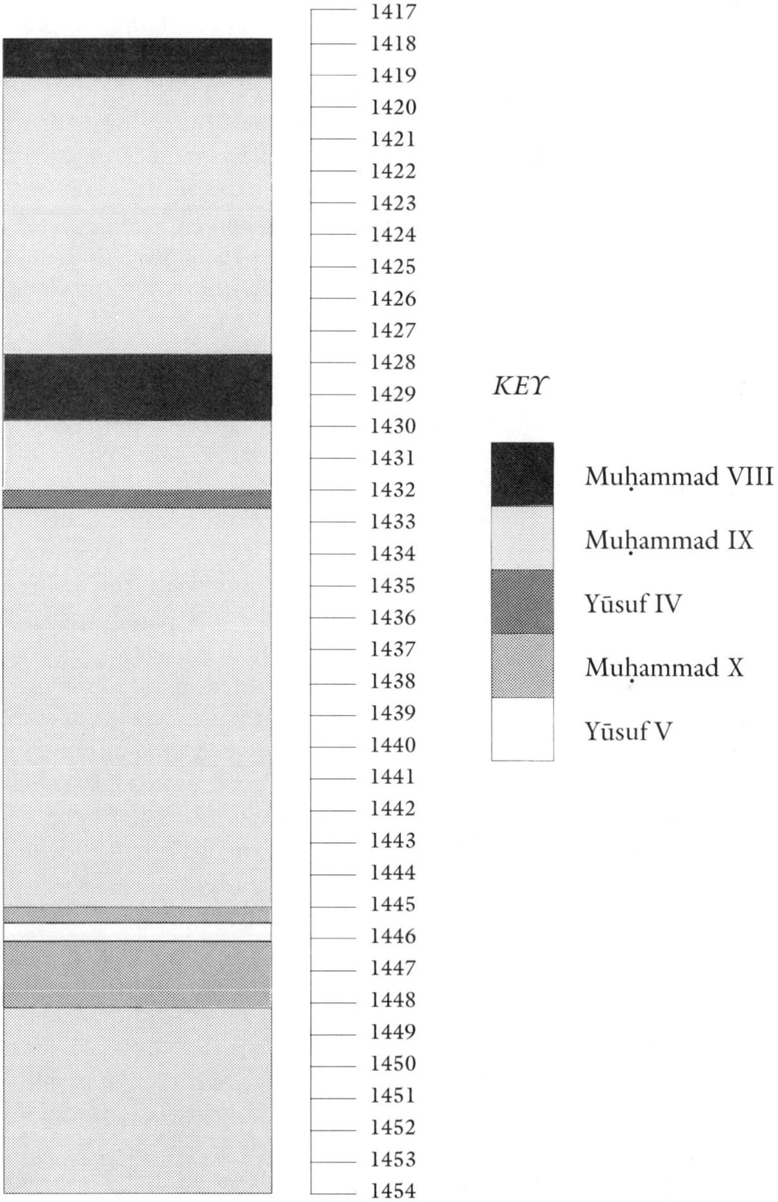

Muḥammad VIII's first short reign (he was to return to the throne for a second reign) lasted two years. He was ousted by Muḥammad IX, grandson of Muḥammad V. Muḥammad IX had early gained a reputation for ambition and cunning, qualities that had brought him imprisonment in the castle of Salobreña (often a detention center for potentially dangerous members of the royal family). The coup which brought Muḥammad IX to power was directed against ʿAlī al-Amīn by the Banū Sarrāj, who enjoyed the support of the Islamic lawyers. In the city Muḥammad IX was proclaimed; in the Alhambra ʿAlī al-Amīn was safe, but he unwisely accepted assurances that Muḥammad VIII could go safely into exile, and that he himself would come to no harm at the hands of Muḥammad IX. His assassination was carried out by men working for Muḥammad IX's wife, Zuhr al-Riyāḍ (Seco de Lucena 1955).

Muḥammad IX, First Period (1419–1427)

Whatever the degree of his responsibility for ʿAlī al-Amīn's death, Muḥammad IX certainly benefited from the crime. No change of policy became apparent, and although the Banū Sarrāj had criticized ʿAlī al-Amīn's regime for its lack of aggression towards the Christian enemy, deep Christian raids into Granadan territory in 1420 led by Alonso de Guzmán and Rodrigo Narváez failed to evoke any violent military response. Muḥammad IX was content to use the machinery that had evolved for resolving frontier disputes peaceably: the *jueces de frontera*, "frontier judges." Given the physical nature of the frontier and the psychological make-up of the tough but ill-disciplined men who faced each other across that frontier, it is hardly surprising that, even in times of peace, incidents not infrequently occurred which constituted infractions of the truce. The frontier judges provided a mechanism of arbitration which helped to prevent the frontier incidents from flaring up into out-and-out war. Finally, in 1427 disaster struck for Muḥammad IX when his inability to secure an extension of the truce from the Castilians led his people in the city of Granada to revolt. Their reaction probably arose from their calculation that he would have to pay a higher price in terms of tribute in order to buy peace (BAE:LXVIII, 405), and this would mean that their taxes would rise. They therefore preferred to take their chance with Muḥammad VIII again. The change of sovereign meant a change of ministers, and the Banū Sarrāj government was replaced by one under Riḍwān Bannigash or Venegas.

As his name indicates, Riḍwān had a mixed background. He is said to have been born of Christian parents, and to have been carried off as a captive when still a child. He was given a thorough Islamic education, which permitted him to rise rapidly through the bureaucracy. Such a pattern of recruitment to the higher echelons of government is, of course, reminiscent of the practices of the Ottomans and others. Their ruling classes were drawn from among imported slaves and captives, but an essential difference between the Turkish practice and that of the Granadans was that no impediment seems to have been placed in Granada in the way of the neo-Muslim's offspring following him into government, whereas Turks and Mamlukes sought to avoid corruption by banning the transmission of offices from father to son. Recruitment by slave raiding was, in any case, never more than sporadic in Granada, whereas in the Ottoman East the practice became institutionalized. Nothing like a corps of janissaries could ever emerge in Spain, and the foreign militia for Granada was, as we have seen, North African.

The Muslim side of the Venegas/Vanegas family were vulnerable to accusations that their loyalty to Islam was suspect. There were members of the family still in Christian service, and the two halves of the clan do seem to have had some contacts across the frontier, but nothing suggests that this faction in Granada was easily suborned. When final defeat came in 1492, it is true that one part of the Muslim family, that led by Sīdī Yaḥyā Alnayar, crossed over, so that Yaḥyā became Don Pedro de Granada, and was baptized (Durán y Lerchundi 1893:II, 167–217). Yuce Vanegas remained a Muslim, and kept up considerable state as a local dignitary (Harvey 1956).

What saved Muḥammad IX's life on the occasion of the change of regime was that he had available to him a place of refuge: Almería, to which he made his way with prudent haste. From Almería he was able to go on to Tunis, where Abū Fāris, the Ḥafṣid ruler, was willing to welcome him.

Muḥammad VIII for the Second and Last Time (1427–1429)

Muḥammad VIII was eighteen when he came to the throne for the second time. He relied on "anti-Abencerrajes" to staff his government. No matter who ruled, the basic problem was the same: how to negotiate a truce, and how to raise the finances for the payment of the tribute exacted by the Castilians. Castile's superior size and greater numbers meant that unless it was embroiled in civil wars, it could easily unleash dangerous raids, and the Granadans were willing to pay to avoid destructive forays. Granada wanted to negotiate long periods of truce in order to secure stability, the Castilians, on the other hand, preferred to keep the Granadans on a short lead, and tended only to allow truces of twelve months or less.

The ways in which relations between Castile and Granada were linked with the state of relations between Castile and Aragon are particularly obvious at this stage. For so long as Castile could count on peace with Aragon, it felt free to develop a hostile policy towards Granada, but if poor relations with the Christian neighbor prevailed, then Castile would seek peace on its southern borders. Thus in 1427 and 1428 the Granadans sought in vain for truces of five years' duration and had to accept single-year renewals. Then, in 1429, Castile suddenly became willing to negotiate a renewal of indefinite duration because Alfonso V of Aragon had made a pact with Navarre and was already infringing Castilian sovereignty. At this point Castile was saved by the return of Muḥammad IX from North Africa.

In earlier days a Granadan pretender from across the seas might expect to land with a North African escort. How times had changed is shown by the fact that what the Ḥafṣids of Tunis sent was a suggestion that the Abencerraje party should turn for help to the Ḥafṣids' good friend and ally the Castilian monarch! (BAE:LXVIII, 488 [*Crónica de Juan II*]) The letters of recommendation were to prove quite worthless. Rather than back either of the existing contenders for the throne, Castile preferred to create its own puppet. But this is to allow the story to run ahead too fast. Let us return to the point when Muḥammad IX was contemplating an attempt to regain the throne under, so he thought, the aegis of the Castilians. The *Chronicle of King John II* does not tell us the whole story, but it provides a point of departure:

> At this time [late 1428] a Muslim gentleman called Yūsuf Ibn Sarrāj [Abenzarrax] arrived at Lorca with thirty mounted men. He had been chief minister of Granada, and a great favorite of King Muḥammad [IX] who had been driven into exile by Muḥammad [VIII], the small. This gentleman came seeking the king of Castile at Illescas, and in his company there came Lope Alonso de Lorca, who was regidor of Murcia and knew Arabic well. The king decided to send them both to the king of Tunis [Abū Fāris the Ḥafṣid] to tell him to send Muḥammad [IX] the left-handed to the kingdom of Granada, so that he would help him get it back again.

> To this end he sent letters of credence and everything needful for the voyage. When they had reached the king of Tunis, and Lope Alonso had explained his mission, the king [of Tunis] was delighted, and immediately had the escort which was to travel with them made ready: three hundred horse, two hundred foot soldiers, and these were all Granadans who had gone to Tunis because of the warm reception they found there. Lope Alonso traveled with them, and through him the king of Tunis sent to the king [of Castile] a gift of clothing made from fine linen and silken cloth, and musk, civet, amber, and many other kinds of perfume. They traveled by land across North Africa till they reached Oran, which belongs to the king of Tlemcen, whence they crossed to Vera, which is in the Kingdom of Granada [near to Almería]. There this King Muḥammad [IX] the left-handed was received as king, and thence Lope Alonso proceeded by sea to Cartagena. Within a few days he was with the king [of Castile], and could relate to him everything which had happened, and hand over the king of Tunis's gift, with which the king was much pleased.
>
> As soon as the people in Almería heard that the left-handed king was at Vera, they sent to ask him humbly to go there to be received as king, and this was done. When [Muḥammad VIII] heard about this he sent one of the princes, a brother of his, against him with up to six hundred horse. They came within sight of each other, and two parts [two-thirds?] of [Muḥammad VIII's] troops went over to [Muḥammad IX], and the rest fled back towards Granada. [Muḥammad IX] set out for Almería and then went to Guadix which immediately surrendered to him, and thence he went to Granada, where most people received him as king. [Muḥammad VIII] withdrew into the Alhambra, while Muḥammad IX set up his headquarters in a castle called Alcahizar, near the Alhambra, with those few men who remained with him. And Malaga, Gibraltar, Ronda, and all the other places in the kingdom, sent to signify their loyalty and to acknowledge him as their king. (BAE:LXVIII, 449)

No doubt the Castilian chronicle gives full emphasis to the extent of the Castilian participation, but it is clear that if Muḥammad IX had succeeded in occupying the Granadan throne at this juncture, it would have been as a puppet of Castile. It is curious that the Banū Sarrāj should have underwritten such an ill-advised venture. What the chronicle has found it convenient to omit is that Muḥammad VIII, when threatened by the advance of Muḥammad IX, turned to John II and asked him for help. He had every right to expect this by the terms of their peace accord. But Muḥammad IX also made diplomatic *démarches* to Castile. At this point a sort of auction began, with the two Muḥammads bidding against each other. Muḥammad VIII made the offer that he thought John II wanted to hear: he would become Castile's vassal. Muḥammad IX, in de facto possession of most of the Granadan kingdom, was not willing to go so far, and held out for independence.

John II could afford to play for time, and in fact sent his negotiator Lope Alonso to Granada to make soundings. Muḥammad IX must have been infuriated, for he had with Castilian support set out to regain his throne, and had almost succeeded in doing so, only to find that Castile was altering the basis of the understanding between them, and demanding full vassalage, not to mention some territory.

It was in late 1429 that the diplomatic game of poker was resolved, for Muḥammad VIII surrendered, and Muḥammad IX became sole master of Granada without being beholden to Castile (CCE:VIII, 57–58 [*Halconero*]). His rivals Muḥammad VIII and his brother were sent to Salobreña. (It may appear that the custom of clemency to defeated rivals was becoming established, but nothing was further from the truth. In Salobreña they were put to death, as we shall see.)

Muḥammad IX, Second of Four Reigns (1430–1431)

Muḥammad IX had refused to be browbeaten by John II's negotiator, and thus emerged as the winner, but he had forgotten the cardinal rule that Granada should avoid appearing to win. He now had to face the peril of John II's wrath.

Muḥammad IX had refused to accept John as his overlord, he had not refused to negotiate. In April 1430 Ibrāhīm ʿAbd al-Barr was sent to John to offer Castile help against Aragon (CCE:VIII, 70). John kept Granada in a state of uncertainty, and renewed his claims: tribute should be paid, prisoners freed. He offered a truce of one year only. Muḥammad IX refused, and John launched a military offensive. Muḥammad IX was diplomatically outmaneuvered, for the Castilians suddenly had peace on their Aragonese frontier, and what was more, Muḥammad's Ḥafṣid backers succumbed to a mission (under Lope Alonso) to Tunis laden with gifts of "fine pieces of scarlet cloth." Tunis had been about to despatch ships to help Muḥammad IX, instead they wrote chiding him for displeasing the king of Castile. "What he should do was to pay in full the tribute due as his forebears had done; he could have no hope of receiving sustenance or assistance from him against his good friend the king of Castile" (BAE:LXVIII, 488).

This last sentence is clearly suspect, and was probably inserted in the *Chronicle of John II* by those anxious to reinforce the case for Castilian suzerainty (even if a Muslim ruler had given advice to this effect, he would have worded the advice quite differently).

Muḥammad IX's great enemy within the Granadan ruling elite was Riḍwān Venegas. Riḍwān's master Muḥammad VIII had died in March 1431, when Muḥammad IX had him assassinated at Salobreña. In May Riḍwān at the head of a small band crossed the frontier to go to see John II in Cordova. What Riḍwān proposed was a third candidate for the throne, a grandson of Muḥammad VI, Yūsuf [IV] (usually known to the Castilians as Abenalmao, "Ibn al-Mawl") (BAE:LXVIII, 496; CCE:VIII, 106; Seco de Lucena 1959:284).

Yūsuf made no difficulties about swearing fealty to John II, and the Castilians endeavored to force this puppet ruler on Granada. John II's great favorite, Álvaro de Luna, took a prominent part in this campaign: "Several times the constable escorted him to near to Alcázar Genil where many Moors were massed. He sent to tell them to accept Yūsuf as their king, or otherwise they would have to have him imposed on them against their will. Although there were talks on this subject, in the end there was no agreement at that time" (CCE:I, 336–37 [*Victorial*]).

The display of Castilian military might which created the conditions for the imposition of the puppet ruler was the so-called battle of La Higueruela (otherwise Andaraxemel). It was an encounter fondly remembered on the Castilian side for many exploits of heroism (it is commemorated on the walls of the Hall of Battles in the Escorial). Strategically the Christians achieved little or nothing, but as a parade of strength it sufficed to persuade the Granadans to open their gates to the Castilians' nominee, Yūsuf IV. Once in possession of the city (or a major part of it) Yūsuf formally acknowledged his vassal status, and agreed to make payments both in money and in kind (BAE:LXVIII, 503; Suárez Fernández 1954:39–42).

Yūsuf in Granada was not able to impose his will elsewhere. Almería and Malaga were outside his control, and finally even those in Granada who had accepted him fell away. Whether they killed him themselves (as Diez de Games states in *El Victorial* [CCE:I, 337, IX, 132]), or handed him over to Muḥammad IX (as the *Chronicle of the Falconer* has it), for him to be put to death, does not really matter. An episode of Castilian policy was at a close. The Castilians did not have the logistic capacity to sustain the sort of campaign which would be needed to reduce the Granadans to surrender, nor was it possible to rule through a mere creature such as Yūsuf IV. The solution that remained for them was Muḥammad IX.

An anecdote and a poem illustrate the limitations of Castilian power. The anecdote concerns, in the first place, Álvaro de Luna, but casts light on the standards of victualing in the Castilian army, and the difficulties of keeping an army in the field so far from base. Shortly after La Higueruela, Álvaro de Luna

> with his army took up position on a hillock called Vizcarao near Antequera. The troops began to complain of the lack of food, which they could not obtain, especially certain bodies of foot soldiers from Biscay and from the Mountains [i.e., Asturias]. They began to desert, saying they could not keep alive without food. The constable said they should make do as best they could, and soon their situation would improve. If there were need, he said, he would together with them eat herbs [*las yerbas,* perhaps simply "grass"] out of duty to his lord the king, and to the good of that land. The captains of the foot soldiers said they were not brute beasts to have to eat *yerbas,* and they would stay no longer, and would lead their troops away. The constable gave orders that some of them were to be subjected to justice and beheaded. (CCE:II, 127 [*C. de Álvaro de Luna*])

Granada would be able to hold out so long as Castile was not able to sustain its troops in the field through the hard slog of a long campaign.

The poem "Ibn Aḥmar, Ibn Aḥmar" ("*Abenamar, Abenamar, moro de la morería*") is one of the most famous of the ancient frontier ballads. It puts into the form of a dramatic dialogue the Castilian attempt to impose Yūsuf IV on Granada. After the Castilian king and the Moorish king (Yūsuf) have spoken of the glittering prize of the city of Granada which they can see in the distance, the city itself, personified as a woman being forced into an unwanted marriage, has the last word, pointing out that her hand is not available:

I am a married woman, King John,	Casada soy, rey don Juan,
A married woman and no widow,	Casada soy, que no viuda;
And the Moor that keeps me	el moro que a mí me tiene,
Loves me very dearly.	muy grande bien me quería.
	(Smith 1964:126)

One of the remarkable qualities of these frontier ballads is that, although written in Castilian, they often achieve remarkable empathy with the Granadan and his predicament. The poem conveys the depth of the emotional commitment of the Granadan people to their by now well-established separate identity, their rejection of the blandishments of those who would wish to see Granada swallowed up by its more powerful neighbor.

Muḥammad IX, for the Third and Longest of His Four Reigns (1432–1445); the Confused Reigns of Muḥammad X (1445 and 1446–1447) and Yūsuf V (1445–1446); Together with the Final Reign of Muḥammad IX (1447–1453), and Muḥammad XI (1451–1452)

The administration of Muḥammad IX which took over in 1432 included a number of able and powerful men associated with the Banū Sarrāj faction: Ibn ʿAbd al-Barr was chief *wazīr;* Ibn Kumāsha and Saʿīd al-Amīn (brother of the assassinated minister of Muḥammad VIII) also served. Meanwhile Riḍwān Venegas prudently sought refuge in Castile. As far as external relations went, the policy was to try to maintain peace, but at the same time to seek to remain independent, and that was what John II refused to accept. At no time in the whole history of Granada was the issue of vassalage posed with greater clarity. In 1432 Castile obtained a bull of crusade, and by the summer of that year, Castilian attacks had begun in earnest, although there was no large-scale single incursion, such as the one that led up to the battle of La Higueruela. Castilian tactics were rather to lay waste (*talar*) crops and agricultural installations with the double objective of inflicting damage on the Granadan economy and, if at all possible, tempting the Granadans out into a fight in the open. The Castilian troops posed a dilemma for the Granadans. The more heavily armed Castilians often had the advantage of the Granadans in pitched battles, which the Granadans in general avoided. But could the Granadans allow their carefully cultivated land to be reduced to a desert?

This process of attrition went on all through the 1430s (Seco de Lucena 1978: 171–79), and the Granadans had some victories: in 1433 as far afield as Álora and Écija, in 1435 at Guadix, Huelma, and Ubrique. But the Castilian strategy was beginning to tell, and one by one Granadan castles and fortified villages could be picked off: in 1433 Benzalema and Xiquena on the eastern front, in 1435 Huéscar, in 1436 both the Vélezs, Rubio and Blanco, with Galera. In 1438 Íñigo López de Mendoza of literary fame took Huelma. Given Castile's superior numbers, this process of nibbling away at the frontier, combined with destructive expeditions aimed at the agriculture of the heartlands, would eventually bring Granada to its knees. Particularly cruel were the attacks on the Granadans' arboriculture (an activity in which the Granadans had excelled). A grove of olive trees or of mulberries represented a sustained investment over many years, and once axed the trees took years to replace. Chopping down trees in their productive prime was a loss even more severe than that of standing crops in the fields.

Suddenly relief came to Granada, and thanks to events quite out of its control. Álvaro de Luna, the most powerful man in Castile, for long chief minister of John II, was challenged in 1439 by the "Infantes de Aragon," Henry and John, princes of the Trastamaran house, who resented this non-royal personage who seemed to control everything. And so with divisions inside the Castilian camp, John II authorized Íñigo López de Mendoza to negotiate a truce, not for just one year but for three.

The respite may have saved Granada from collapse, but paradoxically it led to Muḥammad IX's regime falling. Malcontents who had kept silent for so long as the enemy were actually on Granadan soil, now felt free to voice their pent-up grumbles. Two rival claimants to the throne emerged.

In the east a leader known as *al-Afnah* (*el cojo*, "the lame one") used his position as governor of Almería to strike at the regime in Granada, to drive out the Banū Sarrāj-based administration, and to come to power as Muḥammad X (Arié 1973:138). In 1445–1446 the sequence of events of 1430–1431 was almost repeated. The Castilians, faced with chaos in Granada, decided to impose their own ruler, this time Yūsuf V (Seco de Lucena 1955:402), Aben Ismael in the Castilian sources. This Castilian nominee, grandson (or was it great-grandson?) of Muḥammad V, did not last more than a few months, and Muḥammad IX returned for a fourth reign, which was to last for some six years (1447–1453/4). An old man by now, Muḥammad IX rather puzzlingly began to have recourse to assassination, to eliminate Muḥammad X, and then, in about 1450, he took a step intended to bring to an end the feuding within the Naṣrid house. He tried to win over the partisans of Muḥammad VIII by associating with himself on the throne Muḥammad VIII's son, Muḥammad XI, known as *el Chiquito* (Livermore 1963:331–48).

Rachel Arié (1973:Tableau No. 1) follows Seco de Lucena in placing Muḥammad X as son of ʿUthmān, son of Naṣr, son of Muḥammad V; the Muḥammad who descended through Muḥammad VIII, Yūsuf II, and Yūsuf III is, in her view, Muḥammad XI who reigned from 1451–1452 and 1453–1454. Resolution of the intricate puzzle is not an easy matter, although when numismatic and notarial evidence is sifted, perhaps the details of the succession at this period will be clearer.

It is not always possible to ascribe responsibility for the numerous frontier raids and forays of this period; in particular it is difficult to say exactly who sponsored and planned the Muslim raids into Christian territory. The absence of a Granadan ruler of commanding authority with a broad base of support meant that opportunistic raids could easily be launched by local commanders. To put troops in the field for an inconveniently long and unprofitable campaign was not easy to arrange, but frontiersmen who had heard of some easily rustled herd of cattle could only with difficulty be restrained from setting out to steal them.

The frontier was sinking rapidly into anarchy, and the king of Granada was losing his ability to offer in negotiations with the Castilians some reasonable prospect of peace. This meant that the attractiveness to the Castilians of the policy of controlling the frontier through "vassals" or even puppet rulers diminished (the vassals could not deliver peace or tribute), and the potential advantages of proceeding to the point of outright conquest grew. Granada might hope to survive for so long as Castile was rent by internal discord, but if ever Castile managed to shed the handicap created by its rebellious nobility, its increasing strength (based on a rising population and a healthy economy) would enable it to eliminate the Muslim regime in Granada altogether.

The *Chronicle of John II* paints a picture of disaster for the Castilians in 1447 at the tactical level. The Muslim regime could hope for limited and short-term successes, but what it lacked by this time was any coherent strategy which would permit Granada to build on its tactical successes and survive in the longer term. By the mid-fifteenth century Granada was living on borrowed time.

> The Moors, aware of the dissensions in these kingdoms, made incursions in divers places, and caused great harm, not only carrying off large herds of cattle, and taking men and women captive, but also capturing by assault towns and fortresses formerly won by the Christians at great effort and expense, and at the cost of great loss of life. This year [1447] they took the town of Benamaurel and Benzalema and the town and castle of Arenas, and Huéscar, and the towns and castle of Vélez el Blanco and Vélez el Rubio, the which places were lost not because of any fault on the part of the garrison commanders, but rather was it the fault of those surrounding the king, for he had received many requests from the commanders for supplies and munitions, all of which were ignored. There were even some in the Royal Council who held it would be better for these places to be lost than for them to be held at the cost which was being incurred. (BAE:LXVIII, 654)

This offensive of 1447 pushed the frontier almost back to where it had been when Fernando of Antequera undertook his campaigns; places safe even in those days suffered grievously. At Cieza on the Murcian front, forty kilometers northwest of Murcia itself, a raid in 1449 (and hence presumably authorized by Muḥammad IX) wiped out the Christian community almost completely. So great was the number of captives borne off, from a region which must surely have come to think of itself as at a quite safe distance from the fighting, that the Castilian authorities had to enlist the good offices of Pope Nicholas V to negotiate the ransoms (L. Suárez in HEMP:XV, 194–95). Nor was this type of deep raiding restricted to the eastern frontier. The very same year raiders reached within "five leagues" of Seville itself (CCE:VIII, 532 [*Halconero*]).

In 1449 we find a most unusual pattern of alliances: Granada and Navarre versus Castile. That the two small kingdoms had a common cause is obvious enough; within half a century both were to be gobbled up by Castile. We have also seen how the house of Navarre relied on its own Muslim minority population to provide an important contingent in its army. However, the distance separating the two states made effective coordination of effort difficult.

As the Castilian *Chronicle of John II* tells us:

> Because the king of Granada [unfortunately not further identified] knew of the great rifts and troubles which beset the kingdom of Castile, and the great hardships there, he made every effort to help and favor the king of Navarre and the knights who were of his opinion. In order to give further encouragement to the king of Navarre, he had his knights on many occasions make forays into Castile, and on some of these raids they encountered so little resistance that on one occasion they rode as far as Baena and on others to the outskirts of Jaén, and on others to Utrera. On these forays they were able to inflict much damage, and they drove off great herds of cattle, and they captured many Christians and killed others. In addition they sent to the king of Navarre to incite him to make raids into Castile with such strength as he could command, and the king of Granada assured him that he would come immediately to besiege Cordova, and would not abandon the siege until he had won the city for him.
>
> The king of Navarre replied that he was much obliged and he and the knights of his opinion would shortly invade Castile to claim back what was their own, and when this was done he would inform him and call on his assistance. (BAE:LXVIII, 668)

The chronicle interprets this reply as an attempt by the Navarrese to temporize without committing themselves, but in the circumstances it is not surprising that suddenly John II became willing to conclude a truce. The Granadans accepted: rather than playing for high stakes in Castile they had to deal with dissidence in Malaga where Yūsuf V (Aben Ismael) had briefly managed to establish himself (CCE:VIII, 542).

The idea of a serious attack on Cordova to be mounted at mid-century by Granada's armies sounds a fantasy, and probably was, but Castile certainly was at this point torn apart by the dissensions which arose as Álvaro de Luna's enemies came out into the open.

In Murcia the civil war raged, and Alonso Fajardo, hammer of the Muslims in so many combats, took himself to Granada, where he obtained military assistance on a lavish scale to use against his near namesake Pedro Fajardo, *adelantado* of the province. One thus has in 1450 the extraordinary alignment of Alonso Fajardo being besieged in Murcia by Christian enemies, with the city defended by Muslim troops from Almería under the two al-ʿAbbās (Alabez) brothers, by the *wazīr* Ibn al-Sarrāj, and by the *qāʾid* Mufarraj (Tapia 1986:368).

A note of warning should have sounded for Muḥammad IX in 1451 when on the Murcian frontier Alonso Fajardo and his numerous Christian enemies composed their differences in the face of the dangers of an invasion. Muslim forces were being marshaled at Vera in very great strength, forays had already been launched towards Lorca and Mula, and, for example, all the inhabitants of Molina Seca were borne off into captivity (Torres Fontes 1960:132).

We have seen that at all times the Muslim forces displayed superiority in the capacity of their cavalry to maneuver rapidly and to tempt adversaries into dangerous false positions where they could be destroyed. The Muslim tactic of *karr wa-farr,* of alternating between simulated flight and sudden attack, was the opposite of the heavy cavalry charge of the Christians. The exceptional readiness of the Muslims in this campaign of 1450 to meet the Christians head-on was to prove disastrous for them.

The *Chronicle of John II* narrates the encounter as follows: "On Thursday March 16 [1452] Alonso Fajardo sent word to Diego de Ribera of how he had information of six hundred Moorish horse and fifteen hundred foot soldiers who had invaded Christian territory and driven off forty thousand head of cattle and sheep with forty or fifty Christians" (BAE:LXVIII, 676). Diego de Ribera responded immediately, as did Alonso Fajardo, Garci Manrique his son-in-law, and many others.

> When they came in sight of one another, the Moors drew themselves up in battle array, and the Christian knights did the same. The battle was so keenly fought that the Christians had to make three charges, but finally the Moors were beaten, and more than eight hundred of them killed; the Christians lost forty killed, and two hundred wounded. Those Moors who could escape made their way to the top of a high range of mountains. Although these mountains were extremely steep, some of them were captured along with their mounts and other things. Amongst the Moors who died were fourteen captains, the names of whom were as follows: Ibn ʿAzīz, commander of Baza; Abūʾl-Qāsim, com-

> mander of the region of Granada; al-ʿAbbās, governor of Vera; the commander of Vélez el Blanco, of Almería, of Vélez el Rubio, etc., etc.[2]

This great defeat for the Granadans was known as the battle of Alporchones from the name of a village some fifteen kilometers east of Lorca. The mountains in which the Muslims took refuge were the Sierra de Almenara and the Sierra del Cantal. The battle was a great reverse for Muḥammad IX (with his associated monarch Muḥammad XI). The initiative, which had briefly and against all the odds been wrested by the Granadans from the Castilians, was now lost. The price Granada had to pay for venturing on to the offensive and losing the pitched battle was a heavy one in terms of leaders and men who died, perhaps more so in terms of morale destroyed.

The very extent of the Christian victory all but created a disaster for them in Lorca. That frontier town, principal base for Fajardo, became crowded with Muslims, with many prisoners awaiting ransom added to the existing Mudejar population. In June 1453 the Muslims rose and occupied the town, though not the castle. Alonso Fajardo hastened to Lorca and fought his way through to a point where he could make contact with the defenders of the castle. Once he had established control, the Muslims were massacred. He was not content with taking his revenge in Lorca, and mounted a fierce raid against Mojácar. That beautiful fortified village south of Vera had been thought of as impregnable. "I took Mojácar where such great deeds were done that the streets ran with blood" was how Fajardo reported what happened (Tapia 1986:382).

This was a period of political transition. We do not know when exactly Muḥammad IX died, but it must have been in 1453. The old king's hope of securing a smooth transfer of power to Muḥammad XI was not fulfilled, for the Castilians still had their candidate, Yūsuf V. True, the last attempt to foist him onto the Granadans in 1445 had failed miserably, but in Granadan politics, as Muḥammad IX himself had shown, rulers could sometimes learn by earlier mistakes. The misfortune of Yūsuf V was that his great opportunity came when Castile was rent with the crises arising from the execution of Álvaro de Luna

2. BAE:LXVIII, 676–77. The text only gives nine names, not fourteen.

and within months of the death of John II. There was little time to consider how to defend the interests of the Castilian candidate for the Granadan throne.

Thus one might have expected Muḥammad XI to take over without great difficulties after all. Not at all. To complicate the picture still further, the Banū Sarrāj produced a new claimant to the throne, Abū Naṣr Saʿd.

SEVENTEEN

Saᶜd (1453–1464) and Abūᵓl-Ḥasan ᶜAlī (1464–1482)

Saᶜd, 1453–1464

Abū Naṣr Saᶜd, known as "Ciriza" by the Castilians (presumably "Cirizá," i.e., a deformation of Sīdī Saᶜd) was no child-prince: he was fifty-five when he began his reign. Born in 1398, he was the son of ᶜAlī, brother of Yūsuf III. He was sponsored by the Banū Sarrāj but was also on good terms with Henry IV, who had succeeded John II on the Castilian throne (July 1454). Cirizá sent a delegation of nobles to do homage at Henry's accession, including his son Abū'l-Ḥasan ᶜAlī, known as "Muley Hacén" by the Castilians. Muley Hacén, who had arrived with an escort of three hundred fifty men, stayed on as hostage, and was accorded a palace in Arévalo in which to reside.

In the mid-1450s there were thus two kings in Granada. Muḥammad XI still occupied the Alhambra, the whole of Granada and Malaga, also Almería. Saᶜd's power base was Archidona, and westward from there towards Ronda (Arié 1973:141). Saᶜd had other supporters elsewhere, in Almería for example, but Muḥammad's position seemed the stronger, even though Saᶜd enjoyed both Castilian and Abencerraje support.

Henry IV early in his reign committed himself to the resumption of the fighting, and the strategy he followed was a continuation of the war of attrition and *talas* undertaken by John II. This accorded ill with the policy of "divide and rule," for destructive raids inevitably did harm to partisans of the Castilian-sponsored claimant (Saᶜd) as well as those of

Muḥammad XI. Thus in 1455 when Henry was attacking Malaga he had to desist from destroying the crops of Saʿd's supporters. (BAE:LXX, 107; cf. CCE:IV, 15).

The confused period of two monarchs came to an end in 1455 when Muḥammad XI became so unpopular in Granada that he had to flee. (The reason for his unpopularity was the fact that his representative, Ibrāhīm ʿAbd al-Barr, had bought a truce at what his subjects reckoned to be too high a price.) Saʿd thereupon entered Granada. Once in power, Saʿd, the Castilians' candidate, rejected the Castilian terms, which centered on the familiar demands for vassalage, tribute, freeing of captives, cession of some territory. Once again Castilian policy proved unworkable. If the Castilians found somebody to act as their nominee, either he became so unpopular he could not rule, or he asserted his independence and spoke up for his subjects against the Castilian demands. Saʿd's power was increased when Muḥammad XI, after fleeing the city of Granada, fell into an ambush set by Abūʾl-Ḥasan ʿAlī (released from Arévalo). Muḥammad XI was put to death inside the Alhambra, and with him all his heirs were suffocated (Arié 1973:143; Baeza 1868:5).

Henry IV now took up arms against Saʿd in earnest. Crops were destroyed round Malaga in the spring of 1456, round Granada in the autumn. By October Saʿd had to sue for a truce, but was granted only a five-month respite, which cost him twelve thousand doblas and six hundred prisoners. Saʿd was well advised to buy a little time, for Henry was acquiring enemies fast, and could no longer devote his full attention to the question of Granada. Even in the south he was probably more preoccupied with trouble caused for him by Fajardo. Gonzalo de Saavedra with six hundred men was despatched to besiege him and take him alive. Fajardo was openly condemned "because of his partiality towards the Moors" (BAE:LXX, 110), but for Henry his real crime was disobedience. In 1457 Saʿd was able to secure a truce to run until April 1461 (Arié 1973:144).

When fighting resumed in 1461, Abūʾl-Ḥasan in April defeated Rodrigo Ponce de León near Estepa, and in July Miguel Lucas de Iranzo was defeated at Arenas, but then in August the tide of war turned against Saʿd, with the capture of Gibraltar, that mighty fortress where so much blood had been shed in the past. This time rather than heroism we have black farce, for the garrison appears to have been more anxious to give in than were the besiegers to accept surrender, and the Castilians were as eager to squabble among themselves as they were to fight the enemy.

A Moor who was a fugitive from Gibraltar, Alí el Curro by name, soon to be baptized as Diego, crossed into the Christian lines, and informed the authorities in Tarifa that the fortress was poorly garrisoned and ready to surrender (CCE:IV, 75). The governor of Tarifa, Alfonso de Arcos, made the mistake of inviting a number of nearby towns and two powerful nobles to assist him. The forces that assembled lacked coordination and did little but maneuver for advantage.

The first men to reach Gibraltar were from such nearby places as Vejer and Alcalá de los Gazules. Thinking to gain all the booty for themselves, they rushed into a premature attack and were easily beaten off. Then the men of Cadiz came, only to find the Christians ready to give up and go home, and Alí el Curro doing his best to persuade them to fight!

At this point somebody else slipped out through the lines, and the remaining defenders realized that the weakness of the defense could not be hidden. They hastened to offer to surrender. They had the terms already written out, and must have been doing a lot of packing in advance, since they asked for four days to "tie up their bundles and settle their affairs." The Christians answered that since some of them were the king's men, others in the service of Count Juan Ponce de León, yet others of Duke Juan de Guzmán of Medina Sidonia, they had nobody empowered to negotiate terms (CCE:IV, 77). Not surprisingly the Gibraltarians were not very pleased (*no muy contentos*) to hear that. The count's son, Rodrigo Ponce de León, had by now turned up, but his old father was so infirm that he was still on the road.

The Gibraltarians heard the uproar at Rodrigo's arrival and were delighted. At last somebody to whom they could surrender! Rodrigo had to tell them to wait for the count and the duke, though he did promise to put in a good word for them. "At this reply the Moors went back inside very sad."

The men of Jerez had been watching all this, and when Rodrigo had gone, they told the Gibraltarians that what Rodrigo wanted was an excuse to take the place by storm and cover himself with glory. Now if they would be so good as to open the gates quickly, all two thousand of them would enter and grant them terms. The Gibraltarians agreed. At last somebody who would accept their surrender.

The mistake the Jerez contingent made was to dismount and actually start walking in through the gate. Rodrigo spotted what was going on, turned his horse, and charged full tilt with his men behind him, scattering the men of Jerez. Before long he had occupied all the strongpoints, and collected much booty. The poor men of Jerez, still at the gate, complained that they had spent a hard night in the open, and were allowed in to seek shelter.

The duke of Medina Sidonia was in danger of missing the occasion altogether, and sent messengers ahead asking Rodrigo to wait until he could get there. Rodrigo was just on the point of accepting the formal surrender. The duke was a powerful man, and Rodrigo said he would delay now until not only the duke had come but also his own father.

The duke arrived ahead of the count, and lost no time in sending one of his men, Martín de Sepúlveda, to talk to the Moors. He worked on their fears that if they did not manage to secure terms rapidly, they were in danger of finishing up as slaves. A surrender was drawn up between the Gibraltarians and the duke. Rodrigo was furious: he could point out that the place had already been taken by himself. The duke blustered about the need to render account to the king, and so a compromise was found, whereby the two nobles' banners were to be paraded in side by side. As they went in, one of the Moors "asked for the duke's banner and left that of Don Rodrigo." Precisely what our source means is not clear, but it is obvious that Rodrigo felt he was being unjustly tricked out of his rights, and he set his hand to his sword and dealt the duke's standard-bearer a blow on the arm, knocking the banner to the ground. The duke had to ask Rodrigo to desist (*le rogava que en aquello no oviese mas*).

Once the parade was over, the duke had two hundred of his retinue hurry in, and they managed to take over the keep. Rodrigo in disgust withdrew altogether, and from an encampment at Guadiaro he issued a challenge to the duke, who steadfastly ignored it. After three days the count went back home (CCE:IV, 75–77).

In this ludicrous incident the Muslim garrison became totally forgotten as the Christians wrangled and fought. There could be no better illustration of the disunity within the Christian camp, or of the impotence of the Muslims, who were quite incapable of exploiting the Christians' folly.

Muslim disunity was no less great, and indeed this year is best remembered in Granadan history as the date of the assassination of the Banū Sarrāj on Saʿd's orders. Quite why he turned so violently against his erstwhile backers will never be known; perhaps, under heavy criticism for failing to keep Castilian raiders at bay, he wished to deflect opprobrium from himself by spreading the story that the Banū Sarrāj had kept back for themselves tribute which should have been paid over to the Castilians, and had hence provoked the Castilian incursions. The story is less than convincing. How he allegedly invited them to a banquet in the Alhambra, and had them slaughtered there, is well known. Not all fell into the trap, although his own minister, Mufarrij, did do so among many others. Those who could escape went to Malaga, where, in a further twist of fate, they transferred their loyalties to Yūsuf V. (Yūsuf had been kept in Castile to be exploited in just such a situation.) Yūsuf made his truce with Castile, but in late 1463 he died.

It is possible that one indirect benefit accrued to Castile from these plots: the easy capture of Gibraltar. The garrison was depleted because Banū Sarrāj sympathizers had gone to Malaga, the clan's rallying center.

For a while Saʿd resided in the Alhambra and ruled there. In an altogether unexpected twist, he was overthrown in 1464 by his own son, Abūʾl-Ḥasan ʿAlī. There is no agreement as to what happened to Saʿd after he lost his throne. Arié follows Hernando de Baeza in thinking the old man was consigned to Salobreña, but she also records al-Sakhāwā's assertion that the jail was in Moclín. Tapia has Saʿd ending his days in Almería, citing Conde, an authority who does not inspire confidence, and Pulgar (*Tratado de los Reyes de Granada*) gives the date of his death as April 20, 1465 (Arié 1973:145; Tapia 1984:405).

Abūʾl-Ḥasan ʿAlī, 1464–1482

The rebellion of the Banū Sarrāj had not been stifled by the violent repression undertaken by Saʿd, and Malaga had become the center of their opposition to Abūʾl-Ḥasan. From 1470 that city was the capital of a region set up by Abūʾl-Ḥasan's brother Muḥammad. Abūʾl-Ḥasan did manage to reimpose his authority, and the Abencerrajes, faced with a ruthless campaign of extermination, decided to take refuge with Christian frontier lords, in particular with the dukes of Medina Sidonia.

The impression we gain of the Kingdom of Granada is of a state foolishly and recklessly divided against itself even in the face of the gravest danger. In order to place the feuding of the Granadans in perspective, we should bear in mind that on the Christian side of the frontier equally destructive outbreaks of violence set Christians one against another. A striking example of Christian feuding is provided by the riots in Seville in 1471. These involved the Medina Sidonia (Guzmán) and the Cadiz (Ponce de León) factions, whom we have already met at each other's throats at Gibraltar.

In Seville in 1471 "there was a great uproar [*roido*] between the men of these two lords which lasted for four days: in it many men on each side were killed and wounded, and various sectors of the city were set on fire, and many houses were burned down" (CCE:IV,192). All this in spite of energetic attempts by the authorities to put a stop to the riots. Even when peace was restored to the streets of the city, that did not end the feuding. "From this time onwards the warfare which was waged between the duke and the marquis was as cruel as that between Moors and Christians" (CCE:IV, 196). In the same year that the Christian authorities were being conspicuously unsuccessful in keeping public order in Seville, Abū'l-Ḥasan offered his good offices to arrange for a duel to take place between the elder son of the count of Cabra and Alonso de Aguilar. If they fought in Christian territory they would incur the displeasure of King Henry; the idea of transferring the venue of an encounter in this way was by no means unknown in this honor-ridden age. In this case the duel did not take place.

Abū'l-Ḥasan is a ruler to whom many historical legends and myths have become attached. One such is the story that when negotiating with Isabella for a renewal of a truce he haughtily refused to pay tribute, saying, "The kings of Granada who used to give tribute [*parias*] were dead, and the places in Granada where they used to strike the coins to pay the tribute were now being used to forge lance-heads to prevent it from being paid." Carriazo, in a detailed study (1954) of the various versions of this anecdote, has shown that in all probability the words were never pronounced (*inter alia* because tribute on this occasion was not requested), but, as Carriazo remarks, that will not prevent the story from being repeated.

Other legends concern Abū'l-Ḥasan's private life. To his nobly born first wife (daughter of Muḥammad IX, widow of Muḥammad XI) he is said to have preferred a beautiful captive, Isabel de Solís, known after her conversion to Islam as Zoraya (Thurayya), and the dissension within the royal household which sprang from the harem feud between these ladies is said to have weakened the state. The tale of the disastrous consequences of Abū'l-Ḥasan's loves makes a symmetrical counterpart to the tale of the *destruición de España* as a consequence of the passion of the last of the Visigothic kings of Spain for Count Julian's daughter, and it clearly fascinated readers in the fifteenth century and after, but it does little to help us understand why the Granadan kingdom collapsed when it did. No doubt harem intrigues had some bearing on the way events developed in the 1470s and 1480s, but we need to look beyond trivia of this nature.

Granada fell because it was economically and demographically weaker, and because Castile's cruel long-term policy of wrecking Granadan agriculture was making it difficult for even the hard-working and skilled Granadan farmers to survive. The jealousies of Zoraya and Fāṭima (or ʿĀisha, as the romantically minded historians seem to prefer to call her) were of quite secondary importance. It was obvious by the 1480s that the days of an independent Muslim Granada were numbered unless either dissensions within the Christian camp saved it (as had happened so often before) or Muslim states overseas could effect a rescue and turn back the Castilian advance. It was Granada's misfortune that the reign of Isabella and of Ferdinand, when the Castilian crown began to come to grips with the problem of its own dissident nobles, coincided with a period in the history of Islam when none of the lands which in the past had been in a position to intervene in the Iberian Peninsula were able to do so. North African Islam was itself passing through a period of great weakness (as was demonstrated by the ability of the Portuguese and of the Castilians shortly afterwards to establish bases on the African coast, and by the way that the Turks in the following century were easily able to extend their control so far westwards). We even hear of a Granadan diplomatic mission in 1487 to the Mamluke Qāʾit Bey of Egypt. This elicited sympathy for the plight of the distant Muslims of Spain, but even though the diplomatic support of Qāʾit Bey for the Spanish Muslims did worry Isabella and Ferdinand a great deal (they sent one of the best diplomatists of their court, Peter Martyr of Anghiera, to negotiate with the Mamlukes direct), Egypt or any other Muslim power of the eastern Mediterranean was logistically incapable of intervening effectively in the peninsula at this time. The fact that Granada had to turn to Mamluke Egypt for help is an indication of Granada's despair of securing effective aid nearer home. As for the states of the Magrib, they were sunk in a period of profound decadence. When Granada's hour of need came, no assistance was forthcoming from any quarter whatsoever.

It is clearly absurd to focus exclusively on alleged moral failings or sentimental foibles of members of the Granadan aristocracy in seeking to account for the fall of the Granadan state. Palace plots are of course of legitimate interest to any student of this period, and probably of far greater comparative importance than, say, that of Hitler's relationship with Eva Braun for an understanding of the last days of the Third Reich, but Granada was to fall because its economic viability had been impaired by decades of economic warfare, and because Castile had the capacity to keep in the field an army such that Granada was unable in the long run to resist. Nevertheless, as we shall see, Castile's ability to deliver the coup de grace was in doubt until quite late in the 1480s.

The succession of Isabella to the throne of Castile after the death of Henry IV in December 1474 can be seen with historical hindsight to have provided the necessary conditions for a Christian victory. Her marriage with Ferdinand of Aragon meant that any attempt on the part of the Granadans to play Aragonese off against Castilians was precluded. And Isabella's determination and drive were to prove even greater than the self-interest of her Andalusian nobility. All this we know now, but when she came to the throne on December 13, 1474, it was by no means self-evident. The Catholic Monarchs had to worry about the support being given to the other claimant to the Crown of Castile, Juana la Beltraneja, and so 1475 saw Isabella ready to sign a truce for twelve months, and in 1476 one for five years. As had so often been the case in Granadan history, the existence of a general truce did not prevent local forays being launched, and even some expeditions over considerable distance. In late 1477 Rodrigo Ponce de León captured Garciago, killed three hundred fifty Muslim inhabitants, and took much booty. Cieza, on lands held by the order of Santiago, was taken by a Granadan raiding party in 1478, and two thousand of the inhabitants were roped together and led off into captivity. The year 1478 saw a new truce signed by Abū'l-Hasan and the Catholic Monarchs, who were so anxious to be able to devote their attention to war in Portugal that the customary demand for tribute was not pressed, and the truce was extended for three years. After the end of this truce, Rodrigo Ponce de León captured Montecorto, northwest of Ronda, but a party of Moors came out from the city and took it back on Christmas Eve, 1479. In the same region the castle of Zahara, scene of so much fighting earlier, was taken by the Muslims in 1481–1482. The chronicler Pulgar places the blame squarely on the governor, Gonzalo de Saavedra, guilty of "lack of diligence" (CCE:VI, 3). The Granadans scaled the walls one dark winter's night, and the next morning led all the inhabitants away as captives. It can be seen that Abūʾl-Ḥasan commanded forces full of self-confidence, not at all overawed by the Castilian superior strength. And in any case Abūʾl-Ḥasan's love for developing his military strength meant that, as Pulgar said, "that king called Abūʾl-Ḥasan had at that time more mounted troops and more artillery and all other things necessary for war than any of the other kings of Granada in times gone by. Trusting in his own strength he made raids into Christian territory" (CCE:VI, 5).

The chronicles, including the Arabic *Nubdhat al-ʿaṣr* (which for the final period does provide us with an Arabic source to set against the Castilian chronicles), tell us of a great parade of all his troops which the king arranged as a public spectacle in April 1478. The marching went on for days, but then at noon on the last day, April 16, 1478, there was a disastrous thunderstorm, causing floods and mudslides which washed away buildings and bridges. The king appears to have suffered a nervous breakdown as a result, and from this time onwards he is blamed by the censorious Arabic source for neglecting his army and "giving himself up to pleasures and amusing himself with dancing girls" (*Nubdha* 1940:6). From this point on our one Arabic source is hostile to Abūʾl-Ḥasan, who is said, under the influence of an unnamed chief minister, to have cut back on the pay of his troops (so that they had to sell their equipment to live), and to have overburdened his people with taxes and to have been cruel towards them. It is easy to imagine that the unprecedented natural disaster of the floods will have created a financial crisis for Abūʾl-Ḥasan, forcing him to retrench on military expenditure and to raise taxes suddenly.

It would be hardly surprising if the disaster had not left Abūʾl-Ḥasan and his commanders dispirited. The Catholic Monarchs, by a judicious distribution of offices and functions, seem to have found ways of getting most of their difficult subjects to work together. The great sign that the war had moved into a new and final phase was the surprise Christian assault on the fortified town of Alhama.

The Assault on Alhama

The taking of Alhama was a major exploit. This was not just another attack on a border town. Alhama, although not large, occupied a key position more or less in the center of the kingdom, between Granada and Malaga. Alternative routes between the two great cities were available, but if the Christians could take and hold Alhama, they had a base for the further dismemberment of their enemy's territory. The expedition was prepared with care, but the objective was kept strictly secret until after the troops were on the road. With Rodrigo Ponce de León—now, after twenty years in the frontier wars, a seasoned veteran—in charge of one of the columns, it was wisely decided not to communicate information with regard to the plans to the duke of Medina Sidonia (CCE:VI, 6). That Rodrigo could assemble his force of twenty-five hundred horse and three thousand foot soldiers at Marchena, some forty-five kilometers east of Seville, take them undetected across country for two days' forced march by difficult mountain tracks, and bring them, on February 28, 1482, within half a league of Alhama at dawn speaks very highly of his leadership and of the training of his men (CCE:VI, 6).

Scouts (*escuchas*) were already in post, and could advise him which side of the city was most vulnerable (CCE:VI, 7). One Juan de Ortega was first up the assault ladder, followed rapidly by fifteen others. Once over, they employed their ladders again to scale the citadel, on the battlements of which they stealthily killed the solitary guard, and then his companion who was asleep inside. The main defenses they found unmanned, for the fortress governor (*alcaide*) was away (at a wedding in Vélez-Malaga, according to Pulgar). The *alcaide*'s womenfolk were taken captive, and the gates swung open to let Rodrigo Ponce de León and the militia of Seville inside.

Alhama was taken completely by surprise, but the inhabitants did not panic, and began to fight back. The town's strongpoints had been occupied by the raiders, but Granada was, after all, only fifty kilometers away, and they could reasonably hope for an energetic counterattack to drive the Christians out. The fire from small arms (both crossbows and firearms, or *espingardas*) was so intense that it penned the Christians down inside the castle "confused and uncertain what to do" (CCE:VI, 8). The Christians were desperate, for they too realized that Abū'l-Ḥasan would be on his way. Unable to get out of the castle, in which they were trapped by the hail of missiles, they resorted to the strategem of knocking out a whole section of the castle wall from the inside:

> And the Moors fought from morning until night in the streets of many parts of the city, and many Moors and Christians died. That day the Moors put all their strength and all their heart into the combat, as a courageous man is bound to do when defending his life, his wife, and his children from the threat of death or enslavement. Thus, in the hope of saving some of the survivors, they did

> not flinch from battling on over the corpses of their children, their brothers, and those near and dear to them, fallen before them in the struggle. (CCE:VI, 9)

The townsfolk tried to put up a last-ditch defense in the mosque, but the attackers set fire to that and drove them out:

> There were taken prisoner up to four thousand women and children, and more than a thousand were counted dead in the street. Quantities of household goods, gold, silver, and cattle were taken, for this was a wealthy commercial center. Certain [Christian] gentlemen and foot soldiers, thinking they would have to leave them behind when the town was evacuated, set fire to great jars of oil and honey, and scattered the flour and the wheat which the kings of Granada had stored there from the taxes collected in that place. They set free the Christians who had been held captive by the Moors and who had been kept in the dungeons. (CCE:VI, 10)

Abū ʾl-Ḥasan ʿAlī did arrive the next morning, and set up a siege of the recently occupied town. From their positions on the perimeter, the besiegers could see the piles of corpses, which the Christians had cleared away by the simple expedient of tipping them over the walls. To the horror of the Muslims, the local dogs were gorging themselves on the flesh. Abū ʾl-Ḥasan's men put a stop to this by shooting the dogs, leading Pulgar to remark that "not even the city's dogs could remain alive."

Pulgar wondered at the terrible destruction visited on this town within the space of a few short hours. In the way of the times he was moved to seek a moral explanation for what had happened, and he inquired into the way of life of the townsfolk, to see if it could suggest why "it had pleased God to show his wrath so suddenly and so cruelly against them." He soon found the root cause of all this mayhem—baths.

> We discovered that very close [to Alhama] there are baths in a beautiful building where there is a natural hot spring. Thither men and women used to resort, both from the town itself and from the surrounding region in order to bathe. These baths were the cause of a certain softness in their bodies, and of excessive pleasure [*deleites*], from which there proceeded idleness [*ocios*] and other deceits and evil dealings which they inflicted on one another in order to sustain the ease to which they were accustomed. (CCE:VI, 11)

These, it should be noted, are not the words of a crazed ascetic, but of a secretary and official historian to the Catholic Monarchs.

What can have been the Christian strategic plan with regard to Alhama? Was their intention merely to make a destructive raid, take booty, and get out quickly? Or was it to set up a base and hold it? The evidence is contradictory. Alhama was so deep in Muslim territory that no column returning laden with the spoils of victory could reasonably have hoped to reach home unscathed. Surely an attack on Alhama only made sense if the plan was to hold the town. On the other hand, many of the attackers behaved as if all they had in mind was a classic border raid for booty. We have heard that the invaders went in for senseless destruction of valuable supplies which could not easily be borne off, supplies that would have been much appreciated during the ensuing siege. And when Abū'l-Ḥasan arrived, some of the Christian looters were about to set off. "They found the Christians had brought the men, women, and children who had been captured, and the rich booty, outside the walls, and they had saddled up their horses for the ride back home, but when they saw the Muslim cavalry approaching, they unhitched their baggage, went back inside the town, and began to man the walls in defense" (*Nubdha* 1940:7).

Both the Christian accounts and the Arabic one agree that Abū'l-Ḥasan's counterattack was made in great strength, and that it was carried out with great courage. Our Arabic source tells us how "the common folk were imbued with courage and determination and strove with the sincerest of intentions and with ardent hearts." Pulgar speaks of "the rage of the Moors at the loss of that city, for it was almost at the heart of their kingdom. In order to win it back, they rushed up to the walls, set up ladders in many places, and climbed them with no thought for danger. In these combats they did not wait for the favorable moment, or until equipment had been brought up, but unrelentingly, using as a shield anything which came to hand, they closed in on the wall, thinking that by their very numbers, since they were converging from so many directions, they would confuse the Christians and overwhelm them" (CCE:VI, 12).

The tactic of the massed advance in ceaseless human waves did not work. Somehow the Christians held on and managed to send out messages asking for a relief column. It came. The new spirit which Ferdinand and Isabella had managed to instill could not have been better demonstrated: the duke of Medina Sidonia (along with the count of

Cabra and others) broke the siege in which Rodrigo Ponce de León was trapped, and Abūʾl-Ḥasan ʿAlī had to retreat.

The Arabic chronicle is full of scorn for the decision of the king and his (unnamed) chief minister to retreat. It suggests they invented as an excuse an intelligence report to the effect that "the tyrant king [of the Christians] has assembled a great host, and mobilized a great army, and has as his objective to bring assistance to the Christians besieged in Alhama. They are not far away, and you will not be capable of resisting them" (*Nubdha* 1940:14).

The scorn of the Arabic chronicle is hardly justified. It speaks of just one further attempt by Abūʾl-Ḥasan to retake the town, but Bernáldez completes the story for us, for he tells of a second assault in April and a third in July, and for the second the Muslims are said to have brought up a bombard and to have battered a hole in the wall (BAE:LXX, 607). It would seem quite rational for Abūʾl-Ḥasan to abandon the "human wave" attacks, which were getting nowhere, and to bring up the necessary artillery. By early July, when the siege was finally raised, we know that the Castilians were marching across the mountains from Écija towards Loja in force. The intelligence report was a well-timed warning, and Abūʾl-Ḥasan was fully justified in leaving Alhama and attending to the much more urgent matter of the defence of Loja. What is more, Loja provided the Muslims with a major victory and raised Granadan morale.

Loja had been defended most valiantly by ʿAlī al-ʿAṭṭār, and when the relief party arrived, the Castilians withdrew in confusion, leaving behind, in the field of battle, artillery and siege equipment. This was a disaster for King Ferdinand, who was forced to take the long road back to Cordova to begin to build up his forces anew. Loja was a lesson for the Castilians: the Granadans were not going to surrender territory easily. The war was still to be won.

One of the advantages of the Kingdom of Granada was that it enjoyed relatively short internal lines of communication, even though the terrain was so rough. Whereas the Castilians with their heavy supply trains had to lumber from one side of the perimeter to the other, the Granadans could rapidly switch their forces. While Ferdinand was still entangled at Loja, Abūʾl-Ḥasan could suddenly appear at Tarifa and drive off more than three thousand head of cattle, some compensation perhaps for the losses at Alhama. As Bernáldez says, nobody could put up any defense at Tarifa because "they were all at the siege of Loja" (BAE:LXX, 608).

In seeking to understand Abū᾿l-Ḥasan's inability to keep up a long attack on Alhama, we must also bear in mind that he was having to confront a rebellion by his own son Boabdil (Muḥammad XII) in Granada itself. The Arabic chronicle (*Nubdhat al-ʿaṣr*) tells us of this in language that is indirect and allusive, avoiding naming names where possible:

> The day of the victory at Loja [1482], those there heard that Abū᾿l-Ḥasan's sons, Muḥammad and Yūsuf, had fled to the Alcazaba [of Granada] out of fear of their father. The reason for this was that diabolical individuals [?] had taken to whispering to their mother [i.e., Fāṭima] to incite her to be fearful on their account, because of their father's wrathful temper, and the ill feeling between her and Abū᾿l-Ḥasan's Christian slave [*mamlūka*] called Zoraya. These slanderers kept up their campaign, and finally she yielded on the subject of her sons, and got them out by night and took them to Guadix where they were hailed by the people as rulers, and then were acclaimed in Granada itself. So the flame of discord was propagated in al-Andalus. (*Nubdha* 1940:10).

This intentionally veiled account leaves us uncertain about a number of matters. Who were the "devils" who whispered in Fāṭima's ear? (The Abencerrajes perhaps?) Why are the two sons represented as passive instruments, and as an inseparable pair (in the dual number in Arabic), when it is Muḥammad (Boabdil) alone who has an impact on the course of events?

Abū᾿l-Ḥasan was not to give up his claims to power until shortly before his death in 1495. From this point onwards, however, Granadan resistance was fatally weakened by feuds within the ruling Naṣrid family, feuds which the Castilian leadership managed to exploit with great skill.

EIGHTEEN

The Final Decade of Granadan Independence (1482–1491)

From 1482 there was a grave split (*fitna*) in the Naṣrid camp. Abū'l-Ḥasan with his *wazīr* Abū'l-Qāsim Venegas had as his capital Malaga (where he was accompanied by his brother Muḥammad al-Zagal), whereas Muḥammad XII (Boabdil) with his *wazīr* Yūsuf b. Kumāsha (Aben Comixa), and with behind him the Abencerrajes, held Granada, which he had taken from his father in a bloody interlude of street fighting.

Ferdinand with his regrouped forces returned to the *vega* of Granada in 1482 after the disaster of Loja. He did not try to repeat Rodrigo Ponce de León's success at Alhama—that had only been possible because of the factor of surprise—and so he reverted to the strategy of burning and destroying: a slow and inglorious way of bringing the Granadans to their knees, but one that in the end was bound to succeed.

Farther to the west, in the zone now controlled by Abū'l-Ḥasan, increasingly cut off from Granada since the loss of Alhama, fighting took the form of surprise raids on frontier outposts. It was really a pointless game of tit for tat. Abū'l-Ḥasan, operating in the valley to the north of the Sierra de las Borbollas, some fifty kilometers inland to the north of Marbella, destroyed the village of Cañete without difficulty. Some ten kilometers farther east he took heavy casualties when he failed to break into Teba. In this same zone Rodrigo Ponce de León failed to take Setenil but was compensated by the capture of a fortress in the Sierra de Las Salinas.

The Ajarquía Campaign

Christian strategy in 1483 appears to have been to attempt to build on what had been achieved at Alhama by making a drive into the coastal hinterland to the east of Malaga (the Ajarquía). If successful this would have cut the Kingdom of Granada in two, with Ronda and Malaga to the west, Granada and Almería to the east. Since the divisions between Abū'l-Ḥasan and Boabdil already split these areas, and since these divisions had the effect of enabling the areas to continue to operate as autonomous fighting units, it may be doubted whether it was justified for the Castilians to expose themselves to any great risks, although a successful campaign would have provided a welcome boost to morale. The Christian attack appears to have begun with a council of war as to which way to go.

> All these captains and their men assembled in the city of Antequera where there were differences of opinion. Some wanted to direct the raid in one direction, others in another. Gentlemen familiar with the terrain said the rough country was the defense of its inhabitants, and even if the Christians did capture it, it would be of little use to them because there was no great wealth of cattle, and the inhabitants could keep up a resistance on the mountains and in the steep places. They said that in warfare a great deal ought not to be gambled in order to win a little. Finally on the advice of some of the frontier scouts [*adalides*] they resolved to make the raid. (CCE:VI, 62)

The local people did indeed prove to be masters of their own terrain. Before very long disaster was complete, and when the Christian forces belatedly tried to pull out, they found themselves trapped.

> The scouts to whom they had entrusted the task of guiding them thought to take them by the safest route by following a mountain track so high, so steep, that a man on foot would find it difficult. The Moors, as was their custom, kept fires lit all that day (as they had the night before) on the tops of the mountains and at other high points, so as to summon those who lived in the mountains.

> They lay in wait for the Christians, and inflicted heavy casualties on them with rocks and with arrows shot from the side and rear. As the Christians struggled to extricate themselves from the position into which they had committed themselves, night fell. They feared they would suffer even heavier casualties if they kept to that track, so they went back down a deep river valley under a high mountain which the Moors had already climbed. When they saw that the Christians had taken this narrow defile, they threw rocks and stones down on them, killing many. Some who tried to escape by climbing the cliffs plunged to their death because in the darkness of the night they could not even see the footholds. They could hear the war-cries of the Moors, they were terrified by the darkness of the night and the ruggedness of the terrain, and lost heart, not knowing how to escape from the perdition in which they found themselves. (CCE:VI, 64–65)

Rodrigo Ponce de León, for all his military experience, found himself caught in the same trap, and only extricated himself by ignominiously taking another man's horse and fleeing (CCE:VI, 66). Many of the Christians gave themselves up rather than face the mountainous terrain. The Muslims, rejoicing in their victory, uttered their war-cries (*alaridos*), and so completely demoralized were the Christians "that two unarmed Moors captured five or six of the Christians who were wandering over the mountains, and led them to Malaga, which was not far from the place of this defeat. Some women came out from Malaga, and captured the Christians they found lost in the countryside. More than a thousand Christian prisoners were marched away" (CCE:VI, 67).

This was indeed a major setback for the Christians, and the scouts were of course blamed, though, as Pulgar remarked, "in the judgment of men, it was all shown to have occurred because of the overweening pride of the Christians, who despised the strength of the enemy, and because they were forgetful of the trust which they should have had in God, and placed it in the power of men" (CCE:VI, 69).

The *Nubdhat al-ʿaṣr* is by this point consistently hostile towards Abū'l-Ḥasan, and it did not fail to make a point against him, even though this was a Muslim victory:

> The enemy fled defeated, and left more than two thousand prisoners, including many counts and leaders of note, in Muslim hands. Those who did manage to escape abandoned horses, cattle, and

> pack animals, all of which fell into Muslim hands. The booty was transferred to Malaga, and assembled for it to be shared out among those who had taken part in the fighting, but it all finished up in the hands of the oppressive authorities: those who had fought received nothing. May God accord them due punishment for their misdeeds. (*Nubdha* 1940:12)

Lucena and the Capture of Boabdil

The following month Boabdil made a raid from Granada in a northwesterly direction. Bernáldez suggests that in so doing Boabdil was seeking to exploit the demoralization of the Christians after the Ajarquía disaster (BAE:LXX, 610–11). Boabdil's objective was Lucena, deep in Christian territory beyond Loja and Rute (Arié 1973:160n.1). To secure surprise in this direction would have been almost impossible, and the battle plan may have been betrayed by a convert to Christianity (although this theme of the convert who volunteers vital military intelligence is so much of a stereotype element in Christian accounts that one hesitates to accept it in the absence of confirmatory evidence). Lucena did not fall, and trouble began as Boabdil, having taken some booty, headed back towards Loja across the Sierra de Rute. The alarm had now been raised, and in the ensuing debacle for the Muslims, Bernáldez speaks of seven hundred mounted troops and seven thousand foot soldiers being killed or captured. The Arabic source does not give numbers, but is forthright about the extent of the disaster:

> The Muslims were vanquished by the Christians, who followed them in hot pursuit, killing them and taking prisoners. They caught up with the Emir Muḥammad b. ʿAlī [Boabdil] who mingled in with the generality of the people, hid, and began to fight alongside them. He was taken prisoner without any of the Christians recognizing him. This was a shameful disaster . . . and the most shameful part of it all was the capture of the *emir,* because from that stemmed the ruin of our homeland. (*Nubdha* 1940:12)

Among those who fell that day were ʿAlī al-ʿAṭṭār, hero of the defense of Loja, Yūsuf b. ʿAbd al-Barr (Boabdil's *wazīr*), and Ibrāhīm b. Kumāsha.

The *Nubdhat al-ʿaṣr* tells us that when the Christians did realize who had fallen into their hands, they made much of Boabdil "and bore him off to the king of Castile, who also honored him greatly because he saw that he had acquired a long-desired means to capture the land of al-Andalus" (1940:12). This story of Boabdil being taken to the king conflicts with the account given by Pulgar (CCE:VI, 71, 81ff), who depicts Ferdinand as anxious to avoid having Boabdil brought to his court as a captive. There is every reason to prefer the version given by the Christian historian: Boabdil was a great prize, but it is understandable that when the Christians had such a high card placed in their hand, they should have paused a while before deciding how to play it most advantageously. Boabdil was placed in the castle of Porcuna while the case was considered at the very highest level in the royal council.

Pulgar in his chronicle claims to report in detail, and at times verbatim, the debate in council (CCE:VI, 81–92). This account is clearly much edited and arranged, but there seems no reason to doubt that he articulates the main points of view expressed, and that he conveys the Castilian perception of how matters stood inside the Kingdom of Granada as between Abū'l-Ḥasan and Boabdil.

Among the alternative policies being considered by the council was the possibility of acceding to Boabdil's request that he should not only be released but even given some military assistance. An alternative policy was that Boabdil should be kept captive, and that the war should be prosecuted without any let-up, a hawkish viewpoint which in Pulgar's text is put in the mouth of Alonso de Cárdenas, master of the order of Santiago. His statement of the Castilian war aims is succinct: "to wage and win the war of Granada, and not to cease until you achieve the end which you desire." The Castilian army was well equipped and in a high state of preparedness. Immense expenditure had been incurred. The war should not be ended, and certainly Boabdil's request for help against his Granadan enemies should be refused. "If your troops are to be put into peril to win the country for him, it would be better to have won it for yourself."

> Your royal highness is now prosecuting a war against a king who is aged, infirm, and disliked by the people of his kingdom, and he is not now able to follow the campaign because of his physical impediment and because of the disobedience of his subjects. If you now free this king who has been taken prisoner, you give us an enemy who is young and healthy. The Moors, who now lack a leader for whom they have any liking, would get back the king

> they desire. The consequence would be that these enemies of ours, who now are weak and divided for lack of a good captain, would become strong and united under a good leader [*caudillo*]. Nor should we put any reliance on the discord which exists between them. Granted they are divided now, but what reason have we to suppose the divisions will continue, and the father and son not be reconciled, and be all the stronger in their rebellion against us?

The master of Santiago argued that fear of loss of their hostages would never deter the Granadans from switching their policies if they wished. "The power of the Moors is now diminished because of the imprisonment of the king whom they loved, they feel the lack of trained soldiers, lack of arms and of horses lost in the battle in which he was captured." The war should be continued; Boabdil should not be released; *parias* (as payment for a truce) should not be accepted from Abū'l-Ḥasan.

It will be seen that this speech paints a picture of a Boabdil beloved of his people, and no mere Castilian puppet, indeed feared as potentially able to act as an effective focus for Granadan loyalties.

It is Rodrigo Ponce de León whom Pulgar makes the spokesman of the opposite policy. No doubt he was able to state the case for something less than an all-out campaign because nobody could inpugn his loyalty or his courage. He accepted the master's arguments about the need for continuing the war, but argued for flexibility of response. If Boabdil were kept prisoner, he argued, Boabdil's supporters would begin to waver in their loyalty to him, and think of joining his father, "so that you will not be able to say that you hold a king as your prisoner, only a private individual." Ponce de León is arguing, in effect, that Boabdil as a prisoner was a diminishing asset, which ought to be cashed in sooner rather than later.

He went on to point out that so long as Boabdil had been free, it had been easier to wage effective war on the Moors. "Now, after this king has been captured, some of the leading men in Granada who were in favor of the son have joined the father so as the better to defend their homeland" (CCE:VI, 88). Boabdil should be freed so as to cause the Moors to have to fight on two fronts.

As for the danger that Boabdil might, nevertheless, make common cause with his father, Ponce de León did not deny that that might happen, but a continuation of the rivalry seemed more likely, so that

Castilians should give orders for Boabdil to be favored in order to keep the civil war alive. "If you did not have this king [to release]," he argues tellingly, "you ought to create another one [so as to release him]." He summarizes his policy as: release Boabdil; grant a short truce; and accept any tribute offered, including the release of Christian prisoners. All that did not preclude prosecuting the war once the truce came to an end, when Castile itself would be in a stronger position.

The evenly balanced views expressed in the council led Ferdinand to remit the matter to Isabella for her decision, and the upshot of the whole process was that Boabdil was released, and a truce granted for two years. (There is an interesting additional clause permitting one Mahomad Abencerrax [i.e., Abencerraje] to cross from Africa to join Boabdil [CCE:VI, 90]).

Up to this point Ferdinand had avoided a confrontation with Boabdil but court ritual seemed to demand a leave-taking. Should Boabdil kiss Ferdinand's hands? As Pulgar reports the situation (and on this matter he may not be entirely reliable), Boabdil was anxious to do so, while Ferdinand on the other hand opined that "I would give him my hand [to kiss], for certain, if he were free and in his own kingdom, but I will not give it while he is a prisoner in mine." The anecdote would seem to be inserted to stress Ferdinand's magnanimity, but one can see that Boabdil would have become useless to the Castilians if he had been humiliated by them. "I trust in his goodness, that he will do everything that a good man and a good king ought to do" was what Ferdinand said as he avoided giving ammunition to Boabdil's enemies (CCE:VI, 91).

As the Castilian royal council had realized, Boabdil's disappearance into Castilian detention had given his father's partisans an opportunity to reassert themselves in Granada, although factional strife did not die down. Abū ʾl-Ḥasan was afflicted by a grave illness "which was similar to epilepsy, which affected his sight and which caused loss of sensation in parts of his body" (*Nubdha* 1940:30–31), and presumably because of his incapacity he was deposed. "After him his brother Muḥammad b. Saʿd [Muḥammad XIII, best known as "al-Zagal"] ruled the kingdom, but the enemy were extending their hold over it." It will be seen that the Castilian deliberations failed to take this possibility into account.

During the time he detained Boabdil, Ferdinand undertook in 1483 a large-scale incursion. Although its size was immense—ten thousand light horse, twenty-thousand infantry, thirty thousand "deputed exclusively to carry out the destruction of crops," not to mention a special supply column for Alhama, and a total of eighty thousand pack animals—the purpose of this campaign is difficult to determine. It was far too large an expedition for it to prove profitable in terms of booty captured, yet it was not sufficiently powerful to undertake the siege of Granada or Malaga.

The first place Ferdinand attacked was Illora, and the fighting there well illustrates the prime importance of food crops in this stage of the campaign. The folk of Illora had collected the cereal crops awaiting threshing at the threshing floors near their walls "out of fear of the *tala* which the king was undertaking." Losses inflicted on his men from the battlements overlooking the threshing floors led Ferdinand to call his troops off and to bring up light artillery (*ribadoquines* firing projectiles of some three pounds' weight) with which the battlements were cleared (CCE:VI, 75–76).

After further heavy skirmishing at Tájara (CCE:VI, 76–78), where the Muslims were using a cannon, Ferdinand's men went on to carry out the most perilous part of their mission: to run more supplies in to Alhama. On the long ride to Alhama the army suffered terribly from lack of water, and indeed some of the horses died of thirst. When they reached Alhama, the water there was a blessed relief. Thirty thousand pack animals brought in fresh supplies, one thousand men reinforced the garrison, and a new garrison commander, Iñigo López de Mendoza, count of Tendilla, was left in charge (CCE:VI, 78–79). The counts of Tendilla were to provide what amounted to a dynasty of viceroys for Granada after it was conquered.

After Alhama, Ferdinand rode on to Alhendín, a mere ten kilometers from Granada, and while close to the city he appears to have negotiated with both Abū 'l-Ḥasan's faction and also that of Boabdil's mother, Zoraya (CCE:VI, 80). Zoraya was prepared to pay far more for the release of her son, and it was presumably her terms which were being pondered in the council already described. The settlement appears to have been a tribute of twelve thousand doblas and the release of sixty prisoners a year for five years, and in addition ten noble youths (Boabdil's son Aḥmad among them) were to pass into Castilian hands as hostages.

The response of public opinion inside Granada to this arrangement was overwhelmingly hostile. A *fatwā* (Granja 1971:145–76), which survives because it was included in al-Wansharīshī's *Kitāb al-mi ʿyār,* aligned almost all the known leaders of pious opinion against Boabdil: the chief *qāḍī* Ibn al-Azraq, the *muftī* al-Mawwāq, the *qāḍī* Abū ʿAbdallah Muḥammad Ibn ʿAbd al-Barr, and others. They all declared that there could be no justification for any departure from the loyalty owed to Abū ʾl-Ḥasan or for the proclamation of Boabdil. Anybody who gave support to Boabdil was in rebellion against God Almighty and his Prophet. Boabdil's problems when faced with such opposition were enormous. He does not at this stage seem to have sought to enter Granada itself, and he contented himself with residence in Guadix (Baeza 1868:33).

The Campaigns of 1484

At the beginning of 1484 Ferdinand was required elsewhere in his domains, but the Granadan campaigning went on under Isabella's supervision. The first expedition of the year set out under Rodrigo Ponce de León and the master of Santiago. The aim was to cut through the kingdom from north to south, but once near the coast (at La Churriana, some distance to the west of Malaga) the Castilian troops were to collect seaborne supplies sent from Cadiz and Seville. No attempt was made to capture any fortified places.

As soon as Ferdinand had returned, there was a council of war to determine objectives for the main summer expedition. Once again we must rely on Pulgar's highly edited but still invaluable report. The discussion centered on the policy of systematic destruction (*talas*). Should it be continued, or should an attempt be made to tackle the siege of a town? Ferdinand advocated besieging a town, now that the artillery and manpower were available. He claimed that the *tala* policy could be combined with the attack, scarcely a convincing claim.

Álora was the place selected, and there no surprise of any sort could be expected, for in order to clear the roads for the passage of the artillery, a great detachment of foot soldiers had to "advance over the mountains and passes of that region to flatten the roads and the rough sections so that the wagons could get through" (CCE:VI, 120). The Castilian bombards eventually did their work, the walls were battered down, the town fell.

The balance of advantage in warfare was by now firmly tipped in favor of the attacker, if he were able to deploy artillery. From being unpredictable devices, the cannons had become instruments able to do the work for which they were designed. The only possible military response for the Granadans would have been to revert to a fluid style of mobile warfare at which they had always been so successful. However, this was not an option open to them because of the Castilian policy of the *tala*. Faced with a destructive enemy, the only response was to establish strongpoints where food supplies could be stored in safety. This was a policy begun by Muḥammad I in the early days of the regime, and it had stood the kingdom in good stead. However, the food stocks had to be defended, and now that cannon were so effective, that was difficult to achieve. Granada could not abandon its policy of defending its stocks in castles, unless it were to accept a much lower level of subsistence, and to retreat even further into the hills. That was a policy which eventually in the sixteenth century came to be tried by relatively small numbers (in the Alpujarras, for example), but it implied the abandonment of urban civilization. It is not surprising that the Muslims of Spain did not try this strategy until it was forced on them as a desperate last resort.

After success at Álora, the Christians' double strategy of attrition and sieges continued. Some raided, burned, and destroyed, others bombarded walls and captured towns. According to the economics of this expensive double mode of fighting, the *talas* could the more easily be entrusted to the nobility and their men, whereas the sieges became increasingly the affair of the monarch's army (aided by the infantry of increasing reliability provided by the municipalities and by the Santa Hermandad). The *tala* was much like earlier medieval styles of fighting, but to put cannon on the road, to keep them firing, and to exploit their successes required resources which only the nation-state could furnish. We have seen how in the early days of artillery, gentlemen could be asked to provide their own cannonballs. Such improvisations could no longer work in the wars of the 1480s.

In September 1484 Ferdinand besieged Setenil. The inhabitants were confident of the strength of their great walls, and did little to hinder the great guns being brought up against them (to hit the guns while vulnerable on the road was the only effective form of defense). Setenil fell in a textbook demonstration of the power of the new artillery.

If on the battlefronts things went according to Ferdinand's plans, in politics his scheme to split Granadan resistance by making use of Boabdil failed. The anti-Boabdil forces gained in strength, and although Abū'l-Ḥasan was effectively eliminated, his brother al-Zagal proved a successful leader.

In early 1485 we find al-Zagal driving Boabdil's men out of Almería:

> This prince Bahadalahi [this is the form Pulgar uses: a corruption of Boabdil? The description of the prince as brother of *aquel rey viejo,* the old king, i.e., Abū'l-Ḥasan, leaves us in no doubt that al-Zagal is meant] had an understanding with some of the Islamic lawyers in Almería that they would let him into the city by night, so that he could capture the young king [Boabdil], because of the friendship he showed to the Christians, and because he wished to allow them into the kingdom of Granada. Along with other Muslims, these lawyers acceded to what was proposed in order to encompass the young king's destruction, because of the help he had received from the Christians. So the prince [al-Zagal], with mounted men and a number of foot soldiers (and also other Muslims privy to the plot), entered Almería at a place of which he had been informed by the lawyers. The young king left, and fled to Christian territory, where he was able to save himself. And the prince entered the house where Boabdil had been living, and killed one of the king's brothers, a young child, and others of his persuasion on whom he could lay hands, and took over the city, reducing it to obedience to the old king [Abū'l-Ḥasan] his brother. (CCE:VI, 135–36)

Thus Ferdinand's policy of making use of Boabdil had come to nothing. Boabdil came scurrying back in danger of his life. Once again the religious establishment, the *fuqahā'*, were able to demonstrate their power.

The Campaigns of 1485

Ferdinand's campaigning in 1485 began, as in 1484, with probing in the area to the west of Malaga; his principal prizes were Coín and Cártama. He was in a position to operate in force as far as the coast, but not yet to take the city of Malaga. With the kingdom of Granada now cut in half, Ferdinand turned on Ronda. This natural strongpoint of the western region had been largely left alone hitherto (and no doubt the North African garrison still based there inspired respect). It is thus a matter of some surprise that although Rodrigo Ponce de León did not begin to deploy his troops round the city until May 8, after an intensive artillery bombardment and the cutting of the water supply, the town was surrendered by May 22. The rapid collapse of resistance at Ronda led the whole region to seek terms. The smooth triumph of this part of the campaign is to be ascribed to the peak of efficiency to which the Castilians had brought their artillery. The psychological effect of the weapons is commented on by Pulgar:

> The bombardment was so heavy and so continuous that the Moors on sentry duty could only hear one another with great difficulty: they did not have the opportunity to sleep, nor did they know which sector most needed support, for in one place the cannon knocked down the wall, in another the siege engines destroyed the houses, and if they tried to repair the damage wrought by the cannon they could not, for the continuous hail of fire from the smaller weapons killed anybody on the wall. . . . The inhabitants of the city had felt safe and confident because of their massive fortifications, but now their confidence was suddenly converted into terror [*turbacion*]. (CCE:VI, 170–71)

The surrender terms offered to the bulk of the population were not generous—they were allowed to leave with what chattels they could transport—but Pulgar tells of a separate deal struck with the "*alguacil mayor*" (unnamed, probably Ibrāhīm al-Ḥakīm). He was allowed to go to reside in Seville and Alcalá de Guadayra, with arrangements made for his accommodation and maintenance (CCE:VI, 173). Others were given safeconducts from the king and allowed to cross to North Africa, "and thus did this town which had for so long been held by the Moors become quite empty of them."

We can see here Ferdinand's flexible policy in operation. If possible he left Muslim masses leaderless by granting very favorable terms to some of the Granadan aristocracy. Some of the old ruling class were encouraged to make the full transition into the Christian ruling class and to convert. The more recalcitrant of the old leaders were allowed to leave. As for the masses, "the townships in the region of Ronda entreated him to permit them to become his vassals, to which end they freely came to make submission as subjects who are obliged to their king, and who wished to bring him their tribute payments, just as they had done with their Moorish kings" (CCE:VI, 175).

All the inhabitants of these towns and villages remained and became Mudejar serfs (*sierbos mudejares*) of the king and queen. And the *alfaquís* and the elders of each of these places swore an oath on "the unity of God, who knows what is public and what is secret, the living Creator, who gave the law to Muḥammad his Prophet," promising to be loyal subjects and vassals of the king and queen, to carry out what they commanded, to wage war as ordered, to bring such tribute and taxes as were customarily paid to the Moorish kings, and to do this loyally and without fraud (CCE:VI, 175–76).

In return Ferdinand promised to "preserve the law of Muḥammad" (CCE:VI, 176) and to allow the Muslims' legal disputes to be dealt with by their own judges according to the *sharīʿa* and the *sunna* (*xaraçuna*). This was, in fact, a classic type of Mudejar agreement, such as we are familiar with from Castile or Aragon. In this way, in the years immediately before 1492, a considerable number of new Andalusian Mudejars were created. We must inevitably ask ourselves how sincere Ferdinand and his negotiators were in offering guarantees for the continued existence of Islam. Was the granting of Mudejar status a mere ruse? We will rightly blame the Castilians for granting such status and then within less than a generation withdrawing it, but there is no indication that at the time the new Mudejars were created the Castilians were doing anything other than to carry on a well-established traditional policy. It was well understood that if a town or a region were taken by force, the Muslims there might be driven out; if, on the other hand, it were surrendered, terms would normally be granted, and the Muslims allowed to become Mudejars. The surrender terms of Ronda (and eventually those of Granada) simply followed the ancient pattern. Nobody seems to have posed the question of how the delicate balance on which Mudejar society rested would be affected by the extension of Christianity to every corner of the Iberian Peninsula. We can blame Ferdinand for failing to keep his word, but we are not justified in accusing him of bad faith in agreeing to the surrender terms in the first place.

From Ronda the army advanced southeast to the sea at Marbella, and thence along the coast towards Malaga. The roads were very bad, and the Castilian army suffered a great deal, but it was felt that a military demonstration of strength was required, and indeed the effect was worth making, for Marbella was surrendered without Ferdinand having to bring his siege artillery to bear.

The negotiations for the surrender of Marbella are of interest from several points of view. In the first place it is noteworthy that the town actually got in touch with Ferdinand before he arrived. Pulgar lists those negotiating on the Muslim side as "the *alcaide, alfaquín, alfaquí, alguazil,* elders, gentlemen, citizens, and community" (CCE:VI, 180), and they request that those who wish to stay should be allowed to do so as Castilian subjects, whereas those who wish to leave should be allowed to "go to any place they wish" in ships provided by Ferdinand. Additional safeconducts should be provided for North African contingents (*gómeres*) in the town, and the governor (*alcaide*), who "out of fear of his lord" did not wish to cross, should benefit from special arrangements. The Muslim chief negotiator (this same *alcaide*?) asked, in return for his "loyal" service, a ship (*fusta*) for himself and his family, and payment of the salary which he should have received from the king of Granada![1]

We recall that al-Wansharīshī records a *fatwā* concerning a pious Muslim who acted as spokesman for the Muslims of Marbella after the surrender. This is presumably not this negotiator but somebody who stepped into the gap created by the disappearance of the Muslim administrative class.

The march on from Marbella took a terrible toll, and in addition, near to Mijas some of the more bellicose inhabitants attempted to pick off the stragglers. After the exhausting campaign Ferdinand decided against any immediate attack on Malaga, a major enterprise which would require special preparations. He accordingly returned to Cordova and set about planning the great battle.

There was one further engagement that summer at Moclín (some twenty-five kilometers northwest of Granada itself). Arabic and Spanish sources are at one in speaking of a confused mêlée fought partly at night, with neither side quite certain what was happening. It ended with the count of Cabra fleeing for his life and al-Zagal in hot pursuit. In spite of this reverse, Ferdinand was able to pick off a small number of border fortresses: Cambil, Montejícar, and Iznalloz.

Ferdinand's major maneuver that autumn of 1485 was a political one: once again Boabdil was released and sent into Muslim territory, through Murcia to far-off Huéscar (forty kilometers northeast of Baza). The *Nubdhat al-ʿaṣr* states that the inducement Boabdil was offering was a promise that districts loyal to him would be spared the ravages of war. By 1486 we find Boabdil back in Granada itself, more precisely on the Albaicín hill, facing the Alhambra. "The majority of the inhabitants

1. CCE:VI, 183 (he pointed out that he was owed three months' back pay).

of this district fell in with what was proposed out of a desire for peace, because they were cattle drovers and country folk" (*Nubdha* 1940:16). Quite why cattle drovers should be particularly susceptible to peace propaganda is not clear. Perhaps belligerence is seen as a noble characteristic.

The consequence of the arrival of this king promising peace was a renewed outbreak of civil strife: the Albaicín fought the rest of the city. And since the rest of the city had at its disposal siege artillery and other instruments of war, stones and shot rained down on the Albaicín from the Alcazaba heights. The bitterness of this fighting inside Granada in the last few years before the conquest has puzzled many historians. Perhaps in the late twentieth century, after the protracted bombardments that have destroyed one Beirut suburb after another, the senseless destructive violence of the last days of Granada may seem, not more comprehensible, but less incredible.

The Campaign of 1486

Ferdinand's military campaigning in 1486 was coordinated with psychological warfare. Loja was his principal objective. The Castilian artillery was more than a match for the defenders, who surrendered on May 29. What may not have been in Ferdinand's planning was that among those taken prisoner at Loja was Boabdil, once more now in Castilian hands. He had suddenly made peace with al-Zagal in Granada and acknowledged him as king, and then rushed into the battle at Loja. One is tempted to find some deep motive for this strange behavior. Was Boabdil perhaps merely putting on a show of fighting, and was it his objective to surrender Loja to Ferdinand? That would seem confirmed by a letter from Ferdinand to Úbeda setting out the terms of the deal agreed (in return for services rendered, Boabdil was to be assisted to take over much territory, including Guadix and Baza). Even if we reject this "letter" as a libel (and the actual treaty is missing), could Boabdil have simply been seeking to get himself safely captured? A dangerous game. It is perhaps more likely that Boabdil was swept along by a genuine current of patriotic enthusiasm.

About the noble participants in this battle we can speculate and doubt. We are in no doubt about the common people, reduced to despair and starvation by fighting which had now been going on for so long that the meaning of the conflict was easily lost. There is a bitter anecdote recorded by Pulgar which is much to the point.

While some of the fiercest of the fighting was going on at Loja, a Muslim weaver continued to work his loom, apparently unconcerned by the slaughter and destruction all round him. His neighbors and his wife pressed him to join them in fleeing to the town itself in order to have some chance of surviving. He refused.

> "Where do you want us to go? Why should we seek to preserve ourselves? For hunger? For cold steel? Or for persecution? Wife, I tell you that since we have no friend to take pity on our misfortunes and to put them to rights, I prefer to wait for an enemy who covets our goods and will kill me, so as to be spared seeing the sufferings of my own people. I would rather die here by steel [*fierro*] than later in shackles [*fierros*]. For Loja, which once defied the Christians and defended the Muslims, has become the tomb of its defenders and the home of its enemies." Refusing to change his mind, the man remained in his own house till the Christians broke in and killed him. (CCE:VI, 223)

The rhetoric of that passage must owe a great deal to Pulgar, but surely the story itself must have a core of truth: it is difficult to think of a Christian historian inventing it.

The important victory at Loja (whether facilitated by Boabdil's treason to his own cause or not) opened the way for a further advance by the Castilians towards Granada from the west: Montefrío, Illora, and Moclín fell, and left them dominating the whole *vega* of Granada. Then, in July, the Castilian command withdrew right back as far as Cordova.

The reason for this withdrawal was twofold. In the first place urgent business in Galicia called Ferdinand north, but it was necessary now to set in hand the preparations for the final push. Before leaving for Galicia, Ferdinand arranged for the supply of

> all material necessary for the next summer [1487] so as to prosecute the war against the Moors. Those to whom they entrusted this task had abundant supplies of iron brought up to forge picks and trenching tools and spades and other iron implements necessary to dig away hills and make roads smooth and construct ditches and embankments in the military camps. They also gave orders to collect food supplies. And because of the unfortunate consequences which could arise from negotiations involving official arbitrators of ransoms [*alhaqueques*] between Christians and

> Moors, orders were given for no Christian ransom-negotiator to enter Moorish territory and for no negotiator or interpreter from the Moorish side to enter Christian territory, under penalty of death and confiscation of property. [The ban on *alhaqueques* was an attempt to improve security.] (CCE:VI, 242)

At the same time that these military preparations were going ahead, at sea a blockade was being maintained which not only affected large merchant ships but also small craft (*zabras*). The Castilian navy moved over to the offensive, raiding the North African coast, and driving the inhabitants of some coastal regions inland, thus reinforcing the effectiveness of the blockade.

While the Christian armies were gathering their strength, the Muslims of the various provinces were at one another's throats. Boabdil, released after Loja, was to go into "Vélez in the *sharqiyya*," or eastern region. There is an unfortunate ambiguity here. The indications of contemporary documents seem to confirm that "Vélez" here means Vélez Blanco or Vélez Rubio in the area to the west of Lorca, which was indeed the easternmost of Granadan regions at that time, but can we exclude the possibility that what was intended was Vélez in the Ajarquía or region to the east of Malaga? Either destination would have been consonant with the Castilian policy of using Boabdil as a puppet in the east while dealing militarily with Granada and Malaga. We hear nothing of Boabdil in the fighting at Vélez-Málaga when it was attacked, but then he seldom was where he was expected to be.

October 1486 had seen Boabdil back in the Albaicín of Granada, engaged in street fighting with the supporters of al-Zagal in the rest of the city. The fact that Castilian-held territory was now so very near meant that Boabdil's partisans could receive supplies. It is presumably to this stage of the hostilities that Pulgar was referring in his *Brief Report on the Great Deeds of the Excellent Renowned Great Captain:*

> The king and queen favored this young king [Boabdil] with a safeconduct and peace which they extended to those of his realm who supported him, such as the people of the Albaicín, who constantly with their merchants entered Andalusia for bread and oil and necessary provisions. These merchants were well treated by the people on the frontier and the guards. Since Illora is the nearest pass to Granada, and since they were well treated there, that was where they always crossed. (NBAE:X, 562)

If this report is correct, the degree of complicity of Boabdil was very great, for it goes on to tell us:

> He [Boabdil] sent to the king and queen to beg them to order the captains and governors on the frontier to increase their military pressure because by squeezing the city in that way he would be enabled to sustain his position in the Albaicín better. When the orders reached the frontier to do as Boabdil had requested, Gonzalo Fernández [i.e., the future Great Captain] took pleasure in pleasing and being of service to this young man in the Albaicín, where the inhabitants were beginning to waver because they saw the old king's party was ever stronger in the city.

A stratagem was thought up whereby forces from Alhama and Padul were to advance down the Padul road, thus provoking a counter-attack from al-Zagal, and then, when al-Zagal was outside the city, Boabdil was to engage the rear of his forces.

Inside Granada, al-Zagal's dilemma was a terrible one. The need to oppose Boabdil's forces in the Albaicín meant that it was risky for him to operate elsewhere, and yet he could not give the Castilians a free hand.

The Campaign of 1487

Vélez-Málaga was the objective for the Castilians during the first stage of the 1487 campaign. This meant bypassing Malaga itself and moving into the Ajarquía region where the Castilians had had such an ignominious defeat inflicted on them. This time the advance was swift and well organized. For a column to set out from Cordova on April 8 and reach Vélez-Málaga on April 16 was an enormous achievement in itself. Once there the engineers set to work to construct the siege-works and the scaffolding.

When the news of the Castilian advance spread, pressure on al-Zagal to do something increased. Pulgar depicts him as being criticized by the religious leaders [i.e., the *fuqahā*ʾ] and yet unable to secure a truce with Boabdil.

> The *alfaquíes* and elders, when they heard the Spanish king had his troops in the field and his fleet at sea, standing off Vélez, were afraid that if it were lost, Malaga and all the mountainous region

> round it would also fall, and so they went to where the king [al-Zagal] was in the Alhambra, and questioned him, saying that if what he wished was to be king, of what country did he wish to be king, if it was all to be lost? In addition they told him that it would have been better if all the fighting which was taking place between his brothers and members of his family, all the deaths they had caused one to the other, had taken place in defense of the country, against its enemies rather than inflicted on friends, and this they preached all through the city. They ought to grieve, they said, to see the homes which they had built being taken over by Christians, the fruits of trees planted by their fathers and their grandfathers being gathered by them, to see their brothers and relatives exiled from their own land, which had been held by their forebears for so long. Their blood had been shed to win it, now blood was being shed to lose it. (CCE:VI, 271)

Al-Zagal was torn. To leave Granada would open the way to Boabdil. Pulgar tells us that al-Zagal offered to surrender his title of king to Boabdil, and to fight under his banner in order to save Vélez. Boabdil, full of distrust, refused the offer.

Al-Zagal now with all the troops he could muster took the mountain tracks across to Vélez-Málaga from Granada, "and in the evening of one day he appeared at the top of the mountain near the town of Bentomix. He spent the night there, lighting great bonfires through the mountains in many directions" (CCE:VI, 272).

The secret journey from Granada, followed by the open lighting of bonfires, is at first puzzling, until we remember the use made of beacon fires in the earlier fighting in the Ajarquía. This was the signal to rally the scattered inhabitants of that barren region. Al-Zagal was going to fight.

The Castilians were briefly vulnerable, since the slow column bringing up the artillery was still on the road, stretched out over such a distance that it could never be protected at all points from attacks from the flank. Al-Zagal was attempting to employ the only tactic that had any hope of success: to knock out the guns before they could be brought into action. Ferdinand detached troops to protect his artillery, and al-Zagal wavered and thought of striking at the besiegers already deployed round Vélez-Málaga. A curious half-engagement then took place by the light of the great beacon fires "which lit all those mountains so brightly, that they could see one another quite well," and so they began to shoot. The Muslims were at the top of the slopes, the Christians below, and it was by no means easy actually to come physically to blows. When dawn came, the expected battle did not ensue; al-Zagal and his forces had vanished from the hilltops (CCE:VI, 276).

Probably what had happened was that news had reached al-Zagal of Boabdil's triumph in Granada, so that he decided it would be pointless to engage in a protracted struggle for Vélez-Málaga. Al-Zagal made his way first into the Alpujarras and thence to Guadix (*Nubdha* 1940:23). To have remained near the coast would have been to expose his followers to complete ruin.

At this stage we can have no reasonable doubt that Boabdil was acting in close collaboration with Ferdinand and Isabella. We have already seen how favorable terms were available to Boabdil's supporters, who were allowed food supplies, whereas al-Zagal was being subjected to a blockade.

It is not surprising that Vélez-Málaga quickly decided to surrender. Al-Zagal had appeared as a savior on the mountaintops, and had then ridden away. The surrender was negotiated in terms that permitted the inhabitants to leave not only with their goods and chattels but also with their arms. No doubt this unusual deal was struck because the Castilians were anxious to get on with their principal task—the siege of Malaga. In addition to the surrender on these terms for the town itself, a peace settlement was concluded in the presence of the local *alfaquíes* for the whole region, and the Ajarquía was granted what amounted to Mudejar status.

The Siege of Malaga

The Castilians at first attempted to negotiate the surrender of Malaga without a fight. They could point out that no help could be expected from al-Zagal. However, in command at Malaga was one Hamete Zeli (Aḥmad al-Thagrī?), and his garrison was stiffened, as that of Marbella had been, by Berbers (*gómeles*). Aḥmad contemptuously rejected the offer of a negotiated settlement.

In the Castilian camp some were for a long blockade in order to starve the Malagans into surrender, others for a close siege and a military assault. The argument in favor of the second course was that an effective blockade would be difficult to achieve (supplies would slip into the city by sea). Ferdinand decided on a military assault. It was to prove the bloodiest and toughest part of the whole campaign, and in the course of the fighting, as we shall see, the king and queen only narrowly escaped with their lives. Quite naturally the conquest of Granada attracts more attention because it marks the end, but the fighting at Malaga was in reality more important. If Malaga had not been taken first, then supplies and reinforcements could have reached the Muslims in Spain from abroad. Even though none of the North African states (still less any of the eastern Mediterranean states) was in any position to intervene with massive force, even a trickle of aid might have enabled the Granadans to fight on for a considerable time. Malaga was to be the most important battle of the whole war.

The great city of Malaga posed to the Castilian forces a problem of an altogether different order of magnitude from that which had been presented by the small ports of the coast, such as Marbella and Vélez-Málaga. At the heart of the built-up area were the immensely strong linked twin castles of the Alcazaba at the lower level and the Gibralfaro on a hilltop, dominating the whole city. The landward side of the Gibralfaro was protected by steep slopes. The city is built on a comparatively narrow strip between the mountains and the Mediterranean, and these fortifications could cut off east-west traffic. An attacker could not avoid tackling what before the days of artillery had been an impregnable complex of defenses, what were still in the 1480s walls and towers of daunting solidity. The defense was, moreover, conducted in a determined and ruthless fashion. All houses and buildings near the walls, for example, were torn down and destroyed so that the besiegers when they arrived would not find any of their work done for them. No ground was yielded without a fight, and a whole day was lost, for example, in hand-to-hand combats on the slopes of a hill leading up to the castle:

> [The Muslims] seemed to have a greater desire to kill Christians than to preserve their own lives. The fighting went on for six hours, and the sounds of the trumpets, the shouting, the alarms, the clash of weapons, the noise of the matchlock guns and of the crossbows on both sides were so loud that the hillsides re-echoed. . . .
>
> So great was the desire for vengeance that it predominated

> over the desire for gain, and nobody made any attempt to take prisoners, only to kill and to maim. (CCE:VI, 286)

Eventually the hill was taken, the Christians advanced over the bodies of their comrades, the Muslims withdrew behind the walls of the Gibralfaro, and the Castilian army began to construct with extraordinary speed out of timber and earthworks a fortress to face the Muslims' ramparts. It was provided with its own artillery and its own field workshops, and was garrisoned by twenty-five hundred mounted men and fourteen thousand foot soldiers, all under the command of Rodrigo Ponce de León. This enormous fort by no means completed the picture. All round the perimeter strong temporary structures went up. *Estanças* was the term used for them (from the Italian military term *stanza,* a word which in the form *estancia* was to become widely used in Spanish America). "Because the circuit of the city from sea to sea was such a great distance, it was decided to ring it with these *estanças*. They were all fortified with bulwarks and trenches, and at intervals all along the walls there were men with matchlocks and crossbows, with men-at-arms to guard them" (CCE:VI, 290).

When completed, the outer ring of Christian palisades and earthworks faced inwards towards the Muslim stone walls, and both sides then engaged in static warfare, each side making use of artillery to equal effect. "The Moors were provided with many bombards and other cannon, and had skilled gunners and all things necessary for defence and attack. When they saw that the king's tent was pitched there, they shot at it with so many cannons and field pieces that it was necessary to remove the tent to a safe position behind a hill" (CCE:VI, 291).

The Christians soon had more guns in action than the Muslims. The naval guns were brought ashore from the fleet, and ordnance was even brought by sea from Flanders in a ship commanded by Ladrón de Guevara. Ferdinand remembered the stone cannonballs prepared for use at Algeciras, and had them sent for. But all was not well in the Christian camp.

> In some places near Malaga there was plague, and the men of the army feared it would reach the camp. When the ships or the trains of pack animals were delayed, food shortages arose. And as so

> often happens in great armies, some men began to complain. Some bad Christians, men with light heads imbued with corrupt desires, thought that for these reasons the king would be forced to abandon his campaign. Incurring great harm to their souls, and peril to their bodies, they crossed over to the Moors, and told them what was going on, even exaggerating, and saying the soldiers were discontented, and every day some slipped away without permission from the king and his officers (CCE:VI, 295).

Isabella was herself urging Ferdinand to give up. She was reasonably worried lest her forces suffer irreparable losses. Thus we can see that any decision on the part of the defenders to attempt to hold out was quite a reasonable calculation. The Castilian morale was weak, and Ferdinand could think of no better way of demonstrating his determination than to persuade the queen in person to come and share the hardships of the campaign. At length she agreed, and in June 1485 she set out from Cordova.

Ferdinand made maximum use of the propaganda effect of the arrival of the queen and the ladies of her court, both to raise the spirits of his own troops and to try to bring his adversaries to the point of surrender. The Muslims did not allow themselves to be overawed; they knew that the harbor was still in their hands, and any equipment for the Christians had to be landed on open beaches. The continuous cannonade was using up unheard-of quantities of powder. Ferdinand's position was by no means secure. And even when the cannonade succeeded in breaching the city walls, the defenders did not panic, and managed to keep the enemy out.

Clearly morale inside the walls was high. We have no Arabic account of what life was like in the beleaguered city, but the Spanish chronicles are full of admiration for the defenders: "Although they had no food supplies inside, and could hope for none from outside, although they saw their fellows fall dead and wounded in the fighting, it was worthy of note how bold this barbarous folk was in battles, how obedient to their commanders, how hard-working as they repaired the fortifications, how astute in the ruses of war, how constant in the pursuit of their objectives" (CCE:VI, 312).

Some in the Christian camp were for a hurried assault before the winter weather came, but more prudent counsel prevailed, and instead a program of tunneling and sapping was undertaken. This failed to get under the main Malaga defenses, and the Muslims appear to have been successful with counter-saps, so that Pulgar remarks on fighting going on by land, by sea, and beneath the ground as well.

Good news came to Ferdinand from Boabdil. Al-Zagal in Granada had heard of the siege of Malaga, and sent a relief column of men who undertook it as a suicide mission "believing that if they did manage to get in to Malaga, that would be a mighty exploit, and if they did not they would save their souls, so they resolved to die or enter the city" (CCE:VI, 307). Boabdil had this column intercepted and routed it; the remnant had to take refuge in Guadix. Pulgar tells us that the king and queen lavished their favors on Boabdil in gratitude for this. The incident is not confirmed in any Muslim source, but there would seem to be no reason to doubt that Boabdil made such a treacherous attack on al-Zagal's expedition.

Another attempt to bring relief from outside met with some success. This was led by a mysterious marabout-like figure, a man from Jerba in Tunisia called Abraen by Pulgar (Ibrāhīm al-Jarbī). This holy man had been living in a village near to Guadix, and he formed a plot to assassinate the king and queen. "This Moor gave out that he was holy, and that God had revealed to him through an angel what was going to happen. In this way he knew the Moors were to be saved, and Malaga would be victorious against the Christians who were besieging it" (CCE:VI, 314).

He was successful in rallying some four hundred followers, some Berbers, some native Granadans, "and they agreed to follow him and face any danger, doing what he said." The contingent made their way across country, traveling by night, and in order to penetrate the perimeter of the siege they chose to attack one of the temporary forts (*estanças*) at the eastern end of the line, on the seashore. They struck at dawn. The Christian response was swift, and many of the raiders were killed, but nevertheless two hundred did manage to rush the Christian lines and get inside, some swimming round the fort, some leaping the barriers.

Ibrāhīm al-Jarbī had assigned to himself a different role. He was to remain outside and get himself taken prisoner. The primary danger was that the soldiers who seized him would simply despatch him on the spot, but he relied on his undoubted charisma to protect him. He stationed himself half-hidden in a gully with his hands raised to heaven as in prayer, and remained perfectly still, even when the troops sent to mop up after the raid caught sight of him. They took him alive, and bore him off to Rodrigo Ponce de León (CCE:VI, 315).

Under interrogation Ibrāhīm pretended to let slip that he had had a revelation, but when Rodrigo pressed him to be more specific, he replied he would only reveal the secret to the king and queen in person. Rodrigo does not seem to have taken this seriously, but did report the matter to the king and queen, who gave orders for the Moor to be brought in. And so, still dressed as when he was taken, in a burnous with a dagger in his belt, he was brought to the royal tent. People thronged round to see the captive, for the story had spread that he was a holy man.

Now when the Moor and his escort arrived, it so happened that Ferdinand had just had a large meal, and fallen asleep. People wanted to wake him up, but the queen wisely would hear none of that, and insisted that the Moor be kept waiting until Ferdinand awoke. He was accordingly put to wait in a tent belonging to some of the ladies of the court, the marquesa of Moya and Felipa, wife of the son of the duke of Braganza, Álvaro de Portugal.

Ibrāhīm knew no Castilian, and finding himself in an ornate tent, seeing the fine clothes of Álvaro de Portugal and his wife, Felipa, he assumed he had reached his target, so he drew his dagger and aimed a blow at Álvaro, wounding him about the head and almost killing him. He then struck out at Felipa, but in the excitement the blow went wide, and at this point a treasury official called Ruy López de Toledo rushed in. With great presence of mind he grappled bodily with Ibrāhīm, who was thus prevented from striking another blow. Soon people crowded in to see what was going on, and within a few moments the Moor was cut into pieces (CCE:VI, 316).

Somebody then had the idea of taking the pieces of the corpse and projecting them over the wall with a siege catapult. The Muslims who picked up the pieces inside the ramparts piously sewed them together with silken thread, washed and perfumed the body, and gave it an emotional funeral. They then selected a prisoner of some status, killed him, and mounted his corpse on an ass, which they sent out through the defenses in the direction of the Christian camp.

Still the people of Malaga fought on, although hunger was intense. The Arabic *Nubdhat al-ʿaṣr* asserts that when food stocks ran out "they had to eat whatever was edible: horses, asses, donkeys, dogs, skins, the leaves from the trees, and when even these things ran out, the pangs of hunger were indeed terrible. Many of the finest of those who had sustained the siege died, and at that point many gave up and sought peace" (*Nubdha* 1940:24–25). Thus there emerged a "peace party" led by two of the city dignitaries, ʿAlī Durdūsh and Amar Benamar, together with a *faqīh* called Ibrāhīm b. Ḥārith, but the North African garrison held out in the Alcazaba and would not consider surrender.

Finally ʿAlī Durdūsh and his associates crossed the lines and sued to be allowed to become Mudejar subjects of Ferndinand. The Catholic Monarchs said that it was too late for such terms: the choice was death or captivity. The response of the Malagans was to threaten to hang from the battlements all the prisoners they were holding and burn the city, but Ferdinand and Isabella issued the counterthreat that if a single Christian prisoner were harmed, all Malagans without exception would be put to the sword. Finally they softened to the extent of offering a safeconduct to those, like ʿAlī Durdūsh, known to have been advocating peace, and so the Castilian troops went into Malaga. The king and the queen at first did not go: there was such a stench of death from the corpses strewn everywhere that the city had to be cleaned up before they would enter in August 1487.

In the city a Christian administration was set up. The Muslim townsfolk were turned out of their houses and kept in enclosures (*corrales* is the word used) until they could be shared out. One-third were set aside for exchanges of prisoners with North Africa, one-third were given as slaves to those who had fought in the siege, one-third went to defray all the crown expenses. A hundred Berber *gómeres* were sent as a present to the pope, fifty maidens went to the queen of Naples, thirty maidens to the queen of Portugal, and there were various other gifts made. The chronicles speak of no rights for Malagan Muslims at all, but, of course, ʿAlī Durdūsh had his safeconduct and appears to have remained in the city for a time. Another anomalous group were the remnants of the Jewish community who had been trapped inside the walls during the siege: complicated negotiations took place in order to secure ransoms for them. But Malaga, that great commercial seaport of al-Andalus, was no more, and the city was firmly incorporated into the Castilian realm of Isabella.

We have seen that in the campaign against Malaga, the Catholic Monarchs had derived no small assistance from their association with

Boabdil, assistance that was not limited to his negatively hanging back from protecting his fellow Muslims in the city, but which went so far as to include the positive help he gave in driving off al-Zagal's relief column. We are not certain what Boabdil's reward was to have been for his collaboration. The records of the negotiations do not survive complete, but from a fragment of an agreement it would seem that in exchange for Boabdil's assistance the Catholic Monarchs were prepared to make over to him a crescent-shaped zone comprising the central northern area and the eastern area of the Granadan kingdom: from Guadix to Baza through Vélez Rubio and Vélez Blanco and down to the sea at Mojácar (HEMP:XVII(1), 728; Garrido Atienza 1910:Doc. IV).

The events of 1488 form the most enigmatic part of this puzzling war. We are sure that Boabdil was the secret ally of the Castilians up to 1488. As we will see, from 1489 the evidence with regard to his loyalties is ambiguous, and it could be that in the final days of the Naṣrid state he became a true leader of his people. The year 1488 may provide the key to this transition. After the victory at Malaga it became much easier for the Castilians to negotiate the surrender of areas without fighting, and this happened in the eastern zone just mentioned, the area promised as Boabdil's reward. Vera offered its surrender, as did Cuevas, Huércal, Mojácar, Cabrera, Sorbas, Belefique, Níjar, Júrcar, both Vélezes, Cantoria, Alboj, Galera, and other villages. The terms were that those who wished to leave could do so, those who wished to stay became Mudejars. It is unclear whether this was the acquisition for transfer to Boabdil of the lands promised, or whether on the contrary the granting of Mudejar status to this area was taken by Boabdil as an indication that the Castilians were not going to keep the promise they had made in their secret negotiations.

The Campaign of 1489

Remaining in Muslim hands at this time were Granada, Guadix, Baza, and Almería, and the last three were in the hands of al-Zagal's men and well defended. Since Almería was so far away from Castilian bases, and protected by the difficult terrain in its hinterland, and since Granada was clearly being left until last, the choice of objective for 1489 lay between Guadix and Baza. Perhaps the successes in the region of Vera led to the selection of Baza.

The commander of Baza is named as Cid Hiaya in the Castilian sources: Sīdī Yaḥyā al-Najjār (although Pulgar makes him only one of the "captains" and says the *caudillo* of Baza was Mahomed Hacen and the *alcaide* Hamete Alhahali, and alongside Yaya Alnacal he names, among others, Mahomed and Hamete Alatar [al-ʿAṭṭār], Reduan Çafarja, and Ali Çahadon). Baza did not offer to surrender, and Ferdinand had to deploy his artillery. There was a false start to the siege, for the Castilians initially pitched their camp in the *huerta* or cultivated gardens round the city. The terrain proved hopelessly soft, and the camp had to be repositioned, but soon the machinery of war was grinding forward. Five months after the start in June, very little seemed to have been achieved, and the strain of keeping up the blockade of the city as winter began to approach was considerable. The townsfolk were conscious that if they could resist until winter, the Castilians might be driven to abandon the siege. To protect the troops from the worst of the weather more than a thousand (!) mud-brick houses were hastily constructed. (Some of them collapsed, killing those inside.) As for the roads, the thousands of pack animals required to bring up supplies rapidly destroyed the surface, and when there was rain they became impassable. And if "for a single day the supply columns ceased to function, there was a lack of bread and barley in the camp, and the troops lost hope of being able to hold out there, and for fear of hunger that was threatening, they wanted to leave" (CCE:VI, 409).

As at the siege of Malaga, the queen and her ladies were brought in to bolster up morale, and to try to demonstrate to the Muslims that the Christians intended to persist. The queen arrived on November 5, and a great spectacle was witnessed not only by the Castilian army but by the townspeople lining the walls. This time the move did break the deadlock in the negotiations. Hardly had she arrived when Yaḥyā wrote, and serious negotiations began between him and Gutierre de Cárdenas, *comendador mayor de León*. By the end of the month there was an agreement. This hardly mentions the fate of the Muslim people who had been laying down their lives in defense of their homelands, it is concerned instead with the interests of the Muslim ruling class and with the subterfuges that would permit Sīdī Yaḥyā, Muslim commander, to transmogrify himself safely and profitably into Don Pedro de Granada Venegas.

The agreement is a good illustration of the way in which some of the Granadan aristocracy were willing to sell out to the Castilian enemy at the point in time when they perceived that to switch loyalties was the only way in which they could preserve their wealth and their estates:

1. Yaḥyā became Ferdinand's vassal.
2. He became a Christian, and would be baptized in the king's own chamber, but this conversion was to be kept secret until Guadix was surrendered.
3. He was confirmed in possession of his lands, "towns, fortresses, and villages" (i.e., he was to be lord of his own domain).
4. He was exempted from the duty of lodging royal troops (always thought of as a humiliating obligation).
5. He was exempted from certain taxes, including the *pecho*.
6. He was entitled to keep an armed escort.
7. Various financial settlements were made to his advantage, and if Guadix was surrendered, but not until then, he was to receive an extra gratuity (*merced*) of ten thousand reales.[2]

The *Nubdhat al-ʿaṣr* tells us of these same negotiations as seen from the Muslim side:

> The men of consequence in the town had a survey made of the remaining food stocks without the common folk being aware of it. Since they found sufficient for a few days only, they sent to the Christian king asking for a safeconduct on certain terms which they proposed. They found him amenable, and the truce was concluded. In conversations conducted behind the backs of the common folk [ʿ*āmma*] all requests were favorably received. And so on Friday Muharram 10,895 [1489] the *alcaides* brought in a contingent of Christians who took over the castle and coerced [*qaharū*] the common folk, who were overwhelmed and fell into their power. Then they [the Christians?] allowed some of the noble horsemen and foot soldiers who had been helping in the fighting to leave in safety with their horses, arms, and possessions. These men went to Guadix. After the people had been evacuated, and the town occupied, the inhabitants moved out into the suburbs, in safety and with their possessions: all they left in the town were the roofs of the houses. (*Nubdha* 1940:26–27)

2. CCE (VI, 426) gives the version for public consumption, but Durán y Lerchundi (1893:II, 213–16) transcribes the confidential "Asiento e promesa de su Alteza" from Simancas.

Having concluded such a handsome settlement for his family, Yaḥyā, still calling himself that (his conversion was still secret), went to Guadix to see al-Zagal. We know little of these talks, but from the outcome we can say that Yaḥyā earned his ten-thousand-real bonus. By December 22 al-Zagal had surrendered Almería, by December 30 Guadix (in return for an estate to include Andarax, Orgivas, Lanjarón, and other places in the Alpujarras). This was to be a semi-independent territory barred to Christians. Al-Zagal was to be permitted to keep his arms, and a considerable payment (twenty thousand castellanos) was to be made to him (Arié 1973:175).

There is no indication that al-Zagal even toyed with the idea of conversion. He did not settle in his little principality; he allowed his estates to be bought out (for a further thirty thousand castellanos) and crossed to North Africa with his followers. This is how the *Nubdhat al-ʿaṣr* views what happened:

> All the knights and commanders of the Emir Muḥammad b. Saʿd [al-Zagal] accepted the *dhimma* [protection of the king of Castile] and began to help him against the Muslims. The whole country with its villages and with its castles became obedient [to the king] from Almería [in the east] to Almuñécar [in the west], and from Almuñécar [on the south coast] as far as Padul [inland but short of Granada], so that the ruler of Castile could take all that over without a fight, or the need to conduct sieges, with no effort or trouble at all. "We all belong to Allah and to him we will return [Koran]." In each of the castles he appointed a Christian commander [*alcaide*] with a group of Christians to take control in that district.
>
> In the same month of Safar 895 (1489) the land of al-Andalus finally fell into the hands of the ruler of Castile, and entered into obedience to him. All the inhabitants accepted Mudejar status [*tadajjana*], the only district remaining in Muslim hands being the city of Granada and the villages in its immediate vicinity.
>
> Many people assert that the Emir Muḥammad b. Saʿd [al-Zagal] and his commanders sold these villages and districts ruled by them to the ruler of Castile, and that they received a price for them. All this was with a view to taking revenge [*intiqām*] on the son of his brother Muḥammad b. ʿAlī [i.e., Boabdil] and on his commanders who had remained in Granada, with just the city under their government and with benefit of a truce from the

> enemy. By his action he [al-Zagal] wanted to cut Granada off, so as to destroy it in the way that the rest of the country had been destroyed. (*Nubdha* 1940:27–28)

Although this Arabic source does not seem alive to all the ins and outs of the negotiations (it seems quite unaware of the role of Yaḥyā/Pedro de Granada at Baza, the catalyst for the sudden realignments elsewhere), it does seem to provide a plausible explanation for the major mystery of this final period: why al-Zagal, staunch hero of the resistance to Castile, suddenly became Ferdinand's man and left Granada in the lurch.

We have seen that Boabdil in the Albaicín had enjoyed a privileged position, with permission for his merchants to bring in food from outside. The Muslim communities elsewhere had learned that they could expect no help from him (indeed we have seen that there were suggestions that he had prevented help getting to Malaga). For a long time Boabdil was the leader of those who were ready to come to terms, al-Zagal the leader of those prepared to fight. Al-Zagal's sudden change of policy in 1489 is understandable if we see him (*a*) exasperated by Baobdil's cynical (or supine) subservience to Castile; (*b*) arriving at a fresh military appreciation of the situation after the loss of Ronda (the west), Malaga (the central coast), Baza, and Vera (the interior and the east), to the effect that the remaining portion of Muslim territory was quite simply untenable; (*c*) animated by a bitter family feud. There would be a certain poetic justice in having Boabdil, a traitor who did so much to undermine and enfeeble Muslim resistance, left to endure the final stages of the siege. Perhaps that is even what really occurred, but it must be said that we cannot know with certainty either what exactly happened, or what secret motives people had for doing what they did. All that can be stated with certainty is that at the end the Granadan aristocracy failed to provide either effective military leadership or realistic political guidance to those whom they ruled.

The war was now lost, but the last battle had yet to be fought. Granada had still to be occupied. Since al-Zagal had just handed over cities as potentially difficult to take as Guadix and Almería, Ferdinand must have hoped that Granada too would fall into his hands without fighting. But Granada in 1489 was a city torn by internal dissension. There was the rift between the Albaicín and the rest of the city, there were the partisans of fighting to the death and the advocates of negotiations, there were the religious leaders who proclaimed to the faithful their uncompromising views as to where the duties of a Muslim lay. There were Boabdil and his advisors, who may or may not have had as their ultimate objective the yielding of the city to the Castilians. To understand how the various groupings interacted is not always possible, and one suspects that to seek rational explanations for what went on in the terrible final days of Granada may be to seek in vain.

NINETEEN

The Conquest of Granada (1490–1492)

Boabdil sent out his *wazīr* al-Mulīh to enter into talks with the Castilians at the beginning of 1490. Al-Mulīh returned to the city with two young but experienced officers deputed by Ferdinand to prepare the way for the final takeover of the beleaguered city. These two men were Gonzalo de Córdoba (then thirty-seven) and Martín de Alarcón. It is easy to see why they were selected. Martín de Alarcón had been in charge of the arrangements for Boabdil's detention when he was first held by the Castilians, at Porcuna in 1483. From that point on Boabdil had been a tool of Castilian policy. One might even suspect that the sort of psychological ascendancy which a jailor and interrogator can establish over a detainee had been forged at Porcuna. As for Gonzalo de Córdoba, he had already in 1486 successfully completed a mission inside the city of Granada, supporting Boabdil against the faction of al-Zagal, and had again at Loja been given the task of persuading Boabdil to surrender that town (if we are to believe the *Brief Report of the Great Deeds of the Great Captain*) (NBAE:X, 574). He had patched up relations between his master and Boabdil, and renewed the secret compact whereby Boabdil was to be rewarded for help against his uncle al-Zagal by a dukedom or some title (and control of the Guadix-Baza-Mojácar crescent).

The Castilian negotiators who had been so successful in the past this time failed. Boabdil, full of distrust, far from yielding the city, initiated hostilities. What his intentions were can only be guessed. The attacks he launched were aimed at Padul (recently acquired by Ferdinand from al-Zagal) and Adra on the coast. Padul was taken by Muslims from Granada. Adra was taken by North African Volunteers. In all probability Boabdil was attempting to establish a chain of bases that would provide a tenuous lifeline for reinforcements and supplies to pass from North Africa to Granada. (An attack on Salobreña, which would have provided an alternative harbor to Adra, failed in September. A number of other places useful as part of a supply corridor were taken, such as Alhendín and Andarax, although the rising of the Mudejars of the Marquesado of Cenete, on the northern slopes of the Sierra Nevada, was repressed by Ferdinand.) Boabdil must have been exploring the possibility of establishing a link between Granada and the outside world across the mountaintops, but he could never have hoped to use the route to pass more than a tiny trickle of men and supplies.

Meanwhile in the *vega* the Castilians kept up their policy of harassment and destruction—and now the *tala* was aimed at Boabdil and his men.

The year 1490 thus was uneventful. The Granadans did not surrender. The Castilians did not launch a full-scale offensive. We must ask ourselves what Boabdil hoped to achieve. Was he now belatedly converted to the policy of making a last-ditch stand? Was he playing the game of acquiring as many counters as possible to use in eventual negotiations? Was he secretly entirely subservient to Castilian plans, and only acting as an agent provocateur in order the better to undermine Granadan resistance when the right moment came? It is likely that the second of these possibilities is nearest to the truth, but one wonders whether Boabdil and his ministers always understood what their long-range interests were. Long-range objectives are a luxury which the leader of a country in its death throes cannot always afford.

We know a great deal about the events of the last year of campaigning, 1491, from the Christian side. The last battle of the long-drawn-out Reconquest was an event everybody wished to have recorded. We have long lists of the names of the men who took part, and day by day, sometimes hour by hour, we know how things happened. The campaign in the *vega* of Granada had some aspects in common with the sieges of the other major cities of the Granadan kingdom. A solid camp was constructed (after an unfortunate fire had burned down the tented camp) at a place called by the Granadans ʿAtqa (or perhaps ʿUtqo) and renamed Santa Fe. The queen and her ladies were again brought in to grace the heroic scene. Many Castilian heroes performed deeds which are still rightly remembered and celebrated. Knowing what we do now of what was going on behind the scenes, however, there was one major difference. At Malaga or at Alhama there was a real battle to win. At Granada, from the end of August onwards, the Castilian command knew that Granada was ready to surrender, and what was to be decided was when and how the city was to be taken over. The fighting and the bloodshed were, of course, no less real at the level of the men engaged, but there is little point in seeking to follow the tactical struggle when we know that the important developments were taking place round the negotiating table and in secret. On the Muslim side we have little more information than what the *Nubdhat al-ʿaṣr* tells us:

> The King of Castile returned to besiege Granada and pitched his camp at a hamlet called ʿAtqa, where he set about building work, erecting a great walled enclosure in a very short time. He knocked down villages and extracted building materials from them, loaded them onto carts and transported them to the town he had under construction.
>
> Meanwhile he was waging war on the Muslims, who fought back hard. The Christians attacked the fortresses in the villages round Granada, and captured them, so that in the end all that there was left in Muslim hands was the village of al-Fakhkhār [Alfacar nowadays]. To this place he gave no respite, and assaulted it with his cavalry and with his infantry, but got nowhere, and many Christians met their end there. Round Alfacar there was fierce fighting because the Muslims feared that the next step would be the evacuation of the villages on the slopes of the mountains, leading to the tightening of the siege of the city. (*Nubdha* 1940:27)

This aspect of the battle for Granada does not bulk large in Christian accounts, but the Muslims appreciated that Alfacar was important because it is on the foothills of the Sierra Nevada, and so long as it was in Muslim hands, supplies might reach Granada across the broken ground.

From this point on, the account in the Arabic source of the actual fighting ceases to be of much use: we simply have lists of points where skirmishing took place, and there is ludicrously contradictory information about forays made for food. (We are boastfully told that cattle raiders were so successful that the price of meat fell on the city market to one dirham a *raṭl,* but in contrast to this we are soon being told of the extreme pangs of hunger suffered.) The Arabic source, however, does give us in precious detail a description of the process of public debate which led to the emergence in the city of a consensus for surrender.

> When the month of Safar of the year in question [897 = 1491] came, the situation of the people became very much worse because of starvation and lack of food supplies, even many rich people being affected by hunger.
>
> So there came together the leading men, nobles [*khāṣṣa*] and common folk alike, with the Islamic lawyers [*fuqahāʾ*], the guild wardens, the elders, learned men, such courageous knights [*anjād al-fursān*] as were still alive, and anybody in Granada with some insight into affairs. They all went to see their Emir Muḥammad b. ʿAlī [Boabdil], and informed him of the condition of the people, how weak they were, and how afflicted by hunger, how little food there was. Their city was a great one, for which normal food imports were hardly sufficient, so how could it manage when nothing was being brought in at all? The route used to bring in food and fruit supplies from the Alpujarras had been cut. The best of the knights were all dead and passed away, and those that remained were weakened by wounds. The people were prevented from going out to seek food, or to cultivate the land, or to plough. Their heroes had been killed in the battles.
>
> They then went on to say to him: "Our brethren the Muslims who live across the sea in the Magrib have already been approached, and none of them has come to help or risen to our assistance. Our enemy has already constructed siege works and is getting ever stronger, whereas we are getting weaker. They receive supplies from their own country, we receive nothing. The winter season has already begun, and the enemy's army has dispersed and is thus not at full strength, and military operations against us have been suspended. If we were to open talks with them now, our approach would be well received, and they would agree to what we ask. If we wait till spring has come, his armies will assemble to attack us, and we will be weaker still, and the famine even worse.

> He will not again be prepared to agree to the terms we are seeking, and we and our city may not be saved from military conquest. What is more, many of our folk have fled to his camp, and they will act as guides to point out to him our vulnerable spots, and he will make use of them against us."
>
> The Emir Muḥammad b. ʿAlī [Boabdil] said to them, "Give consideration to what seems best to you, and reach a unanimous agreement on what will be to your good."
>
> It was agreed by nobles and commoners alike that they should send an emissary to have talks with the Christian king about their concerns, and those of the city.
>
> Many people alleged that the emir of Granada and his ministers and military chiefs had already made an agreement to hand over the city to the Christian king who was invading them, but they feared the common people, and so kept them duped, and simply told them what they wanted to hear. This was why, when they [the people] came saying what the king and his ministers had been keeping secret from them, they pardoned them on the spot. This was why military operations had been suspended at that time, to give scope for them to find a way of introducing the idea to the common people. So when they sent to the king of the Christians, they found he readily agreed, and was happy to grant all their requests and all their stipulations. (*Nubdha* 1940:40–41)

There are a number of points which need to be made with regard to this passage.

1. The assembly that called for peace was broadly based, and included, besides classes of society which might expect to have a voice in existing consultative assemblies (the knights, the elders, the Islamic lawyers, etc.), members of the common people. Now it is true that elite (*khāṣṣa*) plus common folk (*ʿāmma*) in Arabic often make up an inclusive pair, and mean little more than "all and sundry," but in this context it does not seem that such an interpretation is possible. In this debate it is the common people whose reaction is *feared*. Their fighting spirit might have led to a prolongation of the war. The Naṣrid ruling class feared that it would be trapped into a destructive conflict by the very patriotic spirit which the Naṣrids had created among the common people.

2. Ferdinand's timing was very well judged. We have seen that in

some sieges the advent of winter could put the besiegers under greater pressure than the besieged. He had brought his campaign to its peak in such a way as to make the Granadans anxious to reach a settlement before conditions for them got much worse.

3. Boabdil pretends to be noncommittal in his reply: "Do what you think best. Come to a unanimous agreement." Too enthusiastic a response might have provoked a negative reaction on the part of the patriots or the pious. By cunningly throwing the whole moral onus on his subjects, he got them to renegotiate the deal he had already accepted!

4. The readiness of the Castilian negotiators to agree to whatever was put to them shows up in the Capitulations, which include the most ridiculously detailed petty concessions. As far as the Castilian authorities were concerned, the "real" agreement was the secret one, and they wanted at all costs to secure acceptance for the Capitulations. In order to achieve that settlement, they would seem to have been prepared to make almost any adjustments and emendations to the text which were demanded. This shows in the illogical way in which matters of minor concern are grouped with matters of major importance (the first clause provides a good example). No Castilian negotiator would wish to quibble over minor concessions when what Ferdinand wanted above all else was to hold the keys of the city safely in his hands.

One cannot help feeling that in any real negotiations some of the petty Granadan demands would have been dismissed with scorn: the demand that Christians would not be allowed on part of the city wall, or that young ladies who eloped with the family jewels should have to hand them back, for example. (These are legitimate matters of concern, but should they figure in the surrender document of a mighty city?) In contrast with the Capitulations, as eventually agreed, is the brutally frank response made by Gonzalo Fernández de Córdoba to Boabdil's emissary al-Mulīh when Boabdil was demanding cast-iron guarantees that Ferdinand would fulfill the pledges he was giving.

"Tell me, sir," said Muley (al-Mulīh) to Gonzalo Fernández, "what certainty can he [Boabdil] have that the king and the queen will let my lord the king have the Alpujarras, which is the first clause in our negotiations, and that they will treat him as a relative as is promised?" "The obligation, and the [grant of] lands will last, Mr. Governor, sir, for so long as his excellency [Boabdil] remains in the service of their highnesses" (NBAE:X, 577). The future Great Captain was making the point that it was not in the nature of such agreements to be enforceable for all eternity.

One of the many unsatisfactory aspects of the Capitulations of 1491 was that, although ostensibly they were an agreement arrived at independently, in fact they were a secondary agreement, which arose out of a primary deal struck between Ferdinand and Boabdil. A solemn settlement concerning a whole nation was thus dependent on a private and secret understanding relating to the personal and family interests of one individual: Boabdil. When the primary accord, that between Ferdinand and Boabdil, became a thing of the past—and that happened very soon, when Boabdil crossed over to North Africa—the secondary agreement, the Capitulations, at once began to be at risk. The Capitulations failed to provide lasting protection for the Muslims of Granada. We will shortly see how the *Nubdhat al-ʿaṣr* comments that Ferdinand made his promises "on the assurance of their deceitful religion that he would indeed fulfill all the conditions stipulated." There was possibly an element of bad faith already present in the Capitulations as signed in November 1491, and there was certainly bad faith in the way they were only selectively implemented, and then in less than ten years ignored and abandoned. The memory of this bad faith vitiated all subsequent relations between the two religions in the peninsula. The working out of the consequences of those broken promises is the history of the Moriscos in the sixteenth and early seventeenth centuries.

In speaking of the allegations that a secret understanding existed between Boabdil and Ferdinand, the Arabic account in the *Nubdhat al-ʿaṣr* uses a word, *zaʿama* (people asserted), implying an absence of conclusive proof (1940:41). The Muslim author of the account did not know for certain whether or not there was any collusion. Many Christians must have been privy to the negotiations, but it did not fit in with the powerful myth of the Reconquest for the truth to be known. Nobody wished it to be public knowledge that the gates of the city were waiting to be opened, with the only outstanding obstacle a problem of public relations and of news management. In January 1492 it would not have been thinkable that the campaign to end all campaigns was consummated thanks to treason at the top of the Granadan state rather than to the heroism of the Castilians. The Christians in 1492 knew very well that they fully deserved a triumph, and that is what they got. It has really only been in modern times, and thanks to such studies as María del Carmen Pescador del Hoyo's "Como fue de verdad la toma de Granada a la luz de un documento inédito" (1955) that the inner truth of what was going on in those days has been understood.

The Capitulations of 1491

The Capitulations have survived in a number of texts (Garrido Atienza 1910; al-Maqqarī 1949:VI, 277–78), both in Castilian and in Arabic, although the Arabic texts are by no means as authoritative as the Castilian ones. Whereas in Castilian we have several official transcripts dating from 1492, as well as early summaries, in Arabic we have only the brief résumé contained in the *Nubdhat al-ᶜaṣr* and a not much fuller later text contained in al-Maqqarī's *Nafḥ al-Ṭīb*. We do not know whether al-Maqqarī had access to any "official" Arabic text, and the possibility cannot be excluded that what he gives us is merely an Arabic translation made from one of the Castilian versions.

Let us first look at the summary given in the *Nubdhat al-ᶜaṣr,* not because it has any primacy or authority, but because it must reflect in some way the preoccupations of the Spanish Muslims.

> Of the Capitulations agreed between the people of Granada [*sic: ahl Garnāṭa*] and the king of the Christians [*Rūm*] there were:
>
> - A promise of security for themselves and their townships and womenfolk and children and cattle and homes and gardens and farms and all possessions.
> - Those wishing to remain in Granada were to pay no tax other than the *zakāt* and the *ᶜushr* [tithe], and those who wished to leave might sell their estate at any agreed price to any agreed purchaser whether Muslim or Christian without fraud.
> - Anybody wishing to cross to North Africa might sell his estate and be transported with all his effects in a ship to any Muslim country he wished, without payment of passage money or other expenses, for three years.
> - Any Muslim wishing to remain in Granada was granted secure status on the terms set out above.
> - This was all recorded by the [Christian] king in a document in which he promised on the assurance of their deceitful religion that he would indeed fulfill all the conditions stipulated. (1940:41)

To translate the full text of the Castilian versions would take up an inordinate amount of space, but it is necessary to give the full text of some clauses and at least a summary of the rest of the document. (Clauses rendered in full are marked [F], those summarized are marked [S].) The first clause shows particularly clearly how matters of prime importance were jumbled up with secondary and even petty considerations, presumably as a result of last-minute drafting changes made in committee.[1]

"*Firstly* that the Moorish king and his *alcaides* and lawyers, judges, *muftīs,* ministers, learned men, military leaders, good men, and all the common folk of the city of Granada and of its Albaicín and other suburbs will in love, peace, goodwill, and with all truthfulness in their dealings and their actions yield and surrender to their highnesses, or to a person by them appointed, within forty days from this date, the fortress of the Alhambra and the Alhizan with all towers, gates to the city and the Albaicín and to suburbs connecting directly with the open country, so that they may occupy them in their name with their own troops, at their own free will, on condition that orders be issued to the justices that they should not permit the Christians to climb onto the wall between the Alcazaba and the Albaicín from where the houses of the Moors may be seen; and if anybody should climb up there, he should be punished immediately and sternly." [F]

2. The second clause related to the arrangements for the actual surrender: it should be carried out within forty days "freely and spontaneously," and in order to ensure against trouble, one day before the actual handover, Yūsuf b. Kumāsha (Aben Comixa) and fifty other hostages from important families should give themselves up (once the city, etc., was surrendered, they were to be released). [S]

3. Isabella, Ferdinand, and Prince John (their son) would after the surrender accept all Granadans, from King Abi Abdilehi (Boabdil) down, "great and small, men and women," as their vassals and natural subjects. In return the monarchs guaranteed to let

1. Mármol 1573 (and facsimile 1953): fol. 247v. The sequence is as given in Janer 1857:222–28. See also Fernández y González 1866:421–30 and Ladero 1969:172–85.

them remain in their "houses, estates and hereditaments now and for all time and for ever, nor would they allow any harm to be done to them without due legal process and without cause, nor would they have their estates and property nor any part thereof taken from them, rather would they be honored and respected by all their vassals." [S]

4. To avoid creating an uproar (*escándalo*), those who came to take over the Alhambra would enter by two named gates or from the side facing the country. [S]

5. The same day that Boabdil surrendered the fortresses, the king and queen would return to him his son and all the other hostages and their families, unless they had turned Christian. [S]

6. "Their highnesses and their successors will ever afterwards [*para siempre jamás*] allow King Abi Abdilehi and his *alcaides,* judges, *muftīs, alguaciles,* military leaders, and good men, and all the common people, great or small, to live in their own religion, and not permit that their mosques be taken from them, nor their minarets nor their muezzins, nor will they interfere with the pious foundations or endowments which they have for such purposes, nor will they disturb the uses and customs which they observe." [F]

7. "The Moors shall be judged in their laws and law suits according to the code of the *sharīʿa* which it is their custom to respect, under the jurisdiction of their judges and *qāḍīs*." [F]

8. "Neither now nor at any future time will their arms or their horses be taken from them, with the exception of cannons, both large and small, which they will within a short space of time hand over to whomsoever their highnesses appoint for that purpose." [F]

9. "Those Moors, both great and small, men and women, whether from Granada or from the Alpujarra and all other places, who may wish to go to live in Barbary or to such other places as they see fit, may sell their property, whether it be real estate or goods and chattels, in any manner and to whomsoever they like, and their highnesses will at no time take them away, or take them from those who may have bought them." [S]

10. Those who wished to leave with their families and all their possessions of any kind whatsoever, except firearms, might do so. Those wishing to cross immediately might make use of the ten

large ships provided for the purpose for the next seventy days from the port of their choice to "those ports of Barbary where Christian merchants normally trade." After this, and for three years, ships would be made available free at fifty days' notice. [S]

11. After the end of the three years, they should be free to go, but would have to pay one ducat a head and also the cost of the passage. [S]

12. If those going to Barbary were not able to sell their real estate in Granada (etc.) they could leave it in the hands of a trustee who would be entirely free to remit to Barbary any proceeds. [S]

13. "Neither their highnesses nor the Prince John their son nor those who may follow after them for all time will give instructions that those Moors who are their vassals shall be obliged to wear distinctive marks like those worn by the Jews." [F]

14. Neither Boabdil nor any other Moor of Granada would have to pay taxes on their houses, etc., for three years, they would simply have to pay a tax of one-tenth in August and in autumn and one-tenth on cattle in their possession in April and May "as the Christians are accustomed to pay." [S]

15. All Christian captives were to be handed over at the moment of surrender, with no entitlement for ransom or compensation, although if the Granadan owner of the captive had taken him to North Africa and already sold him before the Capitulations came into force, he would not have to hand him back. [S]

16. Boabdil and his principal officers, etc., were exempt from having their transport animals requisitioned for any form of service (apart from work willingly undertaken for payment). [S]

17. No Christians might enter mosques where the Muslims perform their prayer without permission of the *alfaquíes:* anyone entering otherwise was to be punished. [S]

18. Their highnesses would not permit the Jews to have power or command over the Moors, or to be collectors of any tax. [S]

19. King Boabdil and all his dignitaries, and all the common people of Granada, etc., would be well treated by their highnesses and their ministers, "and that what they have to say will be listened to, and their customs and rites will be preserved, and all *alcaides* [*sic*] and *alfaquíes* will be allowed to collect their incomes and enjoy their preeminences and their liberties such as by custom they

enjoy, and it is only right that they should continue to enjoy." [S]

20. "Their highnesses order that the Moors should not against their will have boarders forced upon them, nor have their linen, or their poultry or their animals or supplies of any sort taken from them." [F]

21. "Law suits which arise between Moors will be judged by their law *sharīʿa,* which they call of the *sunna,* and by their *qāḍīs* and judges, as they customarily have, but if the suit should arise between a Christian and a Moor, then it will be judged by a Christian judge and a Moorish *qāḍī,* in order that neither side may have any grounds for complaint against the sentence." [F]

22. No Moor may be tried for another. [S]

23. A general pardon would be accorded to Moors found in the prison of Hamet Abi Ali "his vassal," and neither they nor the villages of Captil would be prosecuted for any Christians they had killed, nor would any harm be done to them, nor would they have to restore stolen goods. [S]

24. Any Moorish captives in Christian hands who succeeded in fleeing to Granada or other places included in these Capitulations would become free, and their owners were barred from attempts to recover them making use of the law. Not included under this clause were Canary Islanders, and negroes from "the islands" (Cape Verde?). [S]

25. "That the Moors will not be obliged to give or pay more tribute to their highnesses than they used to give to the Moorish kings." [F]

26. Any Granadan Moors in North Africa could, if they wished, be included in the terms of the Capitulations; they had three years to return if they wished to do so. (If they had had Christian slaves and sold them, they would not be obliged to return them or the money so obtained.) [S]

27. If any Moor were to go to North Africa and then find he did not like the way of life, he could return and have all the benefits of the Capitulations, so long as he returned within three years. [S]

28. Any Moors accepting the Capitulations who wished to cross to North Africa for purposes of trade would be freely permitted to do so; also to any places in Castile or Andalusia, with no tolls to pay other than those commonly paid by Christians. [S]

29. Nobody would be permitted to abuse by word or by deed

any Christian man or woman who before the date of the Capitulations had turned Moor, and if any Moor had taken a renegade for his wife, she would not be forced to become a Christian against her will, but might be questioned in the presence of Christians and Moors, and be allowed to follow her own will; the same was to be understood of children born of a Christian mother and a Moor. [S]

30. "No Moor will be forced to become Christian against his or her will, and if for reasons of love an unmarried girl or a married woman or a widow should wish to become Christian, she will not be received [into the church] until she has been questioned. And if she has taken away from her parents' house clothing or jewels, these will be restored to the rightful owner, and guilty persons will be dealt with by the law." [F]

31. Neither the King Abi Abdilehi nor any of the Muslims included in the Capitulations might be called to account for any cattle, property, etc., taken during the war, whether from Christians or from Muslims who were Mudejars or who were not Mudejars. If any persons recognized objects as theirs, they were not entitled to ask for them back and indeed could be punished if they did. [S]

32. If any Moor had wounded or insulted any Christian man or woman held in captivity, no legal proceedings could be instituted against him ever. [S]

33. After the initial three-year tax holiday the Muslims would not have heavier taxes imposed on them than was just, bearing in mind value and quality. [S]

34. "The judges, *alcaldes,* and governors which their highnesses appoint in the city and region of Granada will be persons such as will honor the Moors and treat them kindly [*amorosamente*], and continue to respect these Capitulations. And if anyone should do anything which he ought not to do, their highnesses will have him moved from his post and punished." [F]

35. Neither Boabdil nor anybody else would be called to account for things done before the city surrendered. [S]

36. "No *alcaide,* squire, or servant of the King al-Zagal may hold any office or command at any time over the Moors of Granada." [F]

37. As a favor to King Abi Abdilehi and the inhabitants both

men and women of Granada, the Albaicín, and other suburbs [no mention of the Alpujarras here], they would give orders for the release of all Moorish prisoners, whether male or female, without any payment at all: those in Andalusia within five months, those in Castile, eight. Within two days of the handover by the Moors of any Christian captives in Granada, their highnesses would have two hundred Moorish men and women released. "And in addition we will place at liberty Aben Adrami, who is held by Gonzalo Hernández de Córdoba, and Hozmin [ʿUthmān] who is held by the count of Tendilla, and Ben Reduan, held by the count of Cabra, and Aben Mueden and the *alfaquí* Hademi's son, all of them leading residents of Granada, also the five *escuderos* who were taken when Brahem Abencerrax [Ibrāhīm Ibn Sarrāj] was defeated, if their whereabouts can be discovered." [S]

38. The Moors of the Alpujarras who had accepted vassalage would surrender all their Christian captives within two weeks for no payment. [S]

39. "Their highnesses will order that the customs of the Moors relating to inheritances will be respected, and in such matters the judges will be their own *qāḍīs*." [F]

40. "All Moors other than those included in this agreement who desire to enter their highnesses' service within thirty days may do so and enjoy all the benefits of it, other than the three-year period of tax exemption." [F]

41. "The pious endowments [*habices*] and the emoluments of the mosques, and the alms and other things customarily given to colleges [*madrasas*] and schools where children are taught will be the responsibility of the *alfaquíes,* to distribute them as they see fit, and their highnesses and their ministers will not interfere in this nor any aspect of it, nor will they give orders with regard to their confiscation or sequestration at any time ever in the future." [F]

42. North African ships in Granadan ports would, so long as they carried no Christian captives, be free to leave, and while in port were free from vexation and requisition of property, but they must submit to inspection on departure. [S]

43. Muslims would not be conscripted for military service against their will, and if their highnesses wished to recruit cavalry [no mention of infantry] for service in Andalusia, they would be paid from the day they left home until the date of return. [S]

44. No changes would be made in regulations affecting water courses and irrigation channels, and anybody throwing any unclean thing in a channel would be prosecuted. [S]

45. If any Moorish captive had arranged for someone else to stand as proxy for him in captivity and had then absconded, neither of them would have to pay a ransom. [S]

46. Nobody as a result of the change of sovereignty would be allowed to escape from contractual debt obligations. [S]

47. Christian slaughterhouses would be separated from Muslim ones. [S]

48. "The Jews native to Granada, Albaicín, and other suburbs, and of the Alpujarras and all other places contained in these Capitulations, will benefit from them, on condition that those who do not become Christians cross to North Africa within three years counting from December 8 of this year." [F]

"And their highnesses will give orders for the totality of the contents of these Capitulations to be observed from the day when the fortresses of Granada are surrendered onwards. To which effect they have commanded that their royal charter and deed should be signed with their names and sealed with their seal and witnessed by Hernando de Zafra their secretary, and have so done, dated in the *vega* of Granada on this 28th day of the month of November of the year of our salvation 1491." [F]

The Capitulations of November 1491 contain a number of clauses envisaging a relatively slow timetable of implementation (in forty days, etc.). Pescador del Hoyo's study showed that this had to be accelerated because once the process of the handover of power had begun, it became expedient to present the people with a fait accompli and to avoid giving dissidents time to rouse public opinion. Bernáldez may not have been fully informed of all circumstances, but in the following passage of his *Chronicle of the Catholic Monarchs* (BAE:LXX, 643), he conveys the essence of the problem Boabdil and Ferdinand had to face.

> After the aforementioned hostages had been handed over, because the Moors are very easily moved, and very excitable, and given to uproar and to auguries, many of them gave credence to a Moor who began an outcry in the city, saying that they were bound to win, if only they exalted Muḥammad and if they challenged the settlement. He went about the city shouting; and twenty thou-

sand Moors rose with him. When the king heard of the uproar, he dared not leave the Alhambra to stop him until the next day, a Saturday, when he went to the Albaicín and summoned his council, and when they came, they were in an uproar. He asked them why, and they told him, so he told them his opinion, and calmed them down as best he might, saying that that was no time to be shifting ground, partly because of the dire straits in which they found themselves, with their food exhausted, partly because the hostages had already been handed over, so they should think about that great danger, death, which was staring them in the face, with no possible hope of help to come. After saying this he went back to the Alhambra.

The agreement had been made for the Alhambra to be handed over at the Epiphany [January 6] as stated. King Boabdil, perceiving the difficulty arising from the excitable temperament of the Moors, and the uproar which had taken place, wrote to King Ferdinand about all that had happened, how the Moors had, like foolish people, shifted their ground on what had been agreed, whereas he had not shifted from what had been agreed, so that he now asked his highness to come immediately, with no further delay, to receive the surrender of the Alhambra, and not to wait until the Epiphany, because he already had his hostages, so in spite of the riots he should go ahead with what had been initially agreed and stipulated in the Capitulations.

Thus it was that a hasty and almost improvised handover took place with Gutierre de Cárdenas acting on behalf of the Catholic Monarchs. He was brought by Ibn Kumāsha and Abū'l-Qāsim al-Mulīh into Boabdil's presence in the Comares tower of the Alhambra, where he received the keys of the palace and proceeded to occupy key points (Pescador del Hoyo 1955). Boabdil got a suitable written receipt. All this took place on January 1, 1492.

The public ceremony on the following day at which Boabdil handed over a bunch of keys (the same keys? a purely symbolic bunch?), kissed Ferdinand's hand, and received back his hostage son, was all performed with the Alhambra already under Castilian military control. The count of Tendilla, first Castilian governor of the Alhambra, took over in fact not from the Granadan garrison, but from his colleague Gutierre de

Cárdenas. What took place on January 2 was a splendid pageant, a piece of memorable street-theater.

The last Muslim stronghold in the Iberian peninsula was in Christian hands. The final period of the history of Spanish Islam had begun: the period when all Muslims who lived in Spain were subjects of Christian rulers.

TWENTY

All Mudejars Now: Islamic Spain (1492–1500)

In Spanish history 1492 is remembered for three great events: in chronological order, the Christian conquest of Muslim Granada, the Christian expulsion of the Jews from Spain, and the discovery by Columbus of an island on the far side of the Atlantic. Columbus's logbook, or rather the abridgement of it by Las Casas, which is all that survives, actually starts in Granada:

> On January 2 in the year 1492, when your Highnesses had concluded their war with the Moors who reigned in Europe, I saw your Highnesses' banners victoriously raised on the towers of the Alhambra, the citadel of that city, and the Moorish king come out of the city gates and kiss the hands of your Highnesses, and the prince, my Lord. And later in that same month . . . your Highnesses decided to send me, Christopher Columbus, to see those parts of India and the princes and peoples of these lands, and consider the best means for their conversion. . . . Therefore having expelled all the Jews from your domains in that same month of January, your Highness commanded me to go with an adequate fleet to these parts of India. . . . I departed from the city of Granada on Saturday May 12 and went to the port of Palos, where I prepared three ships. (Columbus 1969:3 [trans. J. M. Cohen])

The surrender of Granada was of course of transcendental importance to the Muslims of Spain, but neither of the other events was without its bearing on their fate. The expulsion of the Jews was the first step towards the ending of the old Spain of three monotheistic religions, which had existed in the Middle Ages. Spain was moving towards the period when one religion only would be tolerated: Christianity. We speak of the expulsion of the Jews, but in fact there was a choice: forcible conversion or expulsion from Spain. Those sufficiently fond of their native land might choose to pretend to be Christians in order to live on in Spain. The eventual extension of the policy of forcible conversion to Muslims as well as Jews brought into being a community of crypto-Muslims alongside the community of crypto-Jews. The conversion/expulsion of the Jews in 1492 thus prepared the way for the creation of the Morisco problem of the sixteenth century.

The discovery of the New World may seem altogether more remote from the history of the Muslims of the peninsula. From the enterprise of America, Muslims (and Jews) were, in theory at least, totally excluded. The indirect impact that Spain's possession of a New World empire had was considerable. Spain's economic and military power and its prestige in international affairs grew immeasurably. The victory at Granada in 1492 might have been expected to evoke a military response, a counterattack from somewhere in the Islamic world. Not only was Islamic North Africa weak, but Spain's might was increasing all the time. Before long its superiority over any Islamic state within striking distance was overwhelming.

Thus all three of the events of 1492 combined to make the Christian victory at Granada a final and a conclusive one. The Mediterranean seacoast might be open and vulnerable to pirate raids from the far Islamic shore, so that at times there was almost a Spanish psychosis related to the cry "*Moros en la costa*" (the Moors have landed), but in fact there was no landing in strength on Spanish territory by troops from any Muslim power, no attempt to regain what had been lost.

All this undoubtedly had its effect on the way in which Spanish policy towards the minority religions developed. Because we now know that within the space of some eight years the Capitulations of Granada were unilaterally declared to be null and void, there is a risk that we will pass too rapidly over the period when most of the provisions of the Capitulations were respected: when Granada was a largely Mudejar city. Nobody now has reason to cherish the memory of this Mudejar interlude, but for those eight years Granada, although ruled by a small Christian upper class of soldiers, lawyers, and ecclesiastics, was still an almost totally Islamic city, with most of the personnel of its own Islamic machinery of administration and local government still in post.

Continuity between Naṣrid Granada and Granada after 1492 was considerable. We have a list (Durán y Lerchundi 1893:I, 122) of those who held office in the first *ayuntamiento* of Granada under the Catholic Monarchs. The Castilian orthography does not always permit us to reconstruct the Arabic forms (although often it does), but there can be no doubt that this was no rump of disreputable collaborators, but a municipal senate of weight and authority.

1. El Cadi Mahomad Ben Abdilmet el Chorrut.
2. Cadi Mahomad el Pequenni el motacen.
3. El Alfaqui Jucef el mudéjar.
4. El Alfaqui Mahomad Fat.
5. El Hatib de Axares Adulhazis.
6. El Hatib de la Alcazaba Mahomad Adera.
7. El Hatib Forés el Basti.
8. El Alfaqui Hamete el Pequenni.
9. Hamete Abenzulema.
10. Abul Cacim el Guadixi.
11. Hamete el Comayde.
12. Bexir el Gibi.
13. Alí Bennaur.
14. Adul haid el Mugeri.
15. Yaga el Xarif.
16. Hamet Abulfat.
17. Hamet Azafar.
18. Mahomet el Guadixi.
19. El Alfaqui Aben Cobdi del Alacaba.
20. Zaad Afin.
21. Abraen el Cayci.

What is most striking about this list is the predominance of the religious elite, clearly the largest single element in the city's ruling class.

No fewer than nine out of twenty-one are identified as *qāḍī, khaṭīb,* or *faqīh*. The religious leaders were not exempt from pressures to convert. Alonso de Santa Cruz tells us (1951:I, 99) that in 1493, when Ferdinand was severely wounded in Barcelona by a would-be assassin, "a low fellow, unknown, some sixty years of age, a Catalan," who struck at him with a sharp sword "so that it was a miracle he did not lop his head clean off," Boabdil had a delegation of the gentlemen of his household visit the convalescent king, "and with them was el Pequenni, who was a very important man among the Moors, and who afterwards became a Christian and was called Fernando Enriquez."

Outside the city there were a number of residences where dignitaries who had accepted Mudejar status could live in some state: chief among these, of course, was at the beginning Boabdil himself. Fernando de Zafra, the royal secretary, reports in a letter to Ferdinand dated December 9, 1492, that Boabdil and his servants were continually out hunting on his Alpujarras estate. "He is at present in the country near Dalia and Verja although his house is at Andarax. They say he has gone for a month" (CODOIN:XI, 543). Boabdil did not remain long. By September or October he had left for North Africa (Tlemcen) (HEMP: XVII[1], 909). His wife had died in Andarax and is buried in Mondújar (*Actas* 1978:II, 341).

We meet with contradictions if we attempt to trace Boabdil into exile. Al-Maqqarī (1949:VI, 281), who presumably ought to have been in a position to find the truth, in 1628 visited Fez where he met members of Boabdil's family: according to him Boabdil died in 1533 or 1518 (he indicates exactly where he was buried). On the other hand Luis de Marmol Carvajal in the *Descripción general de Africa* (1573) tells us Boabdil was killed fighting for the ruler of Fez against the Sharifian forces at the battle of Abū ʿAqba (Buacuba). As Mercedes García-Arenal points out in her edition of the *Relación del origen y succeso de los Xerifes* by Diego de Torres (1980:107n), this battle took place in 1536, when Boabdil would have been about 80 years old, so we should perhaps reject the anecdote as spurious. Mármol is quite specific, however: "with him was Muley Abi Abdallah el Zogoibi, king that was of Granada, who, having surrendered such a famous city as that to the Catholic Monarchs, Ferdinand and Isabella, had passed across to Barbary and resided with the King of Fez. . . . In this battle el Zogoybi died, which made a mockery of Fortune, for death struck him as he was defending the kingdom of somebody else when he had not dared to defend his own."[1] Probably deserving more credence is al-Maqqarī's report that in his day Boabdil's descendants were drawing charitable relief in Fez.

To encourage the emigration to North Africa of the military aristocracy was the policy of the new Castilian rulers of the kingdom of Granada. No doubt by removing the old leaders, Ferdinand and his administrators hoped that the Muslim masses would not be able to organize themselves. José Szmolka (*Actas* 1978:II, 406) regards Zafra as the "main author" of the policy which, he says, "by 1495 bore fruit as there only remained in Granada a minority totally amenable to the wishes of the Castilian authorities." This is how Zafra reports to his royal master: "The Abencerrajes have taken their womenfolk up to the Alpujarras. After selling off all their property, they are preparing to leave by the end of March. As I see it, most people are packing their bags to leave. Your Highness may believe that by the summer all that will be left here, and in the Alpujarras too, I think, will be farm workers and craftsmen [*labradores y oficiales*], for, as far as I can see, all the rest are on their way out, and not on account of any harsh treatment they have received, for never were people better treated" (Caro Baroja 1957:9).

On September 22 he reveals a little more of his underlying sentiments: "These Moors are all very quiet, and entirely at the service of your Highnesses, to such an extent that nobody in the world could be more so, as it appears. However, I would rather there were not so many of them [*yo no querría tantos*], not because I have any grounds for suspicion, thank God, but with an extra turn of the screw [*un garrote*, perhaps "a big stick"] the person of least importance whom your Highnesses have in your kingdoms might expel them" (Caro Baroja 1957:13).

The Christian authorities took over this society unchanged, and although Zafra might be constantly hearing of wealthy people leaving, the city remained full of Muslim workers. Crafts were organized in guilds, each with its *amīn* or syndic. Since in Islamic times such guilds usually had a religious (and sometimes a Sufi) dimension, we can reasonably suppose that such trade organizations would have been impenetrable to the Christian immigrants. The two societies were not merged or integrated, they coexisted.

The first strong indication of the arrival of a tide of Christian immi-

1. Marmol 1573 (and facsimile 1953):fol. 247v. See also Marmol (1600) for the legend of Boabdil's last sigh; cf. Alarcón 1947:10.

grants comes in 1498 with the reorganization of the city into two halves, Christian and Muslim. In spite of the Capitulations, the city proper was to be made over to the newcomers, the Albaicín reserved for the Muslims. Muhammad el Pequenni served as spokesman for the Muslims in this apportionment of living space.

It was not simply that the city was being geographically divided, it was also becoming socially compartmentalized at many levels. On March 22, 1498, the church promulgated regulations (backed up by the ecclesiastical penalty of excommunication) preventing Christians from renting accommodation to Muslims for such ceremonies as weddings, barring the consumption of meat sold by *ḥalāl* butchers, the use of Moorish bath-houses, and the employment by Christian women of Moorish midwives if Christian practitioners were available (Caro Baroja 1957:14). The rationale for all these bans was religious, but the effect would be social and economic as well.

There is no reason to think that the man charged with being the first archbishop of Granada went about his task in a spirit of anything other than true christian charity and self-abnegation. Fray Hernando de Talavera respected all those parts of the Capitulations which protected the religious beliefs of the new Mudejar community, and he became well loved and trusted by the Muslims of the city. His preaching was largely by Christian example. As far as success in bringing about conversions was concerned, he had little or none: hardly surprising, for no Christian missionary to any Islamic community has ever been successful. Yet he was much criticized for his slow progress, notably by Francisco Jiménez de Cisneros, whose forceful personality and aggressively militant Christianity made him quite unable to sympathize with Talavera's quietism. Cisneros, because of the key posts he occupied at court and in the national church, was well placed to make his views prevail.

The immediate cause of conflict between Cisneros and Talavera was the issue of the *elches* or Christian converts to Islam. A clause protecting the rights of such people to continue in their adopted religion was included in the Capitulations. It was quite explicit and unambiguous, so that Christians could certainly not plead that the implications of this aspect of the peace settlement had unfortunately been overlooked. The Granadan negotiating team had foreseen only too well the problems likely to arise over the *elches* and had protected the rights of those neo-Muslims with wording of admirable clarity.

Yet the freedom of the *elches* to choose their religion stuck in the throats of pious Christians, who were being asked to accept what had never before been accepted: the inclusion *within* a Christian-controlled society of individuals who had known Christianity, and had freely and willingly rejected it. Medieval Christian society had no place for the renegade, and while Christian theology was always quite clear on the need for the exercise of free will by the believer entering into the obligations of the faith, it did not envisage such exercise of free will as would lead to the abandonment of that faith.

Alonso de Santa Cruz in his *Chronicle of the Catholic Monarchs* summarizes Cisneros' point of view effectively:

> The archbishop of Toledo, Fray Francisco Jiménez, wished [in 1499] to remain in Granada with the zealous desire and intention of trying to see if he could convert the Moors to the faith of Jesus Christ, and if he could not, at least of seeing to it that those who were of Christian descent should be converted. This he set about doing, and had persons known to be of such descent brought before him. With kind words he persuaded them to return to our holy Catholic faith, because, as he said, it could not without the gravest sin be permitted for people to belong to the religion of the Moors, if their forebears had been Christian. (1951:II, 191)

Perhaps if he had limited himself to such "persuasion" all might have been well but

> those converted in this way were given assistance by him, and he bestowed gratifications on them: those who refused, he had put in prison, and kept locked up until they were converted. As this affected many Moors, there was a great outcry. On the day of Our Lady of the O,[2] when a bailiff sent by the said archbishop went to arrest a Moor in the Albaicín, and was seen by many Moors, they assembled together, and killed him. After the perpetration of this murder, the whole of the Albaicín was in an uproar, and the inhabitants took up arms.

2. "Our Lady of the O" is not, as I first thought, an abbreviation, simply one of the advocations of the BVM. I am indebted to Dr. Angel García for this information.

Of course anybody who deliberately flouts an explicit and binding engagement deserves opprobrium, but in order to put this action by Cisneros into perspective, it should be pointed out that his attitude towards Christian renegades was an exact mirror image of the Muslim attitude to Muslim renegades. Under no circumstances whatsoever would Islamic law condone a Muslim exercising his free will and becoming a Christian. If a Muslim ruler were to sign a treaty acknowledging the right of a convert to continue in his newly adopted faith, the *fuqahā'* could be relied on to denounce such a document in the strongest terms, and a public outcry might be expected. What Cisneros was doing, presumably quite unconsciously, was to imitate his adversaries. Cisneros with his stubborn intransigeance drove the Muslims of Granada (described, as we have seen, by Zafra as quite peaceful) into armed insurrection.

The infractions of the Capitulations of which Cisneros was guilty were by no means limited to those relating to the *elches*. As we have seen, it is possible to make some form of a plea in mitigation of Cisneros' activities where people of Christian background were concerned. (The Capitulations if fully and loyally implemented would have set up a state which was truly neutral as between Islam and Christianity, and for that there was no precedent anywhere.) What was utterly indefensible was his brutal treatment of some Muslims. It is difficult to relate what he did without being overwhelmed by outraged indignation, and it is perhaps safer to let his "official biographer," Alvar Gómez de Castro, tell the story. Gómez de Castro was fully convinced of Cisneros' righteousness, but what we hear is startling:

> A great number of the Granadans had already been pleased to accept the Christian faith when some arose who were stubbornly opposed to it, excessively attached as they were to the traditions of their forefathers. They regretted that the original religion of the Moors was dying out, and with impassioned speeches they tried to persuade people to abandon Christianity. Cisneros, so as to protect the congregations of the New Christians from harm, imprisoned all the dissidents in chains, and though it ran counter to his temperament, he allowed them to be dealt with by methods which were not correct.
>
> Among those arrested, one man called Zegrí Azaator was

preeminent, partly because of his noble descent, partly because of his spiritual and physical attributes. It was commonly said that he descended in direct line from that Abenhamar [Ibn al-Aḥmar] who is celebrated by our countrymen in their ballads. He was a powerful obstacle in the way of Cisneros' pious schemes with his constant sharp reminders to his fellows. For this reason, Cisneros decided to strike firmly, and to use harsh measures against one who had proved immune to more generous approaches. This task he entrusted to his sacristan, Pedro León, who did indeed prove to be such a lion in his handling of this case that he changed an exceedingly tough spirited person with great powers of resistance into a gentle humble man completely subject to the will of Cisneros.

After a few days, Zegrí, vanquished in spite of himself—or perhaps inspired by the divine grace which leads all men to seek their own salvation—begged to be conducted to "the *alfaquí* of the Christians" (his very words, it was said) and they led him in as he was, in chains and filthy.

He asked Cisneros to order his chains to be struck off, so that he could talk freely, for, as he said, the statements of a captive in manacles and chains might not be held to carry authority. With the chains removed he knelt and kissed the ground first, then his own hand, in accordance with Moorish custom [?], and declared his wish to become a Christian, saying that, the night before, Allah (that is their name for God) had told him to do so in a vision, and he was sure he had been called by God, and had the confidence unhesitatingly to give account of his Christian faith. "But I would be foolish," he smiled, "to seek reasons other than this wild lion [León] of yours; if you were to entrust our people to him, there is not one but would convert immediately." It was as if, by his smile, he wished to underline León's fierceness to himself. Cisneros, happy at an outcome beyond his hopes, ordered all his prison garments to be stripped from him, and had all the filth which had become caked on him in his prolonged and harsh imprisonment washed away, so that in a red silk robe he could go to the baptismal font. When he was born again through baptism, he changed his name and decided to call himself Gonzalo Fernández Zegrí, since in his youth he had fought against that great Gonzalo Fer-

> nández [the Great Captain] and had stood his ground against him on the plain of Granada. (Gómez de Castro 1984:98)

Quite enough is said here to enable us to see that the conversion techniques of the late fifteenth century were remarkably similar to the methods of brainwashing as employed in the twentieth: the switching from kindness to cruelty, the attack on the victim's self-respect by depriving him of the elementary means of keeping himself clean, and so on. Alvar Gómez de Castro's account links indirectly with another action of Cisneros which is perhaps even more notorious: his burning of Arabic books. (There may well be no such link.)

> Joyous at this success, and thinking he must profit from such a favorable occasion, Cisneros sought to extirpate all Mahometan error from their souls, and did not allow himself to be deflected by those advocating the prudence of proceeding little by little when seeking to eradicate such a deeply ingrained habit. Cisneros considered that such an approach might have its place in matters of little moment, but not when the salvation of souls was at stake. Thus without difficulty, and with no need for decrees or force, he managed to get the *alfaquíes* (who were prepared to do him all manner of favors) to bring out into the street the copies of the Koran, that is to say of the most important book of their superstition, and all the books of the Mahometan impiety, of whatsoever author or kind they might be: more than five thousand volumes with ornamental bindings, even of gold and silver and of admirable artistry. These caught the eye of some who asked for them as gifts, but he would give none to anybody, and all were burned together on a great bonfire with the exception of certain works on medicine, a study to which people of that race had always devoted themselves to great effect. These works, rescued from the flames by the merits of the healing art, are to this day kept in the library at Alcalá. (1984:99)

Cisneros' harrying of the *elches,* his attempt to terrorize the Islamic elite into conversion, combined with other grievances to drive the Muslims of Granada into armed revolt. The triumphalism of Cisneros in his relations with Muslims in general, the plain brutality of his treatment of some, undid the work of all those (Tendilla, Talavera, Zafra, Ferdinand himself) who had over the years since 1492 labored to establish a modus vivendi between Castilian rulers and Granadan Muslim subjects: a new form of Mudejarism. The archbishop of Toledo's zeal for conversion had military consequences. To the pessimists among the Castilian ruling class it almost seemed that the Granadan war needed to be fought all over again. It fell to others, of course, not to Cisneros, to repair the damage: to the first governor of the Alhambra and captain-general of the Kingdom of Granada, the count of Tendilla, to the first archbishop of Granada, Talavera. They had, during their years of service in Granada, built up a relationship of trust with the Muslims they ruled. With immense courage, patience, and tact they were able to restore public order in Granada itself without great bloodshed. Cisneros was for a short while out of favor with his royal patrons, but in the long run it was the policy of Cisneros which prevailed.

The damage done by Cisneros in Granada had its impact elsewhere in the kingdom. When in January 1500 the Muslims of the Alpujarras (as we have seen, a preferred place of residence for those who wished to avoid the close proximity of Christians) heard of the disturbances in the city, many of them rose, and some Christians in isolated areas were put to the sword. It was perhaps fortunate for Ferdinand that Gonzalo Fernández de Córdoba was back in Spain after the triumphs of his Italian campaigns in the 1490s, and he and Tendilla launched an attack aimed at Lanjarón. There were reports that a "king" was being summoned from North Africa. The Castilian authorities took this rising with the utmost seriousness, but the rebels, confronted as they were with some of the best and most experienced military leaders in Europe at this time, stood little chance. As ever, disunity prevailed among the Muslims until the end. Instead of concerting their revolts, it seems they rose in one place after another, giving the Castilian forces the chance to deal with one area at a time. In October 1500 Almería was in revolt, and it was not until early 1501 that the last of the insurgents were put down in the west, in the mountains near Ronda.

The risings gave to the Christian authorities the opportunity to rid themselves of the Capitulations of Granada, and to modify or rescind the Mudejar status of other Muslims elsewhere. This is how Santa Cruz describes the end of Mudejar status in Granada itself:

> The day following this [rebellion and its repression] proclamations were made in places where the Moors of the Albaicín could

> hear, saying that all those who wished to become Christians would be pardoned for their rebellion, and for the deaths which they had caused, and for the robberies and other crimes which they had committed, but those who refused would be prosecuted. As soon as they heard this they came in to make their peace, and handed in the arms which they had, which were short spears [*gorguces*], lances, and crossbows. All went peacefully, and they all turned Christian, up to fifty thousand souls. All the mosques of Granada, both large and small, were consecrated and turned into churches. (1951:I, 193)

Here then in 1499 is the effective end of Islam in Granada, at least of Islam as a public religion. (Such enforced conversions are rarely sincere, so that the end of Islam as a public religion was the beginning of crypto-Islam, but that is another story.) The further decrees confirming this policy elsewhere in the lands of the Crown of Castile did not come until 1501 and 1502, and in Aragon and Valencia it was not until the 1520s that forcible conversions were pushed through (against some opposition from a minority of the Christian aristocracy), but 1499 saw the policy of bringing the Mudejar compacts to an end in the key Muslim community, that of Granada.

After the risings of 1499, as after the conquest of 1492, some members of the Islamic elite must have found ways of reaching an accommodation with Ferdinand and his ministers. Indeed, if we are to judge by the document from which I am about to quote, some Granadan notables must have collaborated actively with royal officials, and received as their reward safeconducts which permitted them to live unmolested on estates where they continued to practice their own religion.

The source in question is an unusual one: a sixteenth-century manuscript written in Arabic characters, but in a form of Spanish (*aljamía*). Most of the manuscript consists of Islamic texts, but the passage that concerns us was copied out by the Morisco author from what he describes as a *conduta* (safeconduct) "in Latin" (by which he seems simply to mean "in Latin characters"). This "very splendid" document he had found in the house of one ʿAlī Sarmiento, an aged scholar who had been *imām* (*catredatico* [*sic*]: it surely cannot mean professor?) in Granada before the conquest. We are told that "so as not to see the affronts which are committed every day in such a noble city as Granada, he exiled himself from there, although he was suffering from three afflictions: a very painful sciatica, a liver complaint, and deafness on one side. We arrived at his house on the twentieth of the honored month of Ramadan, and he made much of us. He was very rich, had married sons and daughters, and was delighted to see us. He possessed a safe conduct in Latin from King Ferdinand, which was very splendid. I read it, and the tenor of what it said was as follows" (Harvey 1956). In what follows the text as given in *aljamía* is translated. Although some of the original phraseology reflects Castilian chancery practice, there are words and expressions which would never have been used in such a document—words that belong exclusively to the Romance speech of the Moriscos. Their presence in the document as copied out in *aljamía* need not make us reject it as totally spurious, but clearly what it contains needs interpreting with care.

> Don Ferdinand and Doña Isabella, Monarchs of Aragon and Sicily, through the grace of the holy spirit set over this Kingdom of Granada, confirmers of the Christian religion against the holy presence and our hidden Jerusalem [*sic:* surely a corrupt passage?].
>
> By this royal deed [*data*] granted by our holy and royal Council with our accustomed mercy, and confirmed by us and our sacramental religion, *ʿAlī Sarmiento* and all his descendants may and can enjoy that liberty and freedom which their forebears enjoyed, to the satisfaction of the said ʿAlī Sarmiento, because he was very obedient and truthful to his sole King, and no less fidelity have we found in him in matters which concern us, and thus, by reason of his merits, we give him frank and free liberty [*franca y libre libertad*] through all our potentates [*sic*?], by land and by sea, to live and travel without hindrance, whether going, returning or staying, or in any further return journeys he may make, whether in our own days or after them, and we so pledge our faith and commend our will to our successors [the MS curiously reads *predecesores,* but the context seems to require *sucesores*] and to governors and to those who serve our royal persons, as also we pledge it by our Holy Religion that in the name of the Sacrament this observance should be maintained and is conceded to the said ʿAlī Sarmiento, and to all his heirs [here again *predecesores*] in the male line, that they be honored and respected, just as is the person of the same ʿAlī Sarmiento, and on pain of being disobedient to us. We order

> those who hold high office under us to regard both their [his family's?] persons and possessions as a special trust, so that they may live in, dwell in and enjoy fields, irrigated lands, all fresh waters from rivers, springs and standing pools, and privileges [corrupt text?], with all enclosures of cattle, sheep and goats. They may not be rejected by [Muslim] communities [*aljamas*], nor may they on account of rancor be made to go short of bread, meat or other communal services such as fire [wood], smiths, carpenters, masons, doctors and surgeons. Let them enjoy all communal rights as are enjoyed by great and small, let them not be vexed by any *preces* [?] by the nobility or by deans or ecclesiastical dignitaries, and since the said ʿAlī Sarmiento in no way is in conflict with our Holy Religion, let him live and maintain his state in whatsoever religion or law may be his will. Given in our royal Alcazar of the Alhambra of Granada; sealed with our royal seal, on May 22 of this present year of 1499. (Harvey 1956)

ʿAlī Sarmiento was visited by the Morisco author of the book in which the document is copied many years later, and he could still say, "After the loss of Granada, there did not remain any Moor [*sic*] with such riches, for since this man remained so much in the good graces of the Christian king and his prelates, he had what he wanted."

This protection permitted him to keep up a great Muslim household, and fulfill what he saw as his obligations: "For so long as the month of Ramadan lasted, never was there lacking meat for poor folk nor for servants." Yet, inevitably the final impression is of the pathetic isolation of this collaborator, clinging to the vestiges of past glories that would never return:

> One Friday, also in the month of Shawwāl, he got up into his pulpit [*minbar*] in his house, and wearing the robe [?] of his donation [?] which he used to wear when he used to go to give greetings to the Kings of Granada on festivals or other special days, with an appearance that was more moving than admonitory, he began to preach to us. His speech was as carefully chosen as any I have heard, nor do I expect to witness anything similar. With just the four of us and a widowed daughter of his, he addressed us, fixing us with his eyes, and saying: "Beloved children, faithful Muslims . . . "

The final words[3] of this account of the Muslims of Spain at the end of the Middle Ages must be those of a member of a distinguished Granadan family: Yuce Banegas. He was visited by the same Morisco author. Like ʿAlī Sarmiento, Banegas preached a little sermon, although not from a formal pulpit, but out in the *vega* in the Cuesta de la Higuera, a league only from the city, and beside a stream (*junto a un arroyo*):

> "My son: I am quite aware that you know little of the things of Granada, but do not be surprised if I recall them, for there is not a moment when it does not all reverberate within my heart; there is no minute, no hour when it does not tear at my entrails. . . . In my opinion nobody ever wept over such a misfortune as that of the sons of Granada. Do not doubt what I say, because I am one myself, and an eye-witness, for with my own eyes I saw all the noble ladies, widows and married, subjected to mockery, and I saw more than three hundred maidens sold at public auction; I will tell you no more, it is more than I can bear. I lost three sons, all of them died in defense of the religion [he uses the word *addin*], and I lost two daughters and my wife, and this one daughter was left to be my consolation: she was seven months old at the time."
>
> He said more: "Son: I do not weep over the past, for to it there is no return. But I weep for what you will see in your own lifetime, and what you can expect in this land, in this Peninsula of Spain. May it please God, because of the nobility of our honored Koran, that what I have to say be proved unfounded, and that it does not turn out as I see it, but even so our religion will suffer. What will people say? Where has our prayer gone to? What has happened to the religion of our forefathers? It will all be bitterness for anybody with feelings. And what hurts most is that the Muslims will be just like the Christians: they will not reject their dress and they will not avoid their food. . . .

3. Harvey 1956. The passage quoted is from MS. Biblioteca Nacional, Madrid, Vitrina reservada 245 fol. 87–88. "Si el rey de la Conquista no guarda fidelidad, ¿qué aguardamos de sus suzesores?"

"If after such a short space of time it appears that we are having to struggle to survive, what will people do when the end of the season is upon us? If parents now make little of the religion, how are their great-great-grandchildren [*choznos*] to exalt it? *If the King of the Conquest does not keep faith, what are we to expect from his successors?*"

BIBLIOGRAPHY

(Including Bibliographical Abbreviations)

al-ʿAbbādī, Mujtār

1955. "Los móviles económicos en la vida de Ibn al-Jaṭīb." *Al-Andalus,* 20:214–21.

1973. *El reino de Granada en la época de Muḥammad V.* Madrid.

Abellán Pérez, Juan

1978. "Notas sobre el comercio de trigo y la Guerra de Granada." In *Actas* 1978, II:349–56.

1983. "Un documento sobre el infante Yūsuf b. al-Mawl." *Andalucía Islámica,* 2–3:189–94.

El Abencerraje (Novela y Romancero).

1983. Ed. Francisco López Estrada. Madrid.

Acién Almansa, Manuel

1979. *Ronda y su serranía en tiempo de los Reyes Católicos.* 2 vols., Málaga.

1981. (with José Enrique López de Coca Castañer) "Los mudéjares del Obispado de Málaga (1485–1501)." In *Actas* 1981:307–47.

Actas 1978 = *Actas del I congreso de Historia de Andalucía, diciembre 1976: Andalucía medieval.* II. Córdoba.

Actas 1981 = *Actas del I Simposio Internacional de Mudejarismo.* Madrid and Teruel.

Actas 1982 = *Actas del II Simposio Internacional de Mudejarismo: Arte, Teruel, 19–21 de noviembre de 1981.* Teruel.

Actas 1985 = *Actas de las II Jornadas de Cultura Árabe e Islámica (1980).* Madrid.

Actas 1986 = *Actas del III Simposio Internacional de Mudejarismo: Teruel, 20–22 de septiembre de 1984.* Teruel.

Agueda Castellano, María

1982. "El mudéjar en los castillos españoles. Criterios de uniformidad y caracteres diferenciadores." In *Actas* 1982:15–22.

Aguilera Pleguezuelo, José

1985. "El derecho malikí aplicado en Al-Andalus: Teoría y práctica juridicas." In *Actas* 1985:17–20.

Alarcón, Pedro A. de

1947. *La Alpujarra.* 12th edition, Madrid.

Alarcón Santón, M., and García de Linares, R.

1940. *Los documentos árabes diplomáticos del Archivo de la Corona de Aragón.* Madrid and Granada.

Albarracín Navarro, Joaquina
1978. "Un documento granadino sobre los bienes de la mujer de Boabdil en Mondújar." In *Actas* 1978:339–48.
1983. "Abū'l-ʿĀṣī en un documento posesorio arábigo-granadino (1493)." *Andalucía Islámica,* 2–3:179–88.
Alfonso X (el Sabio)
1807. *Las Siete Partidas.* 3 vols., Madrid.
See also *Primera crónica general.*
Andalucía Islámica = *Andalucía Islámica: textos y estudios.*
1979- (= *Anejos de Cuadernos de Historia del Islam,* Granada.)
Aranda Doncel, Juan
1984. *Los moriscos en tierras de Córdoba.* Córdoba.
Argote de Molina, Gonzalo
1588. *Nobleza de Andalucía.* Sevilla.
Arié, Rachel
1965. "Les relations diplomatiques et culturelles entre Musulmans d'Espagne et Musulmans d'Orient au temps des Naṣrides." *Mélanges de la Casa de Velázquez,* 1:87–107.
1973. *L'Espagne musulmane au temps des Naṣrides (1232–1492).* Paris.
1984. *España musulmana (siglos VIII–XV).* Barcelona.
Arribas Palau, Mariano
1960. "Una reclamación de Yūsuf III de Granada a Fernando I de Aragón." MEAH, 9:75–84.
Ashtor, E.
1969. *History of the Jews in Muslim Spain.* Philadelphia.
Asín Palacios, Miguel
1944. *Contribución a la toponimia árabe en España.* Madrid.
See also Ribera and Asín 1912.
Aureum opus
1515 and facsimile 1975. *Aureum opus regalium privilegiorum civitatis et regni Valentie cum historia Christianissimi regis Jacobi ipsius primi conquistatoris.* Valencia.
BAE = *Biblioteca de Autores Españoles*
Baeza, Hernando de
1868. "Las cosas que pasaron entre los reyes de Granada desde el tiempo del rey don Juan de Castilla, segundo de este nombre, hasta que los Católicos Reyes ganaron el reyno de Granada." In *Relaciones de algunos sucesos de los últimos tiempos del reino de Granada.* Madrid, 1–44. Sociedad de Bibliófilos Españoles No. 3.
Ballesteros-Beretta, Antonio
1963. *Alfonso X el Sabio.* Barcelona.

Barceló Torres, María del Carmen
1984. *Minorías islámicas en el país valenciano: historia y dialecto.* Valencia.
Barrientos, Lope
See CCE, IX.
Bejarano-Robles, Francisco, and Vallvé Bermejo, Joaquín
1974. *Repartimiento de Comares (1487–1496).* Barcelona.
Benaboud, M'hammad
1984. "El papel político y social de los ʿulamāʾ en Al-Andalus durante el período de las Taifas." *Cuadernos de Historia del Islam,* 11:1–46.
Ben Cheneb, Mohammed
1907. *Études sur les personnages mentionnés dans l'idjâza du cheikh ʿAbd el Qâdir el Fâsy.* Paris. (Reprinted from *Actes du XIV Congrès International des Orientalistes,* IV.)
Benítez Sánchez-Blanco, R.
1982. *Moriscos y cristianos en el condado de Casares,* Córdoba.
Bermúdez Pareja, J., and García Gómez, Emilio
1966. *La Alhambra: la Casa Real.* Granada.
Bermúdez de Pedraza, Francisco
1608. *Antigüedades y excelencias de Granada.* Madrid.
Bernáldez, Andrés
See BAE, LXX.
Biblioteca de Autores Españoles
1846 (and frequently reprinted). Vols. LXVI, LXVIII, and LXX contain the *Crónicas de los Reyes de Castilla desde Alfonso X hasta los Reyes Católicos,* as follows: LXVI, Crónica de Don Alfonso Décimo; C. de Don Sancho el Bravo; C. de Don Fernando Cuarto; C. de Don Alfonso el Onceno; C. de Don Pedro Primero. LXVIII, Crónica del rey Don Enrique, Segundo de Castilla; C. del rey Don Enrique, Tercero de Castilla e de León; C. del rey Don Juan, Segundo deste nombre en Castilla y en León. LXX, Memorial de Diversas Hazañas por mosén Diego de Valera; C. del rey Don Enrique el Cuarto de este nombre por su capellán y cronista Diego Enriquez del Castillo; C. de los señores Reyes Católicos Don Fernando y Doña Isabel de Castilla y de Aragón, escrita por su cronista Hernando del Pulgar; Continuación de la crónica de Pulgar por un anónimo; Anales breves del reinado de los Reyes Católicos . . . que dejó manuscritos el Dr. Lorenzo Galíndez Carvajal; Historia de los Reyes Católicos por el bachiller Andrés Bernáldez, cura que fue de la villa de Los Palacios. Madrid.
Blachère, Régis
1936. "Ibn Zumruk et son oeuvre." *Annales de l'Institut d'Études Orientales de la Faculté de Lettres de l'Université d'Alger,* 2:291–312.

Boronat y Barrachina, Pascual
1901. *Los moriscos españoles y su expulsión*. 2 vols., Valencia.
Borrás Gualis, Gonzalo M.
1981. "El mudéjar como constante artística." In *Actas* 1981:29–40.
Bosch Vilá, Jacinto, and Hoenerbach, Wilhelm
1983. "Un viaje oficial de la corte nazarí (1347)." *Andalucía Islámica*, 2–3:33–69.
Boswell, John
1977. *The Royal Treasure: Muslim Communities under the Crown of Aragon in the Fourteenth Century*. New Haven and London.
Bowen, Harold
See Gibb and Bowen. 1950 and 1957.
Bramon, Dolors
1986. *Contra moros y judíos*. Barcelona.
Brockelmann, Carl
1937–1949. *Geschichte der arabischen Litteratur*. 2nd edn., 2 vols. and 3 vols. of Supplement, Leiden.
Bulliett, R.W.
1979. *Conversion to Islam in the Medieval Period: An Essay in Quantitative History*. Cambridge, Mass.
Burns, Robert Ignatius
1961. "Social Riots on the Christian-Moslem Frontier: Thirteenth-Century Valencia." *American Historical Review*, 66:378–400.
1967. *The Crusader Kingdom of Valencia: Reconstruction on a Thirteenth-Century Frontier*. 2 vols., Cambridge, Mass.
1971. "Baths and Caravanserais in Crusader Valencia." *Speculum*, 46:443–58.
1973. *Islam under the Crusaders: Colonial Survival in the Thirteenth-Century Kingdom of Valencia*. Princeton, N. J.
1975a. "Immigrants from Islam: The Crusaders' Use of Muslims as Settlers in Thirteenth-Century Spain." *American Historical Review*, 80:21–42.
1975b. *Medieval Colonialism: Postcrusade Exploitation of Islamic Valencia*. Princeton, N. J.
1977a. "Mudejar History Today: New Directions." *Viator*, 8:127–43.
1977b. "The Language Barrier: The Problem of Bilingualism and Muslim-Christian Interchange in the Medieval Kingdom of Valencia." In *Contributions to Mediterranean Studies*. Malta, 116–36.
1978. *Moors and Crusaders in Mediterranean Spain: Collected Studies*. London.
1980a. "Canon Law and the Reconquista: Convergence and Symbiosis in the Kingdom of Valencia under Jaume the Conqueror (1213–1276)." In *V International Congress of Medieval Canon Law*. Città del Vaticano, 387–424.

1980b. "Los límites interiores de la Valencia de la reconquista: un género de tipología documental." *Medievalia,* 1:9–34.

1980c. "Societies in Symbiosis: The Mudejar-Crusader Experience in Thirteenth-Century Spain." *International History Review,* 2:349–85.

1980d. "A Medieval Earthquake: Jaume I, Al-Azrag, and the Early History of Ontoniente in the Kingdom of Valencia." In *Jaime I y su época,* 1–2:209–44.

1981a. "Los mudéjares de Valencia: temas y metodología." In *Actas* 1981: 453–97.

1981b. "Socioeconomic Structure and Continuity: Medieval Spanish Islam in the Tax Records of Crusader Valencia." In *The Islamic Middle East, 700–900: Studies in Economic and Social History.* Ed. A. L. Udovitch. Princeton, N.J., 251–82.

1983. "Rehearsal for the Sicilian War: Pere el Gran and the Mudejar Counter-Crusade in the Kingdom of Valencia, 1267–1278." In *La società mediterranea all'epoca del Vespro. XI Congrés d'història de la corona d'Aragó.* Palermo, II:259–87.

1984a. *Muslims, Christians, and Jews in the Crusader Kingdom of Valencia: Societies in Symbiosis.* Cambridge, England.

1984b. "Los mudéjares de la Valencia de las Cruzadas: un capítulo olvidado de la historia islámica." *Sharq al-Andalus, Estudios Árabes,* 1:15–34.

1985. *Society and Documentation in Crusader Valencia: Diplomatarium of the Crusader Kingdom of Valencia. The Registered Charters of Its Conqueror Jaume I, 1257–1276. Introduction.* I. Princeton, N. J.

Burns, Robert Ignatius (ed.)

1985. *The Worlds of Alfonso the Learned and James the Conqueror: Intellect and Force in the Middle Ages.* Princeton, N. J.

Cabanelas Rodríguez, Darío

1952. *Juan de Segovia y el problema islámico.* Madrid.

Cagigas, Isidro de las

1948–1949. *Los mudéjares.* 2 vols. Madrid. *Minorías étnico-religiosas de la Edad Media española,* III and IV.

Calvert, Albert F.

1907. *Granada and the Alhambra.* London and New York.

Canellas López, A.

See HEMP.

Cantera Montenegro, Enrique

1984. "La comunidad mudéjar de Haro (La Rioja) en el siglo XV." In *Estudios dedicados al Profesor D. Ángel Ferrari Núñez.* Madrid, II:157–74. *En la España medieval,* 4.

1986. "Los mudéjares en el marco de la sociedad riojana bajomedieval." In *Actas* 1986:21–38.

Caro Baroja, Julio
1957. *Los moriscos del reino de Granada: ensayo de historia social.* Madrid.
Carrasco Urgoiti, María Soledad
1956. *El moro de Granada en la literatura: siglos XV al XX.* Madrid.
Carrete Parrondo, Carlos
1978. "El rescate de los judíos malagueños en 1488." In *Actas* 1978:321–27.
Carriazo Arroquía, Juan de Mata
1954. "Las treguas con Granada de 1475 y 1478." *Al-Andalus,* 19: 317–64.
1971. *En la frontera de Granada.* Seville.
1978. "La vida en la frontera de Granada." In *Actas* 1978: 277–301.
See also *Colección de crónicas españolas; Crónica de Juan II de Castilla;* HEMP, XVII(1); and Santa Cruz 1951.
CCE = *Colección de Crónicas españolas.*
Chejne, Anwar G.
1974. *Muslim Spain, Its History and Culture.* Minneapolis.
Circourt, Albert de
1986. *Histoire des Mores mudéjares et des morisques, ou des arabes d'Espagne sous la domination des chrétiens.* 3 vols., Paris.
CODOIN = *Colección de documentos inéditos para la historia de España.*
Colin, Georges S.
1919. "Notes sur l'arabe d'Aragon." *Islamica,* 4: 159–69.
Colección de Crónicas españolas, ed. Juan de Mata Carriazo, 8 vols., 1940–1946. I, El victorial, Crónica de Don Pedro Niño, conde de Buelna por su alférez Gutierre Diez de Games; II, Crónica de Don Álvaro de Luna, condestable de Castilla, maestre de Santiago; III, Hechos del condestable Don Miguel Lucas de Iranzo; IV, Memorial de diversas hazañas, Crónica de Enrique IV ordenada por Mosén Diego de Valera; V–VI, Crónica de los Reyes Católicos por su secretario Fernando del Pulgar; VIII, Crónico del Halconero de Juan II, Pedro Carrillo de Huete; IX, Refundición de la crónica del Halconero por el obispo Don Lope Barrientos. (*Sic:* no VII).
Colección de documentos inéditos para la historia de España 1842–1895. 112 vols., Madrid.
Columbus, Christopher
1969. *The Four Voyages of Christopher Columbus.* Trans. J. M. Cohen. Harmondsworth.
Corriente, Federico
1977. *A Grammatical Sketch of the Spanish Arabic Dialect Bundle.* Madrid.
Crónica de Juan II de Castilla
1982. Ed. J. Carriazo Arroquía. Madrid.

Crònica de Pere III.
See Soldevila.
Crónicas del Gran Capitán
1908. Ed. A. Rodríguez Villa. Madrid = NBAE X.
Crónicas de los Reyes de Castilla desde Alfonso X hasta los Reyes Católicos
See BAE, LXVI, LXVIII, and LXX.
Cròniques, Les Quatre Grans
See Soldevila.
al-Dhakhīra al-Saniyya fī taʾrīkh al-dawla al-marīniyya
1920. Ed. M. Ben Cheneb. Algiers.
Diez de Games, Gutierre
See CCE, I.
Doi, ʿAbdur Raḥmān I.
1984. *Sharīʿah: The Islamic Law.* London.
Dozy, R.
1881. *Recherches sur l'histoire et la littérature des Arabes d'Espagne pendant le Moyen Âge.* 3rd edn., 2 vols., Leiden.
1927. *Supplément aux dictionnaires arabes.* 2nd edn., 2 vols., Leiden and Paris.
Drost, Gerrit Willem
1984. *De Moriscos in de Publicaties van Staat en Kerk (1492–1609): Een bijdrage tot het historisch discriminatieonderzoek.* Valkenburg (ZH).
Dufourcq, Charles-Emmanuel
1966. *L'Espagne catalane et le Maghrib, xiii et xiv siècles.* Paris.
Durán y Lerchundi, J.
1893. *La toma de Granada y caballeros que concurrieron a ella.* 2 vols., Madrid.
Edwards, John
1984. "Mission and Inquisition among *Conversos* and *Moriscos* in Spain. 1250–1550." *Studies in Church History,* 21:139–51.
Eiximenis, Francesc
1927. *Regiment de la cosa pública.* Barcelona.
Epalza, Mikel de
1982–1983. "Dos textos moriscos (árabe y castellano) de viajes a Oriente (1395 y 1407–12)." *Hespéris-Tamuda,* 20:25–112.
Febrer Romaguera, Manuel Vicente
1986. "Los Bellvis: una dinastía mudéjar de Alcaides Generales de Valencia, Aragón y Principado de Cataluña." In *Actas* 1986:277–90.
Fernández y González, Francisco
1866. *Estado social y político de los mudéjares de Castilla.* Madrid.
Ferrari Núñez, Ángel
1984. *Estudios dedicados al profesor A. Ángel Ferrari Núñez.* 2 vols., Madrid. *En la España medieval,* 4.

Ferrer i Mallol, María Teresa
1987. *Els Sarraïns de la corona catalano-aragonesa en el segle XIV: segregació i discrimininació*. Barcelona.
1988. *La frontera amb l'Islam en el segle XIV: cristians i sarraïns al País Valencià*. Barcelona.
Fori antiqui Valentiae.
1950–1967. Ed. Manuel Dualde Serrano. Madrid and Valencia.
Fori Aragonum vom Codex von Huesca (1247) . . .
1979. Facsimile and Introduction by Antonio Pérez, Vaduz.
Furs de València
1970. Ed. Germà Colon and Arcadi García. Barcelona.
Furs e ordinations fetes per los gloriosos reys de Aragón als regnícols del regne de València.
1482 (and facsimile 1977). Valencia.
Galán Sánchez, Ángel
1982. *Los moriscos de Málaga en la época de los Reyes Católicos*. Málaga. *Jábega* 29.
Galíndez de Carvajal, Lorenzo
1946. *Crónica de Enrique IV*. Ed. J. Torres Fontes, Murcia.
Anales breves del reinado de los Reyes Católicos. In BAE, LXX: 533–65.
Gámir Sandoval, Alfonso, and Gallego y Burín, Antonio
1968. *Los Moriscos del reino de Granada según el sinódo de Guadix de 1554*. Granada.
García Gallo, Alfonso
1967. *Manual de historia del derecho española*. 3rd edn., Madrid.
García Gómez, Emilio
1944. *Cinco poetas musulmanes*. Madrid.
García Gómez, Emilio, and Bermúdez Pareja, J.
1966. *La Alhambra: la Casa Real*. Granada.
García de Linares, R.
1940. *Los documentos árabes diplomáticos del Archivo de la Corona de Aragón*. Madrid and Granada.
García Sánchez, Expiración
1983. "La alimentación en la Andalucía islámica: estudio histórico y bromatológico: I, cereales y leguminosas." *Andalucía Islámica*, 2–3:139–78.
García i Sanz, Arcadi
1979. *Els Furs*. València.
García-Arenal, Mercedes
1984. "Los moros de Navarra en la Baja Edad Media." In Mercedes García-Arenal and Béatrice Leroy, *Moros y Judíos en Navarra en la Baja Edad Media*. Madrid.

1986. "Los mudéjares en el Reino de Navara y en la Corona de Aragón: estado actual de su estudio." In *Actas* 1986:175–86.

Garrido Atienza, M.

1910. *La capitulaciones para la entrega de Granada*. Granada.

Gayangos, Pascual de

1840. *The History of the Mohammedan Dynasties in Spain*. London. (A rearranged translation of a large part of al-Maqqarī's *Nafḥ al-Ṭīb;* see al-Maqqarī, 1949.)

1853. *Tratados de legislación musulmana*. Madrid. *Memorial Histórico Español* 5. (The name of the editor is not stated, but the work may safely be ascribed.)

Gibb, Hamilton A.R., and Bowen, Harold

1950 and 1957. *Islamic Society and the West*. Vol. I, Parts I and II. Oxford, London, New York, and Toronto.

Gil García, María Pilar

1986. "Conflictos sociales y oposición étnica: la comunidad mudéjar de Crevillente, 1420." In *Actas* 1986:305–12.

Glick, Thomas F.

1970. *Irrigation and Society in Medieval Valencia*. Cambridge, Mass.

1979. *Islamic and Christian Spain in the Early Middle Ages*. Princeton, N. J.

Glick, Thomas F., and Sunyer, Oriol P.

1969. "Acculturation as an Explanatory Concept in Spanish History." *Comparative Studies in Society and History,* 11:136–54.

Gómez de Castro, Alvar

1984. *De las hazañas de Francisco Jiménez de Cisneros*. Trans. José Oroz Reta. Madrid.

González, Julio

1980. *Reinado y diplomas de Fernando III*. Vol. I, *Estudio*. Córdoba.

González Mínguez, César

1976. *Fernando IV de Castilla (1295–1312): la guerra civil y el predominio de la nobleza*. Valladolid.

González Palencia, Angel

1926–1930 *Los Mozárabes de Toledo en los siglos XII y XIII*. 4 vols., Madrid.

Goytisolo, Juan

1984. "Vigencia actual del mudejarismo." In *Coloquio hispano-islámico de Ronda,* I:25–29.

La Gran Crónica de Alfonso XI

1976. Ed. Diego Catalán. Madrid.

Granja, Fernando de la

1971. "Condena de Boabdil por los alfaquíes de Granada." *Al-Andalus,* 36:145–76.

Gual Camarena, Miguel
1949. "Mudéjares valencianos, aportaciones para su estudio." *Saitabi*, 7:165–99.
Guichard, Pierre
1973. "Un seigneur musulman dans l'Espagne chrétienne: le ʿraʾis ʾde Crevillente (1243–1318)." *Mélanges de la Casa de Velázquez*, 9:283–334.
1987. *Estudios sobre historia medieval*. Valencia.
Guillén Robles, Francisco
1880. *Málaga musulmana*. Málaga. (2nd edn., 1957.)
1889. *Catálogo de los manuscritos árabes existentes en la Biblioteca Nacional de Madrid*. Madrid.
Halperin Donghi, Tulio
1980. *Un conflicto nacional: moriscos y cristianos viejos*. Valencia.
Harvey, Leonard Patrick
1956. "Yūse Banegas: un moro noble en Granada bajo los Reyes Católicos." *Al-Andalus*, 21:297–302.
1958a. *The Literary Culture of the Moriscos, 1492–1609*. 2 vols. Unpublished doctoral dissertation, Oxford University.
1958b. "Un manuscrito aljamiado en la biblioteca de la Universidad de Cambridge." *Al-Andalus*, 23:49–74.
1971. "The Arabic Dialect of Valencia in 1595." *Al-Andalus, 36:81–115.*
1981. "'The Thirteen Articles of the Faith' and 'The Twelve Degrees in Which the World is Governed': Two Passages in a Sixteenth-Century Morisco Manuscript and Their Antecedents." In *Mediaeval and Renaissance Studies on Spain and Portugal in Honour of P.E. Russell*. Oxford, 15–29.
Heers, J.
1957. "Le royaume de Grenade et la politique marchande de Gênes en Occident au XVe siècle." *Le Moyen Âge*, 63:87–121.
HEMP = *Historia de España*.
Henríquez de Jorquera, Francisco
1934. *Anales de Granada; Descripción del reino y ciudad de Granada; Crónica de la Reconquista (1482–1492)*. Ed. A. Marín Ocete. Granada.
Hillgarth, J. N.
1976–1978. *The Spanish Kingdoms 1250–1516*. 2 vols., Oxford.
Hinojosa, Eduardo de
1904. "Mezquinos y exaricos: datos para la historia de la servidumbre en Navarra y Aragón." In *Homenaje a D. Francisco Codera*. Saragossa, 523–31.
Historia de España.
1958–(in progress). Ed. Ramón Menéndez Pidal. Various authors. Madrid.

Hoenerbach, Wilhelm
1965. *Spanisch-Islamische Urkunden aus der Zeit der Naṣriden und Moriscos.* Bonn.
See also Bosch Vilá.
Huici Miranda, Ambrosio
1956. *Las grandes batallas de la Reconquista durante las invasiones africanas.* Madrid.
1956–1957. *Historia política del Imperio almohade.* 2 vols., Tetuán.
1970. *Historia musulmana de Valencia y su región: novedades y rectificaciones.* 3 vols., Valencia.
See Ibn ʿIdhari and Ibn Abi Zarʿ.
Ibn Abi Zarʿ
1845. *al-Anīs al-muṭrib bi-rawḍ al-qirṭāṣ fī akhbār mulūk al-Magrib.* Ed. C.J. Tornberg. Uppsala. (= *Rawḍ al-Qirṭāṣ.*)
1964. *Rawḍ al-Qirṭāṣ.* Trans. A. Huici Miranda. 2 vols., Valencia.
Ibn al-ʿAṭṭār
1983. *Kitāb al-wathāʾiq waʾl-sijillāt.* Ed. Pedro Chalmeta and Federico Corriente. Madrid (= *Formulario notarial hispano-árabe.*)
Ibn Hudhayl
1977. *Gala de caballeros, blasón de paladines.* Trans. María Jesús Viguera. Madrid.
Ibn Khaldūn
1858. *al-Muqaddima.* Ed. E.M. Quatremère. 3 vols., Paris.
1898. "Histoire des Benou'l-Aḥmar, Rois de Grenade." Trans. M. Gaudefroy-Demombynes. *Journal Asiatique,* 9ème Série 12:309–40 and 407–62 (= Banūʾl-Aḥmar), a partial translation of *Kitāb al- ʿibar.* based on the Būlāq edition of A. H. 1284, VII, 167 ss.
1956–1961. *Kitāb al- ʿibar* 7 vols., Beirut.
1958. *Al-Muqaddima.* Trans E. Rosenthal. New York and London.
1969. *Histoire des Berbères et des dynasties musulmanes de l'Afrique Septentrionale.* Trans. Macguckin de Slane; new edn. by Paul Casenove, 1956; reprinted 1969. Paris. (Translates the *K. al-* ʿibar into French).
Ibn al-Khaṭīb, Lisān al-Dīn
1934. *Kitāb aʿmāl al-aʿlām.* Rabat.
1955. *Kitāb al-Iḥāṭa.* Cairo.
1973–1978. *Kitāb al-Iḥāṭa.* 4 vols., Cairo.
1981. *Poesía árabe clásica, antología titulada "Libro de la Magia y de la Poesía." Ed and trans. J. M. Continente Ferrer. Madrid. (Arabic title Kitāb al-siḥr waʾl-shiʿr.)*
A.H. 1347. *al-Lamḥa al-badriyya fī*ʾl-dawla al-naṣriyya. Cairo.
n.d. *al-Katība al-kāmina fi-man laqīnāhu biʾl-Andalus min shuʿarāʾ al-miʾa al-thāmina.* Beirut.

Ibn al-Qāḍī

1907. "Le siège d'Almería en 1309." Ed. and trans. René Basset. *Journal Asiatique,* 10ème Série 10:279–303. (Edits an extract from *Durrat al-ḥijāl* and translates it into French.)

Ibn Shanab

See Ben Cheneb.

Ibn Zamrak

See García Gómez 1944.

See Blachère 1936.

Idris, H. R.

1974. "Les tributaires en Occident Musulman médiéval d'après le 'Miʿyār' d'al-Wanšarīšī." In *Mélanges d'Islamologie: volume dédié à la mémoire de Armand Abel.* Leiden, 172–96.

Les Illes orientales d'Al-Andalus i les seves relacions amb Sharq al-Andalus, Magrib i Europa cristiana (ss. VIII–XIII).

1987. Ed. Guillem Rosselló-Bordoy. Palma de Mallorca. *V Jornades d'Estudis Històrics Locals.*

Jaime I y su época

1980–1982. 2 vols., Saragossa. Publications 746 and 847 of the Institución Fernando el Católico. (The numbering of these two volumes is confusing; the first, published in 1980, bears the numbers "1 y 2," and the second, from 1982, "3, 4 y 5.")

Janer, Florencio

1857. *Condición social de los moriscos de España.* Madrid.

Juan Manuel, Don

1982. *Obras completas.* I. Ed. José Manuel Blecua. Madrid.

al-Khushānī

1966. *Quḍḍāt Qurṭuba.* Cairo.

Kirchner, Helena

1987. "El paper polític i social dels vells a les Illes i Regne de València en la Crònica de Jaume I." In *Les Illes orientales d'Al-Andalus* . . . . Palma de Mallorca, 103–13.

Labarta, Ana

1983. "Reconocimiento de tutela a un mudéjar de Daroca (documento árabe de 1477)." *Aragón en la Edad Media,* 5:207–17.

Lacarra, José Maria

1981. "Introducción al estudio de los mudéjares aragoneses." In *Actas* 1981:17–28.

Ladero Quesada, Miguel Ángel

1967. *Castilla y la conquista del reino de Granada.* Valladolid.

1969a. *Los mudéjares de Castilla en tiempo de Isabel I.* Valladolid.

1969b. *Granada, historia de un país islámico* (1232–1571). Madrid.

1972. "Datos demográficos sobre los musulmanes en el siglo XV." *Anuario de Estudios Medievales.* 8:481–90.
1981. "Los mudéjares de Castilla en la Baja Edad Media." In *Actas* 1981:349–90.
1986. "Los mudéjares en los reinos de la Corona de Castilla: estado actual de su estudio. In *Actas* 1986:5–20.
1987. "Nóminas de conversos granadinos (1499–1500)." (In *Estudios sobre Málaga y el Reino de Granada en el V Centenario de la Conquista.* Ed. José Enrique de Coca Castañer. Málaga.
1988. *Granada después de la conquista: repobladores y mudéjares.* Granada.
Lafuente y Alcántara, E.
1859. *Inscripciones árabes de Granada.* 4 vols., Madrid.
See also *Relaciones de algunos sucesos . . .*, 1868.
Lafuente y Alcántara, M.
1843–1846. *Historia de Granada.* 4 vols., Granada.
Lambton, Ann K. S.
1954. *Islamic Society in Persia.* London.
1974. "Islamic Political Thought." In *The Legacy of Islam.* 2nd ed. Ed. J. Schacht and C. E. Bosworth. Oxford, 404–23.
1981. *State and Government in Medieval Islam: An Introduction to the Study of Islamic Political Theory: The Jurists.* Oxford.
Lapeyre, Henri
1959. *Géographie de l'Espagne morisque.* Paris.
Ledesma Rubio, María Luisa
1980. "Notas sobre los mudéjares del Valle del Huerva (siglos XII al XIV)." *Aragón en la Edad Media,* 3:7–27.
Lévi-Provençal, Évariste
1931. *Inscriptions arabes d'Espagne.* Leiden and Paris.
Livermore, Harold
1963. "El segundo Rey Chico, Muhammad XI, y la sucesión de la casa de Abū Naṣr Saʿd, 1452–56." *Al-Andalus,* 28:331–48.
Longás, Pedro
1915. *Vida religiosa de los moriscos.* Madrid.
López de Coca Castañer, José Enrique
1978. "Sobre historia económica y social del reino nazarí de Granada." In *Actas* 1978:395–404.
1982. "Los mudéjares valencianos y el reino nazarí de Granada: propuestas para una investigación." *En la España Medieval,* 2:643–66.
See also Acién Almansa, 1981.
López Estrada, Francisco, ed.
1983. *El Abencerraje (Novela y Romancero).* Madrid.

López Martínez, Celestino
1935. *Mudéjares y moriscos sevillanos.* Seville.
López Ortiz, J.
1941. "Fatwas granadinas de los siglos XIV y XV." *Al-Andalus,* 6:73–127.
López-Baralt, Luce
1985. *Huellas del Islam en la literatura española: de Juan Ruiz a Juan Goytisolo.* Madrid.
López-Morillas, Consuelo
1982. *The Qur'an in Sixteenth-Century Spain: Six Morisco Versions of Sura 79.* London.
Lourie, Elena
1970. "Free Moslems in the Balearics under Christian Rule in the Thirteenth Century." *Speculum,* 45: 624–49.
Lucas de Iranzo
See CCE, III.
Luna, Álvaro de
See CCE, II.
Macho y Ortega, Francisco
1923. "Condición social de los mudéjares aragoneses (siglo XV)." *Memorias de la Facultad de Filosofía y Letras de la Universidad de Zarogoza,* 1:137–319.
MacKay, Angus
1977. *Spain in the Middle Ages: From Frontier to Empire, 1000–1500.* London
Mahdi, Muhsin
1964. *Ibn Khaldûn's Philosophy of History: A Study in the Philosophical Foundation of the Science of Culture.* Chicago.
al-Maqqarī, Shihāb al-Dīn Aḥmad b. Muḥammad
1939–1942. *Azhār al-riyāḍ fī akhbār* ʿIyāḍ. Ed. Muṣṭafa al-Siqā et al. 3 vols., Cairo.
1949. *Nafḥ al-ṭīb min guṣn al-Andalus al-raṭīb.* Ed. Muḥammad Muḥī al-Dīn ʿAbd al-Ḥamīd. 10 vols., Cairo.
Marçais, George
1954. *L'Architecture musulmane d'Occident.* Paris.
Mármol Carvajal, Luis del
1573. *Primera parte de la descripción general de Africa.* Granada.
1600. *Historia del* [sic] *rebelión y castigo de los Moriscos de Granada.* Málaga.
Martín Pérez, Pascual, ed.
n.d. *Colección deplomática de Sepúlveda.* Segovia. Publicaciones de la Diputación de Segovia, serie 1, IV.
Mas Latrie, L. de
1866. *Traités de paix et de commerce concernant les relations des Chrétiens avec les Arabes de l'Afrique Septentrionale au Moyen Âge.* Paris.

Massignon, Louis
1962. "Ibn Sabʿīn et la 'conspiration hallagienne' en Andalousie et en Orient au xiie siècle." In *Etudes d'orientalisme dédiées à la mémorire de Lévi-Provençal*. Paris, II:661–81.
MEAH = *Miscelánea de Estudios Árabes y Hebraicos de la Universidad de Granada.*
Mem. Hist. Esp. = *Memorial Histórico Español.*
Menéndez Pidal, Ramón
See *Historia de España,* and *Primera crónica general* . . . .
Mogollón Cano-Cortés, Pilar
1987. *El mudéjar en Extremadura.* Universidad de Extremadura.
Montes Romero-Camacho, Isabel
1984. "Un gran concejo andaluz ante la guerra de Granada: Sevilla en tiempos de Enrique IV (1454–1474)." In *Estudios dedicados al profesor D. Ángel Ferrari Núñez.* II:595–651. *En la España medieval,* 4.
Murphy, James Cavanah
1813. *The Arabian Antiquities of Spain: The Alhambra.* London.
NBAE = *Nueva Biblioteca de Autores Españoles*
Neuvonen, Eero
1941. *Los arabismos del español en el siglo XIII.* Helsinki.
Nubdha—Kitāb nubdhat al-ʿaṣr fī akhbār mulūk Banī Naṣr.
1940. Ed. Alfredo Bustani and trans. Carlos Quirós. Larache. (= *Fragmento de la época sobre noticias de los Reyes Nazaritas.*)
Nueva Biblioteca de Autores Españoles 1905–1929. 26 vols. Madrid.
O'Callaghan, Joseph F.
1975. *A History of Medieval Spain.* Ithaca and London.
Ozaki, Ikio
1986. "El régimen tributario y la vida económica de los mudéjares de Navarra." *Anuario de estudio medievales,* 16:319–68.
Palencia, Alonso de
1909. *Guerra de Granada.* Trans. A. Paz y Meliá. Madrid
PCG = *Primera crónica general.*
Pedregal y Fantini, J.
1898. *Estado social y cultural de los mozárabes y mudéjares españoles.* Seville.
Pescador del Hoyo, María del Carmen
1955. "Como fue de verdad la toma de Granada a la luz de un documento inédito." *Al-Andalus,* 20:283–344.
Pitt-Rivers, Julian A.
1954. *The People of the Sierra.* London.
El Poema de Alfonso XI
1956 Ed. Yo Ten Cate. Madrid.
Pons Boigues, Francisco

1898. *Ensayo bio-bibliográfrico sobre los historiadores y geógrafos arábigo-españoles*. Madrid.

Prescott, William H.

1888. *History of the Reign of Ferdinand and Isabella the Catholic*. Ed. John Foster Kirk. London.

Primera crónica general de España que mandó componer Alfonso el Sabio y se continuaba bajo Sancho IV en 1289. 1955. Ed. Ramón Menéndez Pidal. 2nd edn. 2 vols., Madrid.

Pulgar, Fernando del

See CCE, V and VI.

al-Qashtālī, Aḥmad

1974. *Tuḥfat al-mugtarib bi-bilād al-Magrib*. Ed. Fernando de la Granja. Madrid.

al-Qayrawānī, Ibn abī Zayd

1952. *La Risâla*. Ed. and trans. (into French) Léon Bercher. Algiers.

Relaciones de algunos sucesos de los últimos tiempos del Reino de Granada.

1868. Ed. E. Lafuente y Alcántara. Madrid.

Repartimiento de Comares (1487–1496).

See Bejarano-Robles, 1974.

Ribera, J., and Asín, M.

1912. *Manuscritos árabes y aljamiados de la Biblioteca de la Junta*. Madrid.

Roca Traver, Francisco A.

1952. "Un siglo de vida mudéjar en la Valencia medieval (1238–1338)." *Estudios de Edad Media de la Corona de Aragón,* 5:115–208.

Rubiera de Epalza, María Jesús

1969. "El Ḏū'l-wizāratayn Ibn al-Ḥakīm de Ronda." *Al-Andalus,* 24:105–22.

1982. Ibn al-Ŷayyāb, el otro poeta de la Alhambra. Granada.

1983. "Los Banū Escallola, una dinastía granadina que no fue." *Andalucía Islámica,* 2–3:85–94.

Rucquoi, Adeline

1987. *Valladolid en la Edad Media:* I, *Genesis de un poder;* II, *El mundo abreviado (1367–1474)*. Junta de Castilla y León.

Ruzafa García, Manuel

1986. "Los mudéjares valencianos en el siglo XV: un perspectiva bibliográfica." In *Actas* 1986:291–303.

Saavedra, Eduardo

1889. "Indice general de la literatura aljamiada." *Memorias de la Real Academia Española,* 6:237–328.

Sáchez-Albornoz, Claudio

1946. *La España musulmana*. 2 vols., Madrid.

Santa Cruz, Alonso de

1951. *Crónica de los Reyes Católicos*. Ed. Juan de Mata Carriazo. 2 vols., Seville.

Santiago Simón, Emilio de

1985. "Algunas calas en el desviacionismo herético de Ibn al-Jaṭīb." In *Actas* 1985:523–26.

Sastre Moll, Jaime

1987. "Notas sobre la población musulmana de Menorca (1287)." In *Les Illes orientals d'Al-Andalus*. Palma de Mallorca, 145–61.

Seco de Lucena, Luis

1951. "Notas para el estudio de Granada bajo la dominación musulmana." *Boletín de la Universidad de Granada*, 91:5–27.

1952. "Una rectificación a la historia de los últimos naṣríes." *Al-Andalus*, 20:399–402.

1955. "Nuevas rectificaciones a la historia de los últimos naṣríes." *Al-Andalus*, 20:399–402.

1956. "El ḥāŷib Riḍwān, la madraza de Granada y las murallas del Albaicín." *Al-Andalus*, 21:285–96.

1960a. "Panorama político del Islam granadino durante el siglo XV." MEAH, 9:7–18.

1960b. "El Musulmán Aḥmad ʿUlaylaš: espía de los Reyes Católicos en la corte granadina." *Al-Andalus*, 21:157–60.

1961. *Documentos arábigo-granadinos*. Madrid.

1978. *Muḥammad IX, Sultan de Granada*. Granada.

Shabāna, M. K.

1969. *Yūsuf al-awwal Ibn al-Aḥmar, sulṭān Garnāṭa (733–755 h.)*. Cairo.

Shatzmiller, Maya

1982. *L'Historiographie mérinide: Ibn Khaldoun et ses contemporains*. Leiden.

Simonet, Francisco J.

1872. *Descripción del reino de Granada bajo la dominación de los Naseritas*. 2nd edn. Granada.

Smith, C. Colin (Ed.)

1964. *Spanish Ballads*. Oxford.

Soldevila, Ferrán, ed.

1983. Jaume I, Bernat Desclot, Ramon Muntaner, Pere III, *Les Quatre Grans Cròniques*. Barcelona.

Spalding, Frances

1953. *Mudejar Ornament in Manuscripts*. New York.

Suárez Fernández, L.

1954. *Juan II y la frontera de Granada*. Valladolid.

Sunyer, Oriol P.

See Glick, Thomas F., 1969.

Szmolka Clares, José
1978. "Los comienzos de la castellanización del reino de Granada (1492–1516)." In *Actas* 1978, II:405–12.
Tapia Garrido, José Ángel
1986. *Almería musulmana (1172–1492). Almería musulmana,* II and *Historia general de Almería y su provincia,* IV. Almería.
Tilander, Gunnar
1937. *Los Fueros de Aragón según el Manuscrito 458 de la Biblioteca Nacional de Madrid.* Lund.
Torre, Antonio de la
1949–1951. *Documentos sobre relaciones internacionales de los Reyes Católicos: I (1479–1483), II (1484–1487), III (1488–1491).* Barcelona.
Torres, Diego de
1980. *Relación del origen y suceso de los xarifes y del estado de los reinos de Marruecos, Fez y Tarudante.* Ed. Mercedes García-Arenal. Madrid.
Torres Balbás, Leopoldo
1949. *Arte almohade, arte nazarí, arte mudéjar.* Madrid. *Ars Hispaniae,* IV.
1985. *Ciudades hispanomusulmanas.* 2nd edn. Madrid.
Torres Fontes, Juan
1960. "Nuevas noticias acerca de Muḥammad VIII 'el Pequeño'." MEAH, 9:127–34.
1981. "La hermandad de moros y cristianos para el rescate de cautivos." In *Actas* 1981:499–508.
1985. "El adalid en la frontera de Granada." *Anuario de Estudios Medievales,* 15:345–66.
1986. "Los mudéjares murcianos en la Edad Media." In *Actas* 1986: 55–66.
Tyan, E.
1938–1943. *Histoire de l'organisation judiciaire en pays d'Islam.* 2 vols., Paris (I), Lyon (II).
Valera, Diego de
1927. *Crónica de los Reyes Católicos.* Ed. J. de Mata Carriazo. Madrid. *Anejos de la Revista de Fililogía Española,* VIII.
See CCE, IV for *Memorial de diversas hazañas.*
Vallvé Bermejo, Joaquín
See Bejarano-Robles, 1974.
Viguera Molins, María Jesús
1981. "Dos nuevos documentos árabes de Aragón (Jarque y Mores 1492)." *Aragón en la Edad Media,* 4:235–61.
al-Wansharīshī, Abū'l-ʿAbbas Aḥmad
1908–1909. "Consultations juridiques . . . ." Trans. E. Amar. *Archives marocaines,* 12 and 13. (Extensive translations and paraphrases with index.)
1981. *Kitāb al-miʿyār al-mugrib.* 13 vols., Rabat.

Watt, W. Montgomery
1965. *A History of Islamic Spain*. Edinburgh.
Yarza Luaces, Joaquín
1982. "Metodología y técnicas de investigación de lo mudéjar." In *Actas* 1982:99–110.
Ye'or, Bat
1985. *The Dhimmi: Jews and Christians under Islam*. London and Toronto.
Zurita, Jerónimo
1973. *Anales de la Corona de Aragón*. Ed. Angel Canellas López. 4 vols., Saragossa.

INDEX